Endorsements

This is a volume for the mind and the heart, providing a historical and theological perspective of great moves of God. Just as books encouraged John Wesley and George Whitefield to pursue God, reading the penned pictures of *God's Generals* will encourage you to do the same. Roberts Liardon has provided another page-turner—one written in an easy style but with academic rigor. I warmly commend this book to you.

—The Reverend Paul Wilson
Methodist Minister, Knutsford, UK
Chair, Methodist Evangelicals Together, UK

God's Generals: The Revivalists gives us a detailed look into the lives of the people God used to wake and shake their worlds. Roberts brings their stories to life and makes them relevant to God's work on the earth today. It will stir you to take your place as we stand on the threshold of the greatest revival of all time.

—The Reverend Kate McVeigh
Author, *The Blessing of Favor* and *Sharing Your Faith*

Over the years, I have found myself referring to the vast knowledge within the excellent work of Roberts Liardon's best-selling work, *God's Generals.* As a Christian and a minister, I appreciate his commitment to this historical work and look forward to the release of this next book in the series.

—Kim Clement
Author, *Call Me Crazy, but I'm Hearing God's Voice*

In this volume, Roberts again gives honor where it is due, yet remains true to history to include their failures and shortcomings. I appreciate that he never does so in a dishonorable way, but instead uses the opportunity to instruct us now not to repeat the same mistakes. That is the way of the kingdom. *God's Generals: The Revivalists* is sure to become required reading to help prepare the generation that was born for the greatest outpouring of the Spirit in history.

—Bill Johnson
Author, *When Heaven Invades Earth*
Pastor, Bethel Church
Redding, California

I highly respect Roberts Liardon for making the lives and battles of yet another set of God's Generals available to this generation in a powerful and readable book. Because the lives and experiences of God's men continue to minister to us, *God's Generals: The Revivalists* is one of the most useful books a minister could lay his hands on!

—Bishop Dag Heward-Mills
Founder and Pastor, Lighthouse Chapel International
Ghana, Africa

As a historian, Roberts Liardon has captured the seed that was placed by heaven in the lives of these great men and women of God. Their stories, woven together, paint an awesome picture of the truth that the Holy Spirit has done a mighty work, and is still working today, to reach a lost and dying world with the Good News of the Gospel. The message is the same—the vessel and the method may be different—but it is the same Holy Spirit. May you be challenged and stirred to look forward with expectation, because the best is yet to come—He has saved the best wine for last!

—Dr. Rodney Howard-Browne
Revival Ministries International
Tampa, Florida

In the typical Liardon style of thoroughness and detail, *God's Generals: The Revivalists* takes the reader to new levels in biographical studies. The reasons include the author's intensity of presentation, added to the fact that the men and women whose lives are herein chronicled surely stand near the mountaintop of greatness, above all those who have lived and ministered in postbiblical history. Many will be blessed, helped, and changed by reading this splendid work. It deserves to be read by every God-seeking person. A great addition to any library!

—Jack Taylor
President, Dimensions Ministries
Melbourne, Florida

Roberts Liardon has done a great work in writing the *God's Generals* series. In this latest volume, he helps us to see the footsteps of the revivalists and to learn how to overcome the barriers and win the battles they faced. It is a must-read book for Christians who long to see revival happen in their lives, communities, and nations.

—The Reverend Dr. Niko Njotorahardjo
Senior Pastor, Bethel Church of Indonesia
Jakarta, Indonesia

GOD'S *The Revivalists* GENERALS

GOD'S GENERALS

The Revivalists

ROBERTS LIARDON

WHITAKER HOUSE

Unless otherwise indicated, all Scripture quotations are taken from the King James Version of the Holy Bible. Scripture quotations marked (NKJV) are taken from the *New King James Version*, © 1979, 1980, 1982, 1984 by Thomas Nelson, Inc. Used by permission. All rights reserved.

Publisher's note:
Original spellings are maintained in all quoted material, and, because of the numerous differences between British and American English, as well as conventions of the time, these are not noted by a [*sic*]. Original capitalizations are also maintained, so in many cases, "he," "his," and other pronouns are not capitalized when referring to God, Jesus, or the Holy Spirit.

God's Generals:
The Revivalists
hardcover edition

Roberts Liardon Ministries
P.O. Box 2989
Sarasota, Florida 34230
www.robertsliardon.com

Manuscript prepared by Rick and Melissa Killian, Killian Creative
Boulder, Colorado
www.killiancreative.com

ISBN: 978-1-60374-025-8
Printed in the United States of America

Whitaker House
1030 Hunt Valley Circle
New Kensington, PA 15068
www.whitakerhouse.com

Library of Congress Cataloging-in-Publication Data

Liardon, Roberts.
God's generals : the revivalists / by Roberts Liardon.
p. cm.
Summary: "Chronicles the life and legacy of prominent Christian revivalists, detailing their historical context and significant contributions"—Provided by publisher.
Includes bibliographical references.
ISBN 978-1-60374-025-8 (trade hardcover : alk. paper) 1. Evangelists—Biography. I. Title.
BV3780.L46 2008
269'.20922—dc22
[B] 2008009604

12 13 ꟺ 26 25

Dedication

I dedicate this exciting third volume of *God's Generals* to my father, Kenneth D. Craft. He was born on April 13, 1936, in Benton Harbor, Michigan, and grew up on a Native American reservation for the Creek Indians in Washington State. In young adulthood, he joined the Marines, and not long afterward married my mother.

As a young married couple, my parents helped my grandparents run the churches they were pastoring and assisted them with their revival campaigns. My father always had a natural way of making everyone his friend. He considered no person a stranger—just a friend he hadn't met before. Ever an outdoorsman, he loved the world of hunting and fishing. Growing up, my sister and I enjoyed many weekends along the banks of the Grand River in the great state of Oklahoma, catching his appreciation for God's creation.

His death came too early for us all on January 13, 1997, just as our ministry was beginning to have a national voice.

Below is my favorite photo of my father and me. My memories of him grow fonder every time I revisit them. Dad, I look forward to seeing you again when we all get to heaven.

Love, your son,
Roberts

Contents

Foreword

I sincerely believe that Roberts Liardon is one of the foremost church historians of our time. This is clearly apparent from his third and latest installment of the best-selling *God's Generals* series, which he delivers in his own inimitable and masterful way. The biographical studies he presents in this volume of the key revivalists of the last three hundred years are the products of years of painstaking and diligent research. Roberts adds to this research his own outstanding gift for storytelling.

Both educational and inspiring, *God's Generals: The Revivalists* is a must-read for any serious student of Christian history (which, of course, every Christian should desire to be!). Roberts's skill in weaving together the primary and secondary data is second to none. His commentary is pithy, lucid, and insightful. This book is extremely difficult to put down!

The best historians present us with descriptions of the past that also inform the present, and this is the triumph of the entire *God's Generals* series. *The Revivalists* is the opposite of dry, irrelevant church history—every page is packed full of life-application treasures, and Roberts ensures that the stories of these "heroes of the faith" continue to speak to us.

I know that you will feel spiritually refreshed as you read about the lives and revivals led by these men and women. Your cry will be, "Do it again, Lord!" as you see what God can do through seemingly insignificant and imperfect men and women who yield completely to Him.

As you read the following pages, allow the Holy Spirit to intensify His work within you. The revivals that we long for must begin with individual hearts being set on fire—just as was the case with the revivalists outlined in this book.

It is my prayer that through this book, the Holy Spirit will put within you a godly desire to be a "General of God" yourself—someone who will make an impact on history and leave a lasting spiritual legacy. This is the "day of the saints"—the age of the priesthood of all believers—not centered on one superstar "man or woman of God," but on the entire body of Christ being mobilized to do the work of Christ in the world. Learn from these revivalists. Let their failings caution you and their successes challenge you. Adopt their desire to make an impact on your generation as you live your life in total dedication to almighty God.

Roberts has done a great service to the entire Christian world in producing a resource of this magnitude. He has given to the body of Christ a tool that will serve generations to come, and I commend it wholeheartedly to you.

—Colin Dye
Senior Minister, Kensington Temple
London

Prologue

One Hundred Years of Intercession

The effectual fervent prayer of a righteous man availeth much.

—James 5:16

Though the reformation was some two centuries behind them and the martyrdom of Jan Hus more than three hundred years in the past, in 1722 a group of Hus's followers from Moravia (a province in Bohemia, today part of the Czech Republic) fled to Saxony (Germany) looking for religious freedom. Driven by persecution, these "United Brethren," as they called themselves, found sanctuary on the land of a rich, young aristocrat, Count Nikolaus Ludwig von Zinzendorf, who gave them a place to settle and to build a community of believers. The township that emerged was called *Herrnhut*, meaning either "on the Lord's watch" or "under the Lord's watch." Because they had come to Saxony from Moravia, the group became known as *the Moravians*.

Count Zinzendorf was a man of God who, at the time, had been actively looking for ways to use his inherited wealth and influence to serve the kingdom of heaven. In 1715, at the age of fifteen, Zinzendorf banded with four friends to form what they considered a society of Christian knighthood, which they called "The Order of the Mustard Seed." The four vowed "1. To be true to Christ; 2. To be kind to all people; 3. To send the gospel to the world."[1] Over the years, the group grew in membership to include such men as the king of Denmark, Christian VI; the Catholic archbishop of Paris, Cardinal Louis Antoine de Noailles; the archbishop of Canterbury, John Potter; a Scottish member of the British Parliament, Erskine; and eventually, after the Moravians had sent missionaries there, the governor of Georgia, General James Oglethorpe; and the Native American Chief of the Creek nation, Tomochichi.

Even though the count was only twenty-two at the time, hearing the Moravians' plea for something as simple as a place to worship freely ignited his heart. He had recently purchased from his grandmother the town of Bethelsdorf, where he installed a close friend, Johann Andreas Rothe, to be pastor. Building a community based upon the Word of God was what he had hoped to accomplish in Bethelsdorf, and here was a group of people who shared this same determination. Desiring Rothe's help in forming Herrnhut, Zinzendorf gave them a plot for their new village only two miles from Bethelsdorf.

Accustomed to persecution, the Moravians soon wearied of the peace of Herrnhut, and with no pressure from outside, the townspeople began to turn upon one another within. Division and strife took their toll to the point that the Moravians even turned on Zinzendorf and Rothe, calling them the "Beast of the Apocalypse" and his "False Prophet." Zinzendorf and Rothe continued to seek God and pray, and it wasn't long before God answered.

On May 12, 1727, Zinzendorf addressed the congregation at Herrnhut and spoke for three hours on the blessedness of Christian unity. Conviction took the town that summer, and everyone began seeking God for revival. As men, women, and children confessed their sins to one another, prayed together, and found new strength in seeking God, their hearts were knit together afresh and the community experienced a golden summer. This wasn't enough, however. The people of Herrnhut wanted power to take the message of Christ to the ends of the earth.

This became a constant subject of prayer to the point that, on August 5, 1727, Zinzendorf and fourteen other Moravian Brethren

[1] "Where it all began: The History of Zinzendorf's Order of the Mustard Seed," The Order of the Mustard Seed, http://www.mustardseedorder.com/cm/story/3.

spent an entire night in seeking and interceding for God's power to fall on their community. On August 10, Rothe was so overcome with the presence of the Holy Spirit in an afternoon service at Herrnhut that he threw himself to the ground to repent before God. The meeting continued through the night as others did likewise, crying out to God with weeping and repentance, until around midnight, when the congregation burst forth in praise, worship, and singing.

Zinzendorf and Rothe then felt they should have a joint meeting between Bethelsdorf and Herrnhut that Wednesday evening, August 13, to share about what God was doing in Herrnhut. The Count visited every home in the village, urging the inhabitants to attend.

Once the meeting began, the Holy Spirit took over as the congregation again fell into repentance for their sins. At one point, Count Zinzendorf took the podium to voice a remorseful confession on behalf of the entire community for the division they had seen in the previous years and to call for a rededication to the principles upon which the town had first been founded. Once that was voiced, the Holy Spirit fell on the congregation. Count Zinzendorf later described it as "a day of the outpourings of the Holy Spirit…; it was its Pentecost."[2] The congregation began praying for groups still under persecution, for unity in their community, and for the body of Christ the world over—and to increasingly intercede that the Word of God would spread mightily around the world.

Just two weeks later, on August 27, twenty-four men and twenty-four women covenanted together to begin praying around the clock. They agreed that one man and one woman in different places would pray in twenty-four one-hour shifts that would fill each hour of the day, every day of the week, and every week of the year. They would pray for whatever God put on their hearts, but mostly for revival and the spreading of the Gospel of Jesus Christ to every corner of the earth. It was a prayer vigil that would last for the next one hundred years and would be the womb from which revival would be born.

That century of prayer would see the greatest missionary outreaches the world had yet experienced as well as the First and

---

[2] Dr. A. K. Curtis, "A Golden Summer," Zinzendorf Jubilee, Comenius Foundation, http://www.zinzendorf.com/agolden.htm. This article first appeared in *Glimpses of Christian History*, "Glimpses 37: Zinzendorf," from the Christian History Institute.

Second Great Awakenings. In fact, the Great Earthquake of 1727 came just months after the Moravians began praying, an event many historians note as the beginning of the First Great Awakening, while Charles Finney's Rochester revival at the height of the Second Great Awakening and the National Revival of 1831 happened around the time their prayer vigil ended.

It was also the era in which the revivalists—a new form of mass evangelists—were born. Here are their stories.

Introduction

The battle for the hearts of humanity has continued to rage throughout the centuries since Christ first came to remove humanity's stains of sin and guilt two thousand years ago. From the first revival that took place among the original disciples at Pentecost to the ongoing "Pentecostal Revivals" of the twenty-first century, God has breathed new life into the hearts of his followers—time and again calling them to deeper levels of intimacy, holiness, and personal understanding of His love.

Paving the way for the Holy Spirit to bring light and truth were faithful men and women of earnest study and fervent prayer. From the groundbreaking revelations taught by Paul, to the revolutionary reformation launched by Martin Luther, to the evangelical campaigns coordinated by John and Charles Wesley and the revivalists to follow, the Holy Spirit has fought to reveal the power of God's saving grace through faith—not of any work or intervention of man, not of any external force of will or institutional decree, but of the simple, personal acceptance of Christ's sacrifice on the cross. To this day, we continue learning how to more fully accept and apply all that this great sacrifice has provided for the individuals whose hearts embrace it.

The hallmark of every revival is hunger of heart: the heart's pursuit of a personal relationship with Christ, the heart's longing to experience God's presence, and the heart's cry to worship God in spirit and in truth. Revival is the product of an awakening of the heart to the power and presence of the living Christ who loves us unconditionally. Revivalists are those men and women who were able to venture from the safety and conformity of head knowledge into the passionate truths only understood spiritually through faith. These truths cannot be fully comprehended with the intellect, but are instead made apparent as we lean on and trust in God. This is what is spoken of in Proverbs 3:5–7:

> *Trust in the Lord with all thine heart; and lean not unto thine own understanding. In all thy ways acknowledge him, and he shall direct thy paths. Be not wise in thine own eyes: fear the Lord, and depart from evil.*

The great revivalists, as we have come to know them, did just that. They fought hard not to lean on their own understanding but in every way to acknowledge God. They resisted the temptation to be wise in their own eyes and in the eyes of their fellow human beings; they trusted only in the leading of the Holy Spirit. It was a battle for many to learn to hear that still, small voice, but through desperate perseverance, they found the Lord.

Each revivalist overcame his own dark night of the soul—a personal wilderness experience during which he seemed to wander without direction, meaning, and sometimes even hope. Each questioned his faith, and sometimes his salvation. But through prayer, motivated by a deep hunger for truth, each found the assurance so desperately desired. Once these heroes of the faith revived their own hearts in this way, they made sparks that ignited a blaze to set nations on fire for generations to come.

As we will see from their stories, personal revival led to national revival. It began with a complete trust in the Lord, a profound reverence for God, and a determination to overcome the social ills each saw oppressing his generation. The revivalists transformed lives in a way that led to the transformation of communities and nations. The battle lines between righteousness and evil were drawn—and held—for eternity by these great Generals of God. We can follow in their footsteps and learn from the battles they won and the barriers they overcame. Journey with me over the span of two and a half centuries as we visit the battlefields of *God's Generals: The Revivalists.*

Chapter One

☆☆☆☆☆

John & Charles Wesley

(1703–1791)

(1707–1788)

"The Head and Heart of Revival"

"The Head and Heart of Revival"

Leisure and I have parted company. We shall never meet again.

—John Wesley

O for a thousand tongues to sing my great Redeemer's praise!

—Charles Wesley

When John and Charles Wesley were born, Queen Anne was on the throne of England, and Louis XIV was ruling France. Isaac Newton was still alive, the philosopher John Locke had only recently passed away, America was merely a disjointed group of colonies, and the advent of the steam engine and the Industrial Revolution were still decades away. England, especially the Wesley brothers' birthplace of Epworth, was mostly agricultural and provincial. In the past half century, England had suffered a series of civil wars, the most notable being the last, which made Oliver Cromwell the protectorate of England (1653–1659). For more than a decade (1649–1659), England was without a monarch. When the monarchy was restored, the crown had considerably less power, sharing it now with Parliament, and after having had a Puritan for a Protector, the Church of England no longer had a stranglehold on religious life.

John & Charles Wesley

The early eighteenth century was also the dawn of the Enlightenment, coming on the heels of the Age of Reason of the previous century, which emphasized rationalism and science over moral, spiritual, and biblical truth. The scientific discoveries of Galileo and Newton inspired a scientific revolution that caused men to believe in the power of the intellect over the wisdom of God. Humanism was on the rise, and with it came moral decay. The Bible was no longer valued as the sole standard by which people should guide their lives.

England also found itself in the grip of the "Gin Age." Gin was being distilled in one of every four homes in London, and it was sold openly in the streets. Drunkenness and depravity had taken their toll on every level of society. Parliament had to adjourn on frequent occasions because its members were too inebriated to conduct the affairs of state.

Children suffered especially cruel treatment; nearly 75 percent died before their fifth birthday. Not only were living conditions harsh, but drunken parents would often abandon or, worse, sell their children in order to feed their addictions. They sometimes maimed their children in some hideous way so that their apparent deformities would earn them more money as beggars. A petition to Parliament in 1739 to create a hospital for abandoned babies tells of the desperate state of the nation's children who were "left to perish in the street" or "blinded or maimed and distorted in their limbs in order to move pity."[1]

England was growing as ripe for revolution as France; yet the revolution in the British Isles would be very different. England's would be a revival called "Methodism," inspired predominantly by John and Charles Wesley. As one historian put it,

> Methodism and the French Revolution are the two most tremendous phenomena of the [eighteenth] century. [John] Wesley swept the dead air with an irresistible cleansing ozone. To thousands of men and women his preaching and gospel revealed a new heaven and a new earth; it brought religion into soulless lives and reconstituted it as a comforter, an inspiration, and a judge. No one was too poor, too humble, too degraded to be born again and share in the

[1] Keith J. Hardman, *The Spiritual Awakeners* (Chicago: Moody Press, 1983), 76.

privilege of divine grace, to serve the one Master, Christ, and to attain to the blessed fruition of God's peace.[2]

The vast network of Methodist Societies established by the Wesley brothers brought desperately needed assurances of God's mercy and love in this time of uncertainty, economic hardship, and short life expectancy. These "home groups"—what many today might call "cell groups"—orchestrated by the Wesleys provided ongoing instruction, prayer, accountability, and the necessary discipleship and fellowship that are the foundation of spiritual growth. Most importantly, John and Charles Wesley brought the message of "free grace" directly to the masses. Their greatest audience was the "contrite and lowly of spirit," who gladly opened their hearts to God's abundant provision of grace.

Purity's Passion

John and Charles Wesley were born on June 17, 1703 and December 18, 1707, respectively, in Epworth, England, a town located a little less than 190 miles north of London and roughly eighty miles east of Manchester in the English heartland. They were the fifteenth and eighteenth of nineteen children, of whom only ten survived into adulthood. In fact, "John Benjamin" Wesley was named after two brothers who had died before he was born. Though John was the fifteenth child, only six were living after his birth—eight of his older brothers and sisters had already died.

The Wesley children were: Samuel (1690–1739), Susanna (1691, died in infancy), Emilia (1692–1771), the twins Annesley and Jedidiah (1864, died in infancy), Susanna "Sukey" (1695–1763), Mary "Mollie" (1696–1734), Mehetabel "Hetty" (1697–1750), an unnamed child (1698, died in infancy), John (1699, died in infancy), Benjamin (1700, died in infancy), another set of twins who were unnamed (1701, died in infancy), Anne (1702–1742?), John (1703–1791), another unnamed son (?, died in infancy), Martha (1706–1791), Charles (1707–1788), and Keziah "Kezie" (1709–1741).

[2] C. Grant Robertson, *England under the Hanoverians*, (London: Methuen and Company, 1923), 210–11, quoted in John Telford, *The Life of John Wesley* (London: The Epworth Press, 1924), 1.

John & Charles Wesley

Epworth was a market town whose population had hovered around two thousand for the last two hundred years. Its residents were primarily employed in the growing and braiding of rope and weaving of other products from hemp and flax. The parsonage where the Wesley brothers were born was a three-story building of timber and plaster with a thatched roof. It stood on a three-acre plot that also had a thatched barn, a dovecote, and a small garden.

John and Charles were descendents of a long line of ministers. Their parents, the Reverend Samuel and Susanna Wesley, raised them with the hope that they would one day become leaders in the Anglican Church. Samuel and Susanna were the products of the Dissenters, but for the sake of a salary, a home, and providing the region with a believing minister, Samuel had made his peace with the Anglicans and was ordained by them. Because of their Dissenter/Puritan background, however, the Wesley home was governed by strict moral principles, exercised daily through rigorous discipline in manners, study, and prayer.

Samuel Wesley, who for thirty-five years was rector[3] of the small parish in Epworth, worked long hours overseeing the spiritual needs of several neighboring towns. When he was able, he dedicated himself to rigorous study, often locked away in his office constructing sermons, writing poetry, or composing hymns. He joined the family only for meals, which were always eaten in silence.

Susanna Wesley

The Wesley Center Online (wesley.nnu.edu) at Northwest Nazarene University, Nampa, Idaho

Susanna, meanwhile, made the most of every opportunity to educate and train her growing family in a wide variety of subjects and personal disciplines. Under her private tutelage, the Wesley children studied history, literature, classical languages, music, and, most importantly, Scripture. They memorized Psalms, Proverbs, and long passages from the New Testament. Every moment from

[3] The Anglican equivalent of a pastor.

dawn until dusk was structured, beginning and ending with prayer and Bible reading. Every child was exposed to the same pace of rigorous study and devotion. The rod was not spared; formal, mannerly behavior of every kind was taught; and obedience was always required.

From one year of age, they learned to fear the rod and to cry softly and sparingly. As a result, although the house was full of children, it was always peaceful and quiet. Susanna's philosophy was simple and goal-oriented:

> I insist upon conquering the will of children betimes [early in life], because this is the only strong and rational foundation of a religious education, without which both precept and example will be ineffectual.[4]

While this approach may seem harsh to many today, it is easy to see how this upbringing caused John to be a creator of the routines, disciplines, and systematic pursuit of God that characterized Methodism. Susanna's training created the stability and purposefulness in John that made him diligent in his religion and humble enough to be always open to the truth. The habits of quiet study, strict time management, and frugality in all things remained with John and Charles for the rest of their lives.

Each child who grew to adulthood left the Wesley home with a trained mind, a pure heart, and a sincere passion for the Lord. Although most, with the exception of Samuel Jr., Charles, and possibly Anne, found themselves in unhappy marriages, all endured their circumstances with a resolute faithfulness. Each would pursue an ongoing interest in study, writing, and teaching, and several, especially Samuel, Hetty, and Charles, would share their father's passion for poetry. No doubt the solid teaching and sound advice of their mother, along with the influence of seven capable sisters, did not escape John and Charles as they grew up.

Trial by Fire

The Wesley family weathered its share of adversity as the children grew. There were long seasons during which Samuel would

[4] Telford, *Life of John Wesley*, 14.

be occupied in London, leaving the family to suffer financial hardship in his absence. Samuel also accumulated burdensome debts; at times, the family was on the brink of financial ruin. For a short time, Samuel was even placed in debtors' prison when John was only two.

When present, Samuel ruled his home with a heavy hand and a quick temper. Susanna, however, remained steadfast in her dutiful respect of him. Even as sorrow was added to difficulty and nine of their nineteen children died in infancy, she never wavered in her faith. Certainly this strength of witness left a deep impression on John and Charles, as later in life they faced daunting opposition with awe-inspiring poise, grace, and faith.

Samuel Wesley

Mary Evans Picture Library

When John was five years old, his mother began teaching him to read from the Old Testament. As was customary, the children rose at dawn to perform their devotions before beginning their academic studies, ate their three small meals in silence, ended their evenings in prayer at six o'clock, and were ready for bed by seven. No child stirred after eight o'clock. All of the Wesley children applied themselves with quiet diligence so they could be spared the rod.

While Susanna's reputation as a disciplined and devout woman grew, her husband became increasingly notorious for his strong opinions and obstinacy. He was bold and perhaps a little too outspoken about his religious and political views. He alienated the Dissenters of his region when he became deeply involved on behalf of an unpopular candidate in a hotly contested election. In addition, he preached vehemently against the sins he saw his parishioners fall prey to, and those who weren't inwardly convicted resented his condemnations. He had probably also made several enemies through his excessive borrowing. Whatever the reason, his popularity among the local citizenry steadily declined until disaster struck on the evening of February 9, 1709.

As the Wesley household slept, the Epworth parsonage was mysteriously set ablaze sometime between eleven and twelve o'clock at night. The roof of the corn room burned through before anyone noticed. Some of the fire came through the thatch roof and fell on Hetty's bed, waking her. At once, she ran to find her father, crying out, "Fire! Fire!" As smoke and flames quickly overtook the house—the roof was falling fast—Samuel and Susanna gathered the children and hurried them outside. They had no time to grab either clothes or possessions. As they descended the stairs, only a thin wall kept the flames from cutting off their escape route. Susanna, who was near term with their last child, suffered some burns on her legs and face as she strained against the flames to make sure all of her children had escaped. Once outside, everyone was accounted for except one—five-and-a-half-year-old John.

John Wesley is rescued from the Epworth parsonage.

Library of Congress, 6002275

John was upstairs asleep behind the curtains drawn around his bed. He awoke groggily to the light flickering on the other side of the drapes. Thinking that it was morning and not wanting to stir before it was time, he laid still, wondering why no one had called him to come down for prayer. At last he stuck his head out of the canopy to find the room engulfed in flames. He jumped from the bed and cried out, but no one was in the house to hear him. Through the door and down the hall he saw a terrible inferno. He ran to the window, climbed up on a chest, and looked out to see several servants and neighbors scurrying about below, trying to quench the fire.

His mother was searching frantically for him outside. Samuel made two attempts to reenter the house, using his breeches as a shield over his head, but the fire was too much for him to penetrate. Failing, he gathered his family around him in the garden to pray, commending John to God.

Susanna Wesley was convinced that John had a special call of God on his life.

At first, no one noticed as young John waved his arms from the second-story window and shouted for help. But as the flames began to swallow the upper level of the house, he caught the eye of a neighbor, who quickly climbed atop another man's shoulders and pulled John to safety mere moments before the remainder of the roof collapsed. In the matter of a few more minutes, the entire rectory was burned to the ground.

When John was brought to his father, the rector cried out, "Come, neighbors, let us kneel down: let us give thanks to God! He has given me all my eight children:[5] let the house go, I am rich enough."[6] Afterward, Samuel Sr. famously remarked, "Is not this [John] a brand plucked out of the burning?" [7] From that point on, Susanna was convinced that John had a special call of God on his life.

The fire's destruction spared nothing—not even a change of clothes was left for the Wesley family. The children had to be dispersed into several nearby homes where neighbors cared for them. Susanna gave birth to little Kezie only weeks later, and for a time,

---

[5] Samuel and Susanna actually had nine children at this point: Samuel Jr. was off at Westminster School, where he boarded and studied, so he did not include him in the remark above.

[6] Robert Southey, *The Life of Wesley and the Rise and Progress of Methodism* (London: Frederick Warne and Company, n.d., ca. 1820), 11.

[7] Ibid.

with Susanna occupied with the cares of a new baby, the Wesley children were allowed to do what other boys and girls their age would do. They ran about and played, talked openly at mealtimes, and socialized in all sorts of common ways, both good and bad.

When the parsonage had been rebuilt almost a year later, Susanna Wesley wasted no time in instituting a strict reform of behavior and habits. Chief of concerns was the children's careless attitude regarding the Sabbath. She heard her children say things she never imagined she would ever hear, and she felt they had lost their good manners and "acquired a clownish accent and many rude ways."[8]

John's perilous escape from the fire made his mother much more attentive to his education. Two years after the fire, she noted in her journal,

> I do intend to be more particularly careful of the soul of this child, that Thou hast so mercifully provided for, than ever I have been, that I may do my endeavor to instill into his mind the principles of Thy true religion and virtue. Lord, give me grace to do it sincerely and prudently, and bless my attempts with good success.[9]

It is interesting to note how many young people with great calls of God on their lives had stories similar to John's. Had John perished in the fire that day, it is unimaginable what might have happened had England gone the way of the French Revolution instead of having the Methodist Revival. The enemy must have seen the call and anointing on John's life and wanted to destroy it—which is why it is so important for parents to understand God's protection for their children and to keep their families safe by applying God's promises.

It was also about two years later, when John was eight years old, that his father permitted him to take Communion. Looking back on this time of his life years later, John wrote in his journal:

> I believe till I was about ten years old I had not sinned away that "washing of the Holy Ghost" which was given me in baptism, having been strictly educated and carefully

[8] Telford, *Life of John Wesley*, 19.

[9] Ibid., 19–20.

> taught, that I could only be saved "by universal obedience, by keeping all the commandment of God," in the meaning of which I was diligently instructed.[10]

Certainly a large part of that instruction was brought into effect when, during the winter of 1711, John's mother began to read sermons to the children at the kitchen table on Sunday evenings. It was while Samuel was again away in London that Susanna felt the need to fill the remainder of the Sabbath after the morning services with "acts of devotion" solely for the benefit of her children. Her readings and discussions were so inspiring that the servants, the servants' families, and soon the neighbors, joined the meetings, eager to hear Susanna read and teach the Word of God. Those who congregated regularly grew to forty, then one hundred, and at last two hundred, so that there soon was not enough room in the parsonage for all who wanted to hear.

The residing curate[11] was not at all pleased, however, because Susanna's reading drew a crowd that outnumbered those who came to hear him on Sunday mornings. He sent a complaint to Samuel requesting he order his wife to stop these irregular proceedings at the risk of the entire church being scandalized. In response, Mr. Wesley wrote to Susanna requesting she find someone else to read the sermons in her place. She replied that there wasn't anyone else capable of reading them without stumbling over the words. At first, Samuel seemed satisfied with this response; however, after further letters of complaint sent by the curate, Mr. Wesley wrote again requesting the meetings be discontinued.

Susanna again defended her position, stating that she could not in good conscience discontinue the meetings, seeing what good they did the people in compelling them to reform their general habits and inducing them to come more regularly to church. In reference to her own duty as a wife, she concluded in a letter to him:

> If you do, after all, think fit to dissolve this assembly, do not tell me that you *desire* me to do it, for that will not satisfy my conscience; but send me your *positive command*, in such full and express terms as may absolve me from guilt and

[10] Ibid., 20.

[11] Pastor.

> punishment for neglecting this opportunity of doing good, when you and I shall appear before the great and awful tribunal of our Lord Jesus Christ.[12]

Samuel Wesley made no further objections.

John's Formal Education

John and Charles sat under their mother's teaching for two more years before John was nominated to attend a private boarding school called the Charterhouse. He was only ten years old, and, like other boys his age, he was not spared the tyranny older boys were permitted to exercise in English boarding schools at this time. As was the custom, the upperclassmen took the daily allotment of meat given the younger boys. Thus, John, for his first several years, lived on bread alone. Yet he thrived, according to his own account, because he followed his father's suggestion that he run the circumference of the large gardens three times every morning. Like Daniel, his meatless diet made him more resilient, and he remained fit and full of energy even though he had little to eat.

John became known for his unflappable demeanor and self-control.

He also weathered the taunts and practical jokes of the older boys with such composure that he became known among students and teachers for his unflappable demeanor and self-control. He seemed mature beyond his years and proved so sincere and conscientious in his intellectual pursuits that for the remainder of his life, he and the headmaster remained close friends.

Although many historians report that young John strayed from his life of discipline and spiritual devotion during his time at Charterhouse, John himself wrote the following account, which, given careful consideration, reveals that his heart still belonged fully to the Lord:

> The next six or seven years were spent at school, where, outward restraints being removed, I was much more

[12] Southey, *Life of Wesley*, 13.

> negligent than before, even of outward duties, and almost continually guilty of outward sins, which I knew to be such, though they were not scandalous in the eye of the world. However, I still read the Scriptures, and said my prayers, morning and evening. And what I now hoped to be saved by was, 1) not being so bad as other people, 2) having still a kindness for religion, and 3) reading the Bible, going to church, and saying my prayers.[13]

At the age of seventeen, John graduated from the Charterhouse and went on to Christ Church, Oxford. Now fully grown, it is worth noting that John was a small man: only five feet five and a half inches tall and weighing roughly 130 pounds. Yet his diminutive size never seemed to hinder him. This proves that a person's physical stature has little importance compared with how "big" he is spiritually. John Wesley was certainly a giant in faith.

It was near the end of his studies at the university that John had a conversation with a porter who opened a new door to the spiritual awakening that would happen to him some years in the future. The man proved to be the first truly grateful person he had ever met. While the porter had only one coat and had consumed nothing all day but a drink of water, his heart still overflowed with praise to God. John remarked, "You thank God when you have nothing to wear, nothing to eat, and no bed to lie upon. What else do you thank Him for?" The man answered, "I thank Him, that He has given me my life and being, a heart to love Him, and a desire to serve Him."[14] From this testimony, John realized there was something more to following Jesus than he had ever experienced before—and this was something he wanted.

At Oxford, John diligently applied himself to his studies. No doubt he was being drawn closer to the things of God as he read the highly influential writings of Thomas à Kempis, Jeremy Taylor, and William Law. He read Kempis's *The Imitation of Christ*, long considered one of Christianity's greatest manuals on spiritual devotion. With great interest he studied Jeremy Taylor's *The Rule and Exercises of Holy Living*, along with William Law's *A Serious Call to a Devout and*

---

[13] Telford, *Life of John Wesley*, 31.

[14] Ibid.

Holy Life and *A Treatise of Christian Perfection.* These writings, in particular, seemed to lay the foundation for John's spiritual journey and personal "awakening" in the years that followed, as did the advice of his mother:

> And now, in good earnest resolve to make religion the business of your life; for, after all, that is the one thing that, strictly speaking, is necessary; all things beside are comparatively little to the purposes of life. I heartily wish you would now enter upon a strict examination of yourself, that you may know whether you have a reasonable hope of salvation by Jesus Christ. If you have, the satisfaction of knowing it will abundantly reward your pains; if you have not, you will find a more reasonable occasion for tears than can be met with in a tragedy.[15]

Such advice may seem a bit odd to most of us today, but it is important to understand that the doctrine John and Charles grew up with was that of predestination, strongly influenced by the French reformer John Calvin. According to the tenets of Calvinism, people had no say in their own salvation; rather, salvation was predetermined or "predestined" by God. God was absolutely sovereign in all areas of life. Thus, going to church became a quest to know "Am I saved?" more than "How can I be saved?" Throughout their early years, though their hearts pursued God earnestly, neither John nor Charles had any assurance of his own salvation. It would not be until John was already ordained and on his way to his first missions post that he would even begin to wonder at this fact.

The "Bible Bigots"

Despite this lack of inner assurance, John was ordained as a deacon upon graduating and preached his first sermon in the small village of South Lye near the town of Witney. That summer, he returned to Epworth to help his father minister to the parish, remaining there for most of the following year. Interestingly, at the same time John was preparing to leave Oxford, his brother Charles, four years his junior, was just arriving to begin his studies. By the spring

[15] Southey, *Life of Wesley,* 20.

of 1726, to the pride and delight of his father, John was elected Fellow of Lincoln College—a prestigious resident position at Oxford. Eight months later, he was appointed Greek Lecturer and Moderator of the Classes.

It was during this time, just after John turned twenty-one in 1725, that he experienced a turning point in his motivation. Greatly influenced by Kempis's *The Christian's Pattern* and Taylor's *Holy Living and Dying,* John began to pursue a doctrine of complete consecration and holiness in every area of life, the pursuit of which would govern his spiritual aspirations for the next ten years and lay the groundwork for what would later become the Methodist doctrine of Christian Perfection.

In *The Living Wesley*, author James H. Rigg wrote, "He was deeply awakened to a sense of his want of real holiness, and began thenceforth to seek after absolute consecration to God, as the great aim of his life."[16] Rigg recorded the following revealing entry made by John in his diary:

> I saw that simplicity of intention and purity of affection—one design in all we speak and do, and one desire ruling all our tempers—are indeed the wings of the soul, without which she can never ascend to God. I sought after this from that hour....Instantly I resolved to dedicate all my life to God—all my thoughts and words and actions—being thoroughly convinced there was no medium, but that every part of my life (not some only) must either be a sacrifice to God or myself, that is, the devil.[17]

Although John desired to apply himself more fully to the pursuit of holiness, because of the Calvinist doctrines of the day, it was an external, legalistic holiness defined by strict adherence to a set of rules and moral guidelines. It was religion in its worst sense—an external appearance of piety and discipline, but no internal change, no true spiritual transformation of the heart. He had yet to understand that being made truly holy came only through the acceptance of what Christ had accomplished on the cross.

---

[16] James H. Rigg, *The Living Wesley* (London: Charles H. Kelley, 1891), 87.

[17] Ibid., 41.

His hope of salvation was thus dependent on the "holy works" he might accomplish in his own strength. He believed that he could *obtain* grace only by hard work and self-sacrifice, as opposed to receiving the gift of God's saving grace by faith. His Anglican background, which emphasized rules and rituals, added to his renewed determination to make himself more righteous by dedicating himself fully to Christ's service and the precepts for behavior outlined in the Bible. However, he did have a genuine longing to serve God. By the time he turned twenty-two, he felt certain that he was called to what he and his parents felt was the noblest of pursuits: ministry.

John struggled as the external rigors of righteousness did not render within him the inner peace he had hoped for.

Despite his dedication, John struggled, as the external rigors of righteousness did not render within him the inner assurance of peace he had hoped for. From 1725 to 1729, he continued to preach but wrote that he "saw no fruit of [his] labour." This was a time of intense inner turmoil as he struggled with his desire to know God more fully and his own futile efforts to obtain consecration. He believed that preaching about holy living would draw people closer to heaven, and that he himself would come to know the Lord more fully through his own virtuous conduct. However, the personal fellowship with God he sought continued to elude him. No matter how hard he worked, no matter what the degree of self-discipline he achieved, he did not find the inner satisfaction he knew in his heart was possible through Christ. Looking back on this time, John wrote, "From the year 1729–1734,...I saw little fruit.... And no wonder: for I did not preach faith in the blood of the covenant."[18]

It was during this time, in 1729, that Charles started to meet with several like-minded students to study, pray, and observe a series of daily disciplines together. John accepted their invitation to join them, and he was soon serving as their mentor and leader. The group was mockingly called the "Bible Moths," "Bible Bigots,"

[18] John Wesley, *Wesley's Works*, 8: 468, quoted in Rigg, *Living Wesley*, 67.

"Sacramentarians," "Methodists," "Holy Club," or "Enthusiasts" by other students, but over the next few years the group proved to be a force for good in the community as members began visiting prisoners and ministering to orphans and the destitute. The name "Holy Club" stuck, and it soon grew to about twenty-five members. Among the original members was George Whitefield, a fiery young fellow who would later take the flame ignited by John and Charles and carry it farther alone than they would together.

The practice of prayer and fasting was paramount to club membership. This one ingredient may have been the critical characteristic that caused the Wesleys, along with Whitefield and others, to emerge as such powerful forces for Christ. As was recorded by John Gambold, who was an early member of the club and afterward became a Moravian bishop,

> [John] thought prayer to be more his business than anything else, and I have often seen him come out of his closet with a serenity that was next to shining; it discovered where he had been, and gave me double hope of receiving wise direction in the matter about which I came to consult him.[19]

Of John's leadership, Gambold recorded,

> Mr. John Wesley was always the chief manager, for which he was very fit. For he had not only more learning and experience than the rest, but he was blessed with such activity as to be always gaining ground, and such steadiness that he lost none....With a soul always upon the stretch, and a most transparent sincerity, he addicted himself to every good word and work.[20]

Throughout this time John was ever more enamored by the works of William Law. Law's *Christian Perfectionism* and *Serious Call* deepened his earnest, methodical approach to religious strictness and devotion. By 1732, at the prompting of Charles, John sought an audience with Law, and over the next several years, the two corresponded regularly. Greatly influenced by Law's teaching, John and Charles, along with the other members of the Holy Club, devoted themselves

---

[19] Rigg, *Living Wesley*, 74.

[20] Ibid., 72, 74.

to the Doctrine of Christian Holiness. They were accountable to one another for the quality of holiness in each other's lives, studied the Bible together every evening, fasted on Mondays and Fridays, and received Communion weekly. Their critics viewed these practices as another form of "high church asceticism," but the group continued to flourish in spite of such labels.

Interestingly, an anonymous letter submitted to the London paper *Fog's Weekly Journal* claimed, "The university at present is not a little pestered with the sons of sorrow, whose number daily received addition" and who aimed to "make the place nothing but a monastery." The letter's author accused the "sect called Methodists" of "absurd and perpetual melancholy" and urged them to discontinue "this gloomy stupidity."[21]

The ongoing struggle of outward works versus inward holiness continued to rage, however, within John's soul. He wanted to "live out" all that the church prescribed as necessary for a devout life, but time and again he underwent a crisis of faith—a crisis of belief that caused him to doubt assurance of his own salvation, a crisis of conviction he felt every time he was faced with death. As Rigg put it,

> He set himself conscientiously to be an Anglican Churchman, according to the prescriptions of the Rubric; and to be a devout and holy Christian, according to early ecclesiastical examples and traditions. He became accordingly, an ascetic ritualist of the strictest and most advanced class.[22]

For a time, he continued in his efforts to reconcile himself to God through acts of piety and self-discipline. He resolved to spend two hours each day in private devotion, to abstain from every vice, and above all to be efficient and industrious, making the most of every hour of the day.

Back in Epworth, Samuel Wesley's health was failing quickly, and he began to seek a replacement among his sons, hoping to keep the parish and rectory—in which he had invested so much time and where he and his family had called their home for nearly four decades—in the family. Samuel Jr. and John were asked in turn,

---

[21] Elesha Coffman, "Attack of the Bible-Moths," *Christian History* 20, no. 1 [Issue 69] (2001): 22.

[22] Rigg, *Living Wesley,* 89.

but both turned down the position. However, as his father's health deteriorated further, John relented and applied for the position, but he was rejected. Shortly after this, Samuel Wesley Sr. passed away on April 25, 1735, at the age of seventy-two. John and Charles, as well as other family members, were at his side during his last hours. At one point in his final days, he laid his hand upon Charles's head, and said, "Be steady. The Christian faith will surely revive in this kingdom; you shall see it, though I shall not."[23]

"He Is the Savior of the World—But Is He Your Savior?"

Shortly after Samuel Wesley's death, Dr. Burton, a former Oxford associate, and James Oglethorpe, a former friend of Reverend Wesley, suggested John accompany Colonel (later General) Oglethorpe as chaplain to the new settlement in Savannah, Georgia, a settlement named after the reigning King George II. Oglethorpe was a member of Parliament who had great interest in what was happening to the poor in England, and his investigations had led to the release of many from debtors' prison. In June 1732, he and twenty other trustees, including Burton, had obtained a charter from George II and founded the colony for the sake of relieving the poor and giving them a chance to start over. Oglethorpe was appointed governor.

So it was that in February 1733, one hundred and twenty emigrants established the first main settlement of the colony, which would become Savannah. In the following years, Protestant groups from Salzburg, Germany, joined them as they fled the control of the Catholic Church. Scottish Highlanders and some of the Moravians seeking to spread the Word of God among the Native Americans followed.

John was intrigued by the prospect of ministering to the unspoiled natives, and he asked Charles to join him. Oglethorpe appointed Charles as his secretary. John, Charles, and two other gentlemen from the Holy Club, Benjamin Ingham and Charles Delamotte, set out with three hundred passengers aboard the *Simmonds* on October 21, 1735. Charles was ordained on the eve of the voyage.

[23] Telford, *Life of John Wesley,* 72.

The ship was escorted to allay fears of attack by the Spanish. When this escort had to part with the *Simmonds*, the ship docked at Cowes on the Isle of Wight and waited for a more proper convoy before moving on.

Once on board, however, the four Methodists wasted no time establishing a rigorous schedule of private devotion, Bible reading, and public prayer services. The four friends rose at four o'clock each morning and retired between nine and ten o'clock at night. Every moment of the day was mapped out with study, prayer, attending services, meeting their physical needs with meals and the like, and engaging others in discussions about religion.

Among the passengers was a large group of German Moravians—the fifth such group to go to Georgia—who quickly became known for their piety and heart for prayer. The Wesleys and their two friends attended the German Moravians' meeting each evening, and John studied German in order to communicate with them. They observed how the Moravians worshipped with genuine emotion and prayed spontaneous, heartfelt prayers. The Moravians practiced supportive group fellowship, Bible study, hymn singing, and a quiet, personal trust in God for salvation that made an impression on the four "Holy Clubbers." Yet something else would impress them all the more in the days to come.

After several weeks' delay anchored at Cowes on the Isle of Wight, the ship finally left for the broad Atlantic on December 10 with a convoy of forty ships. The journey became a succession of storms. Faced with death at the hands of these tempests, John found himself surprisingly unprepared to die, though he thought he was at peace with God. He even asked himself, "How is it thou hast no faith?"[24]

The Moravians, however, acted in stark contrast to this. No matter how severe the storm, they showed no more fear than they had pride, anger, or unforgiveness previously during the voyage. In fact, in the midst of one of the storms, they were holding a service and singing a psalm when a wave crashed over the vessel, tearing the main sail to pieces, flooding the decks, and pouring into the levels below with such a force that many thought the ship would be swallowed up by the ocean. Yet the Germans sang on as if they hadn't

[24] Telford, *Life of John Wesley,* 78.

even noticed, despite the multitude of English passengers who were panicking and crying out in terror. Never had John met one person, let alone an entire group of men, women, and children, who were so unafraid to die.

John decided to try to model their example of how fearing God meant fearing nothing else in this life. At the same time, however, he realized that these people had something from God that he lacked—and it was something he desperately wanted. Being a man with a call and a title, however, he was still too proud to search it out. This search would have to wait until his efforts in Georgia proved to be a failure several times over and he finally returned to England, hungrier and more desperate for God than ever. So John continued his inner battle to "achieve grace" without the revelation of this type of "heart faith," which he would later discover.

John tried modeling the Moravians' example of how fearing God meant fearing nothing else in this life.

The *Simmonds* landed in Georgia on the morning of February 5, 1736, and the passengers set foot in America for the first time. Eager to begin his work, John consulted with a Moravian pastor, Augustus Gottlieb Spangenberg, for advice. During the course of the conversation, Spangenberg said pointedly, "My brother, I must first ask you one or two questions. Have you the witness within yourself? Does the Spirit of God bear witness with your spirit that you are a child of God?"

John was so surprised by the questions that he didn't know what to answer, so Spangenberg rephrased the question: "Do you know the Christ Jesus?" John paused again, then answered, "I know He is the Saviour of the world." "True," Spangenberg countered, "but do you know He has saved *you*?" Wesley answered, "I hope He has died to save me." Undeterred, Spangenberg rephrased the question again: "Do you know yourself?" John again hesitated before answering "I do" as confidently as he could; however, he felt these were empty words.[25]

[25] Southey, *Life of Wesley,* 52.

Through this conversation, John was again confronted with the fact that the Moravians had something of God that he did not, but he was still too proud to admit it and humble himself enough before God to receive it. However, John became a faithful friend of Spangenberg and the other Moravians, and spent a great deal of time with them in Savannah, continually inquiring about their church in Herrnhut and trying to learn as much from them as he could.

Savannah was still in its early stages when the four Methodists arrived, the entire settlement being a little more than a mile and a third in circumference. There were fewer than two hundred buildings, though some of them were two and three stories high, and the population was roughly 520. Because of the dearth of public buildings, the courthouse doubled as the church. Since the minister John was replacing was still in Savannah when John arrived, it would be three more weeks before John took up lodging in the parsonage, so he continued to live aboard the *Simmonds*. During that time, John made his first contact with the Native Americans, who received him heartily. It gave him great hope for what he would accomplish in the New World.

> ***One evening when John preached, the church was overflowing, the ballroom all but empty.***

In his first sermon, John preached about 1 Corinthians 13, also describing the deathbed of his father and one he had experienced since arriving in Savannah. The congregation seemed deeply moved. In fact, John had an almost immediate effect on the community. Only ten days after his arrival, there was a ball that one of the new gentleman settlers had arranged. It was an utter failure, though, for that very evening, the church was filled to overflowing with people praying; the ballroom was all but empty.

As a rule, new colonies rarely attracted the best type of people to make up their initial populations, especially one such as this that was developed to give people failing in the Old World a fresh start in the New. The poor were also relatively unchurched in Great Britain because the Church of England had little patience with them. People of good reputation and high social standing had little or no reason to leave Great Britain and start over. As a result, most of the settlers in Georgia were seeking adventure, had nothing to lose, or were fleeing from disreputable pasts. Thus, it didn't take long for the Wesley brothers' call to a more holy lifestyle to start rubbing many of them the wrong way.

When Oglethorpe went to help with the settlement in Frederica, situated one hundred miles south of Savannah, Charles Wesley and Benjamin Ingham went with him, leaving John Wesley and Charles Delamotte in Savannah. Though Savannah was still a budding settlement, it was highly civilized compared to Frederica, whose inhabitants were rowdy and hostile. When Charles tried to teach or preach, he was seen as too strict and many in the congregation grew offended by his accusational tone. When he attempted to reform character and settle petty disputes, he succeeded only in giving both sides a common enemy; their common goal was getting him out of their business. One day while Charles was praying in a myrtle grove, a gunshot rang out—the ball only narrowly missed him. Charles did not ignore the warning in this shot.

Shortly after this, Oglethorpe took an expedition to visit the Native Americans in the area. While he was gone, in the midst of a sermon by Charles, the town doctor fired a practice shot with his rifle, aiming so close to the building the church was meeting in that the constable felt it his duty to arrest him. It was Charles who incurred blame, however, because everyone thought he had called for the officer to do this. The doctor's wife ran through the streets, shouting expletives and defaming Charles's character, and the doctor refused to go out to any patients, even though there was a woman who needed him. When Oglethorpe returned, he found the town in an uproar. Many threatened to desert the settlement if something was not done, and all pointed to Charles as the cause of the trouble.

While Oglethorpe did manage the complainers with a stern hand, he also expressed his disappointment with the Wesleys. He had hoped that they would bring some peace and order to the colony, but instead, all he saw were formal prayers, poorly attended church services, and general meddling in the affairs of others. While he did not fault the brothers for the current chaos, he was frustrated that they had done nothing to alleviate it.

While John and Charles maintained unquestionable devotion and sincerity in their religion at this time, it is important to remember that neither man was yet born again, nor did either have the Holy Spirit working actively in his life. Again, they were lacking that something possessed by the porter at Oxford and by the Moravians—that something whose absence John had recognized. John's early conversation with Pastor Spangenberg exhibited, however, that as ordained ministers called to lead the religious life in Georgia, he and Charles were too proud to admit that they were not, in reality, qualified for that job. They were disciplined in practicing religion but knew little of Jesus himself and the benefits of operating in the power of the Holy Spirit.

While John's interventions in Frederica were helpful, the area still seemed hopeless. Moreover, Charles became ill, and Oglethorpe dealt tyrannically with him. He had provided none of the furnishings Charles had expected and barred him from using any of his. Charles did not have as much as a bed to sleep on, and when he arose from a fever to perform a funeral service, he was given the deceased man's bedstead. The next day, Oglethorpe gave the bed to someone else he felt needed it more. It was a trying time for Charles.

Charles and Oglethorpe eventually made amends after Oglethorpe returned from freeing Georgia from a Spanish blockade. Oglethorpe had thought the struggle would cost him his life, but when Charles's prayers that he would return were answered, Oglethorpe's harshness softened. When the governor sent Charles back to England in August 1736 with some important paperwork, however, Charles did not return. His American adventure had lasted only about six months.

While John's primary goal in going to Georgia had been to minister to the Native Americans, obstacle after obstacle prevented him from doing so. He had been appointed minister of Savannah without his consent, and the duties this position entailed kept him tied to the settlement. When he had an opportunity to go elsewhere, his parishioners persuaded him to wait for a replacement before leaving; of course, a replacement never came. All the while, the Native American tribes were in the midst of wars that not only made it dangerous to go, but also gave the men no time to listen to John preach the Gospel. His pattern of keeping busy with good works—teaching catechism on Saturday and Sunday afternoons; reading prayers and holding daily services in English, Italian, and French; attending the Moravian services, and regularly visiting the sick, among other activities—also kept him tied to the colony.

A Mismanaged Romance

Something else—someone else, rather—tied John to Savannah, though he may have been unaware of it at first. She was Sophia Christiana Hopkey, the niece of Thomas Causton, the chief magistrate of Savannah. Upon the Wesley brothers' arrival in Savannah, Causton and Oglethorpe wondered if wedding John to Sophia might not both tie him to the settlement and soften some of the eccentricities Oglethorpe felt were keeping John from being more useful to him. The relationship began roughly one month after John's arrival in Savannah. Sophia was attractive, intelligent, and refined, and she was introduced to John as a wounded spirit, curious about the way to eternal life. The two seemed to be naturally progressing along the path Oglethorpe had hoped they would.

From his writings, it is evident that John was quite smitten with Sophia Hopkey. But something apparently happened, perhaps between them, which prompted Sophia to go to Frederica for a time. Her departure compelled John to send his brother a letter, which he wrote partly in Greek to render the letter undecipherable if intercepted:

> I conjure you spare no time, no address or pains to learn the true cause of my friend's former grief. I much doubt you are in the right. God forbid that she should again err thus. Watch over, guard her as much as you possibly can. Write to me, how it behooves me to write to her.[26]

When John went to Frederica in October of that year, some weeks after Charles's departure, he found that Sophia had suffered from the general unsavory demeanor of the community. He wrote,

> Even poor Miss Sophy was scarce the shadow of what she was when I left her. I endeavored to convince her of it, but in vain; and to put it effectually out of my power so to do,

[26] Southey, *Life of Wesley,* 61.

> she resolved to return to England immediately. I was at first a little surprised, but I soon recollected my spirits and remembered my calling.[27]

However, John soon convinced her to stay in Georgia, and when he returned to Savannah he took Sophia with him.

After this, Sophia seemed to take every opportunity to be with John. She persuaded him to tutor her in French, and when John was seized with a fever, she nursed him night and day for five days until he recovered. She also seemed to hang on his every word. After inquiring about his preferences regarding dress and comportment, she began to wear only white and cast off everything ornate or gaudy. When John advised her not to eat immediately before bedtime for health reasons, she complied. As things progressed, it seemed the two would soon wed.

As the anniversary of their arrival in Georgia approached, however, Delamotte cornered John and asked him if he intended to marry Sophia. John was taken aback and refused to answer. Delamotte tried to persuade him that her intentions would not align with his, and that she was seeking the convenience of a marriage; John was being duped by her charms. John became unsettled about the relationship and went to consult with the Moravian bishop, David Nitschman. The bishop heard him out but offered only to pray and consider the matter.

Some time passed and John grew ever more anxious about the question. He decided to bring the matter before the board of Moravian elders. Knowing that they were meeting, he went to their building and found Delamotte there with them. John told the group why he had come. The bishop explained that he had just had time to consider the case, asking if John was willing to abide by whatever they advised. John was hesitant, but agreed. "Then," replied Nitschman, "we advise you to proceed no further in this business." Wesley could only reply weakly, "The will of the Lord be done." John was heartbroken. In his journal, he likened the requirement of forsaking Sophia to God's commanding him "to pull out my right eye; and by his grace I determined to do so."[28]

---

[27] Telford, *Life of John Wesley*, 84.

[28] Southey, *Life of Wesley*, 62.

John could not bring himself to tell Sophia what had happened, but in the days that followed, his behavior changed so dramatically that his intentions must have become quite evident to her. In response, Sophia was engaged to a reputable young man in the community named Williamson, and they were married four days later, on March 12—exactly one year after the day John was first introduced to Sophia.

While Sophia Hopkey did indeed appear to be fickle and was probably every bit as crafty as Delamotte suggested, John's heart would never be the same. The bitterness of his lost love must have eaten at him, for John's affections had been quite sincere. The mission to Georgia was all but flourishing, and John could have stayed on quite comfortably for some time, but his heart could not bear it. To make things worse, he bottled up his feelings within himself, as he likened God's commandment to give up Sophia equivalent to God's word to Ezekiel:

> *Son of man, behold, I take away from thee the desire of thine eyes with a stroke: yet neither shalt thou mourn nor weep, neither shall thy tears run down. Forbear to cry, make no mourning for the dead, bind the tire of thine head upon thee, and put on thy shoes upon thy feet, and cover not thy lips, and eat not the bread of men.*
>
> (Ezekiel 24:16–17)

John threw himself back into his work. In short order, John began to see flaws in Sophia's character that he had not noticed before, and he pointed them out to her. She chafed at his admonitions, and trouble began to brew. Sophia's uncle Causton, the magistrate, was exactly the type of passionate man colonies often attracted—it was said he had fled England to shirk charges in a financial dispute—and to incite his wrath was a grave mistake of any man. Being ill, however, he let the matter fall to his wife, and Mrs. Causton spoke with John and asked for his reproofs in writing, which he delivered. Several weeks later, John refused to allow Sophia and her new husband to take Communion in church. Williamson took this prohibition as a personal insult and sued John, demanding payment of 1,000 pounds for defamation of character. Causton, John's former friend and confidante, gave him every opportunity to explain himself. But when John tried to hold up the veil of clergyman as a right not to answer, Causton lost all patience with him and said he would not rest until John gave account of himself. John complied by writing to Sophia, stating that she had not properly informed him of her plans to take Communion that day. He also explained that he was not permitted to give Holy Communion to someone who had sinned without repenting.

Things went from bad to worse when Causton took the letter and shared it with everyone who would listen, omitting portions that didn't fit his purpose and exaggerating others to increase their impact. John wrote a letter in response, which he read aloud in a public service. Sophia wrote out an affidavit saying that Wesley had made several successive marriage proposals to her, all of which she had refused, and she insinuated many harmful things about John's character. John asked for a copy of the letter, and Causton told him he could obtain one from any newspaper office in America, as they had spread them everywhere to ensure he would never find another post on that continent. A grand jury of fifty men was called to hear the case, but the population was such that only forty-four could be found. Ten counts were brought against John, only one of which was valid: that he had spoken and written to Sophia without her husband's permission. John demanded that the case be decided immediately, but the hearing was delayed for months. In the meantime, John's financial sources dried up, yet he determined to stay in Georgia no matter what.

John seemed a man with a form of godliness, but none of the power that went with it; that would soon change, however.

The weeks dragged on. After much deliberation and prayer, John decided to return to England, and he set sail aboard the *Samuel* for his native land on December 22, 1737. He was dejected and finally seemed humble enough to search out just what it was that the Moravians had found that he had not. Reflecting on this time in Georgia and lamenting his own spiritual state, he wrote the following entry in his journal on Tuesday, February 24, 1738:

> I went to America, to convert the Indians; but oh! who shall convert me? who, what is he that will deliver me from this evil heart of mischief? I have a fair summer religion. I can talk well; nay, and believe myself, while no danger is near; but let death look me in the face, and my spirit is troubled. Nor can I say, "To die is gain!"[29]

Until this point, John's life had been plagued by a lack of clear conviction about the nature of his true calling from God. While doing good never deserves condemnation, doing good can sometimes be an obstacle that keeps us from doing what is best. John hungered for approval, as we all do, but too often he let this obstruct his path to finding his true purpose. He had rejected his father's appeal to lead the parish in Epworth, but as his father neared death, he had relented and applied, only to be rejected. He had traveled to Georgia to minister to the Indians, but he had busied himself with everything else possible when he got there. When he was named minister for Savannah without his consent, he accepted the appointment to please the local community in lieu of rejecting it and following his heart. The faith of the Moravians tugged at his spirit, but he was not willing to risk his position or self-assurance to answer that call. John showed every sign of being a man who had a form of godliness, but none of the power that went with it. Thank God for all of us, however, this was soon going to change.

"I Felt My Heart Strangely Warmed"

With John Wesley aboard, the *Samuel* dropped anchor in Downs, England, only a few hours after the departure of the ship bearing George Whitefield to Georgia. In fact, the two ships passed within sight of one another, but neither John nor George knew that a good friend was close enough to hear a shouted greeting.

Upon landing in England, John learned that Whitefield had only just left and could still receive a message from him, so he wrote, "When I saw God by the wind which was carrying you out brought me in, I asked counsel of God. His answer you have enclosed." It

---

[29] John Wesley, *The Journal of John Wesley*, Christian Classics Ethereal Library, http://www.ccel.org/ccel/wesley/journal.vi.ii.vii.html.

appeared that John had scribbled advice on several strips of paper; by faith, he drew them as lots to indicate the will of God for Whitefield. George pulled out the slip of paper, which said simply, "Let him return to England."[30]

After his failure in America, John must have found such advice warranted and confirming in a rather self-justifying way. After all, if he couldn't succeed in America, what did Whitefield hope to accomplish? Whitefield, for his part, as he had no confidence in laying fleece before the Lord, laid the matter to prayer. As he prayed, he was reminded of the story in 1 Kings 13 about the prophet who turned from his calling because another man told him to do so. When he disobeyed the Lord, he was attacked and killed by a lion. Whitefield continued on in his mission without giving John's counsel another thought. Ironically enough, Whitefield was sailing for Georgia because John had written to him to request his help there, for "the harvest is so great, and the labourers so few."[31]

Only four days after returning to London, John was introduced to three young Moravians—Wenceslaus Neisser, George Schulius, and Peter Bohler—who had been recently ordained by Count Zinzendorf. Upon making Bohler's acquaintance, John took it upon himself to converse with him in German, and the two began a dialogue that continued over the next several months.

Bohler's discussions with John again showed him the possibility of a greater relationship with God than he had experienced up to this time, but his head still struggled with the Moravians' beliefs, many of which conflicted with his own. John was determined to find holiness through devotion, determination, and discipline, while Bohler emphasized that salvation came only by faith in Jesus Christ alone and would be accompanied by love, peace, and joy in the Holy Ghost. John couldn't see how this belief could be possible, but he couldn't let the matter go, either.

He was so perplexed that he wondered if it would be better for him to stop preaching until he had found this faith instead of continuing with what he felt was hypocrisy. When he asked Bohler whether he should stop preaching, Bohler replied, "By no means."

---

[30] Southey, *Life of Wesley*, 75.

[31] Ibid., 80.

"But what can I preach?" Wesley asked. The Moravian answered, "Preach faith *till* you have it; and then *because* you have it, you *will* preach faith."[32]

Bohler traveled with Wesley back to Oxford, where Charles tutored him in English. He spent more and more time in the company of the brothers, encouraging them in the development of their "Methodist Society." Bohler wrote to Zinzendorf,

> I traveled with the two brothers, John and Charles Wesley, from London to Oxford. The elder, John, is a good-natured man; he knew he did not properly believe on the Savior, and was willing to be taught. His brother, with whom you often conversed a year ago, is at present very much distressed in his mind, but does not know how he shall begin to be acquainted with the Savior.[33]

The Wesley brothers were stretched by Bohler's persistent conviction that grace is obtainable by faith alone, and that salvation immediately follows the recognition of that faith rather than being something that has to be worked for over time. "Would he rob me of my endeavors? I have nothing else to trust to,"[34] Charles famously wrote.

John decided to turn to the Bible for answers, and he was amazed by what he found, particularly in the book of Acts. Almost every salvation proclaimed there was, in fact, instantaneous, and the slowest was that of the apostle Paul—it took a mere three days. John was thirty-five at this time, and he had never seen this in the Scriptures before. He wondered if perhaps something within him had changed. "But," he said,

> I was beat out of this retreat too by the concurring evidence of several living witnesses, who testified God had thus wrought in themselves; giving them in a moment such faith in the blood of His Son, as translated them out of darkness into light, out of sin and fear into holiness and happiness.

---

[32] Ibid., 84. The emphasis is Southey's.

[33] "December 15, 1737: Zinzendorf Ordained Peter Bohler," Christian History Institute, http://chi.gospelcom.net/DAILYF/2003/12/daily-12-15-2003.shtml.

[34] Ibid.

> Here ended my disputing: I could now only cry out, Lord, help Thou my unbelief![35]

Soon more Moravians came to London and began to have regular meetings. Bohler left for Georgia, having long intended to do so. John lamented his departure and continued to struggle with his doctrine, even though he was still preaching passionately in various congregations. He even exchanged letters with William Law expressing his frustration at finding nothing of this teaching in his writing or previous interactions with him.

A surprising letter arrived from Charles, reporting that he had made his peace with God. While sick a second time with pleurisy[36]—which had threatened his life earlier—he went to the house of a man named Bray, a "poor ignorant mechanic…who knew nothing but Christ."[37] While staying there, on May 21, 1738, Charles found the faith and assurance of his salvation that Bohler had taught him and his brother about. In that same hour, his strength returned to him and he rose up, healed. John was pleased for his brother because of his renewed spiritual and physical health, but he could not help feeling much less worthy of salvation than he had felt before. He expressed this feeling of worthlessness thusly:

> I feel I am *sold under sin*. I know that I deserve nothing but wrath, being full of abominations. All my works, my righteousness, my prayers, need an atonement for themselves. I have nothing to plead. God is holy, I am unholy. God is a consuming fire, I am altogether a sinner, meet to be consumed. Yet I hear a voice, Believe, and thou shalt be saved. He that believeth is passed from death unto life. Oh, let no one deceive us by vain words as if we had already attained this faith!...Saviour of men, save us from trusting in anything but Thee! Draw us after Thee! Let us be emptied of ourselves, and then fill us with all peace and joy in believing, and let nothing separate us from Thy love in time or eternity.[38]

---

[35] Southey, *Life of Wesley,* 86.

[36] A severe respiratory illness.

[37] Telford, *Life of John Wesley,* 100.

[38] Southey, *Life of Wesley,* 90. The emphasis is Southey's.

However, on the evening of Wednesday, May 24, 1738, this feeling changed dramatically. It is best to catch this change in John's own words from his journal:

> In the evening I went very unwillingly to a society in Aldersgate Street, where one was reading Luther's preface to the Epistle to the Romans. About a quarter before nine, while he was describing the change which God works in the heart through faith in Christ, I felt my heart strangely warmed. I felt I did trust in Christ, Christ alone, for salvation; and an assurance was given me that He had taken away my sins, even mine, and saved me from the law of sin and death.
>
> I began to pray with all my might for those who had in a more especial manner despitefully used me and persecuted me. I then testified openly to all there what I now first felt in my heart. But it was not long before the enemy suggested, "This cannot be faith; for where is thy joy?" Then was I taught that peace and victory over sin are essential to faith in the Captain of our salvation; but that, as to the transports of joy that usually attend the beginning of it, especially in those who have mourned deeply, God sometimes giveth, sometimes withholdeth, them according to the counsels of His own will.
>
> After my return home, I was much buffeted with temptations, but I cried out, and they fled away. They returned again and again. I as often lifted up my eyes, and He "sent me help from his holy place." And herein I found the difference between this and my former state chiefly consisted. I was striving, yea, fighting with all my might under the law, as well as under grace. But then I was sometimes, if not often, conquered; now, I was always conqueror.
>
> Thursday, 25.—The moment I awakened, "Jesus, Master," was in my heart and in my mouth; and I found all my strength lay in keeping my eye fixed upon Him and my soul waiting on Him continually. Being again at St. Paul's in the afternoon, I could taste the good word of God in the anthem which began, "My song shall be always of the

> loving-kindness of the Lord: with my mouth will I ever be showing forth thy truth from one generation to another." Yet the enemy injected a fear, "If thou dost believe, why is there not a more sensible change?" I answered (yet not I), "That I know not. But, this I know, I have 'now peace with God.' And I sin not today, and Jesus my Master has forbidden me to take thought for the morrow."[39]

The Moravians had given the Wesley brothers the key they needed to transform their nation—the new birth. England was caught in the grip of the Calvinist belief that no one could know who was predestined to be saved, as well as the Church of England's teaching that the sacraments were the necessary duty of anyone who hoped he was predestined for salvation. The Methodist Revival would transform England by teaching that not only could you know that you were saved, but also that you could receive that salvation immediately and have peace in your heart thereafter. Then, when John's "methods" of pursuing holiness were added to this—which included "united societies" for believers to gather together regularly, focusing on prayer, fasting, and searching the Scriptures—revival now had not only a framework, but also the spark of the Holy Spirit and the power of God for transformation.

This was an epochal time for John and Charles, who were suddenly challenged to give up strict adherence to their ascetic piety for a singular passion of seeing the lost saved by personal faith in Christ. Charles burst forth in writing hymns that proclaimed God's goodness and grace. John set immediately to preaching the "good news." Where they had before abounded in zeal for study and discipline, they now overflowed with passionate enthusiasm for saving souls. The simplicity of the Gospel had been made clear at last, and where they had earlier failed to understand or convey it, they now gave themselves over completely to making known to all the simple truth of God's redeeming love.

John and Charles were consumed by a new revelation that faith comes by hearing the genuine Word of God preached rather than by observing sacraments or even making great sacrifices. John

[39] Wesley, *Journal of John Wesley*, http://www.ccel.org/ccel/wesley/journal.vi.ii.xvi.html.

described this time as the second major turning point in his life; the first was in 1725, when he dedicated himself to the work of the ministry and the pursuit of outward holiness. John and Charles now both rejoiced in the knowledge of having been made holy once and for all through the blood of Jesus. They were finally able to let go of their burdensome struggle to "enforce holiness" through their own strength of will, good works, and pious devotion.

Having spoken often about the *means of grace* being achieved through "'works of piety' (spiritual disciplines) and 'works of mercy' (doing good to others),"[40] they would now teach a means of grace provided exclusively through faith in Christ—God alone transforms believers through prayer, Bible reading, meditation, and Holy Communion. They taught that it is the power of God's love at work in us that enables believers to aspire to holiness of heart and life. This shift in perspective led to the brothers' emphatic exhortation that we must acknowledge God's extravagant love for us before we are to begin to love Him in return or to love our neighbor as we should. They also taught that yielding to God's love and allowing it to flow through us will ultimately produce "every Christian grace, every holy and happy temper. And from those springs uniform holiness of [action]."[41] Like Peter and Paul before them, once the Wesley brothers personally experienced the resurrection life of Christ in their own hearts by faith, they could not help giving their lives wholly in order to make that life known to all.

John and Charles gave up their strict adherence to ascetic piety for a passion to see the lost saved by faith in Christ.

On June 11, 1738, eighteen days after his conversion, John preached a sermon entitled "Salvation by Faith," which was based

[40] Charles Yrigoyen Jr., *Holiness of Heart and Life,* 33, quoted in "Spiritual Disciplines: Works of Piety," John Wesley: Holiness of Heart and Life, General Board of Global Ministries, United Methodist Church, http://gbgm-umc.org/umw/wesley/disciplc.stm.

[41] Randy L. Maddox, "Be Ye Perfect?" *Christian History* 20, no. 1 [Issue 69] (2001): 32.

on Ephesians 2:8—*"By grace are ye saved through faith"*—before the university at Oxford. In this sermon, he said,

> Wherewithal then shall a sinful man atone for any the least of his sins? With his own works? No. Were they ever so many or holy, they are not his own, but God's. But indeed they are all unholy and sinful themselves, so that every one of them needs a fresh atonement. Only corrupt fruit grows on a corrupt tree. And his heart is altogether corrupt and abominable; being "come short of the glory of God," the glorious righteousness at first impressed on his soul, after the image of his great Creator. Therefore, having nothing, neither righteousness nor works, to plead, his mouth is utterly stopped before God.[42]

Because it contradicted strict Calvinist doctrine, John's message was considered an open threat to the Church of England. Throughout the course of the following year, John became increasingly unwelcome at every church in London and the surrounding areas. Although John and Charles desired unity, they felt compelled to follow their inner conviction and continued to teach and disciple the growing group of Oxford Methodists. Meetings were held in small rooms, filled to capacity, where the Holy Spirit moved freely and touched lives. After experiencing the deep impact of God's living Spirit, Wesley and his converts could not fit easily into the confines of the Church of England, no matter their willingness to do so. Woefully, John found himself altogether unwelcome in the Church of England.

John Journeys to Herrnhut

Hoping to find his bearings, John decided to travel to Herrnhut in Saxony (Germany) to gain a better understanding of the Moravian Brethren and to see how they had discovered the truths of the new birth and life by the Spirit of God, a discovery he had found nowhere in the teachings of William Law or Thomas à Kempis. In July 1738, he set out with Ingham, who had been with him in Georgia, and six others, for Germany. They landed at Rotterdam, and

---

[42] John Wesley, "Salvation by Faith," Christian Classics Ethereal Library, http://www.ccel.org/ccel/wesley/sermons.v.i.html.

then proceeded on to Ysselstein, where they spent a day with some English acquaintances living there. The next day, they continued on foot to Cologne, then up the Rhine to Mentz, and on to Frankfurt, where they were received by Peter Bohler's parents. The next day, they reached Marienborn, where they found Count Zinzendorf and a group of more than fifty disciples from various nations. Describing the group, John wrote,

> And here I continually met with what I sought for—living proofs of the power of faith; persons saved from inward as well as outward sin by the love of God shed abroad in their hearts, and from all doubt and fear by the abiding witness of the Holy Ghost given unto them.[43]

To his brother Samuel, he wrote,

> God has given me, at length, the desire of my heart. I am with a church whose conversation is in heaven, in whom is the mind that was in Christ, and who so walk as He walked. As they have all one Lord and one faith, so they are all partakers of one spirit, the spirit of meekness and love, which uniformly and continually animates all their conversation. Oh! How high and holy a thing Christianity is! And how widely distant from that, I know not what, which is so called, though it neither purifies the heart, nor renews the life, after the image of our blessed Redeemer. I grieve to think how that holy name by which we are called must be blasphemed among the heathen, while they see discontented Christians, passionate Christians, resentful Christians, earthly-minded Christians. Yea, to come to what we are apt to count small things, while they see Christians judging one another, ridiculing one another, speaking evil of one another, increasing instead of bearing one another's burdens.[44]

John and his companions spent two weeks here, learning what they could before traveling on to Herrnhut, a journey that took them eleven days. At this time, Herrnhut comprised about one hundred

[43] Southey, *Life of Wesley,* 103.

[44] Ibid., 104–105.

houses of inhabitants who had continued their twenty-four-hour-a-day, seven-day-a-week prayer service for more than a decade. While John found many of their customs strange, he grew increasingly uncomfortable with the sway Zinzendorf's "apostleship" gave him over everyone there. Even though he found their neatly organized lifestyle almost monastic, he marveled to find the same love here as he had found among Zinzendorf's disciples at Marienborn. John spent another two weeks in Herrnhut before departing on foot to return to England. While he greatly admired the Moravians and their doctrine, he found he didn't fit in with their community and cultural differences—perhaps, he thought, because he didn't understand them, but also because God had another calling for him. On departing, he wrote, "I would gladly have spent my life here; but my Master calling me to labour in another part of His vineyard, I was constrained to take my leave of this happy place."[45] He arrived back in London on September 16, still hungry to find exactly what it was God was calling him to do with the rest of his life.

Those Shouting Methodists

On New Year's Day, 1739, the Wesley brothers were joined by Whitefield, who had recently returned from his ministry in Georgia, as well as Ingham and about sixty others, for a love feast like the one they had shared among the Moravian Brethren. When the midnight hour struck, they prayed and worshipped; this continued on into the morning as they fervently sought God's will and direction. Then, at approximately three o'clock, the power of God moved in an unusual way. Everyone present fell down, crying and weeping with joy. Then they "broke out with one voice, 'We praise thee O God, we acknowledge thee to be the Lord.'"[46] A renewed compassion enveloped them as the love and mercy they felt for the lost compelled them afresh to lay down their lives for the sake of the Gospel. Whitefield acknowledged the power manifested in this time, saying,

---

[45] Southey, *Life of Wesley*, 113.

[46] John Wesley, *The Journal of John Wesley*, vol. 2, ed. Nehemiah Curnock (London: Epworth Publishing, 1938), 122–125, quoted in Eddie L. Hyatt, *2000 Years of Charismatic Christianity: A 20th Century Look at Church History from a Pentecostal/Charismatic Perspective* (Chicota, TX and Tulsa, OK: Hyatt International Ministries, Inc., 1996), 106.

> It was a Pentecost season indeed: sometimes whole nights were spent in prayer. Often have we been filled as with new wine; and often have I seen them overwhelmed with the Divine Presence, and cry out, "Will God indeed dwell with men upon the earth? How dreadful is this place? This is no other than the house of God and the gate of heaven!"[47]

In the months that followed, they would need the courage and strength of vision they walked away with after those nights. Whatever the Holy Spirit imparted would carry those present—especially John, Charles, and George—to entirely new levels of ministry. It would be the year the great Methodist Revival—or the Great Awakening—would begin.

From that point on, because of their emphasis on the work and ministry of the Holy Spirit, the Wesley brothers and their followers became known as "enthusiasts." Their meetings had a reputation of being emotional and unpredictable. A printed pamphlet was widely circulated that explained the Greek interpretation of "enthusiast" as "possession by a divine spirit." Believing the "enthusiasts" had fallen prey to the wrong kind of spirit, the Church of England shut its doors to them. This didn't seem to matter, though, as God was already planting seeds of insight in Whitefield's heart about what was ahead. In once particular instance when crowds were turned away because the building was already full, Whitefield felt compelled to go out and stand on a tombstone to address the hundreds gathered outside. It wouldn't be long before he was doing regular open-air preaching, which drew audiences bigger than any building in Britain could hold.

Initially opposed to "field preaching," John soon couldn't wait to preach in the open air.

By the spring of 1739, upon the urging of Whitefield, John found there was nothing left for him to do but take his preaching outside the church doors. He followed his friend to Bristol that March. Whitefield had already delved into open-air preaching in the

[47] Southey, *Life of Wesley,* 123.

bustling Bristol area, hoping to reach the multitudes of coal miners and shipyard workers there. On March 29, John and Charles accompanied Whitefield to the town square with the intention of bringing their message of faith to whoever would listen. At first, John opposed preaching out in the open, but as Whitefield got started, a noisy crowd gathered out of sheer curiosity. Were their hearts prepared to hear the sacred truths he was about to impart? While thoughts of uncertainty flooded John's mind, Whitefield, not hesitating to take advantage of this opportunity, spoke boldly, inspiring the eager listeners with God's Word. Looking on, John was moved by the sea of faces so thirsty for the water of the Word.

The next day, John stood on a little hill outside of town and delivered his own first open-air message to a reported three thousand people. He preached from Luke 4:18–19:

> *The Spirit of the Lord is upon Me, because He has anointed Me to preach the gospel to the poor; He has sent Me to heal the brokenhearted, to proclaim liberty to the captives and recovery of sight to the blind, to set at liberty those who are oppressed; to proclaim the acceptable year of the Lord.*

The Spirit of the Lord was upon him from that day forth to preach the Gospel to the poor.

John was ecstatic and so invigorated by the experience that he couldn't wait for the next opportunity to preach in the open air. Once he experienced the thrill of "field preaching," there was no turning back. He had found a willing audience, and although they were not always receptive, he knew that what he had to share was what they needed most. In the words of biographer Basil Miller, "Here was a crowd of people to whom his message came as a bursting light from heaven, and he would not deny them this glimpse of Christ."[48] From then on, almost until his dying day, John preached to whoever would hear him, not only daily, but sometimes three or four times a day. John preached wherever he could—in barns, fields, and town squares. As the Holy Spirit moved among the crowds, people would cry out, shout for joy, and fall down under the power of God. A witness wrote the following:

---

[48] Basil Miller, *John Wesley: The World His Parish* (Grand Rapids, MI: Zondervan Publishing, 1943), 71.

> Blasphemers cried for mercy; sinners were smitten to the earth in deep conviction; even passing travelers were so affected. A physician studied a case of a woman whom he had known for years, and as he saw perspiration break from her face and her body shake he decided this was no mere physical disorder but that it was evidence of God's workings.[49]

Such scenes were frequent in Bristol, in society halls and the open air alike. People would cry out under the conviction of sin as if they were about to die, prayer would be offered for them, and they would rise up, rejoicing in God their Savior.

One such case was that of John Hayden, a weaver known throughout the community as an upstanding churchman. Hearing what was happening under John's ministry, he came to see for himself; he left, unimpressed. After the meeting, he told his friends that it was all a delusion. He sat down to dinner the next day and finished reading a sermon he had borrowed, entitled "Salvation by Faith." After he read the last line, his face changed color and he fell from his chair, screaming and beating himself against the ground. The Wesley brothers were called, and they came as quickly as possible. When they arrived, they found the house full of people; Hayden was in the same unusual state. Hayden's wife had first tried to keep everyone out, but Hayden cried out, "No; let them come; let all the world see the just judgment of God." As John entered, he announced to those present, "Ay, this is he who, I said, was a deceiver of the people. But God has overtaken me. I said it was a delusion; but this is no delusion." Then he roared, "O thou devil! Thou cursed devil! Yea, thou legion of devils! Thou canst not stay. Christ will cast thee out! I know His work is begun. Tear me to pieces, if thou wilt; but thou canst not hurt me." As soon as he had spoken, he began beating himself on the ground again, his chest heaving and sweat rolling off of his face. The Wesley brothers and those with them began to pray earnestly, continuing until the seizures had stopped and Hayden was set free of them. John returned that evening to find that though Hayden was weak and had no voice, he was full of peace and the joy of the Holy Spirit.[50]

---

[49] Ibid., 75.

[50] Telford, *Life of John Wesley,* 122–123.

Similar events and reactions followed John to London and Newcastle as he ministered in those places. Though both George and Charles were more boisterous and emotional preachers, such seizures rarely happened when they ministered. John's words were calm and measured yet seemed to penetrate straight to the hearts of his listeners.

As these things manifested in their meetings, they were also often called upon to pray for those sick or demonically oppressed. The following excerpt from John's journals tells of one such instance:

> Thur. [October] 25 [1739].—I was sent for to one in Bristol, who was taken ill the evening before. (This fact too I will simply relate, so far as I was an ear or eye witness of it.) She lay on the ground, furiously gnashing her teeth, and after a while roared aloud. It was not easy for three or four persons to hold her, especially when the name of Jesus was named. We prayed; the violence of her symptoms ceased, though without a complete deliverance.
>
> In the evening, being sent for to her again, I was unwilling, indeed, afraid, to go: Thinking it would not avail, unless some who were strong in faith were to wrestle with God for her. I opened my Testament on those words, "I was afraid, and went and hid thy talent in the earth." I stood reproved, and went immediately. She began screaming before I came into the room; then broke out into a horrid laughter, mixed with blasphemy, grievous to hear. One who from many circumstances apprehended a preternatural agent to be concerned in this, asking, "How didst thou dare to enter into a Christian?" was answered, "She is not a Christian. She is mine." Q. "Dost thou not tremble at the name of Jesus?" No words followed, but she shrunk back and trembled exceedingly. Q. "Art thou not increasing thy own damnation?" It was faintly answered, "Ay, ay:" Which was followed by fresh cursing and blaspheming.
>
> My brother coming in, she cried out, "Preacher! Field preacher! I don't love field-preaching." This was repeated two hours together, with spitting, and all the expressions of strong aversion.

> We left her at twelve, but called again about noon on Friday, 26. And now it was that God showed He heareth the prayer. All her pangs ceased in a moment: She was filled with peace, and knew that the son of wickedness was departed from her.[51]

In another instant, John was called to a man on his deathbed:

> Wed. [December] 15 [1742].—I preached at Horsley-upon-Tyne, eight (computed) miles from Newcastle. It was about two in the afternoon. The house not containing the people, we stood in the open air in spite of the frost. I preached again in the evening, and in the morning. We then chose to walk home, having each of us catched a violent cold by riding the day before. Mine gradually wore off; but Mr. Meyrick's increased, so that, oil Friday, he took his bed....
>
> Mon. 20.—We laid the first stone of the house. Many were gathered, from all parts, to see it; but none scoffed or interrupted, while we praised God, and prayed that he would prosper the work of our hands upon us. Three or four times in the evening, I was forced to break off preaching, that we might pray and give thanks to God. When I came home, they told me the physician said, he did not expect Mr. Meyrick would live till the morning. I went to him, but his pulse was gone. He had been speechless and senseless for some time. A few of us immediately joined in prayer: (I relate the naked fact:) before we had done his sense and his speech returned. Now, he that will account for this by natural causes, has my free leave: but I choose to say, This is the power of God.
>
> Sat. 25.—The physician told me he could do no more; Mr. Meyrick could not live over the night. I went up, and found them all crying about him; his legs being cold, and (as it seemed) dead already. We all kneeled down, and called upon God with strong cries and tears. He opened

[51] John Wesley, *The Works of the Reverend John Wesley, A.M.*, vol. 3. Edited by John Emory. (New York: T. Mason and G. Lane, 1840), 162.

> his eyes, and called for me; and, from that hour, he continued to recover his strength, till he was restored to perfect health.[52]

The Wesleys faced some of the same challenges that modern Charismatics/Pentecostals do—the challenge of discerning between the godly experiences of grace and other types of spiritual or emotional manifestations. Needless to say, they were operating under the power of the Holy Spirit and that anointing no doubt informed and empowered their preaching—as well as attracting a great deal of controversy and criticism.

The Wesleyan revivals were known for loud volumes and intense emotional displays. Followers became known as the "shouting Methodists," as their cries would literally interrupt the preachers, making the gatherings appear chaotic and unruly. Again, John's journals tell of such meetings:

> Saturday [June] 16, [1739] We met at Fetter-lane, to humble ourselves before God, and own he had justly withdrawn his Spirit from us, for our manifold unfaithfulness. We acknowledged our having grieved Him by our divisions, one saying, I am of Paul, another, I am of Apollos; by our leaning again to our own works, and trusting in them, instead of Christ; by our resting in those little beginnings of sanctification, which it had pleased Him to work in our souls; and above all, by blaspheming his work among us, imputing it either to nature, to the force of imagination and animal spirits, or even to the delusion of the devil. In that hour, we found God with us as at the first. Some fell prostrate upon the ground. Others burst out, as with one consent, into loud praise and thanksgiving. And many openly testified, there had been no such day as this, since January the first preceding.[53]

A witness described a meeting in 1746 as follows: "The assembly appeared to be all in confusion, and must seem to one at a little distance more like a drunken rabble than the worshippers of God."

---

[52] Wesley, *Works of the Reverend John Wesley, A.M.*, vol. 3, 274–275.

[53] John Wesley, *The Works of the Reverend John Wesley,* vol. 1 (London: The Conference Office, 1809), 388.

One convert wrote, "I thought they were distracted, such fools I'd never seen. They'd stamp and clap and tremble, and wail and cry."[54] In his book *The New Mystics*, John Crowder writes that many saw shouting as a form of spiritual warfare, "as an act of worship that 'displaced satan from the camp.'"[55]

As the Wesley brothers traveled together, Charles began composing hymns based on John's sermons. Charles seemed to be stirred as frequently with a new hymn as John was with a new sermon. You could say that John had the oracle's gift while Charles had the psalmist's gift—John had the gift of touching people with God's presence through his sermons and Charles through his hymns. He wrote hymns and poetry so prolifically that less than one year later, he published his first volume of songs, followed by several more volumes in subsequent years. As John once described their relationship to Charles, "I may be in some sense the head and you the heart of the work."[56] The hymns and sermons composed by the Wesley brothers provided the foundation upon which all Methodist doctrine and religious practices would be built. It was not long before they were using the printed page to expand the reach of their ministry. They were among the first evangelists to widely publish sermons, hymns, devotional readings, and even a monthly magazine. Their innovative forms of Bible teaching and corporate worship were so effective at making Christ known that hundreds of converts were added daily.

It is important to note here, that though the Church of England forced the Wesleys out of its doors, John and Charles never left the Anglican Church. For them, Methodism was an enhancement of Anglicanism—even though the doctrines of the two often clashed. John, for example, never let his societies meet on Sundays for fear they might replace attending Anglican services, and never gave up his ordination as an Anglican minister. Though the Wesleys relationship to the Church of England grew more and more tenuous over the years and they took their directions from no one but God

---

[54] John Crowder, *The New Mystics: How to Become Part of the Supernatural Generation* (Shippensburg, PA: Destiny Image Publishers, 2006), 276–277.

[55] Ibid., 277.

[56] Richard P. Heitzenrater, "A Tale of Two Brothers," *Christian History* 20, no. 1 [Issue 69] (2001): 16.

and their own hearts, Methodist ties to the church were never officially cut either by themselves or the Anglican hierarchy until after both John and Charles had passed away.

"All the World Is My Parish"

In 1740, Wesley set up his first base of operations in a building that was formerly a foundry used for casting canons. It had been left damaged and unused for twenty years until Wesley purchased it and made it the first official meeting place of the London Methodist Society. Its main room was large enough to seat 1,500 people, and the building was soon converted into a meeting hall, school, and social welfare center. Not long after the Foundry was established, Wesley set up another headquarters in Bristol, where he had first preached in the open air. Next, he established a base in Newcastle, completing what John called a "far-flung triangular base that will cover all England—from Bristol to London to Newcastle."

The Church of England forced them out of its doors, but the Wesleys never left the Anglican Church.

The Wesley brothers drew larger and larger crowds as they shared God's Word and enlightened listeners through preaching and singing. As early as eight o'clock in the morning, audiences would number five or six thousand. Evening crowds could be even larger. When the townsfolk and surrounding farmers heard that the Wesley brothers were on their way, they would travel from all over the region to experience firsthand John's earth-shattering sermons and Charles's heaven-charged hymns. Success didn't come without persecution, however, and those who flocked to these gatherings were often beaten, threatened with their lives, and thrown out of town. The Wesley brothers faced all these dangers with amazing courage and astonishing composure. John was known to flee an angry mob by jumping into a cold pond, swimming out, and resuming his preaching. He had the uncanny ability to calm a hostile mob and turn the most violent opposition his way. John had such love for the lost that he felt those who persecuted him the most were those who needed him the most. With unwavering conviction of God's call on his life, John wrote,

> God in Scripture commands me, according to my power, to instruct the ignorant, reform the wicked, confirm the virtuous. Man forbids me to do this in another's parish; that is, in effect, to do it at all, seeing I have now no parish of my own, nor probably ever shall. Whom then shall I hear, God or man?
>
> I look upon all the world as my parish; thus far I mean, that, in whatever part of it I am, I judge it meet, right, and my bounden duty to declare unto all that are willing to hear, the glad tidings of salvation.[57]

On an average day, John preached three times, traveling about twenty miles on horseback. Every morning he began preaching at five o'clock in order to reach the workers on their way to the fields. He preached again at noon, when the workers broke for lunch, followed often by two more times in the evening. Weather made no difference to his schedule—the brothers always kept every engagement, no matter the circumstances. John also recorded that he was miraculously healed on more than one occasion. In one such instance, he was so sick he couldn't even raise his head. He wrote:

> Friday, 8.—I found myself much out of order. However, I made shift to preach in the evening; but on Saturday my bodily strength quite failed so that for several hours I could scarcely lift up my head. Sunday, 10. I was obliged to lie down most part of the day, being easy only in that posture. Yet in the evening my weakness was suspended while I was calling sinners to repentance. But at our love-feast which followed, beside the pain in my back and head and the fever which still continued upon me, just as I began to pray I was seized with such a cough that I could hardly speak. At the same time came strongly into my mind, "These signs shall follow them that believe" [Mark 16:17]. I called on Jesus aloud to "increase my faith" and to "confirm the word of

[57] Wesley, *Journal of John Wesley*, http://www.ccel.org/ccel/wesley/journal.vi.iii.v.html.

> his grace." While I was speaking my pain vanished away; the fever left me; my bodily strength returned; and for many weeks I felt neither weakness nor pain. "Unto thee, O Lord, do I give thanks."[58]

Of another occasion, he wrote,

> When Mr. Shepherd and I left Smeton, my horse was so exceedingly lame that I was afraid I must have lain by too. We could not discern what it was that was amiss; and yet he would scarcely set his foot to the ground. By riding thus seven miles, I was thoroughly tired, and my head ached more than it had done for some months. (What I here aver is the naked fact: let every man account for it as he sees good.) I then thought, "Cannot God heal either man or beast, by any means, or without any?" Immediately my weariness and headache ceased, and my horse's lameness in the same instant. Nor did he halt any more either that day or the next.[59]

The Wesley brothers sometimes covered sixty miles a day in order to get to a prearranged destination on time. They traveled tirelessly, meeting the people wherever they were, learning about their needs and how best they could help them spiritually, mentally, and physically.

The Move of God Divided

While England was getting swept up in the Methodist Revival fire, problems began brewing in London. A Moravian minister named Philip Henry Molther, who was on his way to Pennsylvania, arrived in October 1739 and started a controversy almost immediately with his teaching. As has happened too often with various movements of God, it appears jealousy arose over who was truly of God and who wasn't. Both the Moravians and the Methodists were of God, though probably both were in a degree of error. As far as the Moravians believed, their assembly in Great Britain was as much

---

[58] Wesley, *Journal of John Wesley*, http://www.ccel.org/ccel/wesley/journal.vi.iv.v.html.

[59] Ibid., http://www.ccel.org/ccel/wesley/journal.vi.vii.i.html.

a mission to a lost nation as were their groups in America. Count Zinzendorf, though a good man at heart, was unlikely to recognize anyone, including the Wesleys, as an equal. Despite how much they respected him, the Wesley brothers were not interested in submitting Methodism to the Moravians' authority.

So it was that Philip Molther began teaching that salvation was through faith alone, and that there were no degrees of faith—either you had the assurance of God's peace and joy in your heart that you were saved, or you did not. There was no working toward it, only waiting on God to provide it—being "still." This waiting stillness didn't include prayer, good works, or studying the Scriptures. Molther even asserted that those who had followed the ministry of Peter Bohler, who preached that faith could grow until it led to salvation, were mistaken if they thought they were saved. While the Wesley brothers were teaching that salvation came through faith, they also espoused the belief that faith grew through prayer, fasting, studying the Word of God, and doing good works. Though the difference in practical application was rather insignificant, it soon drove a wedge between the Wesleys and the Society at Fetter Lane, where Molther had been welcomed.

With the Wesleys traveling in and out of London to minister, the Moravians' position grew more solid. At one point, a fanatic declared that there were only two true ministers in all of Great Britain: Molther and James Bell (one of the leaders at Fetter Lane). He also asserted that there were no true Christians outside of the Moravian Church. By June 1740, the Fetter Lane society decided that the Wesleys were no longer allowed to preach there. Though John and Charles tried time and again to mend the growing divide, Molther and those with him would not be reconciled. John and Charles decided to move on with what God had called them to do, though from time to time they resumed attempts to repair the rift. Among those who left the Methodists to join the Moravians were the two men who had traveled to Georgia with the Wesleys, Ingham and Delamotte, as well as some of the initial members of the Holy Club. As John later stated, "I marvel how I refrain from joining these men. I scarce see any of them but my heart burns within me. I long to be with them. And yet I am kept from them."[60]

---

[60] Southey, *Life of Wesley,* 187.

Separating from the Moravians for the time being proved a wise move, for in the midst of this controversy the revival had stalled, and now it began to pick up speed again. By 1743, the Methodists in London numbered about 1,950, while the Moravians were still only about seventy-two.

In the months before Molther exerted his influence, the seeds of a rift between the Wesleys and Whitefield were being sown. In March 1740, John had given a message entitled "Free Grace," in which he proclaimed, "The grace or love of God, whence cometh our salvation, is FREE IN ALL, and FREE FOR ALL."[61] This statement was in stark contrast to the doctrine of Calvinist predestination that was the accepted belief of the day, and Whitefield immediately questioned the truth of John's sermon.

The Wesleys taught that salvation comes by faith, but that it grows through prayer, fasting, study of God's Word, and doing good works.

While John and Charles's conversions had consisted largely of a struggle to understand the Gospel of salvation through faith and the impact of their free will in receiving that faith, Whitefield's conversion had been more a revelation of God's saving power and a feeling that God had blessed him and called him to be saved. While John and Charles had needed to deliver themselves from the doctrine of predestination before they could be saved, George Whitefield had been saved in spite of it! And though George was as anointed an evangelist as the Wesleys were, he was not the theologian that John was.

As the controversy began to arise, Whitefield headed for America in August 1740, traveling specifically to New England, land of the Puritan Calvinists. As his letters questioning John's stand for free will (called "Arminianism" after one of its proponents, Dutch theologian Jacob Arminius [1560–1609]) were crossing the Atlantic, he was reading extensively about the subject only in the books

[61] John Wesley, "Free Grace," 1740, http://www.ccel.org/ccel/wesley/sermons.viii.ii.html.

suggested by those around him—the Puritan Calvinists. When John published his sermon in 1740 against Whitefield's advice, tensions only grew worse. Whitefield wrote a reply in defense of predestination, which John answered with a counterargument by publishing "Free Grace" in America. Charles echoed the doctrine in his hymns, writing "Wrestling Jacob" and capitalizing the lyric in it, "PURE UNIVERSAL LOVE THOU ART." When Whitefield was invited to speak at the Foundry that year, he chose to pour even more salt on the wound by expounding "the absolute decrees [of predestination] in the most peremptory and offensive manner"[62] while John and Charles could do nothing but sit and look on. Then, a pamphlet entitled "Free Grace Indeed!" which contradicted the Wesley brothers' stance, was published anonymously[63] in January 1741.

The divide was thus complete. The Great Awakening that the Moravians had seeded and the Wesleys and Whitefield had watered and brought to fruit was now three separate movements: the Wesleyan "United Societies," Whitefield's "Calvinistic Methodism," and Moravianism. In fact, Whitefield's Tabernacle was soon established down the street from the Foundry, in a move similar to Burger King opening up a chain restaurant right next to a McDonald's. For the next several decades, Methodism would follow parallel paths divided by Calvinism.

In the end, however, the schism was perhaps more one of leadership again, than actual doctrine. Whitefield, after his incredible success as a preacher in America that truly dwarfed any crowd John or Charles had ever gathered, was hesitant to return under their leadership; while the Wesleys were no more apt to acknowledge their former disciple as their head then they were Count Zinzendorf. And again, their differences were more on paper than in actual practice. First of all, John allowed that God might indeed call some souls especially to Him, though he believed salvation was open to all. It was also the Wesleys who emphasized works to perfect holiness

[62] J. D. Walsh, "Wesley vs. Whitefield: The conflict between the two giants of the eighteenth-century awakening," *Christian History* 12, no. 2 [Issue 38] (1993): 36.

[63] The author was eventually revealed to have been one J. Oswald, of whom little is known. The pamphlet was reprinted in New England by none other than Benjamin Franklin, who had become a good friend of Whitefield.

(something Calvinists would have said showed that they were elect), while in the midst of their disagreement, Whitefield was preaching "Come, Poor, Lost, Undone Sinner" in Glasgow, Scotland, calling his audience to:

> Open the door of your heart, that the King of glory, the blessed Jesus, may come in and erect his kingdom in your soul. Make room for Christ; the Lord Jesus desires to sup with you tonight; Christ is willing to come into any of your hearts that will be pleased to open and receive him.[64]

While adhering to Calvinism made him fit in with the American Puritans, it still didn't preach well, so in application it was easier to call all to come to Jesus of their own free will, and then let Him sort out who was predestined and who was not.

Though the two camps never again joined, the animosity between Whitefield and the Wesleys had already cooled by 1742. In fact, it was often their lieutenants who more hotly debated the division then they did themselves. It appears soon after that they simply agreed to disagree, and no longer allowed the issue to divide them as friends. So it was that as late as 1749, they were again ministering at the same conferences.

The Wesleys Move On

The Wesleys' rejection of predestination and the Moravians' mystical interpretation of "salvation by faith alone" became key beliefs for the continued development and growth of Methodism. If God's salvation was free to all and free for all, then there were no class restrictions to limit who could join a Wesleyan society, a significant departure from the restrictions imposed by the Church of England regarding who could attend services and receive the sacraments. And, if faith was a free gift that could grow and develop, it made sense that the Wesleyan "methods" of united society meetings, regular prayer, Scripture reading, fasting, and performing good works to help the poor, orphaned, and imprisoned were still immensely important. Thus, the Wesley brothers moved on not only

---

[64] George Whitefield, "Come, Poor, Lost, Undone Sinner," *Christian History* 12, no. 2 [Issue 38] (1993): 19.

to preach the Gospel, but also to organize societies to ensure that God's will for all could be done on earth, just as it was in heaven.

In 1742, the Wesley brothers established an orphanage and Sunday school in Newcastle. Four years later, in 1746, they established the first of many medical clinics for the poor in London. Around this time, John began publishing his sermons to be used as devotionals, using the profits to provide financial support for the clinics. He ministered on behalf of those in workhouses by inspiring them to improve themselves through cleanliness, propriety, and thrift. As he once preached, "Slovenliness is no part of religion....'Cleanliness is, indeed, next to godliness.'"[65] He taught the poor that they could improve themselves from within rather than rely on government assistance. Most importantly, he determined to provide a church not only for the poor and destitute, but also for the common, unchurched worker—those the Church of England turned away because they lacked refined manners and proper attire.

John Wesley observes an electrical experiment.

Mary Evans Picture Library

These were the ruffians who, for the first ten years of the Wesleys' outreach, caused them the most harm. Yet they met the persecutions with such dignity and serenity of spirit that the violence subsided over time, and in those places where the assaults were the worst, the Wesleys received the greatest welcome and honor just a few years later. This will always remain a wonder to historians. Rigg wrote in his 1891 biography of John Wesley,

> His heroism was perfect; his self-possession never failed him for a moment; the serenity of his temper was never ruffled. Such bravery and self-command and goodness, in circumstances so terrible and threatening, was too much for his persecutors everywhere. He always triumphed in the end.[66]

[65] John Wesley, "On Dress." http://www.ccel.org/ccel/wesley/sermons.vi.xxxv.html.

[66] Rigg, *Living Wesley,* 162.

Stories abound of hecklers and riot-leaders who were silenced or chased away by those gathered to hear the Wesleys minister. As the brothers' reputation grew, the crowds themselves provided all the protection the Wesley brothers needed from those who would do them harm. Their supporters began to outnumber their adversaries, and the Wesleys were able to expand their reach with decreasing opposition, especially as the Church of England became more exclusive, corrupt, and irrelevant to the common person.

After ten years of traveling through England, reaching northward and into the more remote areas, John Wesley's itinerancy took him to Ireland, Scotland, and Wales. In August 1747, during his first trip to Ireland, he had such widespread success that he continued to minister there for the next six years, crossing the Irish Channel forty-two times. John's first visit to Scotland was in 1751. He paid the Scots twenty-two visits, stirring up all of the Scottish churches—none of which denied him its pulpit.

The strength of the Wesleys' ministry was their burning desire to seek out and minister to the forgotten people of Britain. This became the driving motivation behind their open-air preaching campaign. It has been said that early capitalism in England was actually strengthened by the Wesleyan emphasis on the spiritual and corporal dignity of every man. John Wesley transformed the character of his countrymen by preaching about the importance of cleanliness, temperance, thrift, and, above all, faith. Societal transformation would be achieved from the inside out, one individual at a time, each person undergoing a personal reformation.

Marrying the Wrong Woman

On April 8, 1749, John officiated at the wedding of Charles to Sarah "Sally" Gwynne. Soon afterward, Charles retired from the greater part of his traveling ministry to settle down with his growing family in Bristol. Charles and Sally enjoyed a happy union, pursuing a common interest in music and worship as they oversaw the Bristol headquarters and ministered together locally. They had eight children, but only the youngest three reached adulthood: Charles Jr. (1757–1834), Sarah (1759–1828), and Samuel (1766–1837). Each grew to become an accomplished musician.

It appears that Charles's marriage inspired John to put the heartache of Sophia Hopkey behind him and finally marry for himself. In the meantime, he had written a good deal on the blessedness of singleness, but he seemed unwilling to settle for bachelorhood for the rest of his life. Fortunately, he knew who his wife should be. The previous August, he had fallen ill in Newcastle and was nursed back to health by a beautiful young woman named Grace Murray. John determined to make her his wife.

The widow of a seaman, Grace Murray had first met John in 1740, when she was still married. She became a member, and soon a leader, of a Methodist society in Newcastle. Leadership for women was unprecedented at the time, but the Wesley brothers valued women's input and respected the call God placed on their lives as ministers. Certainly their attitude toward women was influenced by the roles of their mother and sisters in their spiritual formation. Their older sisters had been cherished confidantes and counselors. Later in her life, their sister Hetty proved invaluable to them as a teacher and administrative aide in London. John once said, "May not women as well as men bear a part in this honorable service? Undoubtedly they may; nay, they ought; it is meet, right and their bounden duty. Herein there is no difference, 'there is neither male nor female in Christ Jesus.'"[67]

Grace Murray's husband drowned at sea in 1742, but she continued to be a dedicated Methodist despite her loss. She traveled through the northern counties of England and into Ireland to meet with the female societies there. She had also nursed many traveling preachers who fell ill from the strain of their ministry. Over the years, she had tended to at least seven such preachers, the most notable of whom were John and another minister by the name of John Bennet, whom she served for six months as a nursemaid. "Wesley commended her work by saying, 'I saw the work of God prosper in her hands. She was to me both a servant and friend, as well as a fellow-laborer in the Gospel.'"[68] It is easy to see why, when John thought of marriage

[67] Ruth Daugherty, *John Wesley: Holiness of Heart and Life* (study guide), 1996, quoted in "Grace Murray," John Wesley, Holiness of Heart and Life, General Board of Global Ministries, United Methodist Church, http://gbgm-umc.org/umw/Wesley/gracemurray.stm.

[68] Ibid.

again, Grace was the first person to come to mind. In fact, after she had nursed him back to health, he had told her, "If ever I marry, I think you will be the person."[69]

John had first proposed to Grace in August 1748, but the timing never seemed right to actually marry until after Charles had wed. At the time, Grace had answered, "This is too great a blessing for me; I can't tell how to believe it. This is all I could have wished for under heaven."[70] Not wanting John to leave, she ended up traveling with him through Yorkshire and Derbyshire, providing great help to him along the way. John finally left her for a time in Bolton, which just happened to be the district of John Bennet, whom she had previously nursed for so long.

It seems that Bennet, too, had become smitten with Grace and soon began pursuing her hand in marriage. Grace seemed unable to decide between her two admirers. At one point, she even wrote to John to tell him she felt it was her duty to marry Bennet. In response, a week after Charles's wedding, John took Grace with him to Ireland, where she helped him as he ministered for three months. In Dublin, she finally agreed to marry John.

When they returned to England, they traveled together extensively and were scarcely apart for the next five months. While they were in Epworth, Bennet came for a visit and told John that Grace had sent him all the letters Grace and John had exchanged. Chafing at this news, John wrote to tell Grace that he now felt she should marry Bennet. She wrote back, however, "I love you a thousand times better than I ever loved John Bennet in my life. But I am afraid, if I don't marry him, he'll run mad."[71] John again hesitated over the matter and decided to win his brother's approval before he pursued marriage any further. This proved a fatal error.

Charles was shocked by the idea of John marrying Grace; he was still caught up in that day's societal expectations. Sarah Gwynne came from a family of high position and notable heritage; Grace Murray had been a servant before marrying her seafaring husband. Charles felt that if John's marriage wasn't of a similar status to his

---

[69] Janine Petry, "The Matchmakers," *Christian History* 20, no. 1 [Issue 69] (2001): 24.

[70] Telford, *Life of John Wesley,* 246.

[71] Ibid., 247.

own, such disgrace would cause the preachers in many of their societies to abandon them. While Grace was at her home in Newcastle, Charles met John at Whitehaven to express his reservations. John replied that Grace's character, piety, and worth far outweighed any shame her lowly birth might cause. Charles saw that John would not be convinced otherwise.

John Wesley preaches at Bolton Cross.

The Wesley Center Online (wesley.nnu.edu) at Northwest Nazarene University, Nampa, Idaho

On the way to Newcastle, Charles met Grace at Hindley Hill. He kissed her on the cheek and said, "Grace Murray, you have broken my heart."[72] They returned together to Newcastle, where they found Bennet. Grace then fell at Bennet's feet and begged his forgiveness for using him so badly. They married less than one week later, October 3, 1749. Oddly enough, it was Whitefield, who John met in Leeds for a conference, who broke the news to him of Grace's sudden marriage. When Charles and Sally arrived there the day after, John told his brother, "I renounce all intercourse with you but what I have with a heathen or a publican."[73] However, Whitefield and another associate, John Nelson, prayed, wept, and entreated the brothers to reconcile until they fell on each other's neck asking forgiveness for what they had done. Bennet and his new wife arrived three days later. John greeted Bennet with a holy kiss, but said nothing more to him. He would not see Grace again for nearly thirty years.

For his part, Bennet soon left the Wesleys' fellowship and struck out on his own. He took with him 110 members of his Bolton congregation of 129. All of those at Stockport joined him as well, except for one woman. Bennet accused Wesley of being a puppet of Catholicism and defamed him bitterly. He died in 1759, leaving Grace with

[72] Ibid., 248.

[73] Ibid.

five sons. She afterward moved to Derbyshire and rejoined the Methodists. Through a mutual friend, she met John again in 1788. Biographer Henry Moore described the meeting:

> Mr. Wesley, with evident feeling, resolved to visit her; and the next morning, he took me with him to Colebrooke Row, where her son then resided. The meeting was affecting; but Mr. Wesley preserved more than his usual self-possession. It was easy to see, notwithstanding the many years which had intervened, that both in sweetness of spirit, and in person and manners, she was a fit subject for the tender regrets expressed in those verse which I have presented to the reader. The interview did not continue long, and I do not remember that I ever heard Mr. Wesley mention her name afterward.[74]

"Those verses" were from a poem written by John entitled "Reflections upon Past Providences, October, 1749." While the poem consists of thirty-one six-line stanzas, here is an excerpt:

> Oft, as through giddy youth I roved,
> And danced along the flowery way,
> By chance or thoughtless passion moved,
> An easy, unresisting prey,
> I fell, while love's envenomed dart
> Thrilled my nerves, and tore my heart.
>
> Borne on wings of sacred hope,
> Long had I soared, and spurned the ground,
> When, panting for the mountain top,
> My soul a kindred spirit found,
> By Heaven entrusted to my care,
> The Daughter of my faith and prayer.
>
> In early dawn of life, serene,
> Mild, sweet, and tender was her mood;
> Her pleasing form spoke all within
> Soft and compassionately good;

---

[74] Henry Moore, *The Life of the Reverend John Wesley, A.M.: Fellow of Lincolnshire College, Oxford,* vol. 2 (New York: N. Bangs and J. Emory, 1826), 103, quoted in Telford, *Life of John Wesley,* 250.

Listening to every wretch's care,
Mingling with each her friendly tear.

I saw her run, with winged speed,
In works of faith and labouring love;
I saw her glorious toil succeed,
And showers of blessings from above
Crowning her warm effectual prayer,
And glorified my God in her.[75]

Two years after his brother's marriage, in the same year he first visited Scotland, John met and married Mary "Molly" Vazeille, the widow of Anthony Vazeille, who had four children, after a close confidante convinced him that he should marry. John had slipped on the ice on the middle of London Bridge and struck his ankle against the stone side so hard he couldn't walk. He was taken to Molly's home to recuperate, and he was there one week. He preached on his knees that Sunday, married Molly that Monday, October 18, 1751, and preached on his knees again Tuesday because of the injury. What conversation must have happened during that week in Molly's home to make him marry her so quickly, one can only speculate.

Where John's hesitancy with both Sophia Hopkey and Grace Murray had cost him a bride, his hasty marriage to Molly would cost him a great deal more. The honeymoon was brief; within two weeks, John was on the road again. Molly had assured him his constant travel would not be an issue, but she quickly discovered she was not cut out to be the wife of an itinerant minister. Molly soon grew lonely and jealous while John was away. Only four months after the marriage, Charles found Molly in tears. He did what he could to reconcile her, and it was agreed she should travel more with John, which she did a great deal over the next four years. But when a mob attacked their carriage in Hull, she ceased to travel with him.

Growing ever more jealous and bitter by John's constant absence, Molly began opening his mail and reading through his personal papers, berating him for any references to or correspondence with other women. Her temper became notorious to those close to the family. In anger, she began passing his private papers to enemies or publishing them in the newspapers, sometimes even rewriting the

[75] Telford, *Life of John Wesley,* 251.

way the letters would appear to make her husband look even worse. She would travel a hundred miles just to see with whom John was traveling in his carriage when he arrived in a town. Once, she locked Charles and John in a room in order to confront them with their faults, and they only escaped by quoting Latin poetry to her until she could stand no more. Another time, one of John's staff members found John and Molly in their hotel room—an enraged Molly was standing over John, clutching a tuft of his hair by which she had been dragging him around the room. Molly left John several times but always returned in response to his entreaties. In 1771, she left him for more than a year before returning. Not until Grace passed away in 1781 was peace restored to John's home. It had been thirty grueling years.

Molly left John several times but always returned in response to his entreaties.

Throughout all of this, John continued to itinerate, keeping up his former pace of preaching daily and managing the increasingly complicated demands of an international ministry. He did his best to meet on a quarterly basis with a majority of the societies in the largest circuits of the chief districts throughout England, Scotland, and Ireland.

"The Peculiar Talent Which God Has Given Me"

For five decades, John Wesley traveled throughout the countryside, preaching, teaching, counseling, and praying with tradesman, laborers, farmers, and common folk of every kind. He left in his wake groups of converts who were instructed to meet among themselves weekly to confess their sins, encourage one another in prayer, and strengthen their faith through common Bible study. He taught adherence to a prescribed standard of moral conduct. John often preached, "The soul and the body make a man; the spirit and discipline make a Christian."[76] Wesley was methodical in how he

[76] Charles Edward White, "Spare the Rod and Spoil the Church," *Christian History* 20, no. 1 [Issue 69] (2001): 28–29.

organized his objectives and schedule, as well as how he structured his sermons, led people to Christ, and discipled his converts. He made a strategic appeal to every audience's situation, speaking directly to people's consciences, bringing them the light of a particular truth they needed, and ushering them straight to the throne of grace. After he had delivered a sermon, he left behind printed materials and precise instructions for how to continue working out their salvation to the saving of their souls. Just as Paul instructed the Philippians, John instructed those who followed him in the faith,

> *Wherefore, my beloved, as ye have always obeyed, not as in my presence only, but now much more in my absence, work out your own salvation with fear and trembling. For it is God which worketh in you both to will and to do of his good pleasure. Do all things without murmurings and disputings: that ye may be blameless and harmless, the sons of God, without rebuke, in the midst of a crooked and perverse nation, among whom ye shine as lights in the world; holding forth the word of life; that I may rejoice in the day of Christ, that I have not run in vain, neither laboured in vain.*
>
> (Philippians 2:12–16)

Converts became so many and their needs so overwhelming that Wesley ordained "lay preachers" who would follow in his wake to continue teaching and ministering to the new societies. These lay preachers were not educated clergy but common men who were knowledgeable about the Bible and had proven themselves fit for the ministry. Wesley took great pains to look after their souls and habits. He published encouraging and instructional materials to nourish and guide them, and he required them to abide by twelve official rules and several more "unofficial" ones. He provided guidance about manners, habits, and time management, urging them to spend no less than five hours a day reading useful books. He insisted all preaching fulfill four objectives only: (1) invite; (2) convince; (3) offer Christ; and (4) build up. He wrote that those called to ministry must "avoid everything in look, gesture, word, and tone of voice that savors of pride or self-sufficiency."[77] Below are some excerpts from the twelve rules of conduct every lay preacher was expected to use to govern his behavior:

[77] Ibid., 29.

1) Be diligent. Never unemployed a minute.
2) Be serious. Avoid all lightness and jesting.
3) Converse sparingly with women, particularly young women.
4) Take no step toward marriage without first consulting with the brethren.
5) Believe evil of no one.
6) Speak evil of no one.
7) Tell everyone what you think wrong in him, "and that plainly, as soon as may be; else it will fester in your heart. Make all haste to cast the fire out of your bosom."[78]
8) Do not [act]...the gentleman. (Do not put on airs.)
9) Be ashamed of nothing but sin: not fetching wood...nor drawing water.
10) Be punctual. Do everything exactly on time.
11) It is not your business to preach so many times, and to take care of this or that society, but to save as many souls as you can.
12) Act in all things, not according to your own will, but as a son in the Gospel.[79]

Most importantly, John emphasized that love must be the motive of all instruction, reproof, and discipline. Quoting his brother's hymn, he wrote,

Love can bow down the stubborn neck,
The stone to flesh convert;
Soften, and melt, and pierce,
And break an adamantine heart.[80]

Wesley's lay preachers became known for their propriety, integrity, and diligence. They formed a formidable army of servant-leaders set on overcoming society's evils with the goodness of God. During Wesley's first five years of itinerancy, from 1739 to 1744, forty-five preachers, including several clergymen, had joined the Wesleys in their Methodist campaign. By 1745, in London alone, there were two

---

[78] White, "Spare the Rod," 30.

[79] Sam Wellman, *John Wesley: Founder of the Methodist Church* (Philadelphia: Chelsea House Publishers, 1999), 126.

[80] White, "Spare the Rod," 29.

thousand members regularly meeting in Methodist societies. "The class meeting was fully developed, the Rules of the United Societies printed and enforced, the quarterly visitation of the classes arranged for, lay preaching instituted, places of worship secured, and the sacraments administered."[81]

In 1744, after the Wesleys had established hundreds of Societies throughout England, the first Annual Methodist Conference was held in London. All lay preachers and leaders congregated to hear directly from John, find encouragement as well as reproof, present significant problems, and propose solutions. This conference was part of John's plan to meet the spiritual and intellectual needs of his traveling preachers and local leaders. In addition to establishing the Annual Conference, he also published books on many various subjects expressly for the purpose of educating his growing band of teachers. He published his best sermons and other classic theological works in inexpensive books and used the proceeds to set up schools to educate individuals who were interested in becoming Bible teachers. Wesley advocated the development of the intellect along with the social and emotional aspects of Christian living—even for those who were not called to full-time ministry.

John's widespread success can be attributed largely to his faithful band of lay preachers and class leaders, a group that grew in rank and number with every passing year. Requirements and methods became increasingly formalized. John published a list of four questions all leaders were to ask their class members in order to guide and discipline them. These questions were:

1) What known sins have you committed?
2) What temptations have you overcome?
3) How did God deliver you?
4) What have you thought, said, or done that might be sinful?

Probably more stirring than his messages about God's plan of redemption was John's plan for continued spiritual formation and discipleship. He felt this plan was a critical ingredient for the success

[81] J. F. Hurst, *John Wesley the Methodist: A Plain Account of His Life and Work* (New York: The Methodist Book Concern, 1903), Wesley Center Online, http://wesley.nnu.edu/john_wesley/methodist/ch13.htm.

of every believer, whether young or mature in Christ. After returning from a trip to Wales in 1763, John made this powerful observation:

> Preaching like an Apostle, without joining together those that are awakened, and training them up in the ways of God, is only begetting children for the murderer. How much preaching has [there] been for these twenty years! But no regular societies, no discipline, no order or connection; and the consequence is that nine in ten of the once-awakened are now faster asleep than ever.[82]

The Annual Conference brought together all types of Methodist leaders and continued to grow over the years. Lay preachers traveled from afar to participate. Beginning in 1767, and for every year thereafter, there came a time in the annual proceedings when the question was asked: "Are there any objections to any of the preachers?" Each preacher's name was called out one by one, followed by a few moments of silence. None was immune to the culture of accountability that governed the growing organization.

In the same respect, lay ministers came with the assurance their concerns would be heard. In addition to accountability, the conferences provided a forum where the needs of the local leaders and their families were made known and formally addressed by the executive committee. Decisions at the conferences included giving a living stipend to traveling preachers and their wives and guaranteeing basic care provisions, such as formal education, to their children. Schools were organized expressly for the children of traveling preachers and their local lay-leaders.

From Methodist societies to classes, bands, circuits, and districts—from traveling preachers to class leaders, delegates, officers, and teachers—Wesley had an unprecedented genius for organization. He was astutely aware that God had given him this special gift, as he noted in a letter to his sister Martha: "I know this is the peculiar talent which God has given me."[83] As a leader, he was willing to incorporate suggestions made by others, and he learned continually

---

[82] White, "Spare the Rod," 30.

[83] John Wesley to Mrs. Martha Wesley Hall, 17 November 1742, Wesley Center Online, http://wesley.nnu.edu/John_Wesley/letters/1742.htm.

from the lessons of experience. He closely observed the strategies that helped believers grow in Christ and wove them into the Methodist machinery.

By October 1768, a Methodist chapel was opened in New York. In 1771, Francis Asbury was commissioned to oversee the work in America. In September 1784, Wesley ordained his clerical helper, Dr. Thomas Coke, as bishop, instructing him to ordain Asbury to administer the sacraments. Following in Wesley's footsteps, Asbury became known as a "circuit-riding preacher" whose dedication to the colonies, even during the War of Independence, was instrumental in helping Methodism to take root in America. Asbury would lead a new generation of American circuit riders, including Peter Cartwright, who would be influential in the dawning of the Second Great Awakening that so stirred America in the early nineteenth century.

As Methodism took hold throughout the Old World and New World alike, the constant demands involved with governing such a burgeoning organization weighed heavily on John. By 1770, he actively sought a successor to oversee the ministry in the future. He hoped John Fletcher, a servant of Christ he considered his equal, would succeed him. Fletcher had been his close travel companion after Charles retired from the itinerant life in 1750, and John could think of no one else who was as close to being a kindred spirit, and certainly no one as knowledgeable. Fletcher died in 1785, however, three years before Charles himself passed away.

John was concerned about the future of the Methodist movement. He knew that maintaining the integrity of the doctrine depended on a delicate balance of knowledge of the Word, experience of the Spirit, discipline of thought, and holy Christian conduct. All of these combined, he felt, to perfect the heart and ensure continued growth in the faith—*"the upward call of God in Christ Jesus"* (Philippians 3:14 NKJV).

A contemporary of Wesley who was a correspondent for the *New York Evangelist* wrote,

> The first time I was in the company of the Rev. John Wesley, I asked him what must be done to keep Methodism alive when he was dead. To which he immediately answered:

> "The Methodists must take heed of their doctrine, their experience, their practice, and their discipline....if they do not attend to their discipline, they will be like persons who bestow much pains in cultivating their garden, and put no fence round it to save it from the wild boars of the forest."[84]

John had a strong conviction that strict oversight of the soul was paramount to lasting victory in Christ. As it was with the individual, so it was with the body of Christ. All aspects of life must be brought into *"the obedience of Christ"* (2 Corinthians 10:5). "Is it any wonder," Wesley asked, "that we find so few Christians? Where is Christian discipline? In what part of England is Christian discipline added to Christian doctrine?" Wesley felt the church as a whole needed discipline and firmly believed that "wherever doctrine is preached, where there is no discipline, it cannot have its full effect upon the hearers."[85]

The Wesleys' Influence Remained until the Very End

In 1770, George Whitefield passed away at the age of fifty-six. When John was asked if he expected to see Whitefield in heaven, he replied, "No....Do not misunderstand me, George Whitefield was so bright a star in the firmament of God's glory, and will stand so near the throne, that one like me, who am less than the least, will never catch a glimpse of him."[86]

In 1775, John published "A Calm Address to Our American Colonies," an open letter exhorting the colonies to remain loyal to England. He would tolerate no civil uprisings. This letter caused a breach between Wesley and the American colonists, and if it weren't for the likes of English missionaries such as George Whitefield and Francis Asbury, there might not be any Methodists in America today.

---

[84] Hurst, *John Wesley the Methodist*, http://wesley.nnu.edu/john_wesley/methodist/ch11.htm.

[85] White, "Spare the Rod," 29.

[86] Hurst, *John Wesley the Methodist*, http://wesley.nnu.edu/john_wesley/methodist/ch13.htm.

The 1780s were a difficult decade for John. As I have already mentioned, his wife passed away in 1781. In 1785, John Fletcher, his chosen successor, unexpectedly died. Then, in 1788, his beloved brother and co-laborer, Charles, went home to be with the Lord. In that same year, John looked over his life and assessed the reasons for his longevity. At eighty-five years of age, John attributed his good health to the following, which he recorded in his journal:

> 1) To my constant exercise and change of air.
> 2) To my never having lost a night's sleep, sick or well, at land or at sea, since I was born.
> 3) To my having sleep at command so that, whenever I feel myself almost worn out, I call it and it comes day or night.
> 4) To my having constantly for over sixty years risen at four in the morning.
> 5) To my constant preaching at five in the morning, for above fifty years.
> 6) To my having had so little pain in my life, and so little sorrow or anxious care.[87]

At eighty-six, during a nine-week tour of Ireland, he preached one hundred sermons in sixty towns and villages; six of those sermons he preached in the open air. On June 28, 1790, he wrote in his journal,

> Monday, June 28—This day I enter into my eighty-eighth year. For above eighty-six years, I found none of the infirmities of old age; my eyes did not wax dim, neither was my natural strength abated. But last August I found almost a sudden change. My eyes were so dim that no glasses would help me. My strength likewise quite forsook me and probably will not return in this world. But I feel no pain from head, to foot; only it seems nature is exhausted and, humanly speaking, will sink more and more, till the weary springs of life stand still at last. [88]

---

[87] Luke Tyerman, *The Life and Times of the Rev. John Wesley, M.A., Founder of the Methodists*, vol. 3 (London: Hodder and Stoughton, 1871), 540.

[88] John Wesley, *The Journal of John Wesley*, (Chicago: Moody Press, 1951; Grand Rapids: Christian Classics Ethereal Library, 2000), 265, http://www.ccel.org/ccel/wesley/journal.html.

Two days prior to his next birthday, he preached to two large audiences who had gathered to honor the venerable John Wesley.

On October 7, 1790, he preached his last outdoor sermon under an ash tree in the churchyard of Rye in Kent, crying, like "the voice of the Woes," "Repent!" On February 22, 1791, he preached his last sermon from the pulpit at City Road Chapel in London. The next day, he preached his last sermon on this side of heaven at a friend's house in Leatherhead on "Seek ye the Lord while He may be found."

On the following day, February 24, 1791, John Wesley wrote his famous letter to William Wilberforce—a Member of Parliament who dedicated his life to ending slavery in the British Empire—encouraging him to carry on his crusade against the slave trade. While he could no longer preach the cause of Christ, he wrote in this letter:

> But if God be fore you, who can be against you? Are all of them together stronger than God? O be not weary of well doing! Go on, in the name of God and in the power of his might, till even American slavery (the vilest that ever saw the sun) shall vanish away before it.

He signed it, "Your affectionate servant, John Wesley."[89]

By February 25, John was feeling weak, and he returned to City Road, where he slept for the next two days. On February 27, he seemed to have recovered a bit, joining his companions for dinner. He retired to his room that evening, exhausted. He did not get up again. On March 2, 1791, surrounded by loved ones, he breathed his last breath.

During his ministry, John Wesley rode over 250,000 miles by horseback (approximately 5,000 miles a year)—a distance comparable to circling the globe ten times. He preached more than forty thousand sermons and published more than five thousand sermons, pamphlets, and books of all kinds. At the time of his death, Wesley had 79,000 followers. Today, in England alone, there are 800,000 members of the Methodist Church; worldwide, there are seventy million members.

---

[89] John Wesley to William Wilberforce, 24 February 1791, John Wesley: Holiness of Heart and Life, General Board of Global Ministries, United Methodist Church, http://gbgm-umc.org/umw/wesley/wilber.stm.

John & Charles Wesley

John Wesley brought the challenge of new life to the English church when it had lost sight of Christ as the ultimate Redeemer. By preaching justification by faith, John and Charles Wesley lifted many thousands of the forgotten masses of England from their unfortunate circumstances and evil habits, making them hopeful of righteousness and salvation. John's passionate efforts to bring the knowledge of redemption to mankind were felt not only in England, but also throughout continental Europe and the developing world—predominantly in America. As Rigg said of him,

> He seems to have had a settled and governing conviction that there was a great work to be done for the Church and the world, for the present and yet more for the future; a work which God had called him to do. He saw around him the need of such a work—a hollow and heartless world full of corruption, vanity, and unrest, and a supine, undisciplined, insensible Church; and he felt stirring strongly within him the power and the call to awaken and organize the Church, and to impress and convert the world.[90]

The world would indeed be touched by the Wesleys as Methodism would provide the way of revival far into the next century.

[90] Rigg, *Living Wesley,* 99.

Chapter Two

☆☆☆☆☆

George Whitefield

(1714–1770)

"The Divine Dramatist"

"The Divine Dramatist"

I can call heaven and earth to witness that when the bishop laid his hands upon me, I gave myself up to be a martyr for Him who hung upon the Cross for me....I have thrown myself blindfold, and I trust, without reserve, into His almighty hands.[1]

—George Whitefield,
on his ordination as a minister

Although George Whitefield was probably the most famous personality of his time in the American colonies—roughly four out of every five colonists heard him preach at least once—few today are familiar with the wake of "experiential evangelism" he left. He shook two continents with his dramatic and penetrating preaching style, transforming the spiritual climate of two worlds—the British Isles as well as the new settlements in America. He took New England by storm during one year of itinerant preaching at the age of twenty-five and returned six times to continue stirring the hearts of countless thousands who thronged to hear his moving sermons.

When Boston's population was about sixteen thousand, Whitefield preached his farewell address in Boston Common to a crowd of twenty-three thousand—probably the largest crowd to have gathered in America up to that point. He was likely the only living person with the exception of royalty that every American colonist could recognize. Never before had a single person commanded such great audiences or garnered such widespread fame with no instrument

[1] Southey, *Life of John Wesley*, 78.

other than his voice, no support other than the horse on which he rode or the box on which he stood, and no word of wisdom other than the gift of salvation.

Though the Wesley brothers were long his mentors, his fame surpassed theirs. John Wesley preached his first open-air sermon at the age of thirty-six in a field outside of Bristol to a mind-boggling three thousand, but Whitefield was still in his twenties when he preached to a crowd of about thirty thousand. When John Wesley's crowds had climbed to six thousand, Whitefield was preaching to an unprecedented sixty thousand.

George Whitefield was known as the Great Orator, the Divine Dramatist, and the Heavenly Comet. He appealed to the emotions and used all of his faculties to bring the message of the "new birth" home to the hearts of his hearers. He undoubtedly adopted this term from John Wesley, who was probably the first to use it to refer to becoming a Christian by being "born again." This idea is taken from Jesus' statement in John 3:3: *"Verily, verily, I say unto thee, Except a man be born again, he cannot see the kingdom of God."* Though Whitefield incurred criticism for his theatrics, his heart was sincere and upright before God. His intentions were pure and his love for his hearers was genuine.

Whitefield was an evangelistic pioneer. Moved with such deep compassion for the lost, he was the first to preach "out in the open" to coal miners and shipyard workers as they passed on their way to and from work, for they had no other opportunities to hear the Gospel. He carried the hope of God's redeeming grace not only to the working classes, but also to the nobility—he attended gatherings of famous lords and ladies, holding them spellbound with his dramatic messages. His charisma and compassion carried him from parlors to prisons in England and from politicians' houses to Native Americans' huts in the New World. He was moved most of all by the plight of widows and orphans in the new colonies, as well as by the welfare of the African slaves he also encountered there.

Whitefield was the catalyst of the Great Awakening that swept America and Britain into evangelicalism—a new move of God that emphasized the authority of the Bible and the need for every person to make Jesus Christ his personal Lord and Savior. The Great Awakening brought to the masses not only the message of redemption, but also an underlying message of social equality. The first waves of revival prompted a shift in values that affected politics, trade, and traditional religious hierarchies, as well as daily social life. It created within the common man a new sense of self-worth. People of all classes became more involved in religious affairs and began studying the Scriptures for themselves.

These attitudes were the beginning of a sense of independence and equality that would set the stage for the American Revolution. As the spirit of freedom was proclaimed in the colonies by the Declaration of Independence, it followed the example of itinerant evangelists such as Whitefield, who had been the first to preach universal equality and liberty in Christ.

Humble Beginnings

George Whitefield was born to innkeepers in the cosmopolitan city of Gloucester, England, on December 16, 1714. He was the youngest of Thomas and Elizabeth's seven children. From an early age, he became familiar with the unrefined life of running an inner-city tavern. The Whitefield family owned the busy Bell Inn on Westgate Street in Gloucester's urban center. Two years after George's birth, his father passed away and his mother was left alone to run the inn and care for her large family.

George's upbringing contrasted starkly with the disciplined and refined parsonage where John and Charles Wesley were raised under the watchful eye of their mother. Whitefield was raised by a single mother who did whatever was required to keep the family business afloat, from serving beer to cleaning up after rowdy patrons. George was exposed to the most decadent of pleasure-seekers, the crudest language, and certainly some of the seediest characters. Of his boyhood tendencies Whitefield recorded:

> I can date some very early acts of uncleanness. Lying, filthy talking, foolish jesting I was much addicted to even when very young. Sometimes I used to curse, if not swear. Stealing from my mother I thought no theft at all, and used to make no scruple of taking money out of her pocket before she was up.[2]

---

[2] Albert D. Belden, *George Whitefield—The Awakener: A Modern Study of the Evangelical Revival* (Nashville, TN: Cokesbury Press, 1930), 14.

Doing what she felt was necessary to keep the inn running, his mother remarried when George was ten years old. The marriage proved disastrous and ended in a divorce that left Elizabeth and her children no better off than before. Shortly thereafter, Whitefield's older brother moved away to start a family of his own, and Whitefield left to attend grammar school at St. Mary de Crypt, where he discovered a love of theater. Although he progressed rapidly in the standard classical studies, his passion for winning the lead role in school plays was all-consuming. He often skipped class to memorize his lines and rehearse his parts, and because of his acclaimed oratory abilities, he was called upon to deliver a speech whenever important people visited the school.

His mother had always loved the theater, and the young, impressionable Whitefield inherited her drive to "be somebody." Whitefield was fifteen when his mother's marriage collapsed, and he persuaded her to let him leave school to help her run the inn. He felt she could no longer afford to support his education, which he resolved "would spoil me for a tradesman."[3] He put on his blue apron and, for a year and a half, "washed mops,...cleaned rooms, and in one word, became professed and common drawer"[4]—that is, a common beer tapster in the tavern.

Whitefield and his mother were always very close. After his birth, she had battled a debilitating illness for fourteen weeks and concluded that she would receive more comfort from George for the rest of her life than from any other of her children. She took special care to look after him and did all that she could to provide him with a suitable education outside of school. Perceiving the special place he held in his mother's heart and the ambitious nature they shared, Whitefield later wrote,

> This, with the circumstance of my being born in an inn, has been often of service to me, in exciting my endeavours to make good my mother's expectations, and so follow the example of my dear Saviour, who was born in a manger belonging to an inn.[5]

---

[3] Robert Philip, *The Life and Times of the Reverend George Whitefield, MA*, (New York: D. Appleton and Company, 1838), 16.

[4] Ibid.

[5] Ibid., 12.

George thus grew up bringing beer and food to patrons who became obnoxiously drunk, and cleaning up after them. He worked as a dishwasher as well as a chambermaid. But at night, he stayed up late reading plays, perfecting his delivery of each line and the development of each part. He attended preachers' sermons just so he could return home and imitate them for his sisters. As he mimicked ministers' prayers, the words started to stir his heart. Soon he began to study the Bible and read devotional books, which planted within him the desire to pursue a dramatic and no less significant life as a clergyman in the Anglican Church. Dreaming of one day becoming a priest, he knew he would have to complete his education by somehow finding his way to Oxford University.

At this time, Whitefield's older brother returned to manage the inn with his wife. It was no longer necessary for Whitefield to remain there, and he floundered a bit in Bristol before returning to Gloucester. He remained faithful in his devotions and read plays both to entertain others and amuse himself. One morning as he read a play to his sister, he told her,

> God intends something for me which I know not of. As I have been diligent in business, I believe many would gladly have me for an apprentice, but every way seems to be barred up, so that I think God will provide for me some way or other that we cannot comprehend.[6]

His mother soon learned from a visiting friend that a student could work for his expenses at Oxford as a "servitor"—basically an errand boy for wealthy students. She appealed to Whitefield and asked if he would be willing to go. "With all my heart," he replied. While Whitefield returned to his old schoolmaster to complete his academic requirements, his mother finished setting up a servitor's position at Pembroke College, Oxford.

The Dawn of Destiny Breaks Forth

George Whitefield was eighteen when he entered Pembroke in November 1732. His abilities as a servitor soon came to be in high demand because of his public-house training at the Bell Inn—he was

[6] Belden, *George Whitefield—The Awakener,* 16–17.

hardworking and knew how to cater to and charm his customers. He developed a reputation for diligence, friendliness, and, above all, humility. His first year was lonely, however, as he struggled to uphold both his duties and studies. Meanwhile, he also struggled in his search for God and his own destiny. At times, he felt called to preach; at other times, he felt unworthy of that call.

He tried to make peace with God by eating and dressing poorly. He prayed and fasted, attended public worship regularly, and abstained stubbornly from worldly pleasures. Young George was a member in the making for the Holy Club, and although the demands of his clients and classes did not give him time to pursue fellowship with the growing band of Methodists, by year's end he at last made himself known to one of the club's leaders, Charles Wesley.

George tried to make peace with God by eating and dressing poorly.

Sometime in 1735, George had learned that a woman in one of the workhouses had attempted to cut her own throat. Knowing that John and Charles Wesley would be willing to counsel her, he sent them word via an apple seller whom he charged not to give away his identity. She did not obey his orders, however, and divulged to Charles that Whitefield had sent her with the message. Upon learning his identity, Charles sought him out to invite him to breakfast. According to George,

> I thankfully embraced the opportunity. My soul at that time was athirst for some spiritual friends to lift up my hands when hung down, and to strengthen my feeble knees.[7]

Charles, a college tutor and six years George's senior, was impressed by the young George and invited him to join the Holy Club. Their friendship flourished rapidly. Charles lent him several life-transforming books, of which the most profound, according to George, was the *Life of God in the Soul of Man* by Henry Scougal, a young Scottish professor of divinity who had died in 1657 at the age of twenty-seven. After reading this book, George would never be the same.

[7] Philip, *Life and Times,* 25–26.

> I wondered what the author meant by saying, "That some falsely placed religion in going to church, doing hurt to no one, being constant in the duties of the closet, and now and then reaching out their hands to give alms to their poor neighbours." Alas! thought I, if this be not religion, what is? God soon showed me; for in reading a few lines further, "*that true religion was a union of the soul with God, and Christ formed within us*," a ray of divine light was instantaneously darted in upon my soul, and from that moment, but not till then, did I know that I must be a new creature.[8]

Through these words, as George himself put it,

> Jesus Christ first revealed Himself to me, and gave me the new birth. I learned that a man may go to church, say his prayers, receive the Sacrament, and yet not be a Christian. How did my heart rise and shudder like a poor man that is afraid to look into his ledger lest he should find himself bankrupt.[9]

He wasted no time delving deeper into the Gospel of Christ while the Wesleys were still "stumbling in the mazes of salvation by conduct."[10] It would take the Wesley brothers three more years to experience the magnitude of God's saving grace by receiving the new birth themselves. "The pupil was the first to become a safe teacher; he knew the 'liberty of the sons of God' while the Wesleys were struggling in chains he had broken."[11]

But George returned to bondage when he struggled to abide by the strict legalism of the Methodists—they misunderstood grace and were still trying to work their way to heaven. John and Charles had to be born again before Methodism became a means of growing closer to God rather than a means of attempting to earn salvation through good works. George fell into this trap, for although he had been born again, he didn't understand that he had received salvation through his faith, not his works. Ambitious and competitive, he also

---

[8] Philip, *Life and Times*, 26. The italics are Whitefield's.

[9] From a sermon given by Whitefield in 1769, quoted in Henry Scougal, *The Life of God in the Soul of Man* (London: InterVarsity Fellowship, 1961), 12.

[10] Belden, *George Whitefield—The Awakener*, 19.

[11] Ibid., 20.

refused to be outdone by anyone around him. He fasted regularly, depriving himself to the point of compromising his health.

George Whitefield lived by strict asceticism—he subsisted on bread and water, slept scarcely, and pushed the limits of his strength by visiting the sick and imprisoned during every spare moment. He also wore drab clothes and looked the part of a pauper—a misguided sign of devotion. Because of his newfound piety, students taunted him, refused to pay him his servitor's wages, and even threw dirt as he walked by, but he did not waver in his determination. The master of the college threatened to expel him, yet he was firm in his commitment to buffet the flesh. Sheer exhaustion took its toll, however—his body began to fail him. He finally collapsed and was bedridden for seven weeks.

George was sent home to Gloucester to recover. What he had seen in Scougal's teaching was, for the time being, smothered, and likewise all inward joy and hope. George described how he felt at this time:

> My whole soul was barren and dry, and I could fancy myself to be like nothing so much as a man locked up in armour. Whenever I kneeled down I felt great heavings in my body, and have often prayed under the weight of them till the sweat came through me. At this time Satan used to terrify me much, and threatened to punish me if I forgot his wiles.[12]

During the course of his recovery, he continued to seek the Lord, minister to the needy, and practice a life of methodical devotion. He read the works of William Law and others, but he also rested. After a reprieve from his duties as a servitor and a student, as well as from the demands of the Holy Club and the constant persecutions that resulted from being associated with it, he experienced for a time the transcendent peace of God. He wrote in his journal,

> After having undergone innumerable buffetings of Satan and many months' inexpressible trials by night and day under the spirit of bondage, God was pleased at length to remove my heavy load, to enable me to lay hold of His dear Son by a living faith, and by giving me the spirit of adoption, to seal me, and I humbly hope, even to the day of

[12] Ibid., 21.

> everlasting redemption. But O! with what joy, joy unspeakable, even joy that was full of, and big with glory, was my soul filled, when the weight of sin went off, and an abiding sense of the pardoning love of God, and a full assurance of faith broke in upon my disobedient soul! Surely, it was the day of my espousal—a day to be had in everlasting remembrance. At first my joys were like a spring tide, and, as it were, overflowed the banks. Go where I would, I could not avoid singing of psalms almost aloud; afterward they became more settled, and, blessed be God, saving a few casual intervals, have abode and increased in my soul ever since.[13]

As he rediscovered the joy of his salvation, his strength returned and he dedicated himself to sharing the gospel message with all who would listen. He began leading Bible studies in private homes, teaching in the local parish, ministering with greater enthusiasm to the poor, visiting prisoners, and calling on the sick. He formed the first Methodist Society in Gloucester, teaching and discipling the small group of newly converted locals. Already he was emphasizing "justification by faith," which Paul wrote about in Romans: *"Therefore being justified by faith, we have peace with God through our Lord Jesus Christ"* (Romans 5:1). George's conversion experience—being "born again"—governed everything he taught and did; without it, there was no meaning to existence.

He returned to Oxford to finish his course work and oversee the Holy Club in the absence of John and Charles Wesley, who had both gone to the missionary field in Savannah, Georgia. They had departed the same year George had found the new birth, leaving the Holy Club in his care. He led the group and continued to teach and minister in local parishes and prisons. Those to whom he ministered were increasingly convinced of his special call and urged him to consider taking holy orders. Only twenty-one at the time, George was hesitant to enter the priesthood prematurely. One day as George was

---

[13] J. F. Weishampel Sr., ed., "Rev. George Whitefield's Conviction and Conversion," quoted in *The Testimony of a Hundred Witnesses* (Baltimore, MD: privately printed by J. F. Weishampel Jr., 1858), 121–123, http://www.mun.ca/rels/restmov/texts/believers/weishampelthw/THW049.HTM.

returning from prayer at the cathedral, the bishop summoned him to his chambers and said, "Notwithstanding I have declared I would not ordain any one under three and twenty, yet I shall think it my duty to ordain you whenever you come; for Holy Orders."[14]

After a great deal of prayer and fasting, George felt he could resist the call no longer. The ordination ceremony took place on June 20, 1736. During the following week, the degree of Bachelor of Arts was conferred upon him at Oxford. Thus began a new era in the history of the church—a new way in which the message of Christ would be made known and experienced in both England and America.

The Boy Preacher

George delivered his first sermon as deacon from the pulpit of St. Mary de Crypt in Gloucester. Not far from this church where he had been baptized stood the tavern where he had served as a common tapster not five years earlier. Probably out of curiosity more than anything else, a surprisingly large crowd gathered to hear him preach a message entitled "The Necessity and Benefit of Religious Society." He spoke boldly about the need for religious accountability, support, and edification only found in this type of regular gathering. He also spoke about the destructiveness of nonreligious gatherings that had recently gained popularity. As a result of this message, fifteen people were reported to have "gone mad" from an overwhelming conviction of their sins. No doubt a strong sense of the Holy Spirit's presence made people appear to be "losing their minds." The bishop responded that he hoped "the madness might not be forgotten before next Sunday."[15]

From the beginning, George's preaching reflected years of theatrical performances and a heart filled with intense devotion. The pulpit was his stage, and he would use every ounce of intellect and talent to convey his sermon points. A famous actor of the time, David Garrick, exclaimed, "I would give a hundred guineas if I could say

[14] Richard Green, *John Wesley—Evangelist* (London: The Religious Tract Society, 1905), Wesley Center Online, http://wesley.nnu.edu/john_wesley/evangelist/JWE-3.htm.

[15] Stuart Clark Henry, *George Whitefield: Wayfaring Witness* (New York: Abingdon Press, 1957), 28.

'Oh' like Mr. Whitefield."[16] It was George Whitefield who would set the mark for passionate speaking among American preachers and politicians on the eve of the American Revolution. They learned from his example how to move a crowd to action.

By the end of the summer he was invited to step in as curate at the famed Tower of London while the regular curate was away. He preached for the first time after arriving in London at the large Bishopsgatestreet Church. At first, the congregation mistrusted him on account of his youth. As soon as he started to deliver his message, however, the congregation was spellbound. George recorded their reaction in his journal:

> As I went up the stairs almost all seemed to sneer at me on account of my youth; but they soon grew serious and exceedingly attentive, and, after I came down, showed me great tokens of respect, blessed me as I passed along, and made great enquiry who I was.[17]

It wasn't long before all of London knew the name of George Whitefield, whom they fondly called the "boy preacher." The crowds who came to hear about the "new birth" far exceeded the Tower's accommodations. From the beginning, George preached to packed houses; the common people seemed to flock to him. He was invited next to stand in as vicar in the small village of Dummer, Hampshire, where his popularity continued to grow. He was soon offered a lucrative position as curate[18] in a prominent London church.

America Calling

During his stint in Dummer, George received a letter from John Wesley, imploring him to come to America "where the harvest is so great and the labourers so few. What if thou art the man, Mr. Whitefield?" "Upon hearing this," wrote George, "my heart leaped within me, and, as it were, echoed to the call!"[19]

---

[16] Harry S. Stout, "Heavenly Comet," *Christian History* 12, no. 2 [Issue 38] (1993): 10.

[17] Henry, *George Whitefield: Wayfaring Witness*, 29.

[18] An assistant to a vicar—in essence, an associate pastor.

[19] Belden, *George Whitefield—The Awakener*, 31.

Within the same year that George answered the call to join the clergy, he sensed a call to become a missionary. Though he spent only two months in quiet Dummer, they were productive months in his preparation for the coming tide of evangelistic success he would experience before leaving England. He studied, prayed, read, meditated—and journaled. He wrote, "I always observed, as my inward strength increased, so my outward sphere of action increased proportionately."[20]

George would not be able to set sail for Georgia for another twelve months, but in preparation for leaving, he had already resolved himself of his position in Dummer and his duties at Oxford. He found himself free to go wherever an opportunity arose to preach, and such opportunities multiplied. His growing popularity left him little time to spend in any one place, and he soon began to refer to himself as a "Gospel rover"—never again being bound to any parish, town, or even continent. He took every congregation by storm and quickly became a household name throughout England. His Methodist affiliation made him yet more of a curiosity, and as a result, he seemed to both impress and dismay the Church of England.

> ***George was a "Gospel rover," never bound to any parish, town, or continent.***

One individual who heard George preach said that he "preached like a lion." George combined dramatic flare with a passionate conviction that left no hearer unmoved. His preaching was not only persuasive, but also persistent. His bellowing voice carried the weight of authority—it prevailed over the drums and trumpet blasts that threatened on occasion to drown it out. George would not be deterred; he "preached through and over" every noisy obstacle that presented itself. His voice could be soft and tender with a similar effect, wooing his audience into utter silence and moving them to quiet tears as he himself wept in the pulpit while meticulously describing Christ's sufferings or the depth of God's sorrow for the lost. While Wesley was meeting with disappointment as a missionary in Georgia, young

[20] Ibid., 25.

George Whitefield, "with the golden voice," was "laying the foundation of that Methodist popularity and preaching repute which was to become the outstanding feature of the century."[21]

Upon his last visit to Bristol, where the Wesleys would first experience the thrill of open-air preaching, George recorded that "multitudes came on foot, and many in coaches, a mile outside the city to meet me, and almost all saluted and blessed me as I went along the street." In his 1876 biography of Whitefield, the Reverend Luke Tyerman wrote that it was "the melting charity, the earnestness of persuasion, the outpouring of redundant love"[22] that characterized the preaching of the young evangelist. Tyerman went on to say, "It may be fairly doubted whether Wesley's preaching in 1739 would have attracted the attention which it did if Whitefield had not preceded him in 1737."[23] When George told those in Bristol about his imminent departure for Georgia, he recorded in his journal, "Multitudes, after the sermon, followed me home, weeping, and the next day I was employed from seven in the morning till midnight, in talking and giving spiritual advice to awakened souls."[24]

In August 1737, he returned to London with expectations of sailing to Georgia. One year had passed since he first landed in London and began his whirlwind preaching tour as a newly ordained deacon, and his notoriety was on the rise even as he prepared to leave the country. George's flair for publicity managed to equal his flair for showmanship, and he published his sermons in newspapers in both Britain and America. No church was large enough to contain the crowds of people who wanted to hear the "boy preacher." At a time when London's population was less than 700,000, George was able to hold captive crowds of 20,000. Listeners swooned as his voice boomed exhortations such as this:

> Lift up your hearts towards the mansions of eternal bliss, and with an eye of faith, like the great St. Stephen, see the heavens opened, and the Son of Man with his glorious retinue of departed saints sitting and solacing themselves

[21] Belden, *George Whitefield—The Awakener*, 33.

[22] Luke Tyerman, *Life of the Rev. George Whitefield, B.A. of Pembroke College*, vol. 1 (London: Hodder and Stoughton, 1876), 51.

[23] Ibid.

[24] Ibid.

> in eternal joys....Hark! Methinks I hear them chanting their everlasting hallelujahs, and spending an eternal day in echoing forth triumphant songs of joy. And do you not long, my brethren, to join this heavenly choir?[25]

Distraught at his impending departure, many offered him large sums of money to remain in London, or, if he preferred, to return to other cities he had visited during the year. It was undoubtedly divine intervention that George was drawn away from so early a rise to fame.

As George's ship, the *Whitaker*, was heading for America, John Wesley was just setting foot back on English shores. Unbeknownst to George, he had seeded the English soil for the Wesley brothers much better than they had seeded the Georgian soil for him. Thanks to George's preaching, the Wesleys would soon reap the fruitful harvest of the Great Awakening.

Aboard the *Whitaker*, George immediately began ministering to sailors, soldiers, and fellow passengers. At first he was despised because of his youthfulness, but he proved his worth and sincerity by caring continually for the sick, singing psalms during rough seas, and preaching his usual stirring messages. Once his shipmates heard him preach and witnessed his manner of discipline and service, their hearts softened toward him and they listened with interest to his daily exhortations.

Two smaller vessels had sailed with the *Whitaker*. The three ships had not been long at sea when the smaller ships pulled in closer to the larger one so that their passengers could hear George preach. Just imagine—even out on the high seas, in the middle of the Atlantic Ocean, there was George, preaching over the waves and wind to captive audiences across the decks of three ships. When the ships docked in Georgia, George gave a moving farewell sermon even though he was ill with fever. Sorrow spread as the passengers parted from George and went their separate ways.

The Next Morning in the New World

The *Whitaker* arrived in America on May 7, 1738. At five o'clock the very next morning, George began his ministry in the New

[25] Stout, "Heavenly Comet," 10.

World. He spoke to a congregation of seventeen adults and twenty-five children. Unlike the Wesleys, George came to the colony bearing gifts and much-needed supplies. He came with a heart ready to meet spiritual and material needs alike. Rather than the burden of rules and rituals commonly associated with spiritual overseers, he brought a message of freedom in Christ. The liberty he had found in his own new birth affected his listeners, and while the congregation had dwindled under John Wesley's oversight, George soon saw its numbers grow. By June, attendance had outgrown the capacity of the Savannah church and news of the engaging young preacher had spread to the surrounding towns.

From the outset, George was moved by the living conditions of the poor, and especially by the growing number of orphans. One month after his arrival, he began to teach the children in the surrounding villages and made arrangements to establish a school in Savannah. He also felt compelled to begin plans for a home for orphans. Although he had not planned to stay long in Georgia for this first visit, it was now clear that he would have to return to England to secure funds for the care of widows and orphans in the colonies and to complete his ordination as a priest.

"What I have most at heart," he wrote, "is the building of an orphan-house, which I trust will be effected at my return to England. In the meanwhile, I am settling little schools in and about Savannah; that the rising generation may be bred up in the nurture and admonition of the Lord."[26] George left Georgia with the desire to return as soon as possible. With the great sorrow among the people that typified his departures, he left for England with the promise to return as quickly as the Lord would permit him.

All the Trees of the Field Shall Clap Their Hands

When George returned to London in December 1738, he found much had changed. Foremost, Charles and John Wesley had experienced their own personal conversions through the work of the

[26] William Bacon Stevens, *A History of Georgia: From Its First Discovery by Europeans to the Adoption of the Present Constitution* (New York: D. Appleton and Co., 1847), 349.

Moravians and were preaching at Oxford and elsewhere on the "new birth" and "salvation by faith." Their message, combined with the strictness of their moral code, had incurred waves of opposition in the city. Church pulpits were increasingly closed to them, and due to George's association with the Methodists, these pulpits had become less welcoming to him as well.

Not only was his affiliation with the Wesleys controversial, but the personal journals he wrote while journeying to America had been widely circulated. He had intended for them to be shared among a close circle of friends and colleagues, but somehow they had been made public. The clergy members who read them were insulted by George's theological presumptions and felt he had become inflated with pride. They were also certain he had exaggerated his success in America and the extent of his philanthropic contributions there.

In spite of their objections, George was ordained to the Anglican priesthood on January 14, 1739. He managed to preach to large crowds at the few remaining churches that would admit him, collecting significant financial contributions to defray construction costs for the orphan house he proposed to build in Savannah. His celebrity, as well as his charity, caught the interest of the Countess of Huntingdon, who invited him to deliver a presentation to a gathering of her aristocratic friends. She and several of her peers were soon counted among his most faithful supporters and patrons.

It was not long before George made his way back to Bristol. Upon his arrival there, he found the clergy cold; the pulpits that had been promised him were firmly closed. But he knew from his prior experience there that the common people would not be so judgmental. Being censored by the established churches of the city, he went to the mining district of Kingswood—where there was no church at all—to preach to the coal miners "without a shepherd." He recorded his first experience preaching out in the open, of which an excerpt follows:

> I went upon a mount, and spake to as many people as came unto me. They were upwards of two hundred. Blessed be to God, I have now broken the ice; I believe I never was more acceptable to my Master than when I was standing to teach those hearers in the open fields.[27]

[27] Henry, *George Whitefield: Wayfaring Witness*, 48.

George went on to write that he could see the "white gutters made by their tears, which plentifully fell down their black cheeks."[28] The more he took to field preaching, the more he received hostility from the churches.

Hardly a month had passed since his ordination, and he was being threatened with suspension and excommunication. He was not deterred in the slightest, however, but continued to preach openly wherever he could attract a crowd. "I now preach to ten times more people than I should if I had been confined to the Churches....Every day I am invited to fresh places. I will go to as many as I can,"[29] he wrote.

It was near the end of March when George again sought to return to Bristol to touch the hearts of the people who had been so moved by his captivating messages only one year earlier. This time, he brought Charles and John Wesley with him. There, in the town center, he stepped up on a low wall and began to exhort the townspeople as they passed by. People stopped to listen with such rapture that John witnessed firsthand how *"the harvest truly is plenteous, but the labourers are few"* (Matthew 9:37).

From that day on, the Wesley brothers took to open-air preaching with equal fervor. Within the next several weeks, the field preachers were commanding crowds of thousands, then tens of thousands. When George preached again in Kingswood, two thousand people turned out to hear him; the following time, five thousand came. At Rose Green Common later that month, there was "so great a multitude of coaches, foot and horsemen, that they covered three acres, and were computed at 20,000 people."[30]

> The open firmament above me, the prospect of the adjacent fields, with the sight of thousands and thousands, some in coaches, some on horseback, and some in the trees, and at times all affected and drenched in tears together, to which sometimes was added the solemnity of the approaching

---

[28] John Gillies, *Memoirs of Reverend George Whitefield* (New Haven, CT: Whitmore and Buckingham, and H. Mansfield, 1834), 39.

[29] Henry, *George Whitefield: Wayfaring Witness*, 48.

[30] *Gentleman's Magazine* (1739), 162, quoted in Green, *John Wesley—Evangelist*, http://wesley.nnu.edu/john_wesley/evangelist/JWE-6.htm.

> evening, was almost too much for, and quite overcame, me.[31]

The tide of revival had begun and would continue to swell as the Wesleys took over where Whitefield left off. He left them preaching to crowds of thousands in Bristol, Bath, and beyond, while he returned to London to prepare for his journey back to America. He continued to collect offerings at every opportunity for the orphan house in Savannah. Although he met with violent opposition, he was able to collect significant sums as he preached to crowds of twenty and thirty thousand at Moorefield and Kensington Common in London. "Now I know," wrote George, "that the Lord calls me to the fields, for no house or street is large enough to contain the people who come to hear the Word."[32]

While the Wesley brothers were occupied in the provinces, George brought revival to London. And while George so captured the attention of his audiences that they seemed mesmerized, it was more common among those who heard the Wesley brothers to cry out, shout, or fall to the ground. Though George Whitefield and the Wesleys' ministry styles were strikingly different, they complemented one another nonetheless. The unemotional John Wesley would produce the most dramatic emotional effects in his hearers, while the passionate George would leave his audiences speechless. George had the gift of opening new territory; Wesley, of taming it. One tilled the field and scattered the seed; the other painstakingly gleaned the harvest—filling the barns and keeping careful watch over the precious yield. The Reverend Albert Belden, author of *George Whitefield—The Awakener*, made this profound statement:

> There are few instances in history of personal influence so perfectly mutual, so profound and far-reaching in their effects on the world at large as the shuttle-like impacts of these three men on one another. They form a triangle of constantly interchanging forces. John captures Charles, Charles lays hold of Whitefield, Whitefield bursts into flame, and in turn, pioneers John and Charles into the

[31] Henry, *George Whitefield: Wayfaring Witness*, 49.

[32] Belden, *George Whitefield—The Awakener*, 71.

> greatest religious achievement of the century, and John, through a long and laborious life, carries on and consolidates the pioneer's work. If ever three men were brought together by God for His purpose it was these three.[33]

Awakening America

On October 30, 1739, George's ship landed in Lewis Town, one hundred and fifty miles north of Philadelphia. He traveled directly to Philadelphia, a city where every church immediately welcomed the famous young preacher from England. It was not long before even the largest of churches proved too limited a venue to hold the throngs of people pushing their way in to hear George Whitefield deliver his epic sermons. Unlike in England, he took to the open streets not because he wasn't welcome in the churches but because the church buildings were too confining. He needed all the space the out of doors could provide, at last taking leave of the city to preach in the open fields.

From Philadelphia to New York, he spoke to record-sized audiences—those who gathered to hear him often outnumbered the local population! From all over, masses of people would descend on a village or field once they learned that Whitefield was to speak there. People came rushing on horseback, in carriages, on barges and ferries, and on foot to witness Whitefield's dramatic interpretations of the Bible. Whether motivated by mere curiosity, the prospect of being entertained, or the earnest desire to hear an inspired word from the Lord, the colonists turned out in greater numbers than even the British people had in London. George Whitefield was a phenomenon.

At the same time that Whitefield was taking America by storm, the Wesley brothers were riding their own wave of revival wherever they preached in England. The Spirit was at work on both sides of the ocean at the dawn of the Great Awakening; nothing could hold back the tide of evangelism from the lost and hungry populace. The light of Christ pierced the darkness that had pervaded the land as a result of the "Gin Age," in which England had nearly drowned. The colonies were entrenched in a darkness of their own as New World

---

[33] Belden, *George Whitefield—The Awakener*, 18.

hardships, including disease and the threat of starvation, pressed them on all sides.

The colonists were pioneering individualists who would not be ruled by any force other than the inner witness of the Holy Spirit. They were open to exploring new frontiers, both geographical and spiritual, and they valued freedom and truth. Thirsty for knowledge, they hung on George's every word. Determination characterized those who came from all directions and distances to hear him preach. Nothing could stop the multitudes from coming or prevent George from preaching at every opportunity. He would push himself to his physical limits to deliver the Bread of Life to the hungry masses who, with equal determination, had made a long and dusty trek on horseback to hear him preach.

George took to the open streets because church buildings were too confining.

George was surprised how crowds "so scattered abroad can be gathered at so short a warning." He was also surprised at how such enormous crowds could listen so attentively that, as he wrote, "even in London, I never observed so profound a silence."[34] Benjamin Franklin heard Whitefield preach when he first arrived in Philadelphia, and wrote in response, "He had a loud and clear voice, and articulated his words and sentences so perfectly, that he might be heard and understood at a great distance, especially as his auditories, however numerous, observed the most exact silence." Franklin calculated that Whitefield's voice could be heard by more than thirty thousand listeners: "This reconciled me to the newspaper accounts of his having preached to twenty-five thousand people in the fields, and to the ancient histories of generals haranguing whole armies, of which I had sometimes doubted."[35]

Franklin and Whitefield would share a lifelong friendship. From the outset, Franklin offered to publish Whitefield's sermons

[34] Stout, "Heavenly Comet," 11–12.

[35] Benjamin Franklin, *The Autobiography of Benjamin Franklin,* http://www.kellscraft.com/FranklinAutobio/FranklinAutobiographyCh11.html.

in his newspaper, the *Pennsylvania Gazette*, and continued to follow Whitefield's ministry with great interest. He published several volumes of George's journals, which sold in record numbers. Both men profited from the arrangement: George, from the publicity; Franklin, from additional newspaper subscriptions. Franklin would even help George raise money for the orphan house. He was so taken with George's fund-raising ability that he wrote the following famous account:

> I happened soon after to attend one of his sermons, in the course of which I perceived he intended to finish with a collection, and I silently resolved he should get nothing from me. I had in my pocket a handful of copper money, three or four silver dollars, and five pistols in gold. As he proceeded I began to soften, and concluded to give the coppers. Another stroke of his oratory made me ashamed of that, and determined me to give the silver, and he finished so admirably, that I emptied my pocket wholly into the collector's dish, gold and all.[36]

George preached throughout the region to such great multitudes that he left in his wake the rumblings of revival. So many thronged to hear him day after day that when he finally left Philadelphia, a company of more than two hundred horsemen escorted him out of town and to his destination, where the crowds continued to pursue him. On through Maryland, Virginia, and the Carolinas, George preached to massive audiences, even in the most sparsely populated areas.

During the next five months, George worked his way back to Georgia, preaching several times a day and raising money for the orphan house. He arrived in Savannah in January 1740 and immediately set to work choosing a site for the orphanage on the five hundred-acre plot of land donated by the city's trustees. He chose a tract of land ten miles north of Savannah and called it the "Bethesda Home for Boys." In 1773, three years after George's death, Bethesda burned to the ground; however, it was rebuilt and still operates today. In fact, it is the oldest operating children's home in America.

---

[36] Franklin, *Autobiography of Benjamin Franklin,* http://www.kellscraft.com/FranklinAutobio/FranklinAutobiographyCh11.html.

According to author Edward J. Cashin, the story of Bethesda is the story of Savannah.[37]

A road had to be created to make the site accessible before construction could begin, and acquiring adequate labor and supplies proved a challenge. There were hardly enough workers available for the enormous undertaking—George had to recruit carpenters, bricklayers, masons, and road workers from distant settlements. Construction finally began, and by March, George noted in his journal that "nearly forty children are under my care, and nearly a hundred mouths are daily supplied with food from our store....The expense is great, but our great and good God will, I am persuaded, enable me to defray it."[38]

Benjamin Franklin and George Whitefield shared a lifelong friendship.

George also expected wealthy friends in Britain and America to provide support, and local merchants and tradesman to donate supplies and services. This did not come about exactly as he had planned, however, and he was compelled to embark on another preaching campaign to raise the necessary funds. Some believed the undertaking was ill-conceived, but George maintained confidence in God's guidance and trust in His divine provision. The financial burden of Bethesda would remain with George for the rest of his life. He was in constant debt and collected an offering for the cause each time he preached.

With unflagging energy and zeal, George began another campaign and headed for Pennsylvania, where his popularity and the demand for his preaching only grew. While George had been overseeing the construction of Bethesda in Georgia, Franklin and other supporters had been busy overseeing the construction of a meeting hall large enough to contain the crowds who came to hear George speak. The hall would later become the site of the University of Pennsylvania. When George returned to Philadelphia, he stayed with

[37] For more on the story of Bethesda, refer to Cashin's book, *Beloved Bethesda: A History of George Whitefield's Home for Boys, 1740–2000* (Macon, GA: Mercer University Press, 2001).

[38] Philip, *Life and Times,* 168.

Franklin, and although the two did not share identical faith, they held one another in the highest esteem and mutual respect. Franklin continued to publish George's sermons and preaching itineraries, and George continued to ensure the printer's publications were best sellers.

As Whitefield worked his way through New England and on to Boston, Massachusetts, he preached three times daily—at such great length, and with such great force, that he pushed himself to the point of exhaustion. "After great labours, which reduced him physically to such a condition that thrice a day he was lifted upon his horse, being unable to mount otherwise, he rode and preached and came in and laid himself along two or three chairs."[39] Attracted by printed itineraries and press coverage in New England, George's audiences continued to grow. In Boston and other port towns along the eastern seaboard, the enthusiasm George generated bordered on panic as crowds "elbowed, shoved, and trampled over themselves to hear of 'divine things.'"[40] On the famous Boston Common, he preached to a crowd of more than fifteen thousand several times a day for several days in a row.

Adding Fuel to the Fire

By mid-October, George found himself in Northampton, Massachusetts, the guest of Jonathan Edwards, a Puritan preacher who would himself continue the American Great Awakening after George's return to England. Edwards was so moved by George's sermons that he was known to break down in tears as he listened to him preach. Edwards's wife, Sarah, was also taken with George's oratorical abilities, and wrote,

> It is wonderful to see what a spell he casts over an audience by proclaiming the simple truths of the Bible. I have seen upwards of a thousand people hung on his words with breathless silence, broken only by an occasional half-suppressed sob....A prejudiced person, I know, might say that this is all theatrical artifice and display; but not so will anyone think who has seen and known him.[41]

[39] Belden, *George Whitefield—The Awakener*, 90.

[40] Stout, "Heavenly Comet," 12.

[41] Ibid., 13.

George was equally impressed with Sarah Edwards, and stated his hope that one day he would find such a wife "adorned with a meek and quiet spirit," who also "talked feelingly and solidly of the things of God."[42] During his stay with Jonathan and Sarah Edwards, George spent some time ministering to their children and preached twice at Edwards's church. As expected, he left a remarkable impression on the entire family, congregation, and community.

When Edwards had taken up the pastorate in Northampton, he had recorded that the entire area was in a sorry moral state. Edwards had prayed for revival, and he preached with such passion and persistence that he eventually influenced the social climate of the entire nation. Of the impact George left on Northampton, Edwards wrote,

> There was scarcely a single person in the town of Northampton, either old or young, that was left unconcerned about the things of the eternal world. Those who were wont to be the vainest and loosest, were now generally subject to great awakenings. The town seemed to be full of the presence of God. It never was so full of love, nor so full of joy; and yet, so full of distress, as it was then. There were remarkable tokens of God's presence in almost every house. Our public services were beautiful.[43]

George Whitefield's presence in Northampton had the effect of fresh fuel applied to an already kindled fire. While Edwards preached fear of God's judgment, George preached God's mercy and acceptance. With impressive insight, George sensed what his listeners needed to hear. He recorded, "I found my heart drawn out to talk of scarce anything else besides the consolations and privileges of the saints and the plentiful effusion of the Spirit upon believers."[44] It was the tender message that the congregations needed to hear, and hearts that had already been "scorched and broken with the fires of judgment"[45] melted at the sound of George's compassionate words—as the Romans 2:4 says, *"the goodness of God leadeth thee*

---

[42] Henry, *George Whitefield: Wayfaring Witness*, 66.

[43] Belden, *George Whitefield—The Awakener,* 113.

[44] Ibid.

[45] Ibid.

to repentance." One of his biographers, the Reverend Albert Belden, wrote,

> The movement started so powerfully by Jonathan Edwards would have smoldered and died after all too brief a blaze, if it had not been gathered up into the tenderer atmosphere and more positively healing revivalism of George Whitefield. Indeed, there are few features of this whole story more impressive than the sense of a "brooding spirit of Revival" hovering over the Churches of the time both in Britain and America, and which brought about the most timely human contact in pursuit of the great end....These form a kind of mosaic of inevitable ordained connection over which the electric current of revival ran with all-consuming energy.[46]

It was not uncommon for shopkeepers to close up their stores and workers to leave their tools and plows to come and hear Whitefield wherever he spoke. One person described the scene of one of the open-air sermons he delivered around this time thusly:

> When we came within about half a mile of the road that comes down from Hartford Weathersfield and Stepney to Middletown; on high land I saw before me a Cloud or fogg rising. I first thought it came from the great river [Connecticut River], but as I came nearer the Road, I heard a noise something like a low rumbling thunder and presently found it was the noise of horses feet coming down the road and this Cloud was a Cloud of dust made by the Horses feet. It arose some Rods into the air over the tops of the hills and trees and when I came within about 20 rods of the Road, I could see men and horses Sliping along in the Cloud like shadows, and as I drew nearer it seemed like a steady stream of horses and their riders, scarcely a horse more than his length behind another, all of a lather and foam with sweat, their breath rolling out of their nostrils in the cloud of dust every jump; every horse seemed to go with all his might to carry his rider to hear news from heaven

---

[46] Belden, *George Whitefield—The Awakener,* 113.

for the saving of Souls. It made me tremble to see the Sight, how the world was in a Struggle, I found a vacance between two horses to Slip in my horse; and my wife said law our cloaths will be all spoiled see how they look, for they were so covered with dust, that they looked almost all of a colour coats, hats, and shirts and horses.

We went down in the Stream; I heard no man speak a word all the way three miles but every one pressing forward in great haste and when we got to the old meeting house there was a great multitude; it was said to be 3 or 4,000 of people assembled together, we got off from our horses and shook off the dust, and the ministers were then coming to the meeting house. I turned and looked towards the great river and saw the ferry boats running swift forward and forward bringing over loads of people; the oars rowed nimble and quick, every thing men horses and boats seemed to be struggling for life; the land and banks over the river looked black with people and horses all along the twelve miles. I saw no man at work in his field, but all seemed to be gone.

When I saw Mr. Whitefield come upon the Scaffold he looked almost angelical, a young, slim slender youth before some thousands of people with a bold undaunted countenance, and my hearing how God was with him every where as he came along it solumnized my mind, and put me into a trembling fear before he began to preach; for he looked as if he was Cloathed with authority from the Great God, and a sweet solemn solemnity sat upon his brow. And my hearing him preach gave me a heart wound; by Gods blessing my old foundation was broken up, and I saw that my righteousness would not save me; then I was convinced of the doctrine of Electron and went right to quarrelling with God about it, because all that I could do would not save me; and he had decreed from Eternity who should be saved and who not.[47]

[47] George Leon Walker, *Some Aspects of the Religious Life of New England* (New York: Silver, Burnett, and Company, 1897), 89–92, http://historymatters.gmu.edu/d/5711.

George commented on the reactions of such crowds:

> Look where I would, most were drowned in tears. Some were struck pale as death, others wringing their hands, others lying on the ground, others sinking into the arms of their friends, and most lifting up their eyes to heaven and crying out to God.[48]

From Northampton, George made his way back to New York through New Haven, Milford, Stratford, Fairfield, and Newark, kindling the flame of revival in each place. He found himself again in Philadelphia, where he had arrived from England exactly one year earlier. Although the roof had not been completed on the meeting hall that had been built during his absence, a podium and platform had been constructed, and the new building welcomed him as its first speaker. While in Philadelphia, he felt impressed by the Lord that it was time for him to return to his native country, and he made plans to check on his affairs in Georgia before setting sail for Britain. Of his whirlwind tour through New England, he wrote,

> My Body was weak, but the Lord much renewed its strength. I have been enabled to preach, I think, 175 times in public, besides exhorting very frequently in private. I have traveled upwards of 800 miles, and gotten upwards of 700 sterling[49] in goods, provisions and money for my poor orphans. Never did God vouchsafe me such assistance. All things concur to convince me, that America is to be my chief scene for action.[50]

George returned to Savannah to find that despite his great fund-raising efforts, he was still five hundred pounds short of paying the debt he owed for the orphanage's construction. In the middle of January, he bid farewell to record-sized audiences in Boston, and from Charleston he boarded the *Minerva* back to Britain in the hopes of securing more funding for the increasingly needy orphan house in Georgia.

---

48 George Whitefield, *George Whitefield's Journals* (London: The Banner of Truth Trust, 1965), 425, quoted in Hyatt, *2000 Years of Charismatic History,* 115.

49 This would be about $160,000 in purchasing power in 2006.

50 Henry, *George Whitefield: Wayfaring Witness*, 68.

George Whitefield

Friends, Foes, and Raving Fans

The year 1741 was an eventful one for George Whitefield. He was invited to Scotland, where a revival greater than any he had yet witnessed broke out under his ministry. He married a widow, Elizabeth Burnell James—the marriage provided more convenience than comfort, however, as George entered into it with a sense of duty rather than a sincere romantic interest.

This was also the year of his break with the Wesleys over the doctrine of predestination—a break that would affect him more deeply than any other event. Divisive public debates that lasted nearly a year created two camps among the Methodists: the Wesleys' "free grace" camp and Whitefield's Calvinist camp. Two separate groups of "Societies" were on the rise, and soon both Whitefield and the Wesleys saw the danger of the split—they realized the opposition they felt toward one another was scarcely as strong as the opposition between their followers.

Furthermore, George never had any interest in the demands that starting his own denomination would entail, while John Wesley was especially gifted in administrative leadership and organization. Neither could bear to be separated "in spirit" from the other for long. Though their friendships would be rejoined, the two movements of Whitefield's "Calvinistic Methodism" and the Wesleys' "United Societies" would not.[51]

Having conquered England and North America, George shifted his aim to awaken Scotland. The Scottish Presbyterians were eager for George to visit them. Calvinists all, Americans and Scots were kindred spirits in the eighteenth century. Both territories perceived themselves to be on the periphery of British control and struggled with their own nationalistic identities. George would visit Scotland fourteen times, experiencing a depth of revival he had not witnessed in the rest of Great Britain or the colonies. He reminisced later in life about the joy he always found in speaking to the Scots; he was "impressed by the 'rustling made by opening the Bibles' as soon as he 'named' his text."[52]

---

[51] For more on this dispute, see chapter one, subtitle, "The Move of God Divided."

[52] Henry, *George Whitefield: Wayfaring Witness*, 79.

He put on the map a small town named Cambuslang, just southeast of Glasgow, after he preached to twenty thousand twice in one day and to thirty thousand the next. The sheer numbers were not as unusual for George as the effects of this particular preaching event. He had never witnessed such a hunger for the presence of God among those to whom he preached. Enormous tents were set up to accommodate the thousands desiring to partake in Communion, while worship and prayer continued into the early hours of morning. He recorded the following:

> You might have seen thousands bathed in tears. Some at the same time wringing their hands, others almost swooning, and others crying out, and mourning over a pierced Saviour....All night in different companies, you might have heard persons praying to and praising God....It was like the Passover in Josiah's time.[53]

In August, an "open-air" Communion unlike any ever seen in Scotland, much less anywhere else, took place. An observer noted,

> Some called it fifty thousand, some forty thousand, and the lowest estimate, with which Mr. Whitefield agrees, makes them to have been upwards of thirty thousand....Of these some were from England and even from Ireland and many were Episcopalians and some even Quakers.[54]

This scene would repeat itself wherever Whitefield ventured to preach; it is said that the fires kindled during these "Cambuslang Revivals" set all of England aflame. Of George's impact on his listeners in Scotland, Dr. John Gillies recorded, "The whole multitude stood fixed, and, like one man, hung upon his lips with silent attention, and many under deep impressions of the great objects of religion and the concerns of eternity."[55]

In addition to the far-reaching impact of the events at Cambuslang, revival was underway in all parts of the British Isles. John Wesley was preaching to a perpetually packed house at the Foundry in London, Charles Wesley was preaching to thousands in Bristol

---

[53] Henry, *George Whitefield: Wayfaring Witness*, 78.

[54] Belden, *George Whitefield—The Awakener*, 135.

[55] Gillies, *Memoirs of Reverend George Whitefield*, 138.

and Gloucester, and Howell Harris, a fellow Calvinist and admirer of Whitefield, had ignited revival in Wales.

George understood that his primary calling was to be a "wayfaring witness," bound by no particular place or church, let alone country—he could never preside as Wesley did over a growing network of Societies. "An itinerant pilgrim life is that which I choose,"[56] he wrote. John Wesley, on the other hand, refused to send preachers where he could not direct the formation of Societies and felt the Great Awakening in America and Scotland subsided largely because George's converts lacked effective discipleship. He felt they failed to stay the course without an effective leadership structure. George appreciated John Wesley's talent for guiding and disciplining his growing flock, and Wesley acknowledged that no other person "since the apostles called so many thousands, so many myriads of sinners to repentance!"[57]

George speaks in the drawing room of Selina, Countess of Huntingdon.

Mary Evans Picture Library

In Wales, George joined his friend Howell Harris, who was single-handedly establishing dozens of Methodist Societies throughout the region. Harris was a field preacher who endured severe persecution, but his persistence ultimately brought revival to Wales. As was happening elsewhere throughout Britain and America, converts were being added daily. George helped Harris form the "Welsh Calvinistic Methodist Association" not long after Harris introduced George to Elizabeth Burnell James, who would become his wife.

Harris was instrumental in arranging the first meeting of George and Elizabeth—a widow who loved the Lord and was dedicated to the Methodist movement. George had told Harris that he was open to the prospect of marriage; he hoped to find a helpmate for his work in the ministry. Elizabeth agreed to marry George even though he made it clear that preaching the Gospel would always be

---

[56] George Whitefield, *The Works of the Reverend George Whitefield, M.A.*, vol. 3 (Poultry, UK: Edward and Charles Dilly, 1771), 48.

[57] Stout, "Heavenly Comet," 15.

his first love. Elizabeth was thirty-six and George twenty-six when they married in November 1741. During their weeklong honeymoon, George preached twice a day. Within the month, he was back on the road; thereafter, he would rarely see, or even speak of, his new wife. Two months after his marriage, he was quoted as saying, "O for that blessed time when we shall neither marry nor be given in marriage, but be as the angels of God."[58] Elizabeth set up residence in London; George would stay there for short periods but could not remain in one place for long, as the call of evangelism tugged constantly at his heart.

There were also the increasing demands to raise funds for the orphanage, and thus the pace of Whitefield's itineration increased steadily year after year to the extent that he did not see his wife for a period of twenty-four months. Elizabeth was faithful in keeping George's affairs in order while he traveled abroad—she copied his letters and sermons and oversaw the mass of correspondence her husband's popularity required. Two years into the marriage, Elizabeth gave birth to a son who died in infancy. This loss weighed heavily on George, and from that point he showed special concern for children everywhere. He was known to speak directly to them when he preached, telling them that if their parents would not come to Christ, they were to come anyway and go to heaven without them.

Following the death of their son, Elizabeth suffered four miscarriages. Although observers noted that George was always respectful and courteous toward his wife, Elizabeth wrote of her marriage to him, "I have been nothing but a load and burden to him."[59] In August 1768, after twenty-seven years of marriage, she entered heaven's gates two years ahead of her husband. After Elizabeth died, George said, "I feel the loss of my right hand daily."[60]

The Upward Call

The years before George set sail again for America in 1745 were filled with incredible evangelistic victories—and with the most violent persecution. He was frequently pelted with stones, rotten vegetables,

---

[58] Mark Galli, "Whitefield's Curious Love Life," *Christian History* 12, no. 2 [Issue 38] (1993): 33.

[59] Ibid.

[60] Ibid.

and dead animal parts. On one occasion, a rock struck his head and nearly rendered him unconscious. Another time, he would have been stabbed had the crowd not intervened on his behalf. One man tried to strike him with a whip as he preached; others attempted to drown out his voice with drums or trumpets. In 1744, the same year that George's infant son died, an intruder broke into his home and attacked him in his bed. His life was preserved thanks to his landlady—when George screamed, "Murder!" she came running and shouting, waking the entire neighborhood and sending the assailant fleeing into the night.

When George made his third trip to America in 1745, he experienced such a tremendous welcome throughout the colonies that it took some months for him to work his way south to Georgia. He stayed at the Bethesda orphanage and observed the condition of the buildings and staff. The orphans appeared to be in good health and were progressing in their spiritual growth and education. He hoped to start a college on the premises that would become a premiere center for religious studies in the South. With a renewed fervor, he headed east to generate support for his expanding vision.

George set out for Philadelphia and Boston, being hailed to preach in every town along the way. People came from forty or fifty miles away when they heard he would be stopping in a certain town. Pushing himself to exhaustion, he preached daily to crowds of tens of thousands, expanding the wave of revival to all corners of the colonies. George was on his way to becoming America's first cultural hero—he unified the young nation as it sought to define its position in the world.

George returned again to England, Scotland, and Wales. He earned the further attention and respect of the wealthy Lady Huntingdon, who had become one of his primary supporters. She appointed him chaplain of a network of chapels she had built, a position that relieved some of his financial burdens. The demand for his preaching did not slacken; persecution did, fortunately. During the 1750s, the Methodists, namely the Wesley brothers and George, had gained popular support as their message became more widely accepted among all ranks of society. As individuals, they had also mellowed in the way they expressed their viewpoints. George learned to use a gentler tone in his letters and public declarations, ruffling far fewer feathers as he grew older.

However, his words still cut to the core. One young man, John Thorpe, and some friends, heard George preach in May of 1750, and they went straight on the tavern. There they began mocking his exuberant style to make one another laugh. When it was Thorpe's turn, he grabbed the Bible, leapt onto a nearby table, and exclaimed, "I shall beat you all!" When his eyes fell to the open page they lighted upon the words, "*Except ye repent, ye shall all likewise perish*" (Luke 13:3 and 5). The words struck him to the core, and he stopped mocking and began sincerely preaching. Two short years later, he was an itinerant preacher for John Wesley.[61]

When George made his fourth trip to the colonies in 1751, he took a group of twenty-two destitute boys with him to Bethesda. Seeing the need for expansion there, he returned to England almost immediately to raise the required capital. On his fifth transatlantic trip in 1754, he received an honorary Master of Arts degree from the College of New Jersey (now Princeton University) and worked closely with Benjamin Franklin as he entered the political arena. By this time, nearly every American had heard George Whitefield speak and esteemed him highly, much as people today esteem Billy Graham. George's endorsement of Franklin must have helped significantly to start Franklin's political career. One year later, in March 1755, George left for England and would not return to his beloved Bethesda for another eight years.

As he grew older, George learned to use a gentler tone in his letters and public declarations.

In 1760, George was in London when he heard about the Great Fire of Boston. He collected a large sum of money on behalf of "the sufferers" and sent it immediately to Boston. When he returned to America in 1763 and passed again through Boston, even the coldest Bostonians were melted by George's attention and "voted unanimously that the thanks of the town be given the Rev. George Whitefield for his charitable care and pains in collecting considerable sums of money for the distressed sufferers."[62] George recorded that in New

[61] Stout, "Heavenly Comet," 13.

[62] Henry, *George Whitefield: Wayfaring Witness*, 91–92.

England, "invitations come so thick and fast from every quarter that I know not what to do."[63]

As tensions mounted between England and the colonies, George sided decisively with the colonists. They considered him their champion and clamored more and more to hear his preaching throughout the colonies. George never refused an opportunity to preach and would stop to give a sermon wherever he was hailed, so it took him more than eighteen months to work his way back to Georgia. The physical demands of traveling worried George's doctors, who exhorted him at least to remain in one location if he insisted on preaching. Nevertheless, when he returned to England in 1765, he continued to itinerate from London to Edinburgh.

His wife passed away in August 1768, and almost exactly one year later, George made plans to return to the colonies. He gave a farewell speech to crowds of thousands in London, and in November 1769, he made his final transatlantic trip to America. Although he was not in good health when he arrived in Charleston, he preached to large crowds for ten consecutive days. He continued his preaching tour throughout New England as if he were still a youthful man. Although battling asthmatic colds, he insisted to his friends that he "would rather wear out than rust out."[64] For the next nine months he did not slow his pace, even though he was often "taken in the night with a violent lax [diarrhea], attended with retching and shivering." [65]

On the morning of September 19, 1770, he preached a moving message in Portsmouth, New Hampshire, to the ever-present multitude that had thronged to hear the legendary George Whitefield. He then set out immediately for his next destination: Newburyport, Massachusetts. Friends and admirers observed his weakened condition and begged him to rest, but he pressed on. By midday, George was implored by a gathering crowd to preach, and he complied. He climbed atop a barrel in an open field to preach what would be his last sermon. The text he spoke about was "Examine yourselves whether ye be in faith," which discussed the new birth. Whitefield's last public words were about the uselessness of works to get to heaven: "Works!

---

[63] Ibid., 91–92.

[64] Stout, "Heavenly Comet," 14.

[65] Ibid.

Works! A man gets to heaven by works! I would as soon think of climbing to the moon on a rope of sand."[66]

George Whitefield breathed his last in the early hours of September 20, 1770, the day after he preached his last sermon. He was fifty-six years old. Six thousand mourners attended his funeral, at which John Wesley delivered the eulogy. Charles Wesley penned the following lines in remembrance of their providential meeting:

> Can I the memorable day forget
> When first we by Divine appointment met?
> Where undisturbed the thoughtful student roves
> In search of truth, through academic groves;
> A most modest youth, who mused alone,
> Industrious the frequented path to shun
> An Israelite, without disguise or art
> I saw, I loved, and clasped him to my heart,
> A stranger as my bosom friend caressed
> And unawares received an angel-guest.[67]

Someone asked Wesley whether he would see George Whitefield in heaven, and he replied, "George Whitefield was so bright a star in the firmament of God's glory, and will stand so near the throne, that one like me, who am less than the least, will never catch a glimpse of him."[68]

In his life's ministry, George preached more than eighteen thousand sermons—an average of five hundred a year for a thirty-year period, or ten a week. He had recorded these prophetic words in his journal: "I believe there is such a work begun as neither we nor our fathers have heard of. The beginnings are amazing; how unspeakably glorious will the end be!"[69]

A Powerful—and Strange—Legacy

After his death, George Whitefield's body was laid to rest beneath the pulpit of the Old South Presbyterian meetinghouse in

---

66 Stout, "Heavenly Comet," 15.

67 Belden, *George Whitefield—The Awakener,* 18.

68 Hurst, *John Wesley the Methodist,* http://wesley.nnu.edu/john_wesley/methodist/ch13.htm.

69 Belden, *George Whitefield—The Awakener,* 129.

Newburyport, Massachusetts, an obscure town that became a destination for people on pilgrimages throughout New England. In 1775, a group of colonial soldiers, led in part by Daniel Morgan and Benedict Arnold, asked if they could hold services in the building before a battle. After the meeting, they asked the pastor if they could view George's body. Having obtained permission, they pried open the casket, took his clerical collar and wristbands, and cut them into pieces, which they divided amongst themselves to take into the battle as protective relics.

For the next century and a half, George Whitefield's corpse and bones continued to be objects of great attention. Jesse Lee, the "Methodist Apostle of New England," visited the church in 1790 and noted the body's slow decay—something long believed to signify the saintliness and holiness of the deceased. Lee found "the greater part of it hard and firm; a small part of it only had putrefied."[70] He took a small section of George's gown and knelt with it to pray.

Over the years, thousands would come to view the body and take pieces of cloth or bone if they could. Abel Stevens (1815–1897), an American editor, historian, and Methodist Episcopal clergyman, viewed the body some years later and even held George's skull in his hands. In 1829, the bones of George's right arm were taken to England, where they remained for twenty years. They were restored later with a procession of two thousand mourners who came to pay their respects. The tomb was finally covered over with glass, and a gas light was installed nearby so that people who came to see his bones could enter the chapel at any hour to pray and observe his remains without disturbing them. Despite these measures, a small part of one of his thumbs made its way to Drew University, where it is stored to this day in the Methodist Archives. The tomb was finally sealed over with slate slabs in 1933 and left to rest in peace.

More than any other eighteenth-century preacher, George Whitefield paved the way for the modern evangelistic techniques with which we are familiar today. Without the aid of television or even amplifiers, his voice reached into nearly every home of Great

---

[70] Clifton F. Guthrie, "Touching Whitefield's Bones: Relics and Saints among Nineteenth-Century Methodists," paper presented at the Southeast Regional Meeting, American Academy of Religion, March 21, 1998, http://www.bts.edu/Guthrie/GuthrieCV&Pubs/Touching%20Whitefields%20Bones.htm.

Britain and America. His oratory skills and irresistible charisma, combined with his great love for the lost and depth of character, made him a potent force for God. At a time when people were desperate for the light of truth, George Whitefield stepped on the scene. He brought the innovation of field preaching to the Wesleys and a fresh revelation of God's mercy to Edwards, thus igniting the flames of revival across two continents.

Chapter Three

☆☆☆☆☆

Jonathan Edwards

(1703–1758)

"God's Intellectual"

"God's Intellectual"

The sense I had of divine things, would often of a sudden kindle up, as it were, a sweet burning in my heart, an ardor of soul, that I know not how to express.

—Jonathan Edwards

Jonathan Edwards is the most complex—and therefore the most misunderstood—of all the revivalists. Born the same year as John Wesley, Edwards was the son of a Puritan minister and almost considered nobility in colonial New England—though their accommodations were closer to the forts and garrisons of the Wild West than the Wesleys' peaceful parsonage in Epworth.

While Jonathan Edwards would become a pastor and revivalist at the center of the Great Awakening in America, he was also an intellectual who cut his teeth on Enlightenment thought and the writings of such men as John Locke and Isaac Newton. During his life, Edwards would write some of the most scholarly theological works, edit the popular *Life and Diary of David Brainerd*, which remains a classic piece of missions literature, breathe life into the hearts of two revivals, be dismissed from the church he pastored, serve as a missionary to the Native Americans, and die as the president of the University of New Jersey at Princeton.

Jonathan was a Puritan, but he was also an evangelical Calvinist—a seeming oxymoron. He believed that only God can elect those who are saved; but almost conversely, he also believed it was the responsibility of every individual to search out his or her own personal destiny with God. Jonathan Edwards was a man of immense integrity who balanced the importance of radical faith with discipline and critical thinking. He was never afraid to ask why or question his own beliefs and then search with all of his heart until he found an answer.

During his short life of fifty-four years, Jonathan Edwards chronicled the incredible signs and wonders of the move of God that he witnessed in the Great Awakening. Questioning the excesses, he argued the necessity of making religion a thing more of the heart than the head. He preached a great deal on the nature of God being defined by His love, yet his most famous sermon was his fire-and-brimstone call to repentance, "Sinners in the Hands of an Angry God." He preached the gravity of the wrath of God out of a heart overflowing with compassion and concern for the lost. He was better acquainted with heaven than with hell but was glad to give his congregation a guided tour of hell in the hopes that they would avoid it at all costs.

Jonathan and his wife, Sarah, are among the most notable parents in American history. By 1900, the descendants of their eleven children included thirteen college presidents, sixty-five professors, one hundred lawyers (including one dean of an outstanding law school), thirty judges, sixty-six physicians (including one dean of a medical school), 135 editors, one publisher, and more than one hundred overseas missionaries. Among these were the writer O. Henry, the publisher Frank Nelson Doubleday, and the writer Robert Lowell. Eighty of their descendants held public office, including three U.S. senators, mayors of three large cities, governors of three states, and one U.S. vice president, Aaron Burr Jr. There was also one U.S. first lady, Edith Roosevelt (the second wife of Theodore Roosevelt), and one controller of the U.S. Treasury, Robert Walker Taylor.[1] The generational legacy of Edwards's children reflects how the influence of a sincere follower of Jesus Christ is passed down through history.

To focus exclusively on the legacy Jonathan Edwards left, however, would be to miss his primary importance to Christianity today. He was a man willing to struggle with thoughts, feelings, and the

[1] A. E. Winship, *Jukes-Edwards: A Study in Education and Heredity*, Project Gutenberg, http://www.gutenberg.org/files/15623/15623-h/15623-h.htm.

rushing tide of change in order to receive the reward of Abraham—friendship with the great "I Am." First and foremost, Jonathan Edwards was a man in pursuit of knowing God, and that pursuit fulfilled everything he desired.

Colonial Beginnings

On October 5, 1703, Jonathan Edwards was born in East Windsor, Connecticut, to Puritan parents Timothy Edwards and Esther Stoddard Edwards. Of their eleven children, he was the only son; Esther had four daughters before giving birth to Jonathan, and six more followed. Although the Puritans came to the New World with high hopes for a religious nation where believers could live out their biblical convictions as they judged best, it didn't take long for a focus on the promise of a prosperous life to stagnate the faith of many.

Ever present reminders of mortality tempered the lure of materialism, however. Life-threatening hardships were ubiquitous, and it was not uncommon for loved ones to perish from epidemics, accidents, or brutal attacks by Indians. Nearly 50 percent of the Pilgrims who had first arrived in Plymouth less than a century before Jonathan's birth died during the first winter. Because of the threat of Indian attacks, the settlements between Northampton and Deerfield (located in present-day Massachusetts) looked more like military outposts than the quaint colonial-era town replicas that tourists visit today.

It is important to remember that throughout his life, Jonathan considered himself a British subject. He did not live to see the American Revolution, and his birth was in the midst of Queen Anne's War (called "The War of Spanish Succession" in Europe), which pitted England against France and Spain in a competition for land in America. While the war started in St. Augustine, Florida, French territorial holdings were just to the north of New England in Canada. War with France and Spain didn't just mean a change in British government; it meant the possibility of a takeover by Roman Catholicism, which most Puritans considered to be the religion of the Antichrist.

Not only that, but the French Canadian neighbors had stronger ties to the Indians than the British colonists did, and the European wars would each spill over into fighting between the French and

Indians and the English colonists. French Jesuits came to America with Catholicism—a brand of Christianity that demanded fewer cultural changes of Native Americans. It was one thing to take the sacraments regularly, and quite another to be born again. This built another bond of loyalty between the French and the Indians, and it wasn't long before the Indians adopted the French disdain for English settlers and their Protestant religion.

The same week that Jonathan was born, Indians ambushed two men in Deerfield (roughly fifty miles north of East Windsor) and carried them to the north as captives. John Williams, Deerfield's pastor and Jonathan's uncle, only narrowly escaped being taken captive. Then, on February 29, 1704, the entire town of Deerfield was attacked by roughly two hundred Native American braves and a small contingent of Frenchmen. In what became known as the Deerfield Massacre, fifty-six of its roughly three hundred residents were killed; another one hundred were carried off to Canada. Another of Jonathan's uncles, John Stoddard, barely escaped with his life. Wearing only his sleeping gown and a coat he grabbed in his flight, he wrapped his feet with cloth cut from his coat and somehow managed to walk ten miles in two feet of snow to summon help. Help came too late, however; Jonathan's uncle and aunt, John and Eunice Williams, watched as two of their children—a six-week-old and a six-year-old—were killed before their eyes. The rest of the family members were carried north to Canada along with the others. Eunice, still weak from having given birth recently to her baby, who was murdered, collapsed in a stream and was killed on the spot by a single blow to the head with a tomahawk.

Williams and four of his children made their homecoming one year later, when sixty of the settlers were ransomed. He and his brother-in-law, John Stoddard, acted as envoys to Canada for the return of the rest of all the captives at the end of the war in 1713. One of Williams's daughters, named Eunice after her mother, had not been ransomed with him and his other children. She married a Mohawk man in early 1713 and remained in Canada. Williams later wrote about the ordeal in a book, *The Redeemed Captive of Zion*, which became a best seller.[2]

---

[2] George M. Marsden, *Jonathan Edwards: A Life* (New Haven, CT: Yale University Press, 2003), 15–17.

The Puritan mind-set interpreted such calamities simply as signs of the times for God's new covenant people, which they believed themselves to be. Like the nation of Israel, Puritans believed they were blessed or punished according to their obedience or disobedience of God. For them, the Deerfield Massacre and kidnappings were like being carried off into Babylon, while their return was likened to Nehemiah's rebuilding of Jerusalem. With death and hardship always near, the Puritans felt they had to hold God even closer if they were to keep any hope of surviving at all. Jonathan remembered being called to pray several times a day to beg God for the protection of family members when he was young.

An Unusual Heritage

Jonathan's family tree, especially on his father's side, represented the two extreme identities of the time: the Puritan and the frontiersman. The first fit the Puritan ideal of perfectionism, held up as an example to all. The second would be best described as the uncivilized, sinful life—a life to be avoided at all costs.

Jonathan's paternal grandfather, Richard, was a successful merchant who had married his bride, Elizabeth, only to find out three months later that she was pregnant by another man. With divorce virtually unheard of in those days, Richard Edwards arranged for the child to be raised by Elizabeth's parents. More scandal and disgrace followed when Elizabeth was diagnosed with mental illness, an imperfection no one knew how to handle in those days. It seems the illness affected other members of her family as well. One of her sisters murdered her own child; another was killed with an ax by her own brother.

Timothy Edwards was the oldest of Richard and Elizabeth's six children. There is little doubt that he was influenced greatly by his mother's vagaries—on several occasions, she abandoned the family, only to reappear suddenly. After Elizabeth's repeated infidelities, rages, and threats of violence—she once warned Richard that she would cut his throat while he slept—Richard finally appealed to the authorities and sought to divorce Elizabeth. His request was initially rejected, but after several more years of chaos, he appealed again and the divorce was granted.

Although Richard's divorce was legal, his son Timothy paid the price in the community of Puritans, who rejected divorce regardless of its lawfulness. Timothy was mysteriously expelled from Harvard, where he had been preparing for the ministry. "All we know is that an 'ominous' mark was entered next to his name in the 'Severe Punishments' column of the Harvard records. Some believe the timing correlates with his father's divorce petition." [3] With perseverance—a Puritan virtue and an Edwards family trait—Timothy continued his ministerial studies under a private tutor. Harvard later recognized his accomplishments and granted him his degree.

Timothy's wife, Esther Stoddard Edwards, grew up in the home of the great Solomon Stoddard, a famous Puritan minister who was held in such high esteem that many called him the "Pope of the Connecticut River Valley." As the daughter of such a respected minister, Esther was introduced to many of New England's most influential people and was privileged to receive the finest education available to a woman at that time. Perhaps it was her love of books and learning that helped to whet her young husband's appetite for knowledge, preparing Jonathan Edwards to become one of the greatest intellectuals of his day.

"Swallowed Up in God"

In those days, the local pastor often served as the local schoolmaster, and Timothy Edwards was no exception. Having his father as both his pastor and his teacher played a significant role in stirring young Jonathan's heart toward God. During his early years of education at home, Edwards learned Greek, Hebrew, and Latin. He also described in his journals how, as a young boy, he would often wander through the fields surrounding his home, sensing God's majesty in everything around him. Jonathan was always a man of books, but he would never allow indoor study to monopolize his time.

Even as a child, Jonathan must have sensed God's calling on his life. He recorded in his journals that he spoke often about God to the other boys his age, and together they built a place in the woods where they could pray. He wrote that for a period of months, he and the other boys would go there as often as five times a day to seek

[3] Marsden, *Jonathan Edwards: A Life*, 23.

God. One can sense the regret expressed in his memoir: "eventually, the nine year old lad 'entirely lost all those affections and delights' and 'returned like a dog to his vomit, and went on in ways of sin.'"[4]

Jonathan continued his pursuit of knowledge by enrolling at the age of thirteen at the Collegiate School of Connecticut, which would later become Yale University. While studying for the ministry, Jonathan devoured books in the largest library in the area, reading works not only particular to ministry, but also from many different fields. He graduated in 1720 at the head of his class but stayed for two more years to pursue a master's degree.

A hot and cold experience with God characterized Jonathan's early years.

It seems that Jonathan put aside his previous longing for God until his senior year at Yale, when, at age sixteen, he had a near-death experience, according to what he recorded in his journal. He became very ill with pleurisy[5] and was terrified that he would die without being adequately prepared for eternity. He described this dreadful feeling as being "shook over the pit of hell"[6]—imagery that would reappear in his most famous sermon. Though he recorded that during this time he committed himself to God in a new way, when he eventually recovered from his illness, he "fell again into his old ways of sin" and continued to have "great and violent [spiritual] struggles."[7]

This hot and cold experience with God went on throughout Jonathan's formative years. One can understand how doubt might have reigned in his mind, given what his father taught him. According to Timothy Edwards, there were three specific steps to conversion: (1) an initial conviction or awareness of God; (2) a sense of unworthiness and being separated from God; and then (3) repentance and, *if* God granted it (as a good Calvinist would believe), ultimate salvation.[8] Timothy Edwards had to be strongly convinced God *had*

---

[4] Marsden, *Jonathan Edwards: A Life*, 26.

[5] A severe respiratory illness.

[6] Marsden, *Jonathan Edwards: A Life*, 36.

[7] Ibid.

[8] Ibid., 33.

indeed granted one salvation. Jonathan wrote a letter to tell his sister saying that after their father presented these steps to his congregation, hundreds in his church had responded to a stirring of the Holy Spirit in their hearts, seeking a closer relationship with God. Thirty had made appointments with Timothy to have him confirm the validity of their experience, a mere thirteen of whom he accepted as sincere and allowed to join the church.

This process of proving one's conversion was difficult for Jonathan Edwards to accept. His maternal grandfather once told him that, ten to one, those converted would surely know that their experience was real. Since Jonathan's experiences came with struggles of uncertainty, he may have wondered whether God had indeed granted his salvation. Even so, he was determined not only to know with his mind the God of the Bible, but also to experience Him personally to the fullest in his own heart. Nothing short of that would do. As someone once said of him, "He had no middle gears."[9]

Finally, in 1721, in a regular time of study, the truth of this passage surpassed his rational mind: *"Now unto the King eternal, immortal, invisible, the only wise God, be honour and glory for ever and ever. Amen"* (1 Timothy 1:17). He wrote,

> There came into my soul, and was as it were diffused through it, a sense of the glory of the divine being; a new sense, quite different from anything I ever experienced before....I thought with myself, how excellent a Being that was; and how happy I should be, if I might enjoy that God, and be wrapped up to God in heaven, and be as it were swallowed up in him.[10]

From this point on, Jonathan determined to understand God and His Word from all points of view, believing that "the more you have of a rational knowledge of divine things, the more opportunity will there be, when the Spirit shall be breathed into your heart, to see the excellency of these things, and to taste the sweetness of them."[11]

---

[9] Ibid., 39.

[10] Ibid., 41.

[11] Jonathan Edwards, "The Importance and Advantage of a Thorough Knowledge of Divine Truth" (sermon), Christian Classics Ethereal Library, http://www.cccl.org/ccel/edwards/sermons.divineTruth.html.

In spite of the darkness around him, Jonathan desired to know the power and wisdom of God, as well as the "sweetness" of God. He was unwaveringly determined to help others to see them as well.

God granted him the abilities required to pursue truth—he looked at the visible things of this world and then used them to understand the truths of the unseen world of God's kingdom. The evidence of this thirst emerged at an early age and continued throughout his life.

The Great Interpreter

Jonathan Edwards was clearly a well-educated man, but much of what he learned about God came from his own process of a disciplined search that included observation, recording his observations and thoughts, making careful interpretation of his recordings, and finally sharing the results and conclusions with others through writing or speaking.

Jonathan would spend his entire life pursuing God's truth with obsessive discipline. He would rise early as a matter of course, a habit he endorsed in his diary by writing, "I think Christ has recommended rising early in the morning, by his rising from the grave very early."[12] He resolved "Never to lose one moment of time, but to improve it in the most profitable way I possibly can,"[13] and "To live with all my might while I do live."[14] For him, this was an ardent intellectual endeavor in which he left no stone unturned in his pursuit of God's glory—and in his pursuit to see God's glory released in the lives of human beings.

Jonathan observed everything he encountered, but he paid especial attention to nature, the Holy Scripture, the writings of scholarly people, and the lives of those around him. His times of tromping through the woods, where he observed the natural world and talked to God, brought many questions to his mind. As a young man, he was captivated by spiders, wondering how their webs were made. He became so fascinated with rainbows that he practiced making them by spurting out a

---

[12] John Piper, "The Pastor as Theologian: Life and Ministry of Jonathan Edwards," paper presented at the Bethlehem Conference for Pastors, April 15, 1988), *Desiring God*, http://www.desiringgod.org/ResourceLibrary/ConferenceMessages/ByConference/16/1458_The_Pastor_as_Theologian.

[13] Ibid.

[14] Ibid.

mouthful of water and then watching the sun create small rainbows as the light was diffracted through each water droplet.[15]

Many have said that if Jonathan had not gone into religious studies, he would have become a scientist like Benjamin Franklin. Instead, he devoured the Word of God, determined to leave no question unexamined. He wrote in one of his journals,

> [I] seemed often to see so much light, exhibited by every sentence, and such a refreshing ravishing food communicated, that [I] could not get along in reading...lingering long on one sentence, to see the wonders contained in it; and yet almost every sentence seemed to be full of wonders.[16]

His quest for truth led him to read books by the likes of Isaac Newton and John Locke. Over the course of his life, he amassed a personal library of more than three hundred books, quite a few in a time when most were blessed just to have a Bible in the house. But it wasn't just reading for reading's sake that Jonathan dedicated himself to devouring books. According to John Piper,

> Edwards was not a passive reader. He read with a view to solving problems. Most of us are cursed with a penchant toward passive reading. We don't ask questions as we read....We don't ferret out the order of thought or ponder the meaning of terms. And if we see a problem, we are habituated to leave that for the experts and seldom do we tackle a solution then and there the way Edwards said he was committed to do if time allowed.[17]

Jonathan's life—and, later on, the life of each of his parishioners—was examined for any gap between the perfection he desired and the results of his personal assessment. He watched carefully for anything that might distract him, especially from spiritual things. Each time he observed a discrepancy in his personal conduct, he drafted a resolution that recorded what he needed to change and how he would accomplish it. He formulated his values intentionally and aligned written goals and plans to ensure that he would live by them.

---

[15] Norma Jean Lutz, *Jonathan Edwards: Colonial Religious Leader* (Philadelphia: Chelsea House Publishers, 2000), 13–14.

[16] Ibid., 23.

[17] Piper, "Pastor as Theologian."

Framing these types of resolutions was a common Puritan practice that truly seemed to empower Jonathan. By the time his personal list was complete, it comprised seventy resolutions that included never doing anything out of revenge, always maintaining strict eating and drinking habits, and only doing what one would do if it were the last hour of one's life. One of the most revealing commitments he made to himself was Resolution Number 11, which stated, "When I think of any theorem in divinity to be solved, immediately to do what I can towards solving it, if circumstances do not hinder."[18] This resolution could be a modern-day mission statement for any church or ministry.

"The Religious Psychologist"

Jonathan determined not only to observe, but also to record, what he saw. The spiders that fascinated him, for example, were classified and described in great detail—we still have Jonathan's detailed account of a spider weaving a web. As a pastor, he was known to carry a pen, ink, and bits of paper along with straight pins when he went for rides in the woods. These rides were prime times for him to think and to talk with God. He would record the ideas that came to him and pin them, in order, to his coat. This checkerboard of thoughts was then carefully unpinned by his wife, vigilant to keep them in order, when he arrived home.

Jonathan once disassembled one of his Bibles—very carefully, of course—and sewed a sheet of blank paper between each pair of pages to allow him to record his notes. Another of his resolutions may reveal part of his reason for doing this:

> 28. Resolved,...to study the Scriptures so steadily, constantly and frequently, as that I may find, and plainly perceive myself to grow in the knowledge of the same.[19]

Constant and deep study of Scripture was a way to make sure he was growing in accordance with the exhortation of the apostle Peter, who wrote in his second epistle, *"But grow in grace, and in the knowledge of our Lord and Savior Jesus Christ"* (2 Peter 3:18).

---

[18] Jonathan Edwards, "The Resolutions of Jonathan Edwards," *Bible Bulletin Board*, http://www.biblebb.com/files/edwards/resolutions.htm.

[19] Ibid.

Jonathan not only observed the perceived gaps in his life and constructed resolutions for solving them, but he also kept a detailed record of his progress. At the end of each month he tallied up the score.

As a pastor, Jonathan later recorded the possible evidences of the spiritual experiences of his parishioners, a practice he had seen his father do. His observations and notes on the emotional and physical responses of the people during the Great Awakening—such as weeping, fainting, laughing, and screaming—caused him later to be known as the "religious psychologist."

After observing and recording what he noticed, Jonathan, according to Sereno Dwight, "then arranged them under their proper heads, ready for subsequent use; of regularly strengthening the faculty of thinking and reasoning, by constant and powerful exercise; and above all of gradually molding himself into a thinking being."[20]

A Chocolate Lover

Jonathan was determined to take time to think about the implications of what he observed, going so far as to skip dinner if it threatened to interrupt the flow of his thinking. As he had done to everything else in his life, he had carefully observed and analyzed which foods best suited his mental labor.

Some said that his discipline in eating left him thin and frequently ill, but Jonathan evidently gave great consideration to his diet. He wrote,

> By a sparingness in diet, and eating, as much as may be, what is light and easy of digestion, I shall doubtless be able to think clearer, and shall gain time. 1. By lengthening out my life. 2. Shall need less time for digestion after meals. 3. Shall be able to study closer without wrong to my health. 4. Shall need less time to sleep. 5. Shall seldom be troubled with the head-ache.[21]

[20] Sereno E. Dwight, *The Life and Works of Jonathan Edwards,* quoted in Piper, "Pastor as Theologian."

[21] Jonathan Edwards, *A Treatise Concerning Religious Affections, in Three Parts* (Philadelphia: James Crissy, 1821), xxi, http://books.google.com/books?id=GC0LAAAAYAAJ&pg=PR21&lpg=PR21.

There is one hint that his disciplined lifestyle had at least a small indulgence. He loved chocolate, which came in "cakes," and could be melted and served as a beverage consumed at breakfast. A letter remains of his request that a courier to Boston be sure to procure chocolate for him.[22] "Though he never totally abandoned his strict spiritual discipline, he did look back on these early days with mature eyes and declare it a time of 'too great a dependence on my own strength; which afterwards proved a great damage to me.'"[23]

The created world he loved to study also caused him to grapple with bigger questions, such as the reason that God created the world in the first place. What desire of God could creation possibly satisfy? In his recorded thoughts of his analysis, Jonathan concluded that God gains nothing from creating; His happiness in Himself is perfect, and nothing can be added to it. But God desired creatures who could see and enjoy the beauty of that perfection—His glory. Jonathan said that everything God has done is for the single purpose of the love and praise of His intelligent, created beings.

The natural world presented Jonathan with all kinds of opportunities to glean spiritual lessons. For example, he once saw a cat taunting a mouse and said it reminded him of how the devil does the same with wicked men. At one point in his life, he had been terrified of thunderstorms, but after his conversion he could interpret them differently. He wrote,

> Before I used to be uncommonly terrified with thunder...but now, on the contrary, it rejoiced me. I felt God, so to speak, at the first appearance of a thunder storm; and used to take the opportunity, at such time...see the lightnings play, and hear the majestic and awful voice of God's thunder.[24]

Jonathan pored over the works of Isaac Newton, intrigued by his findings that the universe operated by certain laws—some of which could even be represented mathematically. He interpreted those findings and concluded that God is a God of order.

---

[22] Steven Gertz and Chris Armstrong, "Did You Know?: Interesting and unusual facts about Jonathan Edwards," *Christian History* 22, no. 1 [Issue 77] (2003), http://www.ctlibrary.com/6341.

[23] Marsden, *Jonathan Edwards: A Life*, 53.

[24] Lutz, *Jonathan Edwards: Colonial Religious Leader*, 21.

A Culture Writer?

Fortunately for us, Jonathan Edwards was also faithful to publish the conclusions of his interpretations. Not surprisingly, he had rules for writing, warning himself to "display modesty of style and to try to gain readers rather than to silence opposition."[25] He also wrote about the arts and sciences and how they were rooted in God. He published these thoughts in a book entitled *The Nature of True Virtue*. Jonathan perceived no conflict between religion and science, believing that correct interpretation would certainly show them to support one another.

It seems that his astute observations, plentiful thoughts, and copious writings carried over into his personal correspondence as well. A young woman in Jonathan's church named Deborah once asked him how she should conduct herself in a Christian way, and he wrote her a fourteen-page letter detailing his recommendations. In a gentle tone, he assured her that even though she might sin, the blood of Jesus could cover it. He also warned her to beware of pride and encouraged her to become a minister to others her own age. This letter was later published as a pamphlet entitled *Advice to Young Converts*.

Early Years as a Pastor

After graduating from Yale, Jonathan accepted his first call to be a pastor in the growing city of New York. His church was small, but to Jonathan that meant he still had time to enjoy his walks in the woods surrounding the Hudson River and to study the Bible. He loved the congregation but could not draw adequate support from the church, which struggled financially. Jonathan was thus forced to move back home to Connecticut. His father convinced him to take a pastorate at Bolton, Connecticut, a job he didn't really want. After only a few months on the job, Edwards was relieved to receive an offer for a teaching position at Yale.

Some thought his reason for taking the job at Yale had to do with the daughter of the pastor there, Sarah Pierrepont. Jonathan was

[25] Marsden, *Jonathan Edwards: A Life*, 59.

twenty and she just thirteen, but he was smitten with her, describing her in his journals as sweet and "beloved of that Great Being."[26]

Even that motivation was not enough to overcome his discouragement with the situation at Yale. He had looked forward to the teaching position, but with no leader appointed to the institution, he was called upon to administrate in addition to teaching. It didn't take long for Jonathan to figure out that this highly coveted job consisted of disciplining wild, wayward young men—a responsibility for which he did not feel gifted. It seems these young men who planned to become clergy members took advantage of their newfound freedom from their strict upbringing. They engaged in excessive drinking and frequent rowdiness, which caused Jonathan to become weary and depressed. Some think his depression could have been due to an illness he suffered during this time, while others believe it was the reverse. Regardless, the depression forced Jonathan to be bedridden for four months, and prolonged illnesses of one type or another plagued him nearly every year thereafter.

Jonathan's grandfather believed that the purpose of evangelism was to ease God's anger.

Jonathan must have been relieved when his grandfather, the Reverend Solomon Stoddard, invited him to become his assistant pastor at the Congregational Church in Northampton, Massachusetts. This was the largest church in New England outside of Boston, and Stoddard, now in his eighties, needed help. Stoddard was a highly influential man, not only in his own town and church but in the whole area. Like other Puritan preachers, he taught that honoring those in authority, including the clergy, was crucial to survival and prosperity.

Disagreeing with Rev. Stoddard must have seemed like disagreeing with God Himself. At one point, he even declared that God was punishing New England because its people were violating His commandments. Stoddard described the people in his congregation

---

[26] John Nichols, *American Literature: An Historical Sketch, 1620–1888* (Edinburgh, Scotland: Adam and Charles Black, 1882), 54, http://books.google.com/books?id=GC0LAAAAYAAJ&pg=PR21&lpg=PR21.

this way: "We live in a corrupt age and multitudes of men take a licentious liberty, in their drinking and apparel, and company, and recreations, and unsavory discourses."[27]

Stoddard believed that the purpose of evangelism was to ease God's anger, and that it was the only means of bringing blessing to His people. The colonists' failure to reach out to the Indians brought punishment, he said, adding that any positive move the colonists made toward the Indians was in the hope of appeasing God.

Jonathan's grandfather held strong opinions about most things. He despised the modern fashion of men wearing wigs—to him, wigs made men look "as if they were more disposed to court a maid, than to bear upon their hearts the weighty concernment of God's kingdom."[28]

There were some points on which Jonathan and his new superior disagreed, mostly having to do with church membership and Communion. Unlike his grandfather, Jonathan believed that being granted church membership, and thereby taking Communion, required proof of having been converted to the Congregational statements of faith. Solomon Stoddard taught that anyone who professed belief and whose life was free from scandal could become a member of the church and partake of the Lord's Supper. Jonathan made a decision to defer to Stoddard while under his authority.

Wedding Bells

With his new position as a pastor—and with the corresponding salary, adequate to purchase land and a home—Jonathan now formally pursued courtship with Sarah. They were married on July 20, 1727; Jonathan was twenty-four and Sarah was seventeen. Sarah wore a bright green, satin brocade dress—an exuberant expression of the Puritan celebration of love and marriage. This is an aspect of Puritan culture that is greatly misunderstood today. While many in the Victorian era viewed the human body negatively, most Puritans acknowledged the wonder of God's creation in ways some of us might even find uncomfortable today. Romantic love between

---

[27] Marsden, *Jonathan Edwards: A Life*, 13.

[28] Ibid., 11.

a husband and wife had an honored place in New England society, and the formation of a new household was a cause for all to rejoice.[29]

Jonathan and his wife were considered a good team. Sarah grew up in a parsonage learning how to be a minister's wife. George Whitefield, famous revivalist from England, once visited their home and said, "A sweeter couple I have not seen."[30] Single when he first met them, Whitefield began to pray that God would give him such a companion as Sarah Edwards. Samuel Hopkins, an apprentice preacher at the time, recalled, "No one of discernment could be conversant in the family without observing and admiring the perfect harmony and mutual love and esteem that subsisted between them."[31]

Jonathan himself said that Sarah's conversation "entertained him"; her spirit encouraged his spiritual life and her presence "brought him peace." He had great respect for what his wife thought, so each night he would read to her what he had written that day and listen to her response before they had devotions together.

Eleven children were born to Jonathan and Sarah: Sarah, Jerusha, Esther, Mary, Lucy, Timothy, Susannah, Eunice, Jonathan, Elizabeth, and Pierrepont. All eleven lived into adulthood, which was extremely unusual for that day and age. There was a long-standing bit of humor enjoyed by the people of Northampton regarding the first four births. Folklore of the day held that a child was born on the same day of the week that he or she had been conceived, and each of their first four children was born on Sunday.[32]

Every evening, Jonathan would spend an hour talking with his children before returning to his study. By all accounts, he was strict but loving. Everyone was to be home by nine o'clock at night. When his daughters were old enough to be courted, their suitors were not allowed to "intrude upon what he considered proper rest and sleep, or the religion and order of the family."[33]

---

[29] Elisabeth S. Dodds, *Marriage to a Difficult Man: The "Uncommon Union" of Jonathan and Sarah Edwards* (Philadelphia: The Westminster Press, 1971), 24.

[30] Ibid., 26.

[31] Ibid.

[32] Gertz and Armstrong, "Did You Know?"

[33] Lutz, *Jonathan Edwards: Colonial Religious Leader*, 34.

Many have commented on the visible influence of many women, including his wife and daughters, on Jonathan. Besides his ten sisters, with whom he remained very close, Jonathan was also exposed to a strong bond of mutual admiration between his father and mother. The high regard in which he obviously held women no doubt started there. According to biographer George Marsden, Jonathan's father Timothy Edwards's letters to his wife, Esther, were filled with love for her and the children. Timothy also preached that a husband's love for his wife should be a "singular peculiar thing" that displayed the "honor and respect" she deserved. He should "not act magisterial or lordly, but in a loving manner with due respect to his wife."[34]

Jonathan Edwards preaches.

Jonathan's sisters were raised to be independent thinkers; all attended finishing school, the women's equivalent of college in that day. Timothy Edwards made sure his daughters developed both intellectually and spiritually. One sister, Hannah, didn't marry until her thirties, not at all a common choice in those days. Pursued by two men, one of whom built her a house and engraved her initials on the mantel, she rejected both offers and eventually married a third man. This delay created quite a stir, but Hannah remarked that women who remained single were at a great advantage if they focused their attention on religion and knowledge.[35]

Earthquake Repentance

The year after Jonathan became assistant pastor at his grandfather's church in Northampton, all of New England experienced

---

[34] Timothy Edwards, sermon on Isaiah 54:5, June 28, 1730, quoted in Marsden, *Jonathan Edwards: A Life*, 21.

[35] Heidi Nichols, "Those Exceptional Edwards Women," *Christian History* 22, no. 1 [Issue 77] (2002): 24.

the Great Earthquake of 1727. According to some accounts, it began with a flash of light, followed by rumbling and shaking that lasted throughout the night. People who were awakened from their sleep crowded together in the streets, believing that judgment day had come. The next morning, churches across New England were filled with penitents. With aftershocks that continued for nine days, the earthquake caused sheer terror to reign in the hearts of all the residents of Northampton, driving them to seek assurance of their salvation. Fasts were called for throughout the land several times in the weeks following.[36]

The governor of Massachusetts called for a day of fasting and prayer on Thursday, December 21, and Jonathan was called upon to give a sermon that day. Would he blast the people for their role in bringing the anger of God upon them all? His grandfather surely would have. Although Jonathan observed sin in the lives of his people—he mentioned cheating, injustice, swearing, trusting in riches, and being insensitive to the things of religion—he instead chose to speak on Jonah and the Ninevites.

Jonathan, being an expert on natural phenomena, expressed the possibility that the earthquake could have merely happened—but he also wondered at the coincidence of it. Was God indeed warning His covenant people as He had warned the Ninevites through Jonah? Because the earthquake came on a Sunday night, was God showing His anger with the young people for their late-night frolicking after sundown on the Sabbath? Jonathan described their practice this way:

> It was their manner very frequently to get together in conventions of both sexes, for mirth and jollity, which they called frolics; and they would often spend the greater part of the night in them, without regard to any order in the families they belonged to.[37]

Jonathan reminded them that God was a God of mercy to the people of Nineveh because they repented. Perhaps it was time for the people of New England to do the same. As a result of the earthquake,

---

[36] Harry S. Stout, "The Puritans and Edwards: The American Vision of a Covenant People," *Christian History* 4, no. 4 [Issue 8] (1985): 24.

[37] Marsden, *Jonathan Edwards: A Life*, 122.

churches throughout the colonies swelled in attendance. Some scholars mark this event as the first light of the Great Awakening.

A Spokesman for the Living God

When Solomon Stoddard died in February 1729, the church decided to make Jonathan the senior pastor of Northampton. It was a position he took as seriously as he did the rest of life. He wrote about climbing the steps to the podium to preach as becoming "the trumpet of God."[38] Some said he turned into an entirely different person while preaching.

After Stoddard's death, Jonathan's health worsened. A brief trip away to rest was helpful, but within a few weeks he was ill again. Stress added to whatever physical ailments he had, and being a pastor certainly entailed stress. Salary was always an issue. Sarah was expected to do a great deal of costly entertaining, which stretched their budget to the limit. Gifts and handouts supplemented many pastors' salaries, including Jonathan's, but that usually required treating those with the most means with bigger gifts and special favor. Edwards wasn't in the habit of playing favorites.

Being fully responsible for more than one thousand parishioners who didn't measure up to his high spiritual standards no doubt caused Jonathan a great deal of anxiety. After Stoddard's death, the congregation seemed totally out of control, especially the young people. It was a time with many similarities to Jonathan's days at Yale, where he was asked to corral unruly youth and didn't feel he had the social skills to rein them in. Family government—the old Puritan structure of power—loosened as parents reacted to their own strict upbringings, swinging to the other extreme of no discipline at all.

Drunkenness among the younger generation was commonplace. Parents seemed surprised when premarital pregnancy rates skyrocketed to one in ten in New England. Jonathan pointed out that they should expect this statistic because they allowed their young sons and daughters to climb into bed together, partially dressed, and

---

[38] Helen Westra, *The Minister's Task and Calling in the Sermons of Jonathan Edwards* (Lewiston, NY: Edwin Mellen, 1986), 7, quoted in Marsden, *Jonathan Edwards: A Life*, 132.

"enjoy each other." The practice, called "bundling," was supposed to allow them to "get acquainted," but much more took place than just friendly conversation. As long as any resulting pregnancy culminated in marriage, the attitude of the people was generally accepting. This bold, new mind-set was most frustrating to Jonathan.

A personal tragedy added to Jonathan's already heavy weight. His family had somehow escaped dying from a disease that had affected most families, but in December 1729, an epidemic of diphtheria took his youngest sister, Jerusha.

The First Tremors of the Great Awakenings

In the early 1730s, the cultural climate of Northampton was beginning to change. The hostilities with the French and Indians during Dummer's War (another outbreak from a war in Europe which had ended in 1727) had forced more communal farming as people stayed closer together for better protection. That meant there was less land available for young men to safely strike out on their own. Marriage was postponed among young couples because there was less room to begin new families. Children lived under the authority of their parents into young adulthood. Jonathan decided to bring the parents together to have them agree to call for godly behavior in their own homes. The young men and women seemed to hear with new ears.

Jonathan's strong preaching against the sinful lifestyles of the young people in his town was balanced by a greater compassion for their souls. No doubt it was all covered with much prayer and the seeking of God's guidance for change. It should be no surprise, then, that the first Great Awakening began with the younger generation.

After the sudden death of a young man in April 1734, Jonathan preached a funeral message that encouraged those present to turn away from their sinful lifestyles and focus instead on their eternal rewards. He spoke from the text of Psalm 90:5–6, which talks about God's protection, rather than from other passages depicting an angry, wrathful God. If one was to die so young, what would he have to show for his life? Jonathan preached,

> How unreasonable is it for one who is so much like the grass and flower of the field...to spend away the prime of his opportunity in levity and vain mirth in inconsideration and pursuit of carnal and sensual delights and pleasures....
>
> Consider. If you should die in youth how shocking would the thought of your having spent your youth in such a manner be to them that see it. When others stand by your bedside and see you gasping and breathing your last or come afterward and see you laid out dead by the wall and see you put into the coffin and behold the awful visage which death has given you, how shocking will it be to them to think this is the person that used to be so vain and frothy in conversation. This is he that was so lewd a companion. This is he that used to spend of his time in his leisure hours so much in frolicking.[39]

It wasn't long until the reports of changed lives began to pour in as young people began to "awaken" to their need for a Savior, just as people had after the Great Earthquake. Another death, along with another funeral message, continued the renewal of spiritual interest. Evenings of "frolicking" were traded for prayer meetings, and soon the great majority of the community—young and old alike—attended such meetings. It was an interesting parallel to Wesley's "United Societies," though it seems quite impossible that the Puritans of New England had ever heard of the Wesley brothers, especially since it would be another five years before the Wesleyan revival broke out in England.

During this time, only the Psalms were sung in corporate praise and worship. Jonathan encouraged the "new singing" of hymns by men such as Isaac Watts in these outside meetings. Watts didn't care for the church music of his day; he found it poorly written and difficult to sing, being simply the Psalms set to music. Although he thought hymns should be doctrinally sound, he didn't believe they needed to be exact renderings; rather, they could be paraphrases of Scripture or even simply based on a scriptural theme. Watts wrote many well-known hymns, such as "When I Survey the Wondrous Cross."

[39] Jonathan Edwards, Sermon (April 1734), quoted in Marsden, *Jonathan Edwards: A Life*, 154.

Jonathan loved music and believed it was a way for the people to release the emotional enthusiasm they experienced. Written in three-part harmonies and accompanied by instruments, these hymns were something new; the traditional Psalms were usually sung according to however each person felt led and thus rarely sounded like a "joyful noise."

Jonathan loved music and saw it as a way for people to release their emotional enthusiasm.

The revival grew further when a young woman known as "one of the greatest company-keepers in the whole town"[40] came to Jonathan and told him the story of her conversion. Jonathan questioned her carefully but was quickly convinced that she was telling the truth. Her changed life was such an unlikely thing to happen that Jonathan worried the news might make people doubt the authenticity of her conversion, thinking the transformation was just for show. Rather than withholding what God had done, however, he spread the story, and it multiplied the number of converts. Within days, a handful of others showed up at his door with similar stories of conversion.

By April 1735, the evidence of a changed spiritual atmosphere in the community was undeniable. Jonathan himself described it this way:

> A great and earnest Concern about the great Things of Religion, and the eternal World, became universal in all Parts of the Town, and among Persons of all Ages....All other Talk but about spiritual and eternal Things, was soon thrown by....The Minds of People were wonderfully taken off from the World; it was treated amongst us as a Thing of very little Consequence....The Temptation now seemed to lie on that Hand, to neglect worldly Affairs too much, and to spend too much Time in the immediate Exercise of Religion.[41]

[40] Marsden, *Jonathan Edwards: A Life*, 158.

[41] Jonathan Edwards, *The Christian History* (1743), quoted in S. Mintz (2007), http://www.digitalhistory.uh.edu/documents_p2.cfm?doc=230. Digital History.

Without being prompted, neighbors took up a collection for the owner of a general store after it burned to the ground. Backbiting and gossiping stopped. Taverns were reported to have emptied. Even church services were transformed:

> Our Public assemblies were then beautiful; the congregation was alive in God's service, everyone intent on the public worship, every hearer eager to drink in the words of the minister as they came from his mouth; the assembly were [*sic*] in general from time to time in tears while the word was preached; some weeping with sorrow and distress, others with joy and love, others with pity and concern for the souls of their neighbours.[42]

Another notable occurrence during the revival was that illness nearly disappeared from the town. When Jonathan later detailed what occurred during the revival in his *Faithful Narrative,* he wrote that although he didn't see this disappearance of disease as evidence required to prove revival, he did feel that it was necessary to acknowledge it. His critics called all that he wrote about "fanaticism," especially the showing of emotions and stories of unlikely people being converted. Some reports say that more than five hundred people—half of them men—joined the church as a result of the revival. Word began to spread in the surrounding areas and people came from other towns to see the excitement. The Edwards household overflowed with visitors. The revival continued to spread throughout the Connecticut River Valley as far as New Haven and the coastal settlements, even reaching outside of New England.

In Boston, a place untouched by the awakening, a minister by the name of Benjamin Colman asked Jonathan to send him a report of the happenings in Northampton. Jonathan's talent for recording details and interpreting them made it a job for which he was well suited. Jonathan's letter was then forwarded to friends of Colman in England.

The report turned into a complete how-to manual for conducting a revival from preparation to onset—the maintenance, regulation,

[42] Jonathan Edwards, "A Narrative of Surprising Conversions," *Jonathan Edwards on Revival* (Carlisle, PA: Banner of Truth, 1984), 13, quoted in Hyatt, *2000 Years of Charismatic History,* 114.

dangers, and effects of revival. This guidebook was eventually published under the title *A Faithful Narrative of the Surprising Work of God.* Even though he penned the words, Jonathan was well aware that it was ultimately God who authored this work of conversion. This publication made Jonathan famous throughout New England, as well as in Scotland and England, where George Whitefield and John Wesley were eventually acquainted with it.

The excitement of revival didn't last, however. In 1735, Jonathan wrote that "Satan seemed to be more let loose, and raged in a dreadful manner."[43] Satan is a destroyer, and he used his influence to cause fear and division. Several people were overcome with fear day and night; others were so afraid of the anger of God that they complained they couldn't sleep. There were even reports of an unnerving invasion of crows that filled the air with loud cawing and landed on the rooftops of homes. An epidemic raged through the valley, killing ninety-nine people in one town alone; eighty-one of them were children. Two people in another town went mad.

Jonathan's own family was affected, too. Joseph Hawley, the husband of Jonathan's Aunt Rebekah, was a respected man in the town. It was understandably quite shocking when he was found to have slit his own throat. When this incident happened, Jonathan had already written the formal report to Colman but had not yet mailed it. Feeling that the exclusion of such information would be deceitful, he broke open the seal and added the account, along with a note saying that his uncle had been mentally unstable.

Jonathan reminded the people that they had a powerful enemy who was very real and was determined to destroy each of them. Finally, his health took a serious turn for the worse, and he left for an extended rest. The move of the Spirit in Northampton and the Connecticut Valley, which began in 1734, came to a close during the summer of 1735.

The Great Awakening Erupts

By March 1737, the spiritual condition of Jonathan's congregation was again cold. He described the people as having "eagerness after the possessions of this life"[44] and noted that there had

[43] Marsden, *Jonathan Edwards: A Life*, 163.

[44] Ibid., 184.

been a return of the heated party spirit. He began to pray again for revival.

The meetinghouse had been deteriorating for some time and the harsh winter had severely weakened the building's supports. As Jonathan began to deliver a sermon to a packed house, the balcony split from its supports and crashed on the people below, mostly women and children. There was screaming and crying, everyone believing that there would be great numbers of dead bodies under the debris. Yet when they cleared the rubble, they found none dead; though they suffered cuts and bruises, they were all alive. No one had even broken a bone.

Jonathan hoped that this "sign from God" would stir their hearts again toward spiritual things. He called the warning "one of the most amazing instances of divine preservation, that perhaps was ever known in the land."[45] Unfortunately, the people failed to be moved by the event. In a letter to Rev. Colman in Boston, Jonathan shared his disappointment that although the people seemed grateful for God's mercy, "it has had in no wise the effect that ten times less things were wont to have two or three years ago."[46] While people around the world rejoiced in reading about the blessings that had come to Northampton, Jonathan was embarrassed that this "city set on a hill" had fallen into decay.

In late winter of 1737, Jonathan began to preach three sermon series that he hoped would turn the hearts of the people back to God. Although little happened outwardly, he held on to a glimmer of hope that things were about to change. Jonathan turned to prayer, spending as many as eighteen hours in prayer before preaching a single sermon.[47] Encouragement finally came from across the Atlantic Ocean—from the Church of England, of all places.

By 1739, George Whitefield was already preaching to crowds of thousands in the streets and fields of England and was now coming to the colonies. Jonathan wrote to him in February 1740 and persuaded him to come to Northampton, warning him that his people might be more hardened of heart than others to whom he had preached.

---

[45] Ibid.

[46] Ibid., 185.

[47] *Change the World School of Prayer* (Studio City, CA: World Literature Crusade, 1976), D–38, quoted in Hyatt, *2000 Years of Charismatic History,* 114–115.

A major publicity campaign helped draw the crowds in the cities to hear Whitefield, and when he moved on to Northampton on October 17, 1740, the attention of the masses followed him.

Whitefield was a powerful speaker, and emotional responses to his speeches were not uncommon. Sarah Edwards described a captivating message she had heard him deliver:

> It is wonderful to see what a spell he casts over an audience....I have seen upwards of a thousand people hang on his words with breathless silence, broken only by an occasional half-suppressed sob.[48]

When Whitefield reminded Jonathan's congregation of their closeness to Christ after the last awakening, many began to weep, including Jonathan himself, as he saw five years of prayer for revival fulfilled. He even reported that some of his own children were brought to Christ.

At the end of Whitefield's time in Northampton, Jonathan rode with him for the next two days and saw the spiritual hunger of thousands who came to hear him speak. The effects on the crowds were unprecedented. It was not uncommon for people to fall out under the power of the Holy Spirit—something Jonathan described as "faintings."

> There were some instances of persons lying in a sort of trance, remaining perhaps for twenty-four hours motionless, and with their senses locked up; but in the mean time under strong imaginations, as though they went to heaven and had there visions of glorious and delightful objects.[49]

The revival continued, and Jonathan and Whitefield stayed in contact by letter. Edwards reported the results of the awakening in his area to be greater than the previous awakening of Northampton in 1734, knowing that he personally had participated little in making this one happen, except by prayer.

---

[48] Chris Armstrong, "The Trouble with George," *Christian History* 22, no. 1 [Issue 77] (2003), http://www.ctlibrary.com/7872.

[49] Jonathan Edwards, "Revival of Religion in Northampton in 1740–1741," *Jonathan Edwards on Revival* (Carlisle, PA: Banner of Truth, 1984), 154, quoted in Hyatt, *2000 Years of Charismatic History,* 116.

Jonathan wasted no time in furthering the progress gained by the revival. He pointed out that "Religion that arises only from superficial impressions is wont to wither away...when it comes to be tried by...difficulties."[50] It would then be up to the pastors to take over from there, and raise the new converts up to maturity in Christ.

Jonathan had no intention of letting the people decline as they had before, so he wrote to some young itinerant preachers and asked them to come. By the time he wrote this letter, the young people of his town had begun holding their own meetings and sharing their experiences. Jonathan met with all the children less than sixteen years of age and talked with them about their souls. The young people cried, prayed, sang, and shared their experiences with one another. Later, Jonathan had a similar meeting with young people aged sixteen to twenty-six; again, they were greatly affected. Some meetings lasted all night because the youth were so overcome.

"Sinners in the Hands of an Angry God"

On Wednesday, July 8, 1741, Jonathan was among a team of preachers at Enfield (near the border of Massachusetts and Connecticut) to minister to large numbers of people who were inquiring about how to be saved. Revival was already brewing in the area; the nearby settlement of Suffield had seen ninety-five people added to its membership the preceding Sunday, though it had not yet touched Enfield. Joseph Meacham, a pastor at Coventry, Connecticut, presided.

Several ministers, including Meacham, had been preaching at the ongoing revival services between Enfield and Suffield. On that Wednesday morning, it was decided that the other would rest and let Jonathan preach. Jonathan searched his saddlebags and found a sermon he had read shortly before to his congregation.They had sat stoic and unaffected when he had preached it. Few acknowledged it further with a "Fine word, pastor,"[51] but it had moved them to nothing beyond that. The passage for the sermon was Deuteronomy 32:35, *"Their foot shall slide* [slip] *in due time."*

---

[50] Armstrong, "Trouble with George."

[51] Stephen R. Holmes, "A Mind on Fire," *Christian History* 22, no. 1 [Issue 77] (2003): 13.

As they entered the church that morning, the congregation seemed more ready for a fashion show than revival. One minister later wrote of the scene, "When they went into the meeting house, the appearance of the assembly was thoughtless and vain. The people hardly conducted themselves with common decency."[52] Jonathan wore thick glasses to read his sermons, and he was purposely monotone as he read for fear of bringing fleshly enthusiasm into his preaching, as many accused George Whitefield of doing. People reported that his style of preaching that day was "easy, natural, and very solemn. He had not a strong, loud voice; but appeared with such gravity and solemnity, and spake with such distinctness, clearness and precision....He made little motion with his head or hands."[53] Here is a brief excerpt of the words he spoke that day:

> Your wickedness makes you as it were heavy as lead, and to tend downwards with great weight and pressure toward hell....There are the black clouds of God's wrath now hanging over your heads, full of the dreadful storm, and big with thunder....
>
> The God that holds you over the pit of hell, much as one holds a spider, or some loathsome insect, over the fire, abhors you, and is dreadfully provoked; his wrath towards you burns like a fire; he looks upon you as worthy of nothing else, but to be cast into the fire; he is of purer eyes than to bear to have you in his sight; you are ten thousand times so abominable in his eyes as the most hateful venomous serpent is in ours. You have offended him infinitely more than ever a stubborn rebel did his prince; and yet 'tis nothing but his hand that holds you

SINNERS

In the Hands of an

Angry GOD.

A SERMON

Preached at *Enfield, July* 8th 1741.

At a Time of great Awakenings; and attended with remarkable Impreſſions on many of the Hearers.

By *Jonathan Edwards*, A.M.

Paſtor of the Church of CHRIST in *Northampton*.

Amos ix. 2, 3. *Though they dig into Hell, thence ſhall mine Hand take them; though they climb up to Heaven, thence will I bring them down. And though they hide themſelves in the Top of Carmel, I will ſearch and take them out thence; and though they be hid from my Sight in the Bottom of the Sea, thence I will command the Serpent, and he ſhall bite them.*

BOSTON: Printed and Sold by S. KNEELAND and T. GREEN, in Queen-Street over againſt the Priſon. 1741.

Jonathan Edwards's sermon manuscript

---

[52] Sereno E. Dwight, *The Life of President Edwards* (New York: G. and C. and H. Carvill, 1830), 605.

[53] Marsden, *Jonathan Edwards: A Life*, 220.

> from falling into the fire every moment: 'tis to be ascribed to nothing else, that you did not go to hell the last night... but that God's hand has held you up: there is no other reason to be given why you haven't gone to hell since you have sat here in the house of God, provoking his pure eyes by your sinful wicked manner of attending his solemn worship: yea, there is nothing else that is to be given as a reason why you don't this very moment drop down into hell.
>
> Oh sinner! Consider the fearful danger you are in....
>
> And now you have an extraordinary opportunity, a day wherein Christ has flung the door of mercy wide open, and stands in the door calling and crying with a loud voice to poor sinners;...many that were very lately in the same miserable condition that you are in, are now in a happy state, with their hearts filled with love to him that has loved them and washed them from their sins in his own blood, and rejoicing in hope of the glory of God. How awful is it to be left behind at such a day![54]

Before Jonathan could even finish his message, the people became agitated and began crying out. As one minister put it, "There was a great moaning and crying out throughout the whole house. What shall I do to be saved. Oh I am going to Hell. Oh what shall I do for Christ."[55] It was as if they believed the floor had opened and they were about to be swallowed up. Another minister wrote, "The assembly appeared deeply impressed, and bowed down with an awful conviction of their sin and danger. There was such a breathing of distress and weeping, that the preacher was obliged to speak to the people and desire silence, that he might be heard."[56] Although he asked the congregation to be quiet, there was no way to be heard. He never finished the sermon.

Of the coming months, Edwards wrote to a fellow minister:

> The months of August and September [1741] were the most remarkable of any this year, for appearances of conviction

[54] Ibid., 223.

[55] Ibid., 220.

[56] Dwight, *Life of President Edwards*, 605.

> and conversion of sinners, and great revivings, quickenings, and comforts of professors, and for extraordinary external effects of these things. It was a very frequent thing to see a houseful of outcries, faintings, convulsions, and suchlike, both with distress and also with admiration and joy. It was not the manner here to hold meetings all night, as in some places, nor was it common to continue them until very late in the night; but it was pretty often so that there were some that were so affected, and their bodies so overcome, that they could not go home, but were obliged to stay all night at the house where they were. [57]

Jonathan's Ministry Heart

It is unfortunate that despite this sermon's importance to the Great Awakening, taken on its own, it greatly distorts the true basis of the movement and the heart of Jonathan's ministry. While Edwards was always a serious man and wasn't afraid to take people to hell in the hope of enabling them to spend eternity in heaven, his tenderness should also be remembered. In a surprising contrast to his most famous sermon, most of the rest of Jonathan's sermons focus primarily on the love of God and on seeing His beauty. He truly desired for all people to know the sweetness of God and His saving power.

Jonathan's second most famous and most published work, *Advice to Young Converts*, though far less remembered, shows his true ministry heart. In it he wrote such things as these:

> We advise persons under convictions to be extremely earnest for the kingdom of heaven, but when they have attained conversion they ought not to be the less watchful, laborious, and earnest in the whole work of religion, but the more; for they are under infinitely greater obligations. For lack of this, many persons in a few months after their conversion have begun to lose the sweet and lively sense of spiritual things, and to grow cold and flat and dark....

---

[57] Jonathan Edwards, letter to the Reverend Thomas Prince in Boston, 12 December 1743, http://www.nhumanities.org/ccs/docs/awaken.htm.

> Don't slack off seeking, striving, and praying for the very same things that we exhort unconverted persons to strive for, and a degree of which you have had in conversion. Thus pray that your eyes may be opened, that you may receive your sight, that you may know yourself and be brought to God's feet, and that you may see the glory of God and Christ, may be raised from the dead, and have the love of Christ shed abroad in your heart....
>
> That you may pass a good judgment on your spiritual condition, always consider your best conversations and best experiences to be the ones that produce the following two effects:
>
> first, those conversations and experiences that make you least, lowest, and most like a little child; and, second, those that do most engage and fix your heart in a full and firm disposition to deny yourself for God and to spend and be spent for him.[58]

We should also recognize that in this sermon, the sinners are still in God's hands, and though God is angry at their sin, his mercy is keeping them from falling into the pit. Though God's wrath is kindled, His lovingkindness will withhold judgment until the last possible second hoping the sinner will turn to Christ for the forgiveness won on the cross. This juxtaposition would have been just the type of intellectual gymnastics Jonathan would have loved, making "Sinners in the Hands of an Angry God" a perfect reflection of the God of love Jonathan was so obsessed with.

Jonathan went on to state that the Great Awakening produced a "remarkable and general alteration in the face of New England."[59] At least 10 percent of the population claimed to be converted. It was not, however, without much opposition. His next few years were spent defending the revivals and conducting his own preaching campaign across the region.

---

[58] Jonathan Edwards, "Advice to Young Converts," http://www.dominiontheology.org/JE-Advice.htm.

[59] Jonathan Edwards, *Edwards on Revival: Containing a Faithful Narrative of the Surprising Work of God in the Conversion of Many Hundred Souls in Northampton, Massachusetts, AD 1735* (New York: Dunning and Spaulding, 1832), 154.

The War of the Old Lights versus the New Lights

As the Great Awakening spread across the colonies, camps divided over whether or not the move was of God or not. Those who clung to the traditional worship and religious practice of churches that excluded the spirit and emotion of the Awakening became know as "Old Lights," and those who embraced these manifestations as the move of God were called the "New Lights." Jonathan was somehow able to explain the awakening with the doctrinal bend and careful analysis that caught the attention of the Old Lights, but still embraced the fact the "surprising works" were truly of God.

God's ability to move in and through Jonathan Edwards's heart, mind, and church was largely due to Jonathan's humble heart; he was always willing to let truth confront his thinking, even if it meant changing his mind on certain issues he had held adamantly to before. His goal was to become more and more faithful to the Gospel of Jesus Christ.

John Wesley had the same humble spirit. Writing about his own thinking on the New Testament, Wesley said of his notations, "I cannot flatter myself so far...as to imagine that I have fallen into no mistakes, in a work of so great difficulty. But my own conscience acquits me of having designedly misrepresented [anything]."[60]

Jonathan was open to understanding doctrinal differences of the Old and New Lights. He had great respect for those whose religious beliefs differed from his, including Wesley—who was not, as we have already discussed, a Calvinist—but he was not willing to accept anything without first studying it for himself.

When Jonathan was young, he read the works of John Locke, for example, like a "greedy miser when gathering up handfuls of silver and gold, from some newly discovered treasure."[61] He didn't agree with everything Locke had to say, however. Locke was an Enlightenment thinker whose approach taught that humans are born with a blank slate, a *tabula rasa*, to fill with information gathered through

---

[60] John Wesley, M.A., *Explanatory Notes upon the New Testament* (London: William Boyer, 1755), http://www.bible-researcher.com/wesley-nt.html.

[61] Lutz, *Jonathan Edwards: Colonial Religious Leader*, 18.

our senses and interpreted by thoughtful reflection. To Locke, truth was derived from experience. Jonathan agreed with the importance of the senses and the necessity of reflecting on what they gathered, but to him, Truth was a person: Jesus Christ. As Jesus said in John 14:6, *"I am the way, the truth, and the life."*

Jonathan was able to look openly at the results of the two great revivals, sorting out the good from the bad—the truth from what might have been exaggerated. Because of certain emotional excesses, there was strong opposition to the awakenings from preachers and lay people alike. The Old Lights disliked the show of emotion that audiences exhibited when they understood their true condition before God without Christ. Nor did they approve of the flamboyant preaching style of people like George Whitefield. Whitefield dramatized the Scriptures, used storytelling techniques, gestured expressively, and even dared to leave the pulpit to walk about while he preached. Before his visit to America, these practices were unheard of. One critic, Charles Chauncy, called the belief that a person could be directly inspired by God simply mad. Some say that Chauncy, a local reverend, tried becoming a revival preacher himself but failed, thus becoming a bitter detractor of others who succeeded.

In his characteristic style, Jonathan began to classify and analyze the perceptions, attitudes, and actions of those who claimed to be regenerated so that he could better divide fact from fiction in defense of the Awakeners. He agreed that there was some excess of emotional expression, but he was convinced that for the most part, the Spirit of God had truly moved on the people. He pointed the doubters to Scripture passages that referred to what he called "affections," noting that emotions such as hope, love, desire, joy, and sorrow were clearly sanctioned by biblical truth. On the other hand, he also said that a person must have more than just feelings: "Religion that arises only from superficial impressions is wont to wither away...when it comes to be tried by...difficulties."[62]

It is possible that Jonathan Edwards was somewhat frustrated when those who expressed overwhelming emotion did not translate that same energy into everyday life. He said that the sign of true conversion was an outward display of love. Christianity, for Jonathan,

[62] Armstrong, "Trouble with George."

was more than just following a set of rules, more than a religion that applied at church. A real experience with God causes change to happen from the inside out and was for everyday living. He advised, "We should get into the way of appearing lively in religion, more by being lively in the service of God and our generation, than by the liveliness and forwardness of our tongues."[63]

Jonathan certainly believed what he taught; more importantly, though, he lived it. There are many stories of him giving charitably to people who needed help, but he always made sure to send the gift to be delivered by a friend who promised not to disclose the giver's identity.

Jonathan said that the sign of true conversion was an outward display of love.

He was also willing to come alongside those who were suffering persecution for their personal beliefs. Jonathan considered one such person to be the young David Brainerd, a university student who was expelled from Yale for embracing the revival movement with excessive zeal. His expulsion didn't dampen his enthusiasm, however, and he became a dedicated missionary to the Indians. Although his health was poor, he traveled three thousand miles on horseback to bring genuine revival to the Native Americans.

Seeing Brainerd as an example of selfless Puritan virtue, Jonathan supported and mentored him. Brainerd was a frequent guest in the Edwards household and was engaged to marry Jonathan's daughter, Jerusha. Unfortunately, Brainerd contracted tuberculosis and died in the arms of his fiancée. Jerusha also contracted the disease and died from it only months later.

Jonathan took it upon himself to see that the diary Brainerd had kept of his missionary work was published. To this day, the *Life and Diary of David Brainerd*, with an introduction by Jonathan, has never gone out of publication. It has influenced many people throughout the centuries, including hundreds of men and women who have been

[63] David W. Kling, "Testing the Spirits: The heart stirring revivalism of the Great Awakening led Edwards to develop a new religious psychology," *Christian History* 22, no. 1 [Issue 77] (2003): 34.

inspired to become missionaries as a result of reading Brainerd's accounts. Here is an excerpt taken from an entry made November 20, 1745, when Brainerd was in Crossweeksung, New Jersey:

> My public discourses did not then make up the one half of my work, while there were so many constantly coming to me with that important inquiry, "What must we do to be saved?" and opening to me the various exercises of their minds. Yet I can say, to the praise of rich grace, that the apparent success with which my labors were crowned, unspeakably more than compensated for the labor itself, and was likewise a great means of supporting and carrying me through the business and fatigues, which, it seems, my nature would have sunk under without such an encouraging prospect....May the Lord of the harvest send forth other labourers into this part of his harvest, that those who sit in darkness may see great light, and that the whole earth may be filled with the knowledge of himself! Amen.[64]

A few days before his death, missionary Jim Elliot (1927–1956), who was martyred by the Auca Indians of South America, entered in his diary, "Confession of pride—suggested by *David Brainerd's Diary* yesterday—must become an hourly thing with me."[65]

When Dead Men Preach

Despite Jonathan's best efforts, by the spring of 1744 the revival fires had cooled significantly. The "emotionalism" of the meetings had taken their toll as churches began to split because the pastor was considered too dry or formal—unlike the new, flamboyant style of revivalists such as Whitefield—or else churches rejected the new, more emotional services as excessive and contrary to the will of God. Adding to this, most likely, were Whitefield's own comments about the state of American churches: "I am verily persuaded, the generality of preachers talk of an unknown, unfelt Christ. And the reason why congregations have been so dead is because dead men

---

[64] David Brainerd, *Journal of David Brainerd,* http://housechurch.org/spirituality/brainerd.html.

[65] Piper, "Pastor as Theologian."

preach to them."[66] Though Whitefield's comments were accurate they made him no friends among those that embraced a more High Church Christianity. Dividing lines become well drawn between the "Old Lights"—more traditional ministers—and the "New Lights"—those who embraced the demonstrativeness in these services as the work of God.

Jonathan's own analytical approach to documenting the revival didn't seem to help, either. While he defended the necessity of emotion as part of conversion, siding with the New Lights, he also seemed convinced that much of what happened was, in fact, too extreme and required restraint, as was being expressed by the Old Lights. However, how did one tell the difference between emotional extravagance that is of God, and someone acting out just to get attention? The move of the Spirit was thus quenched as extraordinary gifts of the Spirit, such as tongues, prophecy, healings, and working of miracles, were quite possibly "delusions" and were suppressed. Religion and men's traditions once again replaced God's will. As Jonathan commented, "The Spirit of God, not long after this time, appeared very sensibly withdrawing from all parts of the country."[67]

Yes, the Holy Spirit is always "sensibly" withdrawing from places He is unwelcome. Had He remained welcome, perhaps the United States would have been founded as a charismatic Christian nation that operated in the power of the first-century church. Instead, the Awakening would fizzle until others again fully opened their hearts to the workings of the Holy Spirit in the Kentucky Camp Meetings that took place about the turn of the next century.

Fired from Northampton

The times in Northampton became difficult and would eventually work to change the course of Jonathan's career. King George's War broke out in 1744, and the colonists again found themselves in open conflict with the French and the Indians. Surrounding towns were being attacked and burned, and several residents of Northampton were killed in surprise attacks.

---

[66] David A. Fisher, *World History for Christian Schools* (Greenville, SC: Bob Jones University Press, 1984), 392.

[67] Jonathan Edwards, "A Narrative of Surprising Conversions," 71, quoted in Hyatt, *2000 Years of Charismatic History,* 117.

With people already on edge, Jonathan was prompted to take a stand regarding church policy on membership and observing the sacrament of the Lord's Supper. There were some issues about which he just could not remain flexible. He had long disagreed with his grandfather's still-standing tradition of allowing anyone to join the church or participate in Communion without a profession of faith, and he finally decided to end this policy. Jonathan demanded evidence of conversion.

To complicate matters, a situation arose that demanded disciplinary intervention by Jonathan. Several young men in the church obtained some books on midwifery and popular medicine, which they shared with their friends, and they proceeded to taunt young women about their menstruation. After investigating the situation, Edwards brought the confessions of three ringleaders before a committee of men who agreed to hear the case—the usual custom of the church in that day. Many thought that it was handled poorly.

This controversy, coupled with Jonathan's seemingly harsh policy regarding those he would allow to take Communion, led to severe opposition among the church leadership. He tried to calm their irritation, but to no avail. In 1750, Jonathan Edwards was fired from the position of pastor—a position he had held for twenty-three years and through two great revivals.

Ministering to the Native Americans

A small band from the church tried to persuade Jonathan to start another church in the same town. With a large family to support and little income to do so, Jonathan must have been tempted by the idea. Being more concerned about the kingdom of God than his own personal needs, however, Jonathan decided that such a decision might cause a bigger divide in the town, and he refused.

There is no evidence of bitterness surfacing in Jonathan's heart. He continued to show brotherly kindness and goodwill to all. A year after he was removed as pastor, he was offered a ministerial position at the Indian Mission at Stockbridge, sixty miles west of Northampton. Though it was a position rather below his station, he humbly accepted the opportunity to minister among the Native Americans.

His days at the Mission offered a simple lifestyle with plenty of quiet time to study. He spent long hours in a four-by-six-foot room next to the chimney of their house. These six years at Stockbridge turned out to be a gift from God, allowing him to do his best theological writing—work that would become famous throughout the coming centuries. The paper he needed to write upon was scarce, so he made notebooks from the scraps of paper he salvaged from anything he could find—the white edges of newsprint, the bottoms of letters received—which he stitched together.

Jonathan and Sarah cared deeply for the Indians, even though they came to church wearing bear grease to ward off insects. Jonathan created the type of worship service that he had wanted to have in Northampton, bringing in the Wesleyan hymns instead of the normal Psalm singing. He encouraged singing in harmony—a practice he loved—and advocated the use of storytelling as a way of teaching the Bible to children.

Jonathan advocated storytelling to teach the Bible to children.

This was also a time of vindication for Jonathan. One of the men who had spearheaded the attack on him wrote an extensive apology, professing shame for all he had done. It's doubtful that Jonathan relished the eventual publication of that apology in the Boston newspaper, though. By then, the French and Indian War had begun, and the Edwards family was busy serving hundreds of meals to the many people who sought refuge in the fort that stood nearby. Yet another turn of events was preparing to propel Jonathan down an altogether different path.

In September 1757, Jonathan received the news that his son-in-law, Aaron Burr, had died of malaria at the age of forty-one. Burr had married the Edwards' third oldest daughter, Esther, on June 29, 1752, after only five days of courtship and an engagement that lasted less than a month. They had been living in New Jersey, where Burr was the president of the College of New Jersey, now called Princeton University.

News of Burr's sudden death was shocking enough, but the rest of the message was that Jonathan had been elected to take his place as the new president of the college. He tried—as Moses once did before the Lord—to convince those who elected him that he was an unworthy candidate. He said he was not in good health and was deficient in certain areas of learning, such as Greek and mathematics. But his strongest objection was that he felt "swallowed up" in his study and writing, desiring above all else to continue at Stockbridge.

The stress of running a college did not appeal to Jonathan. But after much thought, he agreed to seek counsel from some trusted friends. When his advisers expressed their belief that it was his duty and responsibility to accept the appointment, Jonathan broke down in tears before them. He would leave immediately to answer what they believed to be the call on his life.

Last Words: "Trust in God"

Sarah and the rest of the family stayed in Stockbridge, planning to follow Jonathan to New Jersey in the spring. Jonathan traveled with daughter Lucy and arrived in New Jersey in January 1758. To his surprise, he enjoyed preaching to the students and faculty at the university and was comforted by their warm reception. What's more, he actually had more time for study and writing than he had anticipated. Settling in Princeton looked promising.

However, at this time, smallpox had spread throughout New England and many were dying. Prepared as always, Jonathan had already thought through what he would do if the situation ever called for him to be inoculated. Being the scientific progressive that he was, he had decided years earlier that he would receive it. Even so, he consulted the trustees of the college, as there was much controversy over the probable success of the procedure. All agreed he should receive the inoculation. His recently widowed daughter, Esther, also made the choice to receive it, and they went for the treatment on February 13, 1758.

At first, Jonathan showed only some slight symptoms of the disease. But weeks later, a severe fever set in, and on March 22, 1758, at the age of fifty-five, Jonathan died. Days before he died, knowing that eternity was near, he asked his daughter Lucy to record his last words. As expected, he gave his love to his dear wife and children, calling his relationship with Sarah "an uncommon union." He requested that his funeral be simple, and that any designated funeral money would instead be used for the poor. When those standing around his deathbed thought he was no longer capable of hearing or speaking, Jonathan surprised them with these final words: "Trust in God, and ye need not fear."

The doctor who attended Jonathan noted that God had allowed him to pass into eternity with "perfect freedom of pain…he really fell asleep."[68] Barely two months after he had taken up his position as the second president of the university, and just six months after Aaron Burr's death, Jonathan Edwards was buried alongside his predecessor on the grounds of Princeton.

And then, not two weeks later, Esther Edwards died. Some said it was of her inoculation, others of "the fever." She left two small children: four-year-old Sally and two-year-old Aaron Burr Jr. Aaron Jr. would later miss the presidency of the United States by a single vote of the House of Representatives. He went on to become vice president under Thomas Jefferson in 1800.

That fall, Sarah Edwards traveled to Philadelphia to retrieve Esther's children. Not long after her arrival there, she fell gravely ill from dysentery. On October 2, 1758, at the age of forty-eight, she joined her husband in glory, and her body was buried beside his in the cemetery at Princeton.

A Glorious Legacy

John Piper probably best summed up the contribution of Jonathan Edwards:

> The great goal of all Edwards' work was the glory of God. And the greatest thing I have ever learned from Edwards, I think, is that God is glorified not most by being known, nor by being dutifully obeyed. He is glorified most by being enjoyed.[69]

The Great Awakening certainly resulted in a display of God's glory. New England is reported to have had as many as fifty thousand people converted to Christ. That is a phenomenal number when the total population at the time was only about three million. In addition to the number of converts, one hundred fifty new churches were established.[70]

---

[68] Lutz, *Jonathan Edwards: Colonial Religious Leader*, 69.

[69] Piper, "Pastor as Theologian."

[70] Fisher, *World History for Christian Schools*, 392.

Jonathan Edwards was also instrumental in inspiring generations of missionaries by publishing the *Life and Diary of David Brainerd.* Though Brainerd's life was short, its ultimate impact reached further than even he could have imagined. His journals continue to influence countless numbers of people who, like him, are willing to make the greatest of sacrifices as missionaries to every tongue, tribe, and nation.

As for Jonathan himself, it could be said that more than any man in the history of Christianity, he loved God with all his mind, heart, soul, and strength. Ever an ardent intellectual, he was as much a man of the book as he was of the Spirit. He was disciplined to the point of being fanatical, methodical in his pursuit of truth to the point of obsession. His works of theology are still some of the deepest and most important in America today, and the awakening he helped bring about unified the colonies into what would become, soon after his death, the United States of America.

He also insured that America would be considered a Christian nation. Edwards set much of the groundwork for later revivals with his careful documentation of the Great Awakening and how it began. A revivalist of uncompromising integrity, Jonathan Edwards was a man with whose work every minister should be familiar today, especially those looking to stir revival in the twenty-first century.

Chapter Four

★★★★★

Francis Asbury

(1745–1816)

"The Prophet of the Long Road"

"The Prophet of the Long Road"

We should so work as if we were to be saved by our works; and so rely on Jesus Christ, as if we did no works.

—Francis Asbury

Following the First Great Awakening of the 1740s and the American Revolution (1775–1783), a wave of revival hit the newly born United States that looked like nothing that had ever happened before. The colonies, now states, were expanding westward into new territories as the promise of open spaces and free land beckoned settlers to the frontiers. In a time before the telegraph, when New York did not yet have a population of 20,000, American towns must have looked as scattered as the stars. While Edwards's awakening had started in a church in a fair-sized town and Whitefield's preaching had amassed thousands and ten of thousands to come from all around to hear the word of the Lord, this revival would take religion to the people wherever they lived.

On a frontier of scattered farms and small towns stretching from the coastal cities toward the Mississippi River, news was scarce; churches were even scarcer. Before the American Revolution, ministers were concentrated in large cities, but men such as Francis Asbury saw the importance of returning to the pattern set by the apostles when Jesus sent them out two by two. Rather than speaking to record-breaking crowds in city commons, the Methodist circuit riders—of which Francis Asbury was a chief model—took revival to the farthest reaches of the frontier and became the threads that wove together the American people as a nation. Methodism, with its strict disciplines of prayer meetings, Bible studies, and united societies, became the gravitational force that created communities among the independent-minded people of the Western frontier.

Just how important was this binding force? Asbury biographer Darius Salter wrote,

> The National Historical Publications Commission of the United States Government listed sixty-six Americans whose works were considered essential to an understanding of the development of the American nation and its strategic place in world history. Asbury was listed as one of these.[1]

Though neither a political figure nor an American-born citizen, Asbury's name is listed alongside those of George Washington, Thomas Jefferson, John Adams, and Abraham Lincoln as a crucial builder of the democratic republic that serves as a model for the world today. His contribution was so significant that a statue of him on horseback stands in Washington, D.C., looking south down 16th Street toward the White House. It bears the following inscriptions: "If you seek the results of his labor you will find them in our Christian civilization" and "His continuous journeying through cities, villages and settlements from 1771 to 1817 greatly promoted patriotism, education, morality and religion in the American Republic."

Instead of preaching from a stationary pulpit fixed in some large church of a particular city, Francis Asbury rode hundreds of thousands of miles on horseback, taking the Word of God to places it had never been before. Rather than addressing large crowds, he often spoke to a few families at a time who gathered in rustic homes, or to a lonely traveler he encountered along the way. All were equally fallen, as far as he was concerned, and all were in equal need of a Savior. Francis believed he had a divine calling to bring the gift of God's saving grace to anyone who would hear, and he was willing to do whatever it took to deliver the good news to each one—even if he had to do it one by one.

---

[1] Darius L. Salter, *America's Bishop: The Life of Francis Asbury* (Nappanee, IN: Francis Asbury Press, 2003), 9.

Early Years in England

Francis Asbury, or "Franky," as he was sometimes called, was born on August 20, 1745,[2] in Hamstead Bridge, Staffordshire, England, not far from Birmingham. He was the only surviving child of Joseph and Elizabeth Asbury, who became committed Methodists after the loss of an infant daughter, Sarah, before Francis's birth. Elizabeth Asbury was a somber and dedicated believer. Her husband, according to a journal entry Francis Asbury wrote much later in life, was a gardener for some of the wealthy families in the area. This would not have been a position of influence in this rough community whose primary industry was manufacturing metal goods.

Being Methodists did not make them popular there. The people of Birmingham were resistant to any type of religion, and especially to the Wesley brothers' call for personal holiness. Once, when John and Charles Wesley tried to minister there, John was carried off by a mob; Charles was once showered with stones and turnips, and the cacophony of local church bells was often used to drown out his voice. Even the local government seemed opposed to the Methodist preachers. One magistrate offered to pay someone to drive them out. An associate of the Wesleys, John Nelson, was "pelted with eggs and stones, knocked down eight times...dragged through the stones by the hair of his head for twenty yards while he was being kicked in his sides. Nelson's pregnant wife was beaten to the extent that she miscarried her child."[3] Even after the Wesley brothers moved on, the mobs continued to terrorize those who became Methodists, robbing and destroying their homes, as well as physically assaulting them.

Only one story remains from Asbury's—or "little Franky's"—early childhood. It was related by John Wesley Bond, Francis's last traveling companion:

> The Bishop's father being a gardener by trade, used to put up his gardening tools, consisting of long shears, pruning saws, hoes, rakes, etc. in [a room attached to the house].... One day Francis was left in this room; nor was his danger

[2] The exact date of Francis Asbury's birth is actually uncertain. Sources state that it could have been a day earlier (August 19) or later (August 21), but for the sake of simplicity, I have used the most central and commonly cited date here.

[3] Salter, *America's Bishop*, 19.

> thought of until his father, call[ing] to his mother said, "Where is the lad? I heard him cry." His mother ran into the room and found he had crawled into a hole in the floor and fallen through. But by the kind providence of God the gardening tools had been recently removed, and a larger boiler nearly filled with ashes put in their place, into which he fell; this broke his fall, or the world would most probably have been forever deprived of the labours of Bishop Asbury.[4]

Francis's early life was not one of material wealth, but he was blessed with parents who nurtured his character and spiritual growth from a young age. His formal education was nothing to speak of. Beaten often by his teacher and called the "vilest of the vile"[5] by his schoolmates, Asbury made the decision at the age of ten, with no apparent input from his parents, to quit school and take up odd jobs at the wealthy manors. Having learned to read and write, he continued regular study of the Bible on his own.

The modest four-room house of Joseph and Elizabeth Asbury was kept open to preachers, Bible studies, and devotional meetings, so the young Asbury's religious education prospered. Francis himself had difficulty giving an exact date for his conversion, and he left virtually no journal writings about his early life after arriving in America. Yet, along the way, God used many people and mentors to draw him and prepare him for his calling. The Holy Spirit began to deal seriously with him around the age of twelve, but he was soon distracted by his peers. Francis also attributed his lack of sincere progress to the fact that most ministers who came across his path during those early days were themselves uneducated in spiritual matters.

When Francis was thirteen, a traveling shoemaker held prayer meetings in the area. Although the man was a Baptist, Elizabeth Asbury believed he was sincere, and she invited him to speak at the Methodist group meeting in her home. The man's words excited

---

[4] Robert J. Bull, "John Wesley Bond's Reminiscences of Francis Asbury," quoted in *Methodist History* 4 (October 1965), 10, quoted in Salter, *America's Bishop*, 21.

[5] Francis Asbury, *The Journal and Letters of Francis Asbury*, eds. Elmer T. Clark, J. Manning Potts, and Jacob S. Payton, vol. 1 (Nashville: Abingdon Press, 1958), 720, quoted in Salter, *America's Bishop*, 22.

young Francis's heart about salvation. Not long afterward, Alexander Mather, a Methodist circuit rider, was assigned to the Birmingham area. When young Asbury heard Mather explain how a person could have freedom from sin, his heart was again moved to understand the necessity of holiness.

The Methodist society meetings had an indelible impact on Francis as he grew through his teenage years observing men and women who were sincere in their faith sing and praise God. He loved the hymns they sang but was especially impressed by the freedom with which the preachers prayed and spoke. The typical clergy of the day stimulated little thinking—they spoke in a dull monotone and read their prayers from books. Nothing was spontaneous; nothing seemed inspired. Mather, on the other hand, prayed as if God were standing in the room. He preached from his heart without relying on written sermon notes. This would become the model for the type of American Methodism Francis would spread everywhere he went.

A Methodist conference

The Wesley Center Online (wesley.nnu.edu) at Northwest Nazarene University, Nampa, Idaho

During this time of growing and seeking God, Francis developed support systems to maintain his spiritual progress. He bonded with other boys his age who were serious in their faith; they attended four services together every Sunday at two different churches.

Francis attributed a great deal of his spiritual maturation to his mother, who established many of the disciplines he observed throughout his life. For example, Elizabeth Asbury would wake her son at four o'clock every morning so he could perform his duties as a blacksmith's apprentice in order to be free later in the day to preach in the Methodist society groups or at his mother's devotional meetings.

Later in life, if Francis allowed himself to sleep even until six o'clock in the morning, he felt guilty and slothful. He said that he learned perseverance at an early age by observing his mother stand at a window for light as she studied the Bible; she was committed to understanding it when she had no one to teach her. It was from his mother that Francis also saw love in action, for she cared for fellow believers. No doubt her determination to do her part to spread the Gospel profoundly influenced her son.

Francis stayed in close contact with his parents throughout his life, sending them monthly support payments as well as update letters. His continued love and devotion to them is seen in a letter he wrote after hearing they were in financial need: "I have sold my watch and library, would sell my shirt before you should want."[6]

It is heartbreaking to know that when he left for America in 1771 he would never see them again. Years later, after her husband died, Elizabeth Asbury made some unwise financial decisions that put her in serious jeopardy. This tragedy only increased Francis's never-ending guilt for having left his parents behind, even though he knew he was called to give up everything for the sake of the Gospel.

The Making of a Preacher

Francis began preaching publicly when he was about fifteen—he simply read Scripture passages aloud and expounded upon them at his mother's society meetings. From there, he began branching out to the homes of other Methodists. Alexander Mather took notice of him and appointed him to be a local lay preacher and youth leader. Between the ages of seventeen and twenty, Francis traveled throughout the Birmingham area, preaching several times a week wherever he was asked. He recorded that he went "almost every place within my reach for the sake of precious souls; preaching generally, three, four, and five times a week, and the same time pursuing my calling."[7]

When Francis was twenty-two, the Methodist Conference in England gave him a probationary license to preach; one year later, he was assigned his own circuit as a licensed minister. He didn't

---

[6] Ezra Squier Tipple, *Francis Asbury: The Prophet of the Long Road* (New York: The Methodist Book Concern, 1916), 56.

[7] Asbury, *Journal and Letters of Francis Asbury*, vol. 1, 722, quoted in Salter, *America's Bishop*, 28.

consider himself to be a great preacher, confessing, "I wonder sometimes, how anyone will sit to hear me, but the Lord covers my weakness with his power."[8] Being a mediocre preacher wasn't necessarily a bad thing, since Wesley's style of evangelism wasn't as concerned with powerful preaching or establishing permanent churches as it was about reaching the people. Wesley wrote, "Give me one hundred preachers who fear nothing but sin and desire nothing but God, and I care not a straw whether they be clergy or laymen, such alone will shake the gates of hell and set up the Kingdom of Heaven upon earth."[9] Francis's zeal to preach must have fit the qualifications for fearlessness.

For some time, the Wesley brothers had been receiving letters from American pastors calling for experienced men of wisdom to come over and help the new converts who had come to Christ during the revivals of George Whitefield and those who had followed in his wake. John Wesley was unsure of how to do this but prayed regularly about the matter. Among others, a Lutheran missionary had recently returned from the colonies and warned him that the new churches would soon die without adequate leadership. So, at the Bristol Conference in August of 1771, John Wesley decided to solicit volunteers to go to America. He said, "Our [American] brethren call aloud for help. Who are willing to go over and help them?"[10] The call touched Francis's heart deeply, and he, along with Richard Wright, agreed to go. They set sail on September 4, 1771, taking two blankets for a bed, some clothes, and ten pounds that had been given to Francis by some friends. He distilled his own mission statement into these few words:

> Whither am I going? To the New World. What to do? To gain honour? No, if I know my own heart. To get money? No: I am going to live to God and to bring others so to do.[11]

---

[8] Asbury, *Journal and Letters of Francis Asbury*, vol. 3, 4, quoted in Salter, *America's Bishop*, 30.

[9] John Wesley, *The Letters of the Rev. John Wesley, A.M.*, vol. 6, ed. John Telford (London: Epworth Press, 1931), 271, quoted in Salter, *America's Bishop*, 23.

[10] Salter, *America's Bishop*, 36.

[11] Asbury, *Journal and Letters of Francis Asbury*, vol. 1, 4, quoted in Salter, *America's Bishop*, 36.

When I Saw the American Shore

The voyage was long for Francis, who was often seasick. But he held to his calling—he preached on deck every afternoon he could, even if it meant tying himself to a mast in order to resist the pitching of the ship caused by the wind. When the ship docked in Philadelphia on Sunday, October 27, 1771, Francis and Wright went to Saint George's Church, the city's Methodist headquarters, that very night. A few lines from Francis's journal reveal how overwhelming and immense he considered his calling:

> The people looked on us with pleasure, hardly knowing how to show their love sufficiently, bidding us welcome with fervent affection and receiving us as angels of God. O that we may always walk worthy of the vocation wherewith we are called! When I came near the American shore my very heart melted within me to think from whence I came, and where I was going, and what I was going about.[12]

After preaching for the first month in some of the largest churches in Philadelphia and New York, Francis unearthed a growing restlessness in his soul: "The preaching stops were enjoyable, but where was the evangelistic thrust to the countryside and to the more marginalized members of society?"[13] His structured mind wrestled with his frustration that the people in charge had not established any plans to spread much evangelism outside of New York and Philadelphia, let alone given Francis an outlet for his zeal.

In England, Francis had been accused of usurping the authority of another itinerant preacher. Records indicate that a fellow preacher had asked Francis to take his place while he was sick, and although there are no specific details of exactly what Francis did to provoke the accusation, the preacher sent a letter to Francis in which he clearly stated his belief that Francis had tried to take over his district. One might think Francis would have hesitated to risk reaping a similar accusation in America, but he showed no tentativeness in expressing what he saw as the shortcomings of the American mission to date. It had failed to reach far beyond the two major cities

[12] Tipple, *Francis Asbury: Prophet of the Long Road*, 111–112.

[13] Salter, *America's Bishop*, 38.

of New York and Philadelphia and seemed little interested in ever doing so. In addition, Francis saw the work that had been done in these two cities as lax and undisciplined—hardly Methodism as he had learned it from the Wesleys. Unlike his English traveling companions, Francis's forceful personality would not allow him to be satisfied with lingering casually as others ran the Methodist mission with complacency. This dissatisfaction made him few friends among the Methodist leadership in America at the time, but his heart would not let him compromise on these issues.

Soon, Francis persuaded two local churchmen to go with him to Westchester, New York, where he convinced the local judge to let him use the courthouse as his pulpit. It went so well that he returned two weeks later, and although the courthouse was not available, he simply set up church at the home of the tavern owner. Francis spent the night in the home of a local family who, when he invited them to pray after supper, became Methodists. Francis would repeat this pattern of evangelism for the next forty-some years—he would find a place to preach, stay with a local family, and pray with those present to accept Christ. And as he did this, a new Methodist society would be born.

Francis's first decade in America was marked by few such successes, however. He spent much of his time struggling with other Methodists over leadership of the mission. He was caught between three major, rivaling forces: the Anglican church government system, the democratic and independent mind-sets of the Americans who wanted little or nothing of European church patterns in the way they ran their churches, and his own ego versus the egos of other leading Methodists.

The Methodist mission also suffered two principal hardships during this time. The first was that the Methodist movement was inherently English, and tension between America and England was growing exponentially. All the Methodist leaders were men sent from England, and the societies were patterned after those in England, with their members still part of the Church of England. To make matters worse, John Wesley made the unfortunate choice to get involved with politics and urged the colonies to seek reconciliation with the Crown.

The second setback was that Methodism had a hard time finding a home in the pluralistic Protestantism of the thirteen colonies. Why should one become a Methodist when the local Baptist or Congregational church had similar meetings on weeknights? In England, the formality of Anglicanism left a great deal of room during the rest of the week for the societies to meet. Churches in America, however, were much more open, with an emphasis on individual Bible study and prayer rather than the rituals of the sacraments. Methodists could not work in tandem with Congregationalists, Presbyterians, or Baptists as they had with Anglicans. Methodism would have to break new ground as its own denomination before it could gather speed.

Until the Revolutionary War, Francis would be just another one of a squabbling handful seeking to advance Methodism. His success as a revivalist would not come until after he put all of that behind him and became accepted as an American.

"I Am Determined Not to Leave Them"

As the tension with Great Britain continued to grow, leading up to the Declaration of Independence, so did Francis's newfound allegiance to the colonies. The progression of his shifting allegiance is evident in his journal entries. In 1773, he wrote that the people were too disloyal to the mother country; in 1775, he penned, "Surely, the Lord will overrule and make all these things subservient to the spiritual welfare of his Church;"[14] by July 1776 he boldly proclaimed that the British would have little prospect of winning; and finally, in 1779, he prayed that God would "mercifully interpose for the deliverance of *our* land."[15] By spring of 1780, Francis was a recognized citizen of Delaware.

In August 1775, Francis received a letter from the man with whom he had shared leadership for a time, Thomas Rankin, saying the decision had been made that all English Methodist missionaries were to return to England because of the growing unrest. Francis's response was firm:

---

[14] Tipple, *Francis Asbury: Prophet of the Long Road*, 120.

[15] Asbury, *Journal and Letters of Francis Asbury*, vol. 1, 294, quoted in Salter, *America's Bishop*, 71. Emphasis added.

> I can by no means agree to leave such a field for gathering souls to Christ, as we have in America. It would be an eternal dishonour to the Methodists, that we should all leave 3,000 souls, who desire to commit themselves to our care; neither is it the part of a good shepherd to leave his flock in time of danger: therefore, I am determined, by the grace of God, not to leave them, let the consequence be what it may.[16]

As tension escalated with England, people began taking sides. On December 9, British soldiers attacked a group of militiamen at Great Bridge, twelve miles southeast of Norfolk, Virginia. More than one hundred British soldiers were killed that day; the American militia suffered no casualties. Francis lived close by at the time, and he reported that he was keeping his distance from the conflict but maintaining his closeness to Jesus. In 1776, Francis was in Philadelphia when he received a letter from John Wesley trying to calm the Methodists' waning loyalty to England. Instead, his letter seemed to decrease their loyalty to Wesley. Though the number of Methodists continued to drop due to the stress of war, Francis continued his preaching efforts with little interference. He was vehemently determined to focus on spreading the work of Christ and to ignore politics as much as possible. As a result, his journals say nothing about many of the great events and battles of the American Revolution.

By spring of 1778, every English Methodist in leadership but Francis had left the colonies.

But by July 1777, Francis was struggling with depression. It was becoming dangerous to be known as a Methodist, some of which was for good reason, according to the colonists. Francis heard Rankin preach what was promoted as his last speech in America before the English missionaries returned to their homeland. His nerves must have tightened when he heard Rankin preach that until the colonists submitted to the king of England, God wasn't going to bless them. Rankin was later discovered to have remained in the colonies,

[16] Asbury, *Journal and Letters of Francis Asbury*, vol. 1, 161, quoted in Salter, *America's Bishop*, 55–56.

where he was helping the British. Another Methodist leader, Martin Rodda, was found passing out tracts in support of the British, and he took refuge on a British ship anchored in the Chesapeake Bay. Then, there was Chauncey Clowe, the Methodist who led a group of British sympathizers to crash through a company of militia trying to reach the king's army. Clowe was captured, tried in court, and executed. To be a Methodist was as good as admitting to being a spy for King George III.

By early spring of 1778, all the English Methodists in leadership had left except for Francis. He bid farewell to his peers when they set sail for England; some he was undoubtedly glad to let go of, but others he knew he would miss. This difficult time of parting, along with the dangerous atmosphere, would have challenged the faith of the strongest believer. Biographer Darius Salter described what an exceptionally difficult time this was in Francis's life, citing excerpts from his journal entries:

> At first, Asbury transcended with a stiff upper lip. "However, I was easy, for the Lord was with me. And if he will be with me, and bring me to my Father's house in peace, he shall be my God forever." Four days later, however, he broke down, gripped by the stark loneliness of the moment. "I was under some heaviness of mind. But it was no wonder; three thousand miles from home—my friends have left me—I am considered by some as an enemy of the country—every day liable to be seized by violence, and abused."[17]

When residents of Maryland were required to pledge an oath of loyalty to the colony, Francis moved to Delaware, where he stayed in the home of Thomas White for the next eighteen months. He was isolated there and had ample space and time for solitude and study. Biographer Ezra Squier Tipple wrote,

> This period of retirement was as valuable to Asbury as the desert experience of John the Baptist or Paul's stay in Arabia, and it was as much in the order of Divine Providence. He himself seems to have had this belief: "I formerly thought it would be death to me to keep silence from

[17] Ibid., 263–264, quoted in Salter, *America's Bishop*, 65.

> declaring the word of God, but now I am in a measure contented. It appears to be the will of God that I should be silent for a season, to prepare me for further usefulness hereafter. Therefore my time shall be employed to the best advantage."[18]

On one occasion, Francis was forced to hide in a nearby swamp until dark; otherwise, he would have put his host in danger of being accused by the militia of being a British sympathizer. When White was arrested later, Francis left, staying where he could find shelter. He no longer recorded in his journal the names of people who took him in for fear that the records would fall into the wrong hands. He continued to preach when he could, but his body and mind were exhausted. By the end of 1778, he wrote in his journal about his feelings of inadequacy as a man called to preach: "I do the least good in the Church of Christ, of any that I know, and believe to be divinely moved to preach the Gospel. How am I displeased with myself!"[19]

These were difficult days for the American Methodist preachers as well. Some were cruelly whipped, beaten, or tarred and feathered. Joseph Hartley was jailed in Easton, Maryland, but refused to be silent. When he began preaching through the jail windows, he was quickly released because his persecutors feared that he would convert the entire town. Due to British occupation in the cities of New York and Philadelphia, most of the Methodist preachers had shifted to the South; Francis was thus disconnected geographically, and his influence in the organization diminished.

It must have been a surprise to everyone when he received a letter from Wesley, again appointing him over the Methodist work in the colonies. Many wondered why, in the midst of a war with England, Wesley would choose an Englishman to lead the Americans. But then, Francis wouldn't consider himself English for much longer—his heart now belonged to the colonies as well as to his Lord and Savior.

---

[18] Tipple, *Francis Asbury: Prophet of the Long Road*, 129.

[19] Asbury, *Journal and Letters of Francis Asbury*, vol. 1, 287, quoted in Salter, *America's Bishop*, 68.

Freedom Comes to America

In February 1782, the British voted not to continue the war in America. The end of the conflict brought many changes for Francis and for Methodism. The traveling restrictions were minimized, but until a treaty was officially signed, Francis was still suspect and had to obtain a valid pass to move about. Such inconveniences were minor compared to more drastic ministry needs. For example, a currency collapse meant there were no finances to print the books and tracts the Methodists distributed and depended on to aid in believers' maturation, especially since their spiritual leaders came only once every few weeks. More importantly, though, there was a major shift in the hearts and minds of American Methodist leaders—the taste of freedom was sweet. In the newspaper the *Baltimore Advertiser*, one writer expressed the sentiment of those who rejoiced in throwing off the spiritual yoke of England: "Heaven be praised we live in a land of equal liberty, and are determined to exert the prerogative of rational beings, to think for ourselves and to pin our faith on no man's sleeve."[20]

While the attendance and ministry of most churches had diminished during the trials of war, Methodism had actually grown after its initial decline. In 1773, American Methodism had 24 preachers, 12 circuits, and 4,921 members; by the end of the war, there were 82 Methodist preachers, 39 circuits, and a membership of 13,740.[21] Had the movement dwindled, perhaps the Wesleys would have let it go. Given the growth, however, John Wesley probably felt obliged to exercise his leadership again as the father of the movement.

When Wesley tried to regain control from England by sending Thomas Coke as co-superintendent with Francis, however, Coke got an earful about how the people now perceived themselves. The story goes that Coke interrupted American Methodist preacher Nelson Reed to say, "You must think you are my equal," to which Reed

[20] "To the Editors of the Maryland Journal and Baltimore Advertiser," *Maryland Journal and Baltimore Advisor*, 12 (February 15, 1785), 698:1, quoted in Salter, *America's Bishop*, 94.

[21] *Minutes of the Annual Conferences of the Methodist Episcopal Church, 1773–1828* (New York: Mason and Lane, 1840), 7, 17–18, quoted in L. C. Rudolph, *Francis Asbury* (Nashville: Abingdon Press, 1966), 42.

responded, "Yes, Sir, we do; and we are not only the equals of Dr. Coke, but of Dr. Coke's king."[22]

Francis leaned on this independent, democratic spirit to solidify—once and for all—his leadership of the Methodist movement in America by calling for a vote from the combined North and South conferences. This was in direct opposition to John Wesley's method of appointing leaders, who seemed to come and go on a whim. On December 27, 1784, at what would later be referred to as the Christmas Conference, the American leaders voted—they chose Francis to be superintendent of the newly formed Methodist Episcopal Church. With Methodism now its own denomination and Francis Asbury its bishop to travel and appoint ministers as he felt led by God to do, Methodism would flourish in America as never before. Methodism was now American and refused to return to its roots.

Bishop Asbury's ordination service
Library of Congress, 99as

American Methodism was also now an "episcopal" church—*episcopal* means "governed by bishops." In his dedication service, Thomas Coke referred to Francis not as "superintendent," but as "bishop." In spite of numerous complaints about the title, it stuck. Wesley attempted to counter it in a letter to Francis, emphasizing that although he "may be the elder brother of the American Methodists: (but) I am under God the father of the whole family."[23] Subsequent letters expressed John Wesley's efforts to regain control, but these efforts were never fruitful. Francis supposedly told a peer, "Mr. Wesley and I are like Caesar and Pompey. He will bear no equal and I will bear no superior."[24] By 1787, the American leadership had rejected Wesley's directions, effectively declaring American

[22] John Vickers, *Thomas Coke: Apostle of Methodism* (New York: Abingdon Press, 1969), 119, quoted in Salter, *America's Bishop*, 87.

[23] Wesley, *Letters*, vol. 8, 91, quoted in Salter, *America's Bishop*, 97.

[24] Wesley, *Letters*, vol. 3, 183, quoted in Salter, *America's Bishop*, 100.

Methodism's independence. Francis was convinced that he was in the right; he did pay a personal price for his autonomy, however. He wrote of Wesley, "I esteem it as one of the greatest calamities of my life so highly to grieve him, and he has made me feel very sensibly by his letter, as fallen! fallen!"[25]

Francis seemed momentarily distracted by his new title, not quite knowing what to do with it. He disclosed his insecurities in the journal of his private thoughts, writing, "I am sometimes afraid of being led to think something more of myself in my new station than formerly."[26] He even experimented with wearing the professional robes of an Anglican bishop but soon shed them when he was criticized for it. Hiding in his dry sense of humor and his unfamiliarity with such a position of prominence, he once remarked that it was an advantage to have a title as brief as "bishop," since he could "save two souls while he was saying, 'General Superintendent.'"[27]

Whatever his title, his focus now turned to spreading the Gospel in every corner of the new country of America, finally laying hold of the calling that had brought him to the shores of the New World in the first place:

> The Revolutionary war being now closed, and a general peace established, we could go into all parts of the country without fear; and we soon began to enlarge our borders, and to preach in many places where we had not been before....One thing in particular that opened the way for the spreading of the gospel by our preachers was this: during the war, which had continued seven or eight years, many of the members of our societies had, through fear, necessity, or choice, moved into the back settlements, and into new parts of the country; and as soon as the national peace was settled, and the way was open, they solicited us to come among them; and by their earnest and frequent petitions, both verbal and written, we were prevailed on,

---

[25] John Vickers, "Francis Asbury in the Wiltshire Circuit," *Methodist History* 16 (April 1978), 3:187, quoted in Salter, *America's Bishop*, 101.

[26] Asbury, *Journal and Letters of Francis Asbury*, vol. 1, 480, quoted in Salter, *America's Bishop*, 103.

[27] Salter, *America's Bishop*, 96.

> and encouraged to go among them; and they were ready to receive us with open hands and willing hearts, and to cry out, "Blessed is he that cometh in the name of the Lord."[28]

"Live or Die I Must Ride"

Francis now occupied a powerful new role. His heart led him to travel the nation, spreading the Word of God. As Bishop, however, he was also a traveling ordination service. Whenever he came to a new area and found a young man worthy of ministry, he would ordain him as a Methodist clergyman and appoint him to a new circuit. Sometimes, he was called by Methodists who had moved westward to start a work in their area; other times, he just appointed circuit riders over new territories yet to be evangelized. Thus, Methodism grew as a web-like network across the new territories, from one corner of the nation to the other; with it, the Gospel again became the common language shared by most Americans, from the farthest reaches of Kentucky all the way to the original Plymouth settlement.

God certainly knew what He was doing when He prepared Francis Asbury at the blacksmith's anvil and fire rather than in the halls of England's universities, as He had done with Whitefield and the Wesleys. Where Francis was called to go, a college education would have been of little help. His writings, however, have given many historians a window into the hearts and lives of courageous men and women determined to stake their place on the frontier of the new country. Biographer Ezra Tipple described Francis's meticulous journaling in this way:

> The picture which Asbury gives of America is as fine in its way as Wesley's of England, and as valuable. No man of that period traveled as much or as far as Asbury, and in no other book can there be found a more intimate knowledge of the home life of the colonists, especially on the frontiers, or the social and oral conditions which prevailed.[29]

It is from these journals that we learn what life was like for Francis and, undoubtedly, for most of the other circuit-riding preachers.

[28] Tipple, *Francis Asbury: Prophet of the Long Road*, 132–133.

[29] Ibid., 82.

The journals are also the personal window through which we watch a man wrestle with his calling and his relationship with God when things grow difficult. Travel at this time was anything but easy; however, rain, sleet, snow, or cold did nothing to slow his pace. In fact, a popular saying in those days regarding the harsh weather was, "There is nothing out today but crows and Methodist preachers."

It is not only Francis's journals, but his letters, too, that reveal so much about America at this time and the growing Methodist movement. Francis's ministry doubled as a traveling information center and news service; his correspondence connected the scattered settlements of the new nation. Through Francis, news traveled so efficiently and reliably that a letter addressed simply to "The Rev'd Bishop Asbury, North America" would find its way to him. If anything noteworthy was happening in America—and for Francis, "noteworthy" generally meant revival—he was sure to hear about it and spread it far and wide.

Francis learned the system for spreading Methodism from John Wesley while he was growing up in England, and he continued it in America. The system was based on a man's willingness to forgo all worldly comforts in order to gain a heavenly crown by spreading the Gospel wherever he traveled. "No family was too poor, no house too filthy, no town too remote, and no people too ignorant to receive the good news that life could be better."[30]

The life was so hard that half the men assigned to circuits died before reaching age thirty-three because of the toll all of that riding on horseback took on their bodies as well as the constant exposure to inclement weather.[31] Peter Cartwright (1785–1872), who is featured in a later chapter, may well have set the record having itinerated for sixty-seven years.

Despite its stringent demands, however, the system was a brilliant structure that took preaching to the territorial extremes of the new nation—a nation expanding with incredible speed, attested by census figures. In 1770, the part of the country that would later become the states of Georgia, Kentucky, Ohio, and Tennessee had about forty thousand people of European or African descent. By

[30] Salter, *America's Bishop*, 167.

[31] Timothy K. Beougher, "Did You Know?" *Christian History* 14, no. 1 [Issue 45] (1995): 3.

1810, immigration had increased the population of this same area to more than one million.[32]

It must have seemed impossible to the established churches to keep up with this kind of growth, but not to Francis. The old-line denominations simply could not establish new churches at the same speed as the population was expanding. Their institutions for training new clergy members couldn't prepare them quickly enough to be sent out, nor were they equipped to change their strategies. The Methodists, on the other hand, had inherent flexibility with a system that moved their preachers to a new area every six to twelve months in order to keep them fresh. Staying in the same place was the goal of regular churches—70 percent of mainline denominational clergy stayed in the same parish for the duration of their careers. College education was the primary avenue to success for mainline clergy, but Methodist preachers preferred to be without credentials so that they could better relate to the common people they encountered. Asbury certainly didn't discourage learning, but he didn't want anything to distract a man from speaking "the plain truth to plain people."[33] It is said that only four questions were posed to evaluate prospective Methodist itinerant preachers:

1) Is this man truly converted?
2) Does he know and keep our rules?
3) Can he preach acceptably?
4) Has he a horse?[34]

Preaching "acceptably" was a fairly reasonable criterion, since most preachers used a basic set of Scripture passages and then added their own practical applications to everyday life stories. Francis frowned upon anyone who relied on notes when he spoke, a distaste no doubt influenced by the impact of extemporaneous speaking on him during his younger days. Some have said that he often chose his own text just before speaking, allowing himself to be directed by

---

[32] Mark Galli, "Revival at Cane Ridge," *Christian History* 14, no. 1 [Issue 45] (1995): 10.

[33] "A Grassroots Movement," The Methodist Church Web site, http://www.methodist.org.uk/index.cfm?fuseaction=opentogod.content&cmid=1498.

[34] Beougher, "Did You Know?" 3.

the Holy Spirit and the needs of a particular congregation. It wasn't sermon preparation that took up a Methodist preacher's time; it was the rest of his responsibilities.

Each Methodist preacher was responsible for a circuit that was between two hundred and five hundred miles in circumference. He was expected to visit each preaching site every two to six weeks. People were hungry to hear God's Word. One preacher, John Brooks, reported that during a particular revival he was very sick, but the people still made him get out of bed to preach.

In addition to the hours it took him to ride between locations and preach every day of the week—starting at five o'clock in the morning during the summer and six o'clock in the morning during the winter—a circuit preacher was also responsible for meeting with small groups who convened to study the Bible together and practice the disciplined pursuit of God according to the Methodist system. Francis also insisted that visiting the sick and caring for them was part of each man's duty. The salary of a preacher provided little incentive for this job. Up until 1800, the preachers' pay was a mere $64 a year, compared to the pay of pastors in the mainline denominations, who had an annual income of $400. After 1800, circuit riders' annual salary increased to $80. Francis himself admitted that few of them ever received what they were due. Although part of the Methodist preacher's job was distributing books—Bibles, hymnbooks, and other religious literature—and although the sale of these books brought a small commission for the preachers, his minuscule salary was seldom enough to supply even the simplest of clothing. Many circuit riders traveled with mere rags on their backs.

Methodist preachers preferred to be without credentials so they could better relate to the common people they encountered.

Francis, as head of the organization, had scarcely more himself. Everything he owned fit into his two saddlebags. A friend once asked to borrow fifty dollars; he was surprised when Francis showed him that he had no more than twelve dollars. Francis gave him five dollars, commenting, "Strange that neither my friends nor my enemies will believe that I neither have nor seek bags of money."[35]

Francis had no family besides his parents, whom he left in England. He had resolved long before not to marry, saying that it would be unfair to ask any woman to live alone all year with the exception of one week. Although Francis did not demand celibacy from his fellow preachers, he strongly encouraged it and harbored compelling opinions on the topic. He wrote to one man, "Stand at all possible distance from the female sex, that you be not betrayed by them that will damage the young mind and sink the aspiring soul and blast the prospect of the future man."[36] He also set aside time at the annual conferences to speak to the wives of the Methodist ministers, warning them not to behave badly and thereby ruin what their husbands had accomplished.

Life on the trail was brutal. Great portions of Francis's journals contain daily comments about what he encountered. Wolves stalked him, hailstones pelted him, chiggers and ticks preyed on his flesh, and the summer sun and winter winds were unmerciful. His food supply was simple—often, all he ate was bread—but he wrote that he would ride along all the same, enjoying fellowship with God and trusting Him completely to keep him alive. His nightly lodgings never compared to even a moderately comfortable inn. Francis resented having to spend his money on lodging and meals, and he would sleep in any place that agreed to accommodate him. He frequently traveled with a companion, which necessitated finding a room for two. He described bats flying into the holes in the roof as he slept; sharing rooms with dogs, cats, and pigs; and getting a bed for the night that he had to share with two total strangers. He also depicted the deplorable conditions of one particular house where the filth on the floor could have been scooped with a shovel. Francis often rested on flea-infested deerskins on the floor. Once, he barely escaped a burning bed he had placed too close to the fire. Francis sometimes had food for himself and for his horse only if he had money to pay or his host had anything to spare.

---

[35] Tipple, *Francis Asbury: Prophet of the Long Road*, 179.

[36] Asbury, *Journal and Letters of Francis Asbury*, vol. 3, 19, quoted in Salter, *America's Bishop*, 174.

Circuit riders depended greatly on their horses, and the Methodist progression would have been impossible without these creatures. Their significance is reflected in the fact that the *American Minutes*, the list of Methodist rules for preachers, records rule number one as "Be merciful to your Beast. Not only ride moderately, but see with your own eyes that your horse be rubbed and fed." Francis could have been driven around in a fancy carriage, but he declared, "The pomp of a wagon is too great for me, and the danger; perhaps no one in five hundred could drive to please me...besides, I can better turn aside to visit the poor; I can get along more difficult and intricate roads; I shall save money to give away to the needy; and lastly, I can be more tender to my poor, faithful beast."[37]

Francis had to concern himself with finding food, water, shelter, and rest not only for himself, but also for his horse. His experience as a blacksmith's apprentice came in handy when he had to fashion an improvised fix for a lost shoe. Francis seemed to have great concern for his equine traveling companions, which was vital, considering that he often put twenty-five thousand miles on one horse in its lifetime (this would have meant he owned more than ten different horses). There were times when there simply wasn't enough food for both Francis and his horse, but they would press on together. He told of one instance when his horse, weak from lack of food and drenched by pouring rain, fell down twice with Francis on its back. This horse's suffering pained Francis more than many other circumstances he encountered. One of his horses, Sparky, had to be left behind because he went lame. Known for his rough exterior, Francis unmasked his tender heart as he wrote that when he left Sparky, his faithful companion "whickered (neighed softly) after us: it went to my heart."[38]

Francis and the other circuit riders were not part of some romantic image of frontier life, but rather part of the realities of life and death, pain and misery, played out on the sometimes hidden trails and roads to nowhere. He described one road as being as steep as the roof of a house; for nearly a mile, he rode his horse, then got off and walked, sweating and trembling until his knees failed him. But he

---

[37] Asbury, *Journal and Letters of Francis Asbury*, vol. 2, 652, quoted in Salter, *America's Bishop*, 110.

[38] Tipple, *Francis Asbury: Prophet of the Long Road*, 186.

and his horse trudged on. Some accounts describe Francis's horses bolting into the trees, with Francis still riding them; others describe his horses falling on ice and pinning his leg beneath them; still others depict his horses swimming raging rivers. One humorous account tells of Francis's obtaining a horse that had been used for racing. When he rode past the familiar racing grounds, the horse suddenly took off toward the track and gave the preacher quite a ride.

Francis traveled virtually everywhere. He visited practically every state and traveled between four thousand and six thousand miles each year. He wrote in his journal, "I seldom mount my horse for a ride of less than twenty miles on ordinary occasions; and frequently have forty or fifty in moving from one circuit to another. In traveling thus I suffer much from hunger and cold."[39]

Sadly, by the time he reached the end of his life, Francis had spent so much time in the saddle that his body was in worse condition than the body of a man decades older. His feet were inflamed from the iron stirrups, and he could seldom wear shoes, walking instead with crutches. At one point, a traveling companion used soft leather and wool to pad Francis's stirrups in order to protect his bruised and hurting feet. Seldom, though, did he let any kind of sickness stop him, even if it required him to be tied upright in the saddle. He traveled with fevers, boils, terrible headaches, influenza, sore throats, and badly infected teeth. At times, people were sure he was close to death; sometimes, death likely would have been a welcome relief. Francis became his own doctor and frequently gave medical advice to others who were equally distanced from proper medical care. A poor diet, combined with inadequate rest and frequent interaction with disease-carrying people and creatures, ate away at his once strong constitution.

"My Heart Pitied the People"

Why would anyone endure such a life? Francis's heart beat for the people he ministered to because he knew God loved them without measure. There were no guarantees of who would be in his audience when he arrived at his preaching locations, but this mattered

[39] Francis Asbury, *The Journal and Letters of Francis Asbury*, vol. 1, ed. Elmer T. Clark, J. Manning Potts, and Jacob S. Payton (Nashville: Abingdon Press, 1958), 561, quoted in Rudolph, *Francis Asbury*, 72.

little to him. Once, Francis had to break ice to cross a stream. He rode with much pain to reach his destination, only to find that no more than nine people had showed up. Another time, he tried to persuade a woman to be baptized, but she refused. Later, she changed her mind and sent her son to fetch Francis, asking him to come back. Even though both he and his horse were exhausted, he returned for this audience of one, calling the time "solemn."

As Methodism spread in the South, Francis made his first trip to Tennessee. He was tempted to complain about the bad roads but instead was drawn to focus on the people traveling the same road with him:

> A man who is well mounted will scorn to complain of the roads when he sees men, women, and children, almost naked, paddling barefoot and barelegged along, or laboring up the rocky hills, while those who are best off have only a horse for two or three children to ride at once. If these adventurers have little or nothing to eat, it is no extraordinary circumstance, and not uncommon, to encamp in the wet woods after night—in the mountains it does not rain, but pours.[40]

Francis's heart was touched when people came out to hear him speak, even in freezing cold weather. He wrote in his journal of a time when he preached in Baltimore in a house with just openings where the windows and doors would normally be. He finished one sermon and then took a one-hour intermission; the people didn't leave, but waited for him to return and speak again. He said that his "heart pitied the people when I saw them so exposed."[41]

There were plenty of other places where he was not received as eagerly. One night, as he was preaching, Francis was struck by a stone someone had thrown through an open window; nevertheless, he continued to speak. Various types of speaking venues brought different types of responses. Taverns, for example, included drunkards in the audience, along with drinking and swearing. In the South, Francis was grieved to see how lost were those whom he encountered

---

[40] Tipple, *Francis Asbury: Prophet of the Long Road*, 167–168.

[41] Asbury, *Journal and Letters of Francis Asbury*, vol. 1, 56, quoted in Salter, *America's Bishop*, 44.

along the way; he described them as tattered and dirty, starving, and cruel to one another. He cared about children especially, making sure his preachers made an effort to talk with and pray for them wherever they met them.

As his watchful eyes observed the people, he feared that the same expansion of freedom that brought opportunities for enlarging the footprint of Methodism could also keep the hearts of people from focusing on God. As new land brought new prospects for success, new distractions threatened to diminish people's focus on the importance of the Gospel. Francis was determined to help make sure the Gospel never lost its place of priority. As frontier boundaries expanded, new circuit riders were put in place to care for the new homesteads. In 1796, when the Northwest Territory made new land accessible to farmers, preachers were not far behind.

One rider followed the wagon tracks to a new settler's location and was greeted by a man and his family who had come from Virginia. Unfortunately, when the farmer saw the preacher's clerical garb, he informed him that he and his family had left Virginia to get away from preachers; lo and behold, before they could even unload their wagon, they had found preachers again. The wise preacher admonished him, saying, "My friend, if you go to heaven you will find Methodist preachers there, and if to hell, I am afraid you will find some there; and you see how it is in the world, so that you had better make terms with us and be at peace."[42]

New areas for preachers meant new territory for Francis to travel to as well. Going to the new West necessitated adding more people to his traveling party for protection from the threat of Indians. Yet worries about warriors didn't seem to bother him nearly as much as the obligation to ride with men who swore and drank excessively.

The Holy Spirit Explosion on the Western Frontier

Around the turn of the century, a new phenomenon appeared: the camp meeting. The West was now growing populated enough that instead of merely waiting for circuit riders to pass through,

[42] Emory Stevens Bucke, D. D., ed., *The History of American Methodism*, vol. 1 (Nashville: Abingdon Press, 1964), 502, quoted in Salter, *America's Bishop*, 161–162.

settlers could gather in central locations to hear the best preachers, sing new hymns, and take Communion from an ordained clergyman.

In June 1800, James McGready, the pastor of three small congregations at Red River, Gasper River, and Muddy River, invited the local ministers to join him at the annual Communion gathering at the Red River Church. The event would take place over a weekend with Communion to be taken on Monday. The initial days were quiet, but when one of the local preachers spoke on Monday, the Spirit of God fell on a woman and she began shouting and singing. Presbyterian minister John McGee, who was sitting in the congregation as the minister brought his message to a close, began weeping; soon, the rest of the congregation was weeping as well, crying out for salvation.

Then, McGee spoke and exhorted the crowd to let "the Lord God Omnipotent reign in [your] hearts, and to submit to Him." He later recalled, "I turned to go back and was near falling; the power of God was so strong upon me. I turned again and, losing sight of the fear of man, I went through the house shouting and exhorting with all possible ecstasy and energy, and the floor was soon covered with the slain."[43] The power of God was falling on the people and pulling them to the ground.

The ministers at this meeting then made arrangements for a similar gathering at the Gasper River Church the next month. Many people came after hearing what had happened at Red River—so many, in fact, that the church was not big enough to hold them all. Therefore, the meetings were moved outside. The camp meeting was born.

In the following months, similar meetings would be organized and reach a height at the Cane Ridge camp meeting in August 1801. It was a literal Pentecost of revival, with spiritual manifestations that would sweep the camp meeting into popularity for many decades to come. Under the power of the Spirit, people fell into apparent trances, shook with the presence of the Holy Spirit, danced exuberantly, fell into convulsive Holy Spirit laughter, ran like Elijah (see 1 Kings 16:46) around the outskirts of the gatherings, sang inspired songs, and even barked out incomprehensibly under the influence

[43] Galli, "Revival at Cane Ridge," 11.

of the Spirit—"The people report they bark and snatch, and make strange noises."[44]

It didn't take long for many mainline ministers to condemn this emotionalism, as their predecessors had during the Great Awakening. Francis, however, saw God rather than excess, and he embraced the camp meeting movement to the point that he even urged Methodists in the East to imitate the format for themselves and their districts, hoping for the same movement of God to revival souls.

Such excitement had never concerned the Wesleys in England, so it did not concern Francis, either. As L. C. Rudolph, one of Asbury's biographers, put it,

> Wesley did not want noisy physical manifestations, but if there was noise it was only the devil resisting and so no grounds for let up....Asbury was intoxicated by the full-bodied form of American revival; from now on he would always want more noise than Wesley or Coke.[45]

Francis wrote of what he heard:

> The work of God is running like fire in Kentucky. It is reported that near fifteen if not twenty thousand were present at one Sacramental occasion of the Presbyterians [this was at Cane Ridge]; and one thousand if not fifteen hundred fell and felt the power of grace.[46]

Though the meetings were Presbyterian, the Presbyterians seemed to be dropping the ball on ministering to the numbers coming out of these revivals. They had the attitude that if God was moving to save these people, He was also able to take care of what He had started. Francis felt otherwise. These people needed to be shepherded, and if the Presbyterians and the Baptists weren't going to do it, then the Methodists certainly would. Francis was not one to limit the power of God. "God hath given us hundreds in 1800, why not thousands in 1801, yea, why not a million if we had faith. 'Lord

---

[44] Francis Asbury, "Letter to George Roberts," 18 August 1803, *Journal and Letters of Francis Asbury* 3: 269, quoted in Rudolph, *Francis Asbury*, 118.

[45] Rudolph, *Francis Asbury*, 113, 116.

[46] Francis Asbury, "Letter to Mrs. John Dickens," 12 September 1801, *Journal and Letters of Francis Asbury* 3: 226, quoted in Rudolph, *Francis Asbury*, 117. Insert added.

increase our faith.'"[47] Methodism thus continued to grow by leaps and bounds throughout the rest of his life.

Always Out Among Them

When Francis came to the American colonies in 1771, "there were four Methodist preachers in the thirteen colonies caring for about three hundred people. By 1813, three years before Francis's death, official Methodist records reported 171,448 white and 42,850 African-American members 'in full society'"[48] His administrative mind was the key to managing such a huge organization. He was convinced that Methodism was God's cause—above even other denominations—and that it would not flourish without strict controls.

He intended to make sure those controls were implemented in bringing up the next generation, especially children educated in the Methodist schools that Francis is credited with having started. For example, the students were to "be indulged with nothing which the World calls *Play*. Let this Rule be observed with the strictest Nicety; for those who play when they are young, will play when they are old." [49] Francis later realized the severity of this policy. "*That matter might have been managed better.* We were to have the boys to become all angels."[50]

Biographer Ezra Tipple told about one man, Nicholas Snethen, who categorized Francis as controlling, among other things. Snethen was a traveling companion to Francis, and he wrote, "It cannot be concealed that he was not incapable of the exercise of that awful attribute of power, hard-heartedness, to those individuals, feelings, and interests which seemed to oppose the execution of public plans." Tipple then questioned whether Snethen was justified in his

---

[47] Francis Asbury, "Letter to Stith Mead," 20 January 1801, *Journal and Letters of Francis Asbury* 3: 196, quoted in Rudolph, *Francis Asbury*, 118.

[48] Salter, *America's Bishop*, 9.

[49] Asbury, "An Address to the Annual Subscribers for the Support of Cokesbury College," *Journal and Letters of Francis Asbury* 3: 58 59, quoted in Rudolph, *Francis Asbury*, 126.

[50] Asbury, "November 1, 1804," *Journals and Letters of Francis Asbury* 2: 445, quoted in Rudolph, *Francis Asbury*, 126.

description, preferring to say that Francis was "fixed in his purposes, immovable in his resolves."[51]

Whatever words one uses to describe Francis, he got the job done. He insisted on being the one to decide each year at the Methodist Annual Conference where the itinerant preachers would be assigned next. That decision in itself was no small task—by 1812, there were 678 ministers to be placed. Making the decision required that Asbury know each man, or at least make inquiries from someone who did know each man, and be acquainted with the particulars about each preaching location. Matching an itinerant with a circuit was far from a random process. Early on, Francis wrote to Wesley that he found it impossible that anyone could rightly assign the men unless he knew them and their gifts, which, in his estimation, required his always being out among them.

Needless to say, his decisions were not always popular. He once commented, "One preacher wishes to go where another dreads to be sent, and smiles at the fears of his more timid brother."[52] His usual way of handling the grumbling was to announce the assignments at the end of the conference, then mount his horse immediately and ride off. But he would never ask his men to go anywhere that he was not willing to go or to endure anything he was not ready to endure. "Comfort" was not a word in his vocabulary.

It wasn't just the circuit-rider assignments that Francis controlled. He insisted on signing every document, overseeing every financial transaction, and approving the plans for most of the buildings the organization constructed to make sufficient space for people to hear and learn. After more than forty years of this commanding position, he seemed to tire of it and long for some freedom and retirement. He wrote, "I wish that a trinity of superintendents might be in operation—that after forty years, I might be at liberty to travel into any part of the New or Old World, if called."[53]

One wonders if it was a longing for home; however, Francis had no home this side of heaven. When asked by a stranger in Ohio

---

[51] Tipple, *Francis Asbury: Prophet of the Long Road*, 324.

[52] Asbury, *Journal and Letters of Francis Asbury*, vol. 2, 342, quoted in Salter, *America's Bishop*, 126.

[53] "Unpublished Letters of Francis Asbury," *Methodist History* 16 (April 1978), 3:49, quoted in Salter, *America's Bishop*, 291.

where he was from, he answered, "From Boston, New York, Philadelphia, Baltimore, or almost any place you please." A biographer summed up Asbury's life in this way: "When he came to America he rented no house, he hired no lodgings, he made no arrangements to board anywhere, but simply set out upon the Long Road, and was still traveling forty-five years later when Death finally caught up with him."[54]

With nothing to tie him to this earth, it was easy for Francis to have tunnel vision, which brought accusations of insensitivity to the desires and feelings of others. His longing for unity often clashed with his desire for authority. When a particular vote at a leadership conference didn't go the way he wanted it to, Francis told the men they were all out of the union, and then took his papers and left. A few days later he asked for their forgiveness. There is no doubt that his negotiating skills were one of the major factors that kept the fledgling organization together and allowed it to develop. Darius Salter said, "No one mastered the art of simultaneously exercising inclusive participation and exclusive authority better than Asbury."[55]

> ***Francis had no home this side of heaven.***

Two issues required more of this ability than any other issue with which Francis dealt. The first had to do with whether Methodist preachers could administer the sacraments of Communion (this was while Methodism was still a mission and not yet a denomination); the second was the issue of slavery. Both threatened at different times to divide American Methodism.

In the early years, according to Wesley, lay preachers were not ordained; they were to establish societies, not recognized churches. Thus, the lay preachers had no authority to serve the sacraments. People were to go to an ordained minister for that purpose. The leadership in the South took exception with that rule since there were few ordained ministers available, leading Francis to write that he would rather accept the sacraments from an "unconverted" minister than from an unordained Methodist—something with which John

[54] Tipple, *Francis Asbury: Prophet of the Long Road*, 158–159.

[55] Salter, *America's Bishop*, 123.

Wesley would likely have concurred. A division of the Northern Societies—which adhered to true Wesleyanism—from the Southern Conference seemed imminent. A meeting of the minds took place in the South, and although Francis presented the perspective of Wesley, the Southern leadership would not budge. They intended to continue ordaining ministers with full authority to administer the sacraments.

Feeling rejected, Francis planned to leave the next morning; but when he returned to say his good-byes, he discovered that the men had changed their minds. They would abide with Francis's ruling and continue to seek direction, focusing on the bigger picture of spreading Methodism. It would not be the last time this subject was hotly debated.

Dinner with President Washington

Slavery was a troubling subject for Francis and for the Methodist organization in general. Francis could not understand how a country that fought for freedom could make slaves of other human beings. He made sure that the slaves felt welcomed by every preacher and were always included with their masters in the preaching times. Asbury even traveled with Harry Hosier, the first African-American Methodist evangelist, to the state of Virginia. Many Methodists considered Hosier to be one of the best preachers in the world.

Francis showed kindness and concern to all he encountered, regardless of their skin color. Once, while he was riding in South Carolina, he greeted a slave as he rode by. Feeling the tug of the Holy Spirit to speak to the man about his soul, Francis turned his horse around and went back. When he asked the man his name, he found that the man didn't know it; because of his affinity for fighting, people called him Punch. As he did with every soul he met, Francis prayed, sang, and read Scriptures to Punch; then, he departed. Twenty years later, when Asbury returned to the same area, he providentially encountered Punch again. Punch told him about the change in his life and of the many other slaves he had influenced, and Francis wrote in response, "Better to witness to one slave than to rule on the highest throne on the face of the earth."[56]

[56] Salter, *America's Bishop*, 324.

Francis's personal opinions did not always translate into Methodist regulations, a gap that history has not always looked upon favorably. Darius Salter explained it this way: "Methodism simply mirrored the inconsistency of a nation that declared that all men are 'created equal' and at the same time held slaves."[57] There were times when Francis did attempt to influence official legislation on the issue of slavery. After the Revolutionary War, he and Thomas Coke made an attempt to get President George Washington to sign a petition to emancipate the slaves. Visiting him at Mount Vernon, Francis felt uncomfortable having black servants wait on them at dinner. Afterward, Washington said that although he agreed with the principle, he would not sign the petition. He explained that the slaves needed to be educated so that they would understand their obligation of freedom; otherwise, freedom would not be a gift. Washington himself owned several hundred slaves, who worked his plantation, but a few months before he died, he changed the specifications of his will so that they would all be set free when his wife died. The degree to which Francis influenced that decision is uncertain.

Francis showed kindness toward everyone he encountered, regardless of skin color.

Many Methodist conferences debated establishing firm rulings on slavery but never passed anything in Francis's lifetime. Francis undoubtedly had much to do with that. Believing that anything that got in the way of evangelizing for eternal purposes was not in anyone's best interest, he rationalized that God's directive to them was saving souls, not liberating bodies. He believed that he was "called upon to suffer for Christ's sake not for slavery."[58]

It would seem that his myopic vision blinded him to the fact that evangelism has to do with more than where one will spend eternity. Only God knows whether Francis's concern over taking a stand on slavery was based on this rationalization or its potential impact on

[57] Ibid., 314.

[58] Ibid.

the growth of Methodism. He wrote that taking an inflexible position against slavery would cripple Methodism's attempt to reach both blacks and whites and that, given what he and others like him had endured, a few years of the physical torture of slavery would be exchanged for "an eternity of spiritual bliss."[59] What brought about this change of heart is difficult to determine, but it is clearly seen in February 1807 when he preached the love of God to the whites and obedient servitude to the blacks.

"What Shall I Do When I Am Old?"

There were times when Francis allowed himself to think about the implications of having neither family nor home. In one of these human moments for a seemingly superhuman man, he wrote a letter to his mother, his confidant: "I am here in a strange land, nothing to depend on but the kindness of friends, am spending the best of my days, what shall I do when I am old?"[60] By age sixty-eight, his body was giving out. He realized that death was imminent. But he would not need to worry about going home to heaven; the God who had called him to this place made sure he was cared for until the very end.

Francis had rheumatoid arthritis; toward the end of his life, the ailment was so severe that he needed to be transported by carriage. But nothing could stop his preacher's heart from wanting to proclaim the good news with his dying breath. Francis and a traveling companion were on their way to Fredericksburg, pushing as hard as they could in hopes of making it to the General Conference, but it was not to be. When Francis could go no farther, they took shelter at the home of an old friend, George Arnold. Francis realized the next morning that it was the Sabbath, and he asked that the family gather around him for worship. His lungs had filled with fluid, so he had to be propped up in a chair. At the end of the singing and preaching by his traveling partner, Francis did as he always did—he called for the plate to be passed so a collection could be taken for the needs of his fellow preachers. He was told that there was only the one family

---

59 Salter, *America's Bishop*, 317.

60 Asbury, *Journal and Letters of Francis Asbury*, vol. 3, 16, quoted in Salter, *America's Bishop*, 46.

present. In a final act of praise, he raised his hands in triumph when asked if he felt the Lord Jesus was precious.

Francis Asbury passed away at four o'clock in the afternoon on Sunday, March 31, 1816. Since the Arnolds lived so far from any town, they decided to bury him in their family plot. Later, the Methodist organization had his body exhumed and moved to Baltimore, where a proper funeral was performed. Asbury's body remains buried in Baltimore beneath a ten-foot pillar whose shape resembles the Washington Monument.

Francis wrote in his will that he didn't want anyone to write a biography about his life, and he even asked that his executor do everything in his power to make sure that didn't happen. He also asked that, at his death, Bibles be given to all the children who had been named after him, and it is said that thousands were handed out.

Many have written about the duty-bound Francis Asbury, who seemed to have a spirit of restlessness, a need to be always on the road. But Ezra Tipple best described the heart of Francis Asbury, saying that it wasn't the love of the road that kept him going, "but love of the man who lived by the side of the Road."[61]

No matter how one views Francis Asbury and his religious doctrine, Methodism endorsed the equality of all believers in America as taught by Jesus Christ. The Good News that salvation could change any life, now and for eternity, shattered divisions between classes and confirmed all the more the reality of the American Dream of rising out of one's class and building a better future for one's family. Asbury's life is a testimony to how God takes simple people and leads them on great journeys with Him. History records that Asbury "rode more than a quarter of a million miles on horseback and crossed the Allegheny Mountains some sixty times....Asbury stayed in 10,000 households and preached 17,000 sermons."[62]

There are roughly thirteen million Methodists in the United States today, second only to the Baptists who have roughly twenty-seven million members.

---

[61] Tipple, *Francis Asbury: Prophet of the Long Road*, 160.

[62] John H. Wigger, "Holy, 'Knock-'em-down' Preachers," *Christian History* 14, no. 1 [Issue 45] (1995), 25.

According to Tipple, Methodism distinguished itself from other denominations, with

> its system of church government, its ardent, effective evangelism, its rational, scriptural, and preachable theology, its aggressive missionary spirit, its teaching concerning experimental salvation, and the freedom and warmth of its services, especially of its preaching and singing....[It] was more nearly a renewal of primitive Christianity than any movement of the centuries since the apostles.[63]

[63] Tipple, *Francis Asbury: Prophet of the Long Road*, 13, 15.

Chapter Five

☆☆☆☆☆

The First Camp Meetings

(1799–1801)

"America's Pentecost"

"AMERICA'S PENTECOST"

I wish you would also hold campmeetings; they have never been tried without success. To collect such a number of God's people together to pray, and the ministers to preach, and the longer they stay, generally, the better—this is field fishing, this is fishing with a large net.[1]

—Francis Asbury,
to the presiding elder of the Pittsburgh District

By the mid 1700s, those wanting more elbow room in the increasingly populous colonies began pushing through the Cumberland Gap out of Virginia to form the first settlements west of the Allegheny Mountains. This wild countryside stocked full of wild turkeys and deer was used mainly as hunting grounds for various Native American tribes. Thick forests, full of excellent timber of many varieties, ran from horizon to horizon. The trees were watered by numerous springs and streams, and the forests held game for settlers and trappers alike. The soil was also marvelously rich for farming, especially around an area that Daniel Boone had dubbed "Cane Ridge" because of a variety of bamboo that flourished there.

Much of this territory was purchased from the Native Americans—by Britain in the Treaty of Fort Stanwix (1768) and by a private company from North Carolina in the Treaty of Sycamore Shoals (1775). The influx of settlers, however, displeased a few of the tribes

[1] Francis Asbury, "Letter to Thorton Fleming," 2 December 1802, *The Journal and Letters of Francis Asbury*, vol. 3, 251, quoted in Rudolph, *Francis Asbury*, 119–120.

to the extent that they sided with the British against the colonists in the Revolutionary War. One of the war's final battles—the Battle of Blue Licks—was even fought in this region, on August 19, 1782. This territory was racked by violence for more than a decade after the war ended. Meetinghouses that weathered this violence are still standing today, their walls bearing rifle slits for colonists to use to protect themselves in case of an attack by Native Americans.

In 1792, this territory became Kentucky, the first state outside of the original thirteen, and the fifteenth state in the Union. (Vermont was the fourteenth state, comprising an area that had been disputed between the states of New York and New Hampshire.) Kentuckians were a rough breed—most were either outlaws on the run, homesteading families, or explorers, of whom Daniel Boone was the most famous. Kentucky was not a place for the faint of heart. Nor did the Kentuckians settle here for the same reasons as those who settled in Plymouth; these were not Pilgrims seeking religious freedom. Kentuckians considered spiritual matters secondary—if they considered them at all. As Francis Asbury put it in 1794, "When I reflect that not one in a hundred came here for religion, but rather to get plenty of good land, I think it will be well if some or many do not eventually lose their souls."[2]

Yet wherever there was a settlement, there was a call for ministers. In many cases, several communities would share a pastor because the early populations were so small. So it was that James McGready, a Presbyterian minister, took charge of the congregations on the Gasper, Red, and Muddy Rivers in Logan County. In 1796 he covenanted with these congregations to pray every Saturday evening, and to pray and fast from sunrise to sunset on the third Saturday of every month. The main focus of these prayer times was to ask God to bring revival.

A Revivalist Comes from the East

Descended from Scots-Irish ancestors, James McGready was born in 1763 in Pennsylvania. When he was a young child, his parents moved to Guilford County, North Carolina, where he grew up and attended David Caldwell's academy. He returned to Pennsylvania for

[2] Galli, "Revival at Cane Ridge," 10.

ministerial preparation studies at Jefferson College, an institution in Canonsburg that would go on to be part of Washington and Jefferson College in nearby Washington, Pennsylvania (near Pittsburgh). It was there that he would hear Dr. John Blair Smith's detailed account of a powerful revival he had experienced in Virginia. James was immediately fascinated by the subject of revival.

James was licensed as a minister by the Presbytery of Redstone on August 13, 1788, and married sometime around 1790. For awhile, James pastored a congregation in Orange County, North Carolina, not far from Guilford. He quickly gained notoriety in the area "for his effective preaching...and for his intense moral seriousness. He touched people by his prayers and sermons, and at the same time troubled them by his denunciation of anything less than perfect holiness in conduct."[3] From time to time, he would minister at Dr. David Caldwell's academy, where he had been educated. There, he touched the lives of future revivalists: William Hodge would become a protégé of James, while Barton Stone, who was pastor at Cane Ridge during the 1801 camp meeting there, would cofound the Churches of Christ denomination. Stone would later say of James,

> Such earnestness—such zeal—such powerful persuasion, enforced by the joys of heaven and miseries of hell, I had never witnessed before. My mind was chained by him, and followed him closely in his rounds of heaven, earth, and hell, with feelings indescribable. His concluding remarks were addressed to the sinner to flee the wrath to come without delay. Never before had I comparatively felt the force of truth. Such was my excitement, that had I been standing, I should have probably sunk to the floor under the impression.[4]

James McGready did not speak with the same emotional charge and drama as George Whitefield or with the calm power of John Wesley, but in the summers of 1800 and 1801, his ministry

---

[3] Paul K. Conklin, *Cane Ridge: America's Pentecost* (Madison: The University of Wisconsin Press, 1990), 53.

[4] Barton Stone, *A Short History of the Life of Barton W. Stone*, 1847, Chapter 2, based on the edition in *Voices from Cane Ridge*, ed. Rhodes Thompson (St. Louis, MO: The Bethany Press, 1954), 31–134, http://www.mun.ca/rels/restmov/texts/bstone/barton.html#ch_two.

left an indelible mark on the history of revivalism. Tall and almost ungainly, James read from carefully written sermons, just as Jonathan Edwards had, though he lacked Edwards's intellectual clout. He exhorted with the authority of an Old Testament prophet—with a voice like thunder—and the careful, logical argument of the apostle Paul. As the Reverend John Andrews, a fellow minister, put it,

> The style of his sermons was not polished, but perspicuous and pointed; and his manner of address was unusually solemn and impressive. As a preacher, he was highly esteemed by the humble followers of the Lamb, who relished the precious truths which he clearly exhibited to their view; but he was hated, and sometimes bitterly reproached and persecuted, not only by the openly vicious and profane, but by many nominal Christians, or formal professors, who could not bear his heart-searching and penetrating addresses, and the indignation of the Almighty against the ungodly, which, as a son on thunder, he clearly presented to the view of their guilty minds from the awful denunciations of the World of Truth.[5]

His zeal provoked a good deal of controversy and opposition. Some said he was causing his parishioners undue anxiety about their souls. James even received a letter written in blood that demanded he leave the county or risk his life, and a band of brigands tore out some of the seats in his church and set fire to his pulpit, burning it to ashes. The following Sunday, he defied them by delivering a sermon based on Matthew 23:37–38:

> *O Jerusalem, Jerusalem, thou that killest the prophets, and stonest them which are sent unto thee, how often would I have gathered thy children together, even as a hen gathereth her chickens under her wings, and ye would not! Behold your house is left unto you desolate.*[6]

[5] James Smith, *History of the Christian Church, From Its Origin to the Present Time; Compiled from Various Authors. Including a History of the Cumberland Presbyterian Church, Drawn from Authentic Documents* (Nashville: Cumberland Presbyterian Office, 1835), 672–673, http://www.cumberland.org/hfcpc/McGready.htm.

[6] Richard Beard, *Brief Biographical Sketches of Some of the Early Ministers of the Cumberland Presbyterian Church* (Nashville: Southern Methodist Publishing House, 1867), 7–17, http://www.cumberland.org/hfcpc/McGready.htm.

In 1796, James left North Carolina for Kentucky and the three Logan County congregations mentioned earlier. There, in one of the roughest parts of Kentucky, he continued to call for moral excellence. The region was known as "Rogue's Harbor" because of those who had fled there to escape the long arm of the law east of the Alleghenies. It was an area rampant with vice and alcoholism, land grabbing, and homesteaders trying to bring civilization to an untamed—and sometimes seemingly untamable—land. Christianity also appeared to be on the ropes as Universalism and Deism were on the rise.

As Methodist minister James Smith put it in 1795, "The Universalists, joining with the Deists, had given Christianity a deadly stab hereabouts."[7] The 1790s were actually seeing a decline in church attendance in Kentucky and Tennessee (which became the sixteenth state in 1796). In 1798, the Presbyterian General Assembly decreed a day of fasting, humiliation, and prayer to call for the redemption of the frontier from "Egyptian darkness."[8] With them, James continued praying.

In May 1797, James saw the first visit of the Holy Spirit as he preached. A woman who had been a faithful church member "was struck with deep conviction," sought salvation anew, "and in a few days was filled with joy and peace in believing."[9] In a letter to a friend on October 23, 1801, he described what happened next:

> She immediately visited her friends and relatives, from house to house, and warned them of their danger in a most solemn, faithful manner, and plead with them to repent and seek religion. This...was accompanied with the divine blessing [manifestations of the Holy Spirit] to the awakening of many. About this time the ears of all in that congregation seemed to be open to receive the word preached, and almost every sermon was accompanied with the power of God, to

[7] Galli, "Revival at Cane Ridge," 11.

[8] Ibid.

[9] James McGready, "Narrative of the Commencement and Progress of the Revival of 1800," letter to a friend, 23 October 1801, Historical Foundation of the Cumberland Presbyterian Church and the Cumberland Presbyterian Church in America, http://www.cumberland.org/hfcpc/McGreaBK.htm#anchor222019.

> the awakening of sinners. During the summer about ten persons in the congregation were brought to Christ.[10]

The seeds of revival were starting to sprout.

The Annual Communions

Ever looking for opportunities to spur renewal in the hearts of his congregation, James adapted a formula that had sparked revivals in Ulster (Northern Ireland) and Scotland. The greatest of these was in 1742 in Cambuslang, where George Whitefield spoke with a number of other ministers. The Reverend McGready called for an annual, multiday Communion service that allowed everyone from the area to come together, hear the Word preached, and then take the sacrament together on the last day. Families from the surrounding area would come to stay with other families in town, and meetings would start on Friday evenings. Services would continue through Saturday and Sunday, followed by a Monday morning service, with Communion observed around noontime. This schedule proved an effective formula for the sparsely populated Logan County. Scattered settlers were able to come together as a community to receive the sacrament, which was impractical on a weekly, or even monthly, basis, because of the time required for travel.

Though these were annual events in James's churches—they probably had been in North Carolina, as well—they were anything but routine after the services at Gasper River in July 1798. Again, in James's own words,

> On Monday the Lord graciously poured out his Spirit; a very general awakening took place—perhaps but few families in the congregation could be found who, less or more, were not struck with an awful sense of their lost estate. During the week following but few persons attended to worldly business, their attention to the business of their souls was so great. On the first Sabbath of September, the sacrament was administered at Muddy River (one of my congregations). At this meeting the Lord graciously poured

[10] James McGready, "Narrative of the Commencement and Progress of the Revival of 1800."

> forth his spirit, to the awakening of many careless sinners. Through these two congregations already mentioned, and through Red River, my other congregation, awakening work went on with power under every sermon. The people seemed to hear, as for eternity. In every house, and almost in every company, the whole conversation with people, was about the state of their souls. [11]

There seemed to be a growing excitement about religion in all of Rev. McGready's congregations.

The first Communion service of summer 1799 took place in July at Red River. Following the formula Whitefield had used at Cambuslang, James welcomed other ministers, including Presbyterians John Rankin, William Hodge, William McGee, and McGee's Methodist brother, John. James described what happened in the same letter to a friend:

> On Monday the power of God seemed to fill the congregation; the boldest, daring sinners in the country covered their faces and wept bitterly. After the congregation was dismissed, a large number of people stayed about the doors, unwilling to go away. Some of the ministers proposed to me to collect the people in the meetinghouse again, and perform prayer with them; accordingly we went in, and joined in prayer and exhortation. The mighty power of God came amongst us like a shower from the everlasting hills—God's people were quickened and comforted; yea, some of them were filled with joy unspeakable, and full of glory. Sinners were powerfully alarmed, and some precious souls were brought to feel the pardoning love of Jesus.[12]

Again, growing revival was seen in the Gasper and Muddy River congregations—but God was far from finished.

The following summer, James called for the Red River Communion to take place even earlier in the summer, on the weekend of Saturday, June 21, to Monday, June 23, 1800. Roughly five hundred

---

[11] McGready, "Narrative of the Commencement and Progress of the Revival of 1800."

[12] Ibid.

people attended. He invited the same group of ministers as he had the year before, but this time, his expectations were exceeded when the Holy Spirit showed up with great power. As James reflected that summer,

> In June the sacrament was administered at Red River. This was the greatest time we had ever seen before. On Monday multitudes were struck down under awful conviction; the cries of the distressed filled the whole house. There you might see profane swearers, and sabbath breakers pricked to the heart, and crying out, "what shall we do to be saved?" There frolickers and dancers crying for mercy. There you might see little children of 10, 11, and 12 years of age, praying and crying for redemption, in the blood of Jesus, in agonies of distress. During this sacrament, and until the Tuesday following, ten persons, we believe, were savingly brought home to Christ.[13]

The Reverend John McGee

Library of Congress, 03001046

The eruption at Red River was truly unexpected from the outset; the first three days had passed with few remarkable happenings. The services had been reverent and orderly.

During the service on Monday morning, however, as William Hodge preached a moving message on Job 22:21—*"Acquaint now thyself with him, and be at peace: thereby good shall come unto thee"*—a woman who had been seeking assurance of her salvation for some time began to shout and sing.

Then, after a short intermission, John McGee rose to speak and came to the pulpit, singing,

[13] Ibid.

> Come, Holy Spirit, heav'nly Dove,
> With all Thy quick'ning pow'rs;
> Kindle a flame of sacred love
> In these cold hearts of ours.[14]

At the sound of this hymn, at least one more woman cried out, probably also coming into a sudden knowledge of saving grace. McGee descended to congratulate these women, and as he did, the glory of God seemed to break out over the people. Some fell to the ground; others were screaming for mercy; some prayed, and others began praising God at the top of their lungs. William McGee, who was sitting nearby, rose to go to the pulpit, but he fell on the floor, apparently under the power of the Holy Spirit. As John McGee turned to him, he felt the power of God fall so heavily on him that he nearly crumbled beside his brother. John later recalled,

> I turned to go back and was near falling; the power of God was strong upon me. I turned again, and, losing sight of the fear of man, I went through the house shouting and exhorting with all possible ecstasy and energy, and the floor was soon covered with the slain.[15]

McGready, Hodge, and Rankin wondered if they should intervene. Never before had their preaching caused people to collapse, and they were unsure how to interpret and deal with what was happening. But John McGee, a "shouting Methodist" himself, assured them that this was the work of God, so they decided to let the service run its course. Rev. Rankin later reported,

> On seeing and feeling his confidence, that it was the work of God, and a mighty effusion of his spirit, and having heard that he was acquainted with such scenes in another country, we acquiesced and stood in astonishment, admiring

[14] T. Marshall Smith, *Legends of the War of Independence* (Louisville: J. F. Brennan, Publisher, 1855), 372–373, quoted in Kenneth O. Brown, *Holy Ground: A Study of the American Camp Meeting* (New York: Garland Publishing, 1992), 18. The hymn "Come, Holy Spirit, Heavenly Dove" was written by Isaac Watts and was widely sung by Methodists.

[15] John McGee to the Reverend Thomas L. Douglas, 23 June 1820, in *Methodist Magazine* 4 (1821): 190, quoted in John B. Boles, *The Great Revival: Beginnings of the Bible Belt* (Lexington: University of Kentucky Press, 1972), 54.

> the wonderful works of God. When this alarming occurrence subsided in outward show, the united congregation returned to their respective abodes, in contemplation of what they had seen, heard, and felt on this most oppressive occasion.[16]

James then decided to have another Communion the following month at the Gasper River Meetinghouse. That summer, the McGee brothers spoke at various locations almost every weekend, and such meetings caught on like wildfire. The word spread quickly, and momentum gathered toward the Gasper River Communion. As Rankin remarked,

> The news of the strange operations which had transpired at the previous meeting had run throughout the country in every direction, carrying a high degree of excitement to the minds of almost every character. The curious came to gratify their curiosity. The seriously convicted, presented themselves that they might receive some special and salutary benefit to their souls, and promote the cause of God, at home and abroad.[17]

In his *"Narrative of the Commencement and Progress of the Revival of 1800,"* James described how the Kentucky revival truly took hold in Gasper, drawing people from far and wide:

> In July the sacrament was administered in Gasper River Congregation. Here multitudes crowded from all parts of the country to see a strange work, from the distance of forty, fifty, and even a hundred miles; whole families came in their wagons; between twenty and thirty wagons were brought to the place, loaded with people, and their provisions, in order to encamp at the meeting-house. On Friday nothing more appeared, during the day, than a decent solemnity. On Saturday matters continued in the same

[16] John Rankin, "Autobiographical Sketch," 1845, quoted in John Patterson MacLean, *Shakers of Ohio: Fugitive Papers Concerning the Shakers of Ohio, with Unpublished Manuscripts* (Columbus, OH: The F. J. Heer Printing Company, 1907), 57.

[17] Rankin, "Autobiographical Sketch," 280–281, quoted in Boles, *The Great Revival*, 55.

> way, until in the evening. Two pious women were sitting together, conversing about their exercises; which conversation seemed to affect some of the by-standers; instantly the divine flame spread through the whole multitude. Presently you might have seen sinners lying powerless in every part of the house, praying and crying for mercy. Ministers and private Christians were kept busy during the night conversing with the distressed. This night a goodly number of awakened souls were delivered by sweet believing views of the glory, fulness, and sufficiency of Christ, to save to the uttermost. Amongst these were some little children—a striking proof of the religion of Jesus. Of many instances to which I have been an eyewitness, I shall only mention one, viz. a little girl. I stood by her whilst she lay across her mother's lap almost in despair. I was conversing with her when the first gleam of light broke in upon her mind—she started to her feet, and in an ecstacy of joy, she cried out, "O he is willing, he is willing—he is come, he is come—O what a sweet Christ he is—O what a precious Christ he is—O what a fulness I see in him—O what a beauty I see in him—O why was it that I never could believe! That I never could come to Christ before, when Christ was so willing to save me?" Then turning round, she addressed sinners, and told them of the glory, willingness, and preciousness of Christ, and plead with them to repent; and all this in language so heavenly, and, at the same time, so rational and scriptural, that I was filled with astonishment. But were I to write you every particular of this kind that I have been an eye and ear witness to, during the two past years, it would fill many sheets of paper.[18]

The Gasper River meetinghouse proved too small to accommodate the large crowds, so areas were cleared to hold meetings in the open air. A makeshift preaching stand was constructed, and logs were converted into pews. Services lasted throughout the first night, and the cries of the penitent threatened to drown out the voice of John

[18] McGready, "Narrative of the Commencement and Progress of the Revival of 1800."

McGee as he spoke on Sunday. The same signs of the move of the Spirit that had been at Red River were at Gasper River: many people fell under the power of God, cried out and prayed under the conviction of the Spirit, and gave loud shouts of joy and praise when they had found the peace with God they had come hoping to receive.

This sketch depicts a meeting with a makeshift stage.

Library of Congress, 98508274

Most historians consider Gasper River to be the first camp meeting ever held, but the term "camp meeting" was not coined for another year or two afterward. This term came about because the Communion services began to draw crowds larger than the local families could accommodate in their homes, and soon, the crowds would outgrow even the capacities of the meetinghouses.

The conviction of the Spirit operated without limits, as believers, Universalists, Deists, and even atheists were all struck down. Revival fire was spreading from Logan County throughout Kentucky and Tennessee. A frenzy of the Holy Spirit continued to take the frontier, and Communion services were held almost every weekend for the rest of the summer.

> At this sacrament a great many people from Cumberland, particularly from Shiloh Congregation, came with great curiosity to see the work, yet prepossessed with strong prejudices against it; about five of whom, I trust, were savingly and powerfully converted before they left the place. A circumstance worthy of observation, they were sober

professors in full communion. It was truly affecting to see them lying powerless, crying for mercy, and speaking to their friends and relations, in such language as this: "O, we despised the work that we heard of in Logan; but, O, we were deceived—I have no religion; I know now there is a reality in these things: three days ago I would have despised any person that would have behaved as I am doing now; but, O, I feel the very pains of hell in my soul." This was the language of a precious soul, just before the hour of deliverance came. When they went home, their conversation to their friends and neighbors, was the means of commencing a glorious work that has overspread all the Cumberland settlements to the conversion of hundreds of precious souls. The work continued night and day at this sacrament, whilst the vast multitude continued upon the ground until Tuesday morning. According to the best computation, we believe that forty-five souls were brought to Christ on this occasion.

Muddy River Sacrament, in all its circumstances, was equal, and in some respects superior, to that at Gasper River. This sacrament was in August. We believe about fifty persons, at this time, obtained religion.

At [Cane] Ridge Sacrament, in Cumberland, the second Sabbath in September [1800], about forty-five souls, we believe, obtained religion. At Shiloh Sacrament, the third Sabbath in September, about seventy persons. At Mr. Craighead's Sacrament, in October, about forty persons. At the Clay-Lick Sacrament congregation, in Logan County, in October, eight persons. At Little Muddy-Creek Sacrament, in November, about twelve. At Montgomery's Meeting-house, in Cumberland, about forty. At Hopewell Sacrament, in Cumberland, in November, about twenty persons. To mention the circumstances of more private occasions, common-days preaching, and societies, would swell a letter to a volume.[19]

[19] McGready, "Narrative of the Commencement and Progress of the Revival of 1800."

John McGee reported that at Desha's Creek,

> many thousands of people attended. The mighty power and mercy of God was manifested. The people fell before the Word, like corn before a storm of wind, and many rose from the dust with divine glory shining on their countences, and gave glory to God in such strains as made the hearts of stubborn sinners to tremble; and after the first gust of praise they would break forth in vollies of exhortation.[20]

One of Rev. McGready's sermons, entitled "A Sacramental Meditation," was based upon Genesis 28:17—*"How dreadful is this place! this is none other but the house of God, and this is the gate of heaven."* This sermon can perhaps begin to give us an understanding of the intensity that led to such extreme reactions. The points of this sermon resemble some that Edwards made in his famous sermon "Sinners in the Hands of an Angry God":

1) A sacramental table is a dreadful place; for God is there.
2) A sacramental table is a dreadful place, because it is a striking exhibition of the most important transaction ever witnessed by men or angels, vis. the redemption of guilty sinners by the bitter agonies, bloody sufferings and dying groans of the incarnate God.
3) A sacramental table is a dreadful place; for the Holy One of Israel here confers and sups with pardoned rebels.
4) A sacramental table is a dreadful place; for here heaven is brought down to earth.[21]

As 1800 drew to a close, God's presence surely seemed to be falling on Kentucky and Tennessee. But these states had seen nothing yet—a fresh dose of Pentecost was just around the corner. The next

[20] John McGee to Douglas, *Methodist Magazine* 4:191, quoted in Boles, *The Great Revival*, 57.

[21] James McGready, "A Sacramental Meditation," quoted in Hughlan P. Richey, "Red River Church and the Revival of 1800," *Adairville* [KY] *Enterprise*, August 14, 1969, 2, Historical Foundation of the Cumberland Presbyterian Church and the Cumberland Presbyterian Church in America, http://www.cumberland.org/hfcpc/churches/RedRivKY.htm.

year, 1801, would see roughly fifty different congregations plan four-day Communions in Kentucky between May and November, the largest and most explosive of all occurring at Cane Ridge. It would be the climax of the revival taking place west of the Alleghenies.

The Holy Spirit Falls on Cane Ridge

When Barton Stone heard that God was moving at James's Communions, he decided to attend in spring of 1801. The scene that greeted him was revolutionary. By this time, the crowds had grown too large to have a service with everyone present, so various areas of ministry would go on concurrently in separate locations. In his autobiography, Stone described what he experienced:

> There, on the edge of a prairie in Logan County, Kentucky, the multitudes came together, and continued a number of days and nights encamped on the ground; during which time worship was carried on in some part of the encampment. The scene to me was new, and passing strange. It baffled description. Many, very many fell down, as men slain in battle, and continued for hours together in an apparently breathless and motionless state—sometimes for a few moments reviving, and exhibiting symptoms of life by a deep groan, or piercing shriek, or by a prayer for mercy most fervently uttered. After lying thus for hours, they obtained deliverance. The gloomy cloud, which had covered their faces, seemed gradually and visibly to disappear, and hope in smiles brightened into joy—they would rise shouting deliverance, and then would address the surrounding multitude in language truly eloquent and impressive. With astonishment did I hear men, women, and children declaring the wonderful works of God, and the glorious mysteries of the gospel. Their appeals were solemn, heart-penetrating, bold and free. Under such addresses many others would fall down into the same state from which the speakers had just been delivered.
>
> Two or three of my particular acquaintances from a distance were struck down. I sat patiently by one of them, whom I knew to be a careless sinner, for hours, and observed with

> critical attention every thing that passed from the beginning to the end. I noticed the momentary revivings as from death—the humble confession of sins—the fervent prayer, and the ultimate deliverance—then the solemn thanks and praise to God—the affectionate exhortation to companions and to the people around, to repent and come to Jesus. I was astonished at the knowledge of gospel truth displayed in the address. The effect was, that several sunk down into the same appearance of death. After attending to many such cases, my conviction was complete that it was a good work—the work of God; nor has my mind wavered since on the subject. Much did I then see, and much have I since seen, that I considered to be fanaticism; but this should not condemn the work. The Devil has always tried to ape the works of God, to bring them into disrepute. But that cannot be a Satanic work, which brings men to humble confession and forsaking of sin—to solemn prayer—fervent praise and thanksgiving, and to sincere and affectionate exhortations to sinners to repent and go to Jesus the Saviour.[22]

When Stone returned to his congregations at Cane Ridge and Concord and shared some of what he had seen, his parishioners were struck to the heart. At Cane Ridge, "the congregation was affected with awful solemnity, and many returned home weeping."[23] At Concord, "two little girls were struck down under the preaching of the word, and in every respect were exercised as those were in the south of Kentucky, as already described. Their addresses made deep impressions on the congregation."[24] Upon returning to Cane Ridge, he found many who were seeking salvation with new vigor. A good friend, Nathaniel Rogers, greeted him by praising the Lord, for he had just gained the assurance of his salvation in his heart. Then, an even more interesting scene transpired:

> As soon as he saw me, he shouted aloud the praises of God. We hurried into each others' embrace, he still praising

[22] Barton Stone, *Short History of the Life of Barton W. Stone*, 1847, Chapter 5, http://www.mun.ca/rels/restmov/texts/bstone/barton.html#ch_five.

[23] Ibid.

[24] Ibid.

> the Lord aloud. The crowd [that had been seeking the Lord while awaiting Rev. Stone's return] left the house, and hurried to this novel scene. In less than twenty minutes, scores had fallen to the ground—paleness, trembling, and anxiety appeared in all—some attempted to fly from the scene panic stricken, but they either fell, or returned immediately to the crowd, as unable to get away. In the midst of this exercise, an intelligent deist in the neighborhood, stepped up to me, and said, "Mr. Stone, I always thought before that you were an honest man; but now I am convinced you are deceiving the people." I viewed him with pity, and mildly spoke a few words to him—immediately he fell as a dead man, and rose no more till he confessed the Saviour. The meeting continued on that spot in the open air, till late at night, and many found peace in the Lord.
>
> The effects of this meeting through the country were like fire in dry stubble driven by a strong wind. All felt its influence more or less. Soon after, we had a protracted meeting at Concord. The whole country appeared to be in motion to the place, and multitudes of all denominations attended. All seemed heartily to unite in the work, and in Christian love. Party spirit, abashed, shrunk away. To give a true description of this meeting cannot be done; it would border on the marvellous. It continued five days and nights without ceasing. Many, very many will through eternity remember it with thanksgiving and praise.[25]

After these events, Stone scheduled a Communion in Cane Ridge for the first weekend of August, only a month after his marriage on July 2. Expecting large crowds, and knowing that the meetinghouse could seat 350 comfortably (500 at maximum), Stone arranged for areas to be cleared so that a large tent could be erected as a secondary place of ministry.

On Friday, August 6, families began arriving on wagons. Hundreds soon turned into thousands, and the houses of local families hosting the attendees—even the more affluent ones, who might

[25] Barton Stone, *Short History of the Life of Barton W. Stone*, 1847, Chapter 5, http://www.mun.ca/rels/restmov/texts/bstone/barton.html#ch_five.

have housed three or four families—were soon overflowing. With so many people coming with the same purpose—to seek the Lord with all of their hearts—the scene passed somewhere between the absolute chaos of a refugee camp outside of a war zone and the Christian equivalent of the Jewish Feast of Tabernacles. In his autobiography, Rev. Stone tried to describe the scene, which quickly spread to fill several acres:

> The roads were literally crowded with wagons, carriages, horsemen, and footmen, moving to the solemn camp. The sight was affecting. It was judged, by military men on the ground, that there were between twenty and thirty thousand collected. Four or five preachers were frequently speaking at the same time, in different parts of the encampment, without confusion. The Methodist and Baptist preachers aided in the work, and all appeared cordially united in it—of one mind and one soul, and the salvation of sinners seemed to be the great object of all. We all engaged in singing the same songs of praise—all united in prayer—all preached the same things—free salvation urged upon all by faith and repentance. A particular description of this meeting would fill a large volume, and then the half would not be told. The numbers converted will be known only in eternity. Many things transpired there, which were so much like miracles, that if they were not, they had the same effects as miracles on infidels and unbelievers; for many of them by these were convinced that Jesus was the Christ, and bowed in submission to him. This meeting continued six or seven days and nights, and would have

Methodists travel en masse to a camp meeting.

Library of Congress, 3g03264

> continued longer, but provisions for such a multitude failed in the neighborhood.[26]

The first Friday evening, rain caused fewer people to come, but the meetinghouse was still filled to capacity. After Rev. Stone's opening address, Matthew Houston delivered the first sermon to an expectant audience. Nothing remarkable happened that evening, though some remained in prayer throughout the night.

Saturday morning was still quiet as the services continued, but by noon, more families were arriving—and by the thousands, despite the intermittent downpours of rain. It was easiest for single men to travel on horseback—during the events, they stayed in taverns or slept in barns as far away as Lexington, a distance of some twenty-five miles. The center could no longer hold; there were simply too many bodies for one area to contain. By the afternoon, both the meetinghouse and tent were filled to overflowing, and preaching continued without interruption.

It wasn't long, however, before preaching began breaking out wherever a crowd had gathered. It was said that during the weekend, there were times when as many as seven preachers were preaching to large crowds simultaneously. Attendance swelled to tens of thousands in the subsequent hours, and when it peaked, one tally counted 1,143 wagons and similar vehicles that had set up camp in the area. These were extraordinary numbers, considering that Lexington's population was a mere 1,795 at the time, and that Kentucky had fewer than 250,000 residents.[27] Another witness said of Saturday morning, "I first proceeded to count the waggons containing families, with their provisions, camp equipage, &c. to the number of 147: at 11 o'clock the quantity of ground occupied by horses, waggons, &c. was about the same size as the square between Market, Chesnut, Second and Third-streets, of Philadelphia."[28] (About four city blocks.)

---

[26] Barton Stone, *Short History of the Life of Barton W. Stone*, 1847, Chapter 5, http://www.mun.ca/rels/restmov/texts/bstone/barton.html#ch_five.

[27] Ray A. Billington, *Westward Expansion* (New York, 1949), 250, quoted in Bernard A. Weisberger, *They Gathered at the River: The Story of the Great Revivalists and Their Impact upon Religion in America* (Boston: Little, Brown, and Company, 1958), 31.

[28] Letter from a man to his sister, 10 August 1801, http://www.mun.ca/rels/restmov/texts/accounts/letter8.html.

In one of the gatherings, a young minister named Richard Nemar proclaimed that he had found a "true new gospel," and it was as if electricity had shot through the crowd. Though no one knew exactly what he meant by this—some were even shocked and offended—the presence of the Holy Spirit fell into the midst of the congregation and was manifest in various ways, some of which no one present had experienced before.

Rev. Stone kept a careful record of every manifestation during the weekend, and the following account essentially composes one chapter of his autobiography:

> The bodily agitations or exercises, attending the excitement in the beginning of this century, were various, and called by various names—as, the falling exercise—the jerks—the dancing exercise—the barking exercise—the laughing and singing exercise, etc. The falling exercise was very common among all classes, the saints and sinners of every age and of every grace, from the philosopher to the clown. The subject of this exercise would, generally, with a piercing scream, fall like a log on the floor, earth, or mud, and appear as dead. Of thousands of similar cases, I will mention one. At a meeting, two gay young ladies, sisters, were standing together attending to the exercises and preaching at the time. Instantly they both fell, with a shriek of distress, and lay for more than an hour apparently in a lifeless state. Their mother, a pious Baptist, was in great distress, fearing they would not revive. At length they began to exhibit symptoms of life, by crying fervently for mercy, and then relapsed into the same death-like state, with an awful gloom on their countenances. After awhile, the gloom on the face of one was succeeded by a heavenly smile, and she cried out, "Precious Jesus," and rose up and spoke of the love of God—the preciousness of Jesus, and of the glory of the gospel, to the surrounding crowd, in language almost superhuman, and pathetically exhorted all to repentance. In a little while after, the other sister was similarly exercised. From that time they became remarkably pious members of the church.

I have seen very many pious persons fall in the same way, from a sense of the danger of their unconverted children, brothers, or sisters—from a sense of the danger of their neighbors, and of the sinful world. I have heard them agonizing in tears and strong crying for mercy to be shown to sinners, and speaking like angels to all around.

The jerks cannot be so easily described. Sometimes the subject of the jerks would be affected in some one member of the body, and sometimes in the whole system. When the head alone was affected, it would be jerked backward and forward, or from side to side, so quickly that the features of the face could not be distinguished. When the whole system was affected, I have seen the person stand in one place, and jerk backward and forward in quick succession, their head nearly touching the floor behind and before. All classes, saints and sinners, the strong as well as the weak, were thus affected. I have inquired of those thus affected. They could not account for it; but some have told me that those were among the happiest seasons of their lives. I have seen some wicked persons thus affected, and all the time cursing the jerks, while they were thrown to the earth with violence. Though so awful to behold, I do not remember that any one of the thousands I have seen ever sustained an injury in body. This was as strange as the exercise itself.

An 1875 camp meeting

Mary Evans Picture Library

The dancing exercise. This generally began with the jerks, and was peculiar to professors of religion. The subject, after jerking awhile, began to dance, and then the jerks would cease. Such dancing was indeed heavenly to the spectators; there was nothing in it like levity, nor calculated to excite levity in the beholders. The smile of heaven shone on the countenance of the subject, and assimilated to angels appeared the whole person. Sometimes the motion was quick and sometimes slow. Thus they continued to move forward and backward in the same track or alley till nature seemed exhausted, and they would fall prostrate on the floor or earth, unless caught by those standing by. While thus exercised, I have heard their solemn praises and prayers ascending to God.

The barking exercise, (as opposers contemptuously called it,) was nothing but the jerks. A person affected with the jerks, especially in his head, would often make a grunt, or bark, if you please, from the suddenness of the jerk. This name of barking seems to have had its origin from an old Presbyterian preacher of East Tennessee. He had gone into the woods for private devotion, and was seized with the jerks. Standing near a sapling, he caught hold of it, to prevent his falling, and as his head jerked back, he uttered a grunt or kind of noise similar to a bark, his face being turned upwards. Some wag discovered him in this position, and reported that he found him barking up a tree.

The laughing exercise was frequent, confined solely with the religious. It was a loud, hearty laughter, but one *sui generis* ["of its own kind"]; it excited laughter in none else. The subject appeared rapturously solemn, and his laughter excited solemnity in saints and sinners. It is truly indescribable.

The running exercise was nothing more than, that persons feeling something of these bodily agitations, through fear, attempted to run away, and thus escape from them; but it commonly happened that they ran not far, before they fell, or became so greatly agitated that they could proceed no farther. I knew a young physician of a celebrated family, who came some distance to a big meeting to see the strange things he had heard of. He and a young lady had sportively agreed to watch over, and take care of each other, if either should fall. At length the physician felt something very uncommon, and started from the congregation to run into the woods; he was discovered running as for life, but did not proceed far till he fell down, and there lay till he submitted to the Lord, and afterwards became a zealous member of the church. Such cases were common.

> I shall close this chapter with the singing exercise. This is more unaccountable than any thing else I ever saw. The subject in a very happy state of mind would sing most melodiously, not from the mouth or nose, but entirely in the breast, the sounds issuing thence. Such music silenced every thing, and attracted the attention of all. It was most heavenly. None could ever be tired of hearing it. Doctor J. P. Campbell and myself were together at a meeting, and were attending to a pious lady thus exercised, and concluded it to be something surpassing any thing we had known in nature.
>
> Thus have I given a brief account of the wonderful things that happened in the great excitement in the beginning of this century. That there were many eccentricities, and much fanaticism in this excitement, was acknowledged by its warmest advocates; indeed it would have been a wonder, if such things had not appeared, in the circumstances of that time.[29]

Estimates of those touched by the Holy Spirit ranged from five hundred to a thousand at a time.

Among those in the audience were some detractors, of whom Robert W. Finley was one, even though he was the son of the builder of the Cane Ridge Meetinghouse, the Reverend James B. Finley. (Finley was also a successful circuit rider who had a powerful ministry among the Wyandot Indians of Ohio.) This is what he had to say of the events:

> On the way to the meeting I said to my companions, "If I fall, it must be by physical power, and not by singing and praying," and as I prided myself upon my manhood and courage, I had no fear of being overcome by any nervous excitability or being frightened into religion. We arrived upon the ground, and here a scene presented itself to my mind not only novel and unaccountable, but awful beyond description. A vast crowd, supposed by some to have amounted to twenty-five thousand, was collected together. The noise was like the roar of Niagara.

[29] Barton Stone, *Short History of the Life of Barton W. Stone*, 1847, Chapter 6, http://www.mun.ca/rels/restmov/texts/bstone/barton.html#ch_six.

The vast sea of human beings seemed to be agitated as if by a storm. I counted seven ministers, all preaching at one time; some on stumps, others in wagons, and one—the Reverend William Burke, now of Cincinnati—was standing on a tree which had in falling lodged against another. Some of the people were singing, others praying, some crying for mercy in the most piteous accents, while others were shouting most vociferously.

While witnessing these scenes a peculiarly strange sensation, such as I had never before felt, came over me. My heart beat tumultuously, my knees trembled, my lips quivered, and I felt as though I must fall to the ground. A strange supernatural power seemed to pervade the entire mass of mind there collected. I became so weak and powerless that I found it necessary to sit down.

Soon after I left and went into the woods, and there I strove to rally and man up my courage. I tried to philosophize in regard to these wonderful exhibitions, resolving them into mere sympathetic excitement, a kind of religious enthusiasm, inspired by songs and eloquent harangues. My pride was wounded, for I had supposed that my mental and physical strength and vigor could most successfully resist these influences.

After some time I returned to the scene of excitement, the waves of which, if possible, had risen still higher. The same awfulness of feeling came over me. I stepped upon a log, where I could have a better view of the surging sea of humanity. The scene that then presented itself to my mind was indescribable. At one time I saw at least five hundred swept down in a moment, as if a battery of a thousand guns had been opened upon them, and then immediately followed shrieks and shouts that rent the very heavens. My hair rose up on my head, my whole frame trembled, the blood ran cold in my veins, and I fled for the woods a second time, and wished I had stayed at home.

While I remained here my feelings became intense and insupportable. A sense of suffocation and blindness seemed to come over me, and I thought I was going to die. There being a tavern about half a mile off, I concluded to go and get some brandy and see if it would not strengthen my nerves.

After some time I got to the bar and took a dram and left, feeling that I was as near hell as I wished to be, either in this or the world to come. The brandy had no effect in allaying my feelings, but, if anything, made me worse.

Night at lengths came on and I was afraid to see any of my companions. I cautiously avoided them, fearing lest they should discover something the matter with me. In this state I wandered about from place to place, in and around the encampment. At times it seemed as if all the sins I had ever committed in my life were vividly brought up in array before my terrified imagination, and under their awful pressure I felt as if I must die if I did not get relief. My heart was so proud and hard that I would not have fallen to the ground for the whole State of Kentucky. I felt that such an event would have been an everlasting disgrace and put a final quietus on my boasted manhood and courage.

At night I went to a barn in the neighborhood, and, creeping under the hay, spent a most dismal night. I resolved in the morning to start for home, for I felt that I was a ruined man. Finding one of the friends who came over with me, I said: "Captain, let us be off; I will stay no longer." He assented, and, getting our horses, we started for home.

We said but little on the way, though many a deep, long-drawn sigh told the emotions of my heart. When we arrived at the Blue Lick knobs, I broke the silence, which reigned mutually between us. Like long-pent-up waters seeking for an avenue in the rock, the fountains of my soul were broken up, and I exclaimed: "Captain, if you and I don't stop our wickedness, the devil will get us both." Then came from my streaming eyes the bitter tears, and I could scarcely refrain from screaming aloud. Night approaching, we put up near Mayslick, the whole of which was spent by me in weeping and promising God if he would spare me till morning I would pray and try to mend my life and abandon my wicked courses....

> Men of the most depraved hearts and vicious habits were made new creatures, and a whole life of virtue subsequently confirmed the conversion.[30]

Robert Finley went on to become a lifelong minister of some importance in the Methodist Church.

Each evening as night fell, campfires were lit, and candles, lamps, and torches provided light for services that continued into the night. Reflected off the trees, this light must have created a wondrous atmosphere and inspired renewed reverence. Another witness gave the following testimony about what the evenings were like:

> The spectacle presented at night was one of the wildest grandeur. The glare of the blazing camp-fires falling on a dense assemblage of heads simultaneously bowed in adoration, and reflected back from the long ranges of tents upon every side; hundreds of lamps and candles suspended among the trees, together with numerous torches flashing to and fro, throwing an uncertain light upon the tremulous foliage, and giving an appearance of dim and indefinite extent to the depth of the forest; the solemn chanting of hymns swelling and falling on the night wind; the impassioned exhortations; the earnest prayers; the sobs, shrieks, or shouts, bursting from persons under intense agitation of mind; the sudden spasms which seized upon scores, and unexpectedly dashed them to the ground;—all conspired to invest the scene with terrific interest, and to work up the feelings to the highest pitch of excitement.[31]

At Cane Ridge, the Communion service had been planned for Sunday instead of Monday, and came off as planned. The tables for this were set up in the meetinghouse in the shape of a cross and could serve as many as a hundred people at a time. Estimates of those who actually participated range from 800 to 1,100, for only those

---

[30] Robert W. Finley, quoted in James R. Rodgers, *The Cane Ridge Meeting-House* (Cincinnati, OH: The Standard Publishing House, 1910), 59–62.

[31] Robert Davidson, *History of the Presbyterian Church in the State of Kentucky: With a Preliminary Sketch of the Churches in the Valley of Virginia* (New York: Robert Carter, 1847), 138.

A camp meeting on the Western frontier.
Library of Congress, 98508373

recognized as converts were allowed—in other words, primarily Presbyterians and Methodists. People from these two groups had been the chief organizers of the event. But because only the Presbyterians presided over Communion, the Methodists began to hold meetings outside, and they soon drew large crowds. A separate African-American service also began nearby. The attendees were likely members of the African Baptist Church.

Small prayer groups also developed during the meetings, and although they were not part of the schedule, they had a similar feel because of the organized agenda by which they operated. Hundreds of people began spontaneously exhorting anyone within earshot as the Spirit of God fell on them. This was the most remarkable manifestation of Cane Ridge, as these exhorters could be anyone—men or women, literate or illiterate, Caucasian or African-American, adults or children—and of any disposition, outgoing or timid. Because of such sights, camp meetings would soon earn the title "carnival of preachers," as one could walk among them and hear preachers from all sides.

In one instance, a seven-year-old girl named Barbara climbed up on a man's shoulder and began to speak with words far beyond her years, and when she was exhausted, she settled down to rest her head on the man's head as if to sleep. When a tenderhearted man nearby remarked, "Poor thing, she had better be laid down," she revived immediately to proclaim, "Don't call me poor, for Christ is my brother, God my father, and I have a kingdom to inherit, therefore do not call me poor, for I am rich in the blood of the Lamb."[32]

As more and more people were touched to exhort, even more were touched and convicted of their sins, which caused a low moaning to arise in the camp. Hymn singing became more pronounced,

[32] Letter from a man to his sister, 10 August 1801, http://www.mun.ca/rels/restmov/texts/accounts/letter8.html.

and all of the manifestations Rev. Stone had documented from the day before began occurring again. The Reverend Moses Hoge tried to describe such a scene in a letter to a friend:

> In time of preaching, if care is taken, there is but little confusion: and when that is over, and the singing, and praying, and exhorting begins, the audience is thrown into what I call real disorder. The careless fall down, cry out, tremble, and not infrequently are affected with convulsive twitchings. Among these the pious are very busy, singing, praying, conversing, falling down in extacies, fainting with joy, exhorting sinners, combating opposers, &c. Those who fall, lie some a longer, some a shorter time. Some get comfort, some do not when first down, when one gets through (it is their own phrase,) that is, obtains relief, the shout is raised glory to God for a new born soul. And the holy embrace follows. Whole nights are spent in this way, and that part of the day which is not employed in divine service. For they stayed upon the ground in both places all the days of the solemnity. Nothing that imagination can paint, can make a stronger impression on the mind, than one of those scenes. Sinners dropping down on every hand, shrieking, groaning, crying for mercy, convulsed; professors praying, agonizing, falling down in distress, for sinners or in raptures of joy! Some singing, some shouting, clapping their hands, hugging and even kissing, laughing; others talking to the distressed, to one another, or to opposers of the work, and all this at once.—No spectacle can excite a stronger sensation. And with what is doing, the darkness of the night, the solemnity of the place, and of the occasions, and conscious guilt, all conspire to make terror thrill through every power of the soul, and rouse it to awful attention.—As to the work in general there can be no question but it is of God.[33]

As people packed their belongings before the journey home on Monday, others were just beginning to show up to experience the outpouring for themselves. Prayer, preaching, exhorting, singing,

[33] Moses Hoge to Ashbel Green, 10 September 1801, http://www.mun.ca/rels/restmov/texts/accounts/letter3.html.

and manifestations of the Holy Spirit would continue until Thursday of that week. Estimates of those who were touched with "exercises of the Spirit" range from one thousand to three thousand—the same numbers that quantify the estimated number of converts.

Peter Cartwright was among those converted at a Communion service that summer, and he said of Cane Ridge,

> At a memorable place called "Cane Ridge," there was appointed a sacramental meeting by some of the Presbyterian ministers, at which meeting, seemingly unexpected by ministers or people, the mighty power of God was displayed in a very extraordinary manner; many were moved to tears, and bitter and loud crying for mercy. The meeting was protracted for weeks. Ministers of almost all denominations flocked in from far and near. The meeting was kept up by night and day. Thousands heard of the mighty work, and came on foot, on horseback, in carriages and wagons. It was supposed that there were in attendance at times during the meeting from twelve to twenty-five thousand people. Hundreds fell prostrate under the mighty power of God, as men slain in battle. Stands were erected in the woods from which preachers of different Churches proclaimed repentance toward God and faith in our Lord Jesus Christ, and it was supposed, by eye and ear witnesses, that between one and two thousand souls were happily and powerfully converted to God during the meeting. It was not unusual for one, two, three, and four to seven preachers to be addressing the listening thousands at the same time from the different stands erected for the purpose. The heavenly fire spread in almost every direction. It was said, by truthful witnesses, that at times more than one thousand

Fervent camp meeting attendees

Mary Evans Picture Library

> persons broke into loud shouting all at once, and that the shouts could be heard for miles around.
>
> From this camp-meeting, for so it ought to be called, the news spread through all the Churches, and through all the land, and it excited great wonder and surprise; but it kindled a religious flame that spread all over Kentucky and through many other states.[34]

Cane Ridge was the high point of the Kentucky revival, but it was far from exclusive. The year 1801 was one of "boiling-hot religion." Such manifestations of the Holy Spirit would continue through the rest of the Communion season of 1801, with the addition of speaking in unknown languages later that year, as described by a witness:

> They swooned away and lay for hours in the straw prepared for those "smitten of the Lord," or they started suddenly to flee away and fell prostrate as if shot by a sniper, or they took suddenly to jerking with apparently every muscle in their body until it seemed they would be torn to pieces or converted into marble, or they shouted and talked in unknown tongues.[35]

Kentucky and the young United States would be forever changed. The camp meeting set the precedent for America's being seen as an "evangelical nation."

The Aftermath

From Kentucky, the revival spread throughout the South and east over the mountains. As powerful a move of God as it was, however, it ended more quickly than it began. It seemed that most of the ministers involved had no idea how to react to the Holy Spirit's manifestations, which literally took over their meetings. While some groups, such as the Methodists, welcomed the format of the camp meetings and the "chaos" of God's Spirit falling on saints and sinners

---

[34] Peter Cartwright, *Autobiography of Peter Cartwright, The Backwoods Preacher*, ed. W. P. Strickland (Cincinnati: Cranston and Curts, 1856), 30–31.

[35] E. Merton Coulter, *College Life in the Old South* (New York: The Macmillan Company, 1928), 194–195, quoted in Vinson Synan, *The Holiness-Pentecostal Tradition: Charismatic Movements in the Twentieth Century* (Grand Rapids, MI: Wm. B. Eerdmans Publishing Co., 1997), 13.

alike, other denominations embraced the camp meeting only as a way of gathering people together annually.

While the camp meetings continued over the years, by the end of the Civil War, they would vary in focus from the Holiness movement, which was a precursor to the Azusa Street Revival, to the Chautauqua meetings, which quickly concentrated more on intellectual pursuits than on spiritual matters. Many camp meetings were also tightly structured, with rules as strict as "No giggling after ten o'clock" and "No chopping wood before six."[36]

Though the abolition movement quickly became associated with most camp meetings—Christians being the most ardent supporters of abolition, temperance, and women's suffrage—African-Americans and Native Americans rarely mixed with others in these camp meetings. They generally had separate gatherings nearby. Revival struck again in the years preceding the Civil War, but racial lines were crossed rarely, if ever, until many years after the war. In spite of this fact, African-American pastors, such as Richard Allen of the Philadelphia African Methodist Episcopal Church, saw their church memberships swell to as many as 7,500. A few years prior to the events in Kentucky, Francis Asbury had dedicated Allen's building, and he later ordained him as a deacon in 1799.

Anyone who tried to fit the works of God witnessed during the summer of 1801 into some kind of man-made, doctrinal box would see no more of such manifestations. Other groups would leave their denominations to form new ones in order to continue pursuing these "exercises of the Spirit." Because of the events that transpired at Cane Ridge, the Cumberland Valley congregations would break away from mainline Presbyterianism to become the Cumberland Presbyterian Church, and Barton Stone would join Alexander Campbell to embrace a "Bible-only" Christianity. They formed a new group, which they called the "Disciples of Christ" or the "Churches of Christ." James McGready, however, was a notable figure who refused to leave the other Presbyterians; he would never become part of the Cumberland group. The Shakers, or "Shaking Quakers," as they were later called, also emerged from meetings

[36] Theodore Morrison, *Chautauqua, a Center for Education, Religion, and the Arts in America* (Chicago: The University of Chicago Press, 1974), 35, quoted in Brown, *Holy Ground*, 39.

similar to the camp meetings of that summer. They would try to start radically new cultures whose aims were serving and seeking God above all else. During the five decades leading up to the Civil War, roughly 120 similar social communities were built to experiment with communities based on the Word of God. Few of these experiments, however, celebrated even temporary success.

Peter Cartwright described these results in his *Autobiography*:

> As Presbyterian, Methodist, and Baptist ministers all united in the blessed work at this meeting, when they returned home to their different congregations, and carried the news of this mighty work, the revival spread rapidly throughout the land; but many of the ministers and members of the synod of Kentucky thought it all disorder, and tried to stop the work. They called their preachers who were engaged in the revival to account, and censured and silenced them. These ministers then rose up and unitedly renounced the jurisdiction of the Presbyterian Church, organized a Church of their own, and dubbed it with the name of Christian. Here was the origin of what was called the New Lights. They renounced the Westminster Confession of Faith, and all Church discipline, and professed to take the New Testament for their Church discipline. They established no standard of doctrine; every one was to take the New Testament, read it, and abide his own construction of it. Marshall, M'Namar, Dunlevy, Stone, Huston, and others, were the chief leaders in this trash trap. Soon a diversity of opinion sprang up, and they got into a Babel confusion. Some preached Arian, some Socinian, and some Universalist doctrines; so that in a few years you could not tell what was harped or what was danced. They adopted the mode of immersion, the water-god of all exclusive errorists; and directly there was a mighty controversy about the way to heaven, whether it was by water or by dry land....
>
> This Christian, or New Light Church, is a feeble and scattered people, though there are some good Christians among them. I suppose since the day of Pentecost, there was hardly ever a greater revival of religion than at Cane

> Ridge; and if there had been steady, Christian ministers, settled in Gospel doctrine and Church discipline, thousands might have been saved to the Church that wandered off in the mazes of vain, speculative divinity, and finally made shipwreck of the faith, fell back, turned infidel, and lost their religion and their souls forever. But evidently a new impetus was given to the work of God, and many, very many, will have cause to bless God forever for this revival of religion throughout the length and breadth of our Zion.[37]

Though the summer of 1802 would be nothing like the previous summer, it would be the first year that the term "camp meeting" was used in everyday vocabulary. The term endures today; for example, organizations such as Kenneth Hagin Ministries sponsor "camp meetings" every summer. For decades following 1802, Methodists would see their own camp meetings spread to every state, as Francis Asbury became a strong proponent of this revival format. Nothing like Cane Ridge would happen again, however, until the Pentecostal Revival at the turn of the next century.

Many people acknowledged that the hand of God was behind what happened in Kentucky in 1801, but glowing reports came only from those who had experienced the Communions of that season. As Paul Conklin, author of *Cane Ridge: America's Pentecost*, put it,

> By the fall of 1801 evangelical visitors to the central counties of Kentucky marveled at a near utopia. The Spirit of God had burned and cleansed the whole area. Practically everyone had been somehow affected by the revival. George Baxter, when he arrived from the Shenandoah Valley, thought he breathed a special, cleansed air in Kentucky. He found "the most moral place I had ever been in," for he heard no profane expressions, everyone was amiable and benevolent, no private quarrels remained, and "a religious awe seemed to pervade the country."[38]

---

[37] Cartwright, *Autobiography*, 31–33.

[38] Conklin, *Cane Ridge: America's Pentecost*, 115–116; quotes from Baxter to Archibald Alexander, 1 January 1802, quoted in *Increase of Piety, or The Revival of Religion in the United States of America, et cetera* (Newburyport, MA: Angier March, 1802), 63–64.

Baxter summed up his impressions with these words:

> I think the revival in Kentucky among the most extraordinary that have ever visited the church of Christ, and all things considered, peculiarly adapted to the circumstances of that country. Infidelity was triumphant and religion at the point of expiring. Something of an extraordinary nature seemed necessary to arrest the attention of a giddy people, who were ready to conclude that Christianity was a fable, and futurity a dream. This revival has done it; it has confounded infidelity, awed vice into silence, and brought numbers beyond calculation, under serious impressions.[39]

This sketch depicts a camp meeting in the countryside of Tennessee.

Mary Evans Picture Library

The Kentucky Communions would be the first winds to fan the flame of the Second Great Awakening. Cane Ridge rang in the nineteenth century, and Azusa Street rang in the twentieth. We Christians of the twenty-first century need to rise up and pray that God will shake this century from its secular complacency—and to a greater degree than He shook Kentucky in the summers of 1800 and 1801. And we need more believers like those whose faith was refined by such revivals—Christians with the courage of Peter Cartwright and the praying tenacity of James McGready and Charles Finney.

---

[39] Baxter to Archibald Alexander, 1 January 1802, quoted in *Increase of Piety, or The Revival of Religion in the United States of America, et cetera*, http://www.mun.ca/rels/restmov/texts/accounts/letter12.html.

Chapter Six

★★★★★

Peter Cartwright

(1785–1872)

"The Pistol-toting Evangelist"

"The Pistol-toting Evangelist"

Love every body and fear no man.

—Peter Cartwright's motto

It is sometimes said that hard times call for hard men, and this statement certainly applies to Peter Cartwright. He would make the American frontier his congregation for roughly seventy years of his life. If ever there was someone who took Paul's advice to *"fight the good fight"* (1 Timothy 6:12) and, like Paul, was able to say, *"So fight I, not as one that beateth the air"* (1 Corinthians 9:26), it was Cartwright. He was never afraid to confront a heckler—with a fist to the jaw, if needed—or discharge his pistol into the air to quiet a crowd.

On the American frontier, the battle for religion was as fierce as the battle for land. It seemed that this was another time when *"the kingdom of heaven suffereth violence, and the violent take it by force"* (Matthew 11:12). Peter Cartwright was just the man to advance the kingdom of God in this time, through his grit and his wit. His nickname, the "Backwoods Preacher," was well earned, and he was an American hero to rival the likes of Daniel Boone and Davy Crockett.

Growing Up on the Frontier

Peter Cartwright was born on September 1, 1785, in Amherst County, Virginia, to Peter Cartwright Sr. and Christiana Garvin, one and a half years before they were married. According to a newspaper story from Civil War times, Peter was born while his mother was hiding in a dense cluster of cane trees to protect herself from an Indian attack.[1] His father was a two-year veteran of the Revolutionary War. When Peter was about five years old, the family moved into the newly opened Kentucky territory. Their harrowing journey attests to Kentucky's wild past.

When the Cartwright family moved westward in 1790–1791, Kentucky was still an unbroken wilderness—the land of "canes and turkeys"—with no roads and few towns. It was a Promised Land to many poor Easterners, complete with warring tribes to withstand and overcome. Violence and fighting between Native Americans was so rife that the group of two hundred families heading west required an escort of one hundred well-armed young men. Because there were no roads, the families traveled with pack horses instead of wagons. This made them attractive targets for the disgruntled tribes, who were unhappy about the settlers taking over their hunting grounds. Less than one day into their passage through the Cumberland Gap, the travelers came across the bodies of another group that had been murdered and scalped by a Native American war party. This discovery was not isolated. They came across several such sites during their trek, and it was not uncommon for the scouts to see small groups of Indians lurking in the trees nearby.

On their first Sunday in Kentucky, the group voted to move on rather than rest. It was a dreary day, with mist and rain. The gloom did not help the settlers' mood, nor did the campsite they chose that night—a place that had been nicknamed "Camp Defeat" after a large group of settlers was massacred there. Rumors of imminent ambush circulated within the camp.

Peter's father was placed as a sentinel at the edge of the brush surrounding the camp. A heavy cloud cover obscured the evening moon and stars, and soon after the camp had grown quiet for the evening, he heard what sounded like a pig rustling and grunting not far from him. Recalling that no one had brought a pig on the journey, he was frightened. He aimed his gun at a dark form he saw moving toward him, fired, turned on his heels, and ran back to camp.

The gunshot roused the entire camp, and everybody wanted to know what had happened. When Peter's father explained himself,

---

[1] Robert Bray, *Peter Cartwright, Legendary Frontier Preacher* (Urbana: University of Illinois Press, 2005), 7.

some scoffed, saying he was just scared and wanted an excuse to return to the camp with the women and children. To prove that he was not a coward, he demanded a lantern and set off with a group of men to investigate the area where he had fired the shot. When they reached the site, the light of his lantern revealed an Indian brave—tomahawk in one hand, rifle in the other—lying dead in the brush. Cartwright's rifle ball had struck near the center of his forehead. Few people slept that night, but there were no further alarms. Never had they seen so beautiful a sunrise as they saw the next morning.

Young Peter was more of a rogue than a Christian, yet his mother prayed constantly for his reform.

A few days later, the group of travelers came upon a man who had been shot in the face. He was the sole survivor of a party of seven. Days later, the party approached Crab Orchard, the first settlement and fort they would reach in Kentucky. Feeling like they had finally reached a safe haven, the party divided as darkness fell, as some wanted to rest and continue on the next day. Seven families stayed behind, while the remainder of the travelers pressed on into the darkness to reach Crab Orchard. Of the seven families that stayed behind, only one man escaped, barefooted, to recount the attack and slaughter of the others at the hands of a raiding party. The captain of the fort organized a group to find the raiding party and recapture all that had been seized from the slaughtered families. Of the twenty-five Indians responsible for the massacre, only one survived.

After this episode, Peter's father took his family to Lincoln County, where they lived for two years on a rented farm. From there, they moved to Logan County, still known at that time as "Rogue's Harbor," even though many of the murderers and horse thieves who had earned it that name had already moved further west. As homesteaders moved in, local men formed a group and called themselves the Regulators. They did what they could to establish a rule of law in this wilderness and to chase outlaws away.

The Cartwright homestead was located about nine miles south of the county seat, Russellville, and just one mile north of the Kentucky-Tennessee border. There were no grain mills for forty miles, so they would grind their own meal and sift it through deerskin with holes turned in it, which was stretched over a hoop. They would typically eat the meat of freshly killed animals, and would gather herbs and tea leaves from the woods. They also made their own sugar and molasses from maple sap.

Though Peter's mother had become a member of the Methodist Episcopal Church, the young Peter was more of a rogue than a Christian, given his passions for card playing, horseracing, and dancing. His father held some sway over him, but it was his mother who wept and prayed constantly for his reform. At times, he was moved by her words, or would attend a meeting where he vowed to seek God more earnestly, but these moments of remorse were fleeting. He would inevitably find himself in the company of other young people fond of gambling and dancing, and he always joined in their pastimes.

To make matters worse, Peter's father bought him a fine horse that proved a strong racer. He also bought him a pack of cards, and while Peter never cheated, he did become rather proficient at gambling to win money, which grew into an addiction. He called himself "naturally a wild, wicked boy."[2]

When Peter was fourteen or fifteen, his family sent him to live with a man named Dr. Beverly Allen so that he could attend a school near Allen's house. Allen had been a Methodist preacher, but an illicit love affair had pitted him against the law. In an effort to escape the Georgia community's retribution for this relationship, he had shot and killed a sheriff who tried to apprehend him. Afterward, he had fled to "Rogues Harbor." His immediate family soon followed him there, and he set up an office to practice medicine. The school Peter attended proved rather poor, but it did teach Peter to read and write.

The Holy Spirit Falls on Kentucky

Peter was sixteen when the four-day Communions of James McGready and others brought revival to Kentucky. Peter found himself in the thick of this wave of the Holy Spirit—a wave that

[2] Cartwright, *Autobiography*, 27.

ultimately converted him. In his *Autobiography*, he described his conversion:

> In 1801, when I was in my sixteenth year, my father, my eldest half brother, and myself, attended a wedding about five miles from home, where there was a great deal of drinking and dancing, which was very common of marriages those days. I drank little or nothing; my delight was in dancing. After a late hour in the night, we mounted our horses and started for home. I was riding my race-horse.
>
> A few minutes after we had put up the horses, and were sitting by the fire, I began to reflect on the manner in which I had spent the day and evening. I felt guilty and condemned. I rose and walked the floor. My mother was in bed. It seemed to me, all of a sudden, my blood rushed to my head, my heart palpitated, in a few minutes I turned blind; an awful impression rested on my mind that death had come and I was unprepared to die. I fell on my knees and began to ask God to have mercy on me.
>
> My mother sprang from her bed, and was soon on her knees by my side, praying for me, and exhorting me to look to Christ for mercy, and then and there I promised the Lord that if he would spare me, I would seek and serve him; and I never fully broke that promise. My mother prayed for me a long time. At length we lay down, but there was little sleep for me. Next morning I rose, feeling wretched beyond expression. I tried to read in the Testament, and retired many times to secret prayer through the day, but found no relief. I gave up my race-horse to my father, and requested him to sell him. I went and brought my pack of cards, and gave them to mother, who threw them into the fire, and they were consumed. I fasted, watched, and prayed, and engaged in regular reading of the Testament. I was so distressed and miserable, that I was incapable of any regular business.
>
> My father was greatly distressed on my account, thinking I must die, and he would lose his only son. He bade me retire altogether from business, and take care of myself.

Peter Cartwright

Soon it was noised abroad that I was distracted, and many of my associates in wickedness came to see me, to try and divert my mind from those gloomy thoughts of my wretchedness; but all in vain. I exhorted them to desist from the course of wickedness which we had been guilty of together. The class-leader and local preacher were sent for. They tried to point me to the bleeding Lamb, they prayed for me most fervently. Still I found no comfort, and although I had never believed in the doctrine of unconditional election and reprobation, I was sorely tempted to believe I was a reprobate, and doomed, and lost eternally, without any chance of salvation.

At length one day I retired to the horse-lot, and was walking and wringing my hands in great anguish, trying to pray, on the borders of utter despair. It appeared to me that I heard a voice from heaven, saying, "Peter, look at me." A feeling of relief flashed over me as quick as an electric shock. It gave me hopeful feelings, and some encouragement to seek mercy, but still my load of guilt remained. I repaired to the house, and told my mother what had happened to me in the horse-lot. Instantly she seemed to understand it, and told me the Lord had done this to encourage me to hope for mercy, and exhorted me to take encouragement, and seek on, and God would bless me with the pardon of my sins at another time.

Some days after this, I retired to a cave on my father's farm to pray in secret. My soul was in an agony; I wept, I prayed, and said, "Now, Lord, if there is mercy for me, let me find it," and it really seemed to me that I could almost lay hold of the Saviour, and realize a reconciled God. All of a sudden, such a fear of the devil fell upon me that it really appeared to me that he was surely personally there, to seize and drag me down to hell, soul and body, and such a horror fell on me that I sprang to my feet and ran to my mother at the house. My mother told me this was a device of Satan to prevent me from finding the blessing then. Three months rolled away, and still I did not find the blessing of the pardon of my sins....

In the spring of this year, Mr. M'Grady [McGready], a minister of the Presbyterian Church, who had a congregation and meeting-house, as we then called them, about three miles north of my father's house, appointed a sacramental meeting in this congregation, and invited the Methodist preachers to attend with them, and especially John Page, who was a powerful Gospel minister, and was very popular among the Presbyterians. Accordingly he came, and preached with great power and success.

There were no camp-meetings in regular form at this time, but as there was a great waking up among the Churches, from the revival that had broken out at Cane Ridge [this remarkable Communion service was actually later that same year]...many flocked to those sacramental meetings. The church would not hold the tenth part of the congregation. Accordingly, the officers of the Church erected a stand in a contiguous shady grove, and prepared seats for a large congregation. The people crowded to this meeting from far and near. They came in their large wagons, with victuals mostly prepared. The women slept in the wagons, and the men under them. Many stayed on the ground night and day for a number of nights and days together. Others were provided for among the neighbors around. The power of God was wonderfully displayed; scores of sinners fell under the preaching, like men slain in mighty battle; Christians shouted aloud for joy.

To this meeting I repaired, a guilty, wretched sinner. On the Saturday evening of said meeting, I went, with weeping multitudes, and bowed before the stand, and earnestly prayed for mercy. In the midst of a solemn struggle of soul, an impression was made on my mind, as though a voice said to me, "Thy sins are all forgiven thee." Divine light flashed all round me, unspeakable joy sprung up in my soul. I rose to my feet, opened my eyes, and it really seemed as if I was in heaven; the trees, the leaves on them, and everything seemed, and I really thought were, praising God. My mother raised the shout, my Christian friends crowded around me and joined me in praising God; and

> though I have been since then, in many instances, unfaithful, yet I have never, for one moment, doubted that the Lord did, then and there, forgive my sins and give me religion.[3]

Held at the Red River Meetinghouse, this meeting was in June, near the start of the biggest Communion season ever. The meeting lasted the entire night with no pauses or breaks, and more than eighty people found peace with God. Peter described what resulted from that summer's revival:

> In this revival originated our camp-meetings, and in both these denominations they were held every year, and, indeed, have been ever since, more or less. They would erect their camps with logs or frame them, and cover them with clapboards or shingles. They would also erect a shed, sufficiently large to protect five thousand people from wind and rain, and cover it with boards or shingles; build a large stand, seat the shed, and here they would collect together from forty to fifty miles around, sometimes further than that. Ten, twenty, and sometimes thirty ministers, of different denominations, would come together and preach night and day, four or five days together; and, indeed, I have known these camp-meetings to last three or four weeks, and great good resulted from them. I have seen more than a hundred sinners fall like dead men under one powerful sermon, and I have seen and heard more than five hundred Christians all shouting aloud the high praises of God at once; and I will venture to assert that many happy thousands were awakened and converted to God at these camp-meetings. Some sinners mocked, some of the old dry professors opposed, some of the old starched Presbyterian preachers preached against these exercises, but still the work went on and spread almost in every direction, gathering additional force, until our country seemed all coming home to God.[4]

Peter spent much of that summer going from one Communion service to the next, hungering continually for God and growing ever

---

[3] Cartwright, *Autobiography*, 34–38.

[4] Ibid., 45–46.

bolder in his faith. He participated in many small prayer meetings that the young men would start on the periphery of the gatherings, and in doing so, he helped several men come to the Lord. At one such meeting, a number of detractors spoke against the meeting, including a rather intelligent man who said he was Jewish and seemed to enjoy opposing Christians. At one point, he observed Peter and several other young men assembling one of these small prayer groups, and he approached them to investigate. Peter recalled this incident in his *Autobiography*:

> In the midst of our little meeting this Jew appeared, and he desired to know what we were about. Well, I told him. He said it was all wrong, that it was idolatry to pray to Jesus Christ, and that God did not nor would he answer such prayers. I soon saw his object was to get us into debate and break up our prayer-meeting. I asked him, "Do you really believe there is a God?"
>
> "Yes, I do," said he.
>
> "Do you believe that God will hear your prayers?"
>
> "Yes," said he.
>
> "Do you really believe that this work among us is wrong?"
>
> He answered, "Yes."
>
> "Well now, my dear sir," said I, "let us test this matter. If you are in earnest, get down here and pray to God to stop this work, and if it is wrong he will answer your petition and stop it; if it is not wrong, all hell cannot stop it."
>
> The rest of our company seeing me so bold took courage. The Jew hesitated. I said, "Get down instantly and pray, for if we are wrong we want to know it." After still lingering and showing unmistakable signs of his unwillingness, I rallied him again. Slowly he kneeled, cleared his throat, and coughed. I said, "Now, boys, pray with all your might that God may answer by fire."
>
> Our Jew began and said, tremblingly, "O Lord God Almighty," and coughed again, cleared his throat, and started again, repeating the same words. We saw his evident confusion, and we simultaneously prayed out aloud

> at the top of our voices. The Jew leaped up and started off, and we raised the shout and had a glorious time. Several of our mourners were converted, and we all rose and started into camp at the top of our speed, shouting, having, as we firmly believed, obtained a signal victory over the devil and the Jew.[5]

The Kentucky Boy Starts Out

At the start of the Communion season the following year, Peter was surprised when his pastor presented him with a letter that acknowledged him as an "exhorter" for the Methodists.

> Peter Cartwright is hereby permitted to exercise his gifts as an exhorter in the Methodist Episcopal Church, so long as his practice is agreeable to the Gospel. Signed in behalf of the society at Ebenezer.
>
> Jesse Walker, A. P.
> May, 1802.[6]

Peter had not sought this office, but he was persuaded to accept it. One provision of the office was that if the Spirit came upon him to preach, he could know that he had the right to do so.

That fall, Peter's father moved the family to Lewiston County, near the mouth of the Cumberland River—an area that just happened to be eighty miles from the nearest Methodist circuit. Peter and his mother asked for letters of membership so that they could hold meetings in their house, and in response, Peter received a letter authorizing him to form a preaching circuit in the area. This permission was much more than he had expected, let alone hoped for. He had been planning to attend school, and had considered circuit preaching too great a responsibility for him. Brother Page, the presiding elder from whom Peter had requested the letters of membership, told him that preaching

> was the very best school or college that I could find between heaven and earth, but advised me, when my father got settled down there, if I could find a good moral school

---

[5] Cartwright, *Autobiography*, 56–57.

[6] Ibid., 58.

> with a good teacher, to go to it through the winter; then, in the spring and summer, form the circuit and do the best I could.[7]

Peter agreed with Page, and he found a school that looked promising. It did not work out, however, because the teacher, though he was a minister, hated Methodists "more than he hated the devil."[8] The other boys at the school branded Peter with the name "The Methodist Preacher" and taunted him, little deterred by the schoolmaster. At one point, two of the boys decided to throw Peter into a nearby creek at a place where the bank was about seven feet high, and the pool about ten feet deep. To lure Peter to the riverbank, they feigned anguish for their sins and asked him to pray for them. He was suspicious of the authenticity of their request, but not wanting to reject them in case they were in earnest, he agreed to go. When they reached the clearing above the bank, the two boys tried to grab Peter, but he ducked and, in an instant, flung one of them over the bank and wrestled the other to the ground. The two boys, being of roughly equal strength, had attempted to overpower Peter's efforts, but they soon found themselves at the brink of the bank, which they proceeded to tumble over together before plummeting into the pool.

Peter prayed for one convert to prove that his call to preach was authentic and God-given.

Not appreciating his classmates' abuse, and feeling he would learn little in this academic environment, Peter went out to form the circuit and reported back as had been requested of him in the fall of 1804. Jesse Walker was appointed to the circuit, and he rode it for the next two years. Methodism was growing rapidly in the Western district.

Peter was eighteen, and he was asked to travel with another circuit rider to aid him with his work. In spite of his father's objections, his mother urged him to accept help, and her exhortations prevailed. Along the route, Peter was asked to give the evening service. Peter

[7] Cartwright, *Autobiography*, 59–60.

[8] Ibid., 60.

had no experience with evening services, let alone assurance that he was called to conduct them. He prayed fervently for God to help him, asking God to give him one convert that night as evidence that his call to preach was authentic and God-given. His preaching that night was met with tears and sighs, and one young man who had been known as a heathen gave his heart to the Lord and joined the church. Peter then felt the certain calling of God on his life. He travelled the circuit for three months, saw twenty-five more people converted, and received a six-dollar payment at the end. Peter became known as the "boy preacher" or the "Kentucky boy," and would ride a circuit for the next sixty-seven years.

A Funeral Service Leads to Revival

Peter was soon summoned to conduct a funeral service in an old Baptist meetinghouse. During the service, the Holy Spirit fell, just as He had during the camp meetings. Peter stayed awhile in order to minister night and day, and every meeting saw a manifestation of the Holy Spirit. Peter saw twenty-three people saved, and would have immediately had them join the Methodist Church, but he had to contend with the local Baptist church for its members. In order to do this, he pretended to be a membership candidate at the Baptist church. He attended their meeting, gave his testimony, and was acknowledged as being saved.

The Baptists invited him to be baptized the next day in a nearby creek. When they had assembled at the creek, Peter made sure he was first in line. He proclaimed that he had already been baptized, through sprinkling of water, to the satisfaction of his conscience; he did not need to be baptized again. When the Baptist minister refused him church membership, he managed to draw the twenty-three new converts away from the Baptist church because of its strict adherence to this doctrine of baptism. Peter then signed twenty-three people into membership in the Methodist Church. Later in life, Peter would say of the Baptists, "Indeed, they made so much ado about baptism by immersion, that the uninformed would suppose that heaven was an island, and there was no way to get there but by diving or swimming."[9]

[9] Ibid., 134.

Peter continued itinerating, and at the Western Conference of 1806, Francis Asbury ordained him as a deacon in the Methodist Episcopal Church. It was not uncommon in the earlier years for Bishop Asbury to travel with an armed guard through the rough Indian country of the West, but he never considered postponing or canceling his personal visits to conferences. Dangers abounded, but the Bishop never had a problem getting through.

Cover of Harper's Weekly, which features the "circuit preacher," modeled after Peter Cartwright

Library of Congress, 98506148

After his ordination, Peter was sent northeast to the Ohio border, where he met his first Yankees. He had been opposed to this trip initially, but when Francis Asbury took him by the arms and said, "O no, my son; go in the name of the Lord. It will make a man of you,"[10] he could hardly refuse. This particular area seemed filled with various sects, including Universalism, Unitarianism, and deism, and exposure to these groups proved a veritable seminary experience for the young Peter, as he had to pore over his Bible to find rebuttals to the teachings and beliefs of these groups. During this time, Peter honed his skill and sharpened his wit as a powerful debater.

Opening Spiritual Territory

The West was in many ways a religious free-for-all at the beginning of the nineteenth century, and saints and scoundrels alike came to preach their gospels. Those who claimed to see visions and to hear God speak to them individually were rife, and many people were gullible, too quick to believe bluffing charlatans. One such charlatan once made his way into the forest a short distance from town, sprinkled some gunpowder on a tree stump, set it off with a cigar, and fell to the ground. When the townspeople heard the bang and

[10] Cartwright, *Autobiography*, 98.

saw the flash, they ran to see what had happened. They found the man lying trancelike on the ground. When the crowd had swelled to a sufficient size, however, he roused himself and began to tell them that God had struck him down in a flash of light and had given him a vision. As he was telling his tale, Peter approached, smelled the sulfur from the gunpowder, and exposed him as the fraud he was.

> As soon as I came near the stump, I smelted the sulphur of the powder; and stepping up to the stump, there was clearly the sign of powder, and hard by lay the cigar with which he had ignited it. He was now busy delivering his message. I stepped up to him, and asked him if an angel had appeared to him in that flash of light.
>
> He said, "Yes."
>
> Said I, "Sargent, did not that angel smell of brimstone?"
>
> "Why," said he, "do you ask me such a foolish question?"
>
> "Because," said I, "if an angel has spoken to you at all, he was from the lake that burneth with fire and brimstone!" and raising my voice, I said, "I smell sulphur now!" I walked up to the stump, and called on the people to come and see for themselves. The people rushed up, and soon saw through the trick, and began to abuse Sargent for a vile impostor. He soon left, and we were troubled no more with him or his brimstone angels.[11]

Unfortunately, not all of the religious scam artists were as easy to expose as this man.

At the end of his apportioned time in Ohio, Peter found himself in dire straits:

> I had been from my father's house about three years; was five hundred miles from home; my horse had gone blind; my saddle was worn out; my bridle reins had been eaten up and replaced, (after a sort) at least a dozen times; and my clothes had been patched till it was difficult to detect the original.[12]

[11] Ibid., 101–102.

[12] Ibid., 102.

He decided to make his way home, but he had only seventy-five cents in his pocket for the journey. Deciding he had no other choice, he struck out, determined to borrow the money to cover the expenses of food and lodging, if necessary. During the journey, however, God supplied his every expense, from ferry tolls to one night's fare at an inn—the innkeeper waived the fee when Peter ministered to his disturbed wife and led her to salvation.

> His wife was subject to spasms, and often had them. I commenced a conversation with her about religion. I found she was under deep concern about her soul. I asked if I might pray for her. "O, yes," she replied, "for there is no one in this place that cares for my soul."
>
> I knelt and prayed, and then commenced singing, and directed her to Christ as an all-sufficient Saviour, and prayed again. She suddenly sprung out of the bed and shouted, "Glory to God! he has blessed my soul." It was a happy time indeed. The old gentleman wept like a child. We sung and shouted, prayed and praised, nearly all night. Next morning the old landlord told me my bill was paid tenfold, and that all he charged me was, every time I passed that way, to call and stay with them.[13]

The next day, Peter arrived home with only six and a quarter cents left. His parents greeted him warmly—his mother, especially warmly—and welcomed the stories of his adventures as a preacher. Before Peter set out for his next conference and circuit assignment, his father gave him "a fresh horse, a bridle and saddle, some new clothes, and forty dollars in cash. Thus equipped, I was ready for another three years' absence."[14] Remuneration was often scant for circuit riders, and tales of barely getting by, surviving on the grace of God, were not uncommon.

Peter Marries Frances

The next conference was in Chillicothe, Ohio, on September 14, 1807, roughly two weeks after Peter's twenty-second birthday. He was assigned a circuit closer to home in the Cumberland district

[13] Cartwright, *Autobiography*, 106–107.

[14] Ibid., 107.

under James Ward, the district's presiding elder. It was in this area that he met and began to court Miss Frances Gaines. Breaking with the tradition of celibacy set forth by Bishop Francis Asbury and Peter's own bishop, William McKendree, he married Frances on her nineteenth birthday, August 18, 1808. Of this departure from tradition, Peter said, "After mature deliberation and prayer...I thought it was my duty to marry,"[15] and that seemed adequate justification for him, as he had consulted none of his superiors on the matter. Peter and Frances celebrated their infare (a combined wedding reception and housewarming[16]) with his parents the following September, on Peter's twenty-third birthday.

Peter would not give up itinerating, even after he was married.

That year, the Western Conference convened in Liberty Hill, Tennessee (just south of Nashville), on October 1. Peter left his wife with his family and headed to Tennessee, weighed down with the knowledge that he would have to inform Bishop McKendree of his marriage. McKendree said that he was sorry, not that Peter had married, but that it meant he would have to settle in one place—an obligation that could hurt his promotion significantly. Peter accepted with grace, but became fired up to show his determination. "It raised my ambitions and I became pretty spunky, and I just said, Now, here goes; I can work for my living, I can split rails, plow, grub, mow, cradle, or reap. I was raised to it."[17] And he would not give up itinerating. He would work his farm and ride his circuit without compromise. McKendree must have appreciated Peter's determination, for he made him an elder in the Methodist Church before the end of the conference.

Peter carried a pistol with him at all times. Once, while he was traveling on horseback with a fellow minister, Brother Walker, a lame man using a large stick as a crutch struck out across the road in front of them. The man asked for a ride a little way up the road, as

---

[15] Ibid., 111.

[16] Bray, *Peter Cartwright, Legendary Frontier Preacher*, 54.

[17] Peter Cartwright, *Fifty Years as a Presiding Elder* (Cincinnati, OH: Hitchcock and Walden, 1871), 217, quoted in Bray, *Peter Cartwright, Legendary Frontier Preacher*, 54.

he feared his strength would give out before he reached lodging for the night. Brother Walker said, "O yes," and started to dismount his horse, but Peter immediately felt impressed to say, "Keep your horse; we are a long way from home, have a long journey before us; under such circumstances trust no man."[18] So, the two men rode past, thinking they had left the man a hundred yards behind them. Suddenly, with Walker slightly ahead of him, Peter's horse started, and he turned to see the man running toward him "as fleet as a deer."[19] Obviously, his lameness had been a ruse by which he had hoped to rob the two preachers. Peter wheeled his horse around, pulled and cocked his gun, and bolted toward the man, who then disappeared into the thick forest brush at first sight of the pistol. Peter pursued him no further. He would later say that the words of warning had come into his mouth by the saving power of the Holy Spirit.

Issues of Slavery

As an elder, Peter was expected to engage actively in church politics, and he soon found himself embroiled in the debate over slavery. While the Methodist *Disciplines* forbade the purchase, sale, and ownership of slaves, southern Methodists in the United States had long disregarded that stipulation. Now it was becoming an issue in the West, where slavery, though sanctioned by law, was quickly losing popularity in the wake of the revivals and the growing support of abolitionism they had inspired. Slavery was an issue that Peter had avoided, at first; he considered it more political than spiritual. He did believe, however, that owning slaves was immoral, and his office as elder would not long permit neutrality on the issue. Members of the Methodist conferences soon became divided along pro-slavery versus abolitionist lines. This spirit of divisiveness came up whenever a slave owner was nominated for ordination as a minister, raising the question, "Could a man who owned slaves be welcomed as a minister for the Methodist Episcopal Church?" In his *Autobiography*, Peter had this to say about the matter:

> Slavery had long been agitated in the Methodist Episcopal Church, and our preachers, although they did not feel it to

---

[18] Cartwright, *Autobiography*, 201.

[19] Ibid.

> be their duty to meddle with it politically, yet, as Christians and Christian ministers, be it spoken to their eternal credit, they believed it to be their duty to bear their testimony against slavery as a moral evil, and this is the reason why the General Conference, from time to time, passed rules and regulations to govern preachers and members of the Church in regard to this great evil. The great object of the General Conference was to keep the ministry clear of it, and there can be no doubt that the course pursued by early Methodist preachers was the cause of the emancipation of thousands of this degraded race of human beings; and it is clear to my mind, if Methodist preachers had kept clear of slavery themselves, and gone on bearing honest testimony against it, that thousands upon thousands more would have been emancipated who are now groaning under an oppression almost too intolerable to be borne. Slavery is certainly a domestic, political, and moral evil.[20]

Not all of Peter's fellow elders felt this way, however, for many of them owned slaves. And while Peter's cantankerous nature won him much support in the fight to end slavery, it also made him a focal point for the opposition, who said he was merely opposing slavery to cause trouble and advance his position in the church leadership. The issue was tabled at the 1808 conference because the debate seemed so heated, but it would only grow more so in the coming years.

Peter at War with "The Shakers"

Peter was assigned to the Salt River circuit, an area where he had been assigned during his first tour of duty from 1804 to 1805. Though he had left the area strong in its Methodism, it was now being overrun with Shakers, or, as they also called themselves, the "United Society of Believers in Christ's Second Appearing." This group's leader was an Englishwoman they called "Mother Ann Lee," supposedly an embodiment of the returned Christ, whom they called upon to prepare communities for the millennial reign of Jesus on the earth, as foretold in the book of Revelation. It was a cult of preposterous self-proclaimed authority, and not one with which

[20] Ibid., 128.

Methodism could comfortably coexist. Therefore, Peter went to war with them, so to speak—he battled through debate. Peter and his "armor bearer," John Davison, shook the Shakers rather thoroughly and brought many people back to Methodism, reestablishing the area as a strong circuit.

Sometime during the winter of 1808 or the spring of 1809, Peter's father passed away. As soon as he heard the news, Peter returned home, but not in time to attend the funeral or burial. The following year, Peter was appointed to Livingston Circuit, where his father's farm was located—the land that constituted the homestead he had claimed upon his eighteenth birthday. He would make the area his home until 1813. It was here that Peter and Frances's first two daughters were born: Eliza B. on May 11, 1810, and Maria H. on September 20, 1812. In 1813, the family sold the farm and moved to a new homestead near Hopkinsville in Christian County, Kentucky.

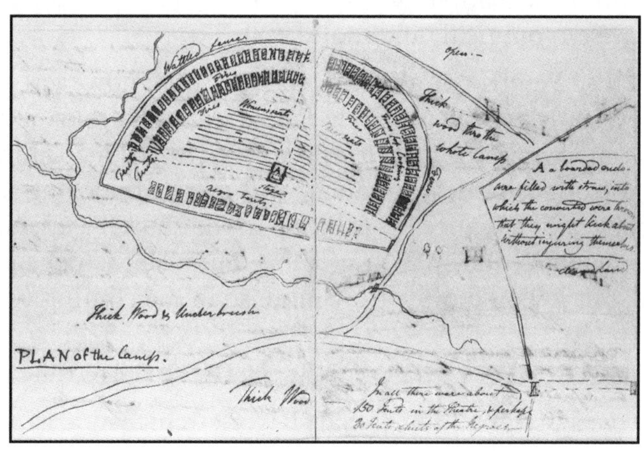

The plan of a camp meeting from 1809

Library of Congress, 006753

In 1811, in addition to his scheduled travels and preaching engagements, Peter was challenged to a debate by a scholarly preacher from the East who believed all Methodist preachers to be "illiterate, ignorant babblers."[21] Peter was never one to back down from a challenge, so even though he had little schooling, he accepted. Hoping to prove Peter's ignorance, the scholar posed a question in Greek—a

[21] Cartwright, *Autobiography*, 80.

language that, of course, Peter could not understand. He had, however, picked up some German along the way, so he responded in that language, which was unknown to the scholar. Caught off guard, the scholar assumed the language to be Hebrew, and he caved in, proclaiming to the crowd that Peter was the first educated Methodist preacher he had met.

Andrew Jackson and Peter Cartwright

Cartwright's *Autobiography* includes few details about the War of 1812, which began the year after Peter's famed debate with the scholar. Aside from providing recruits, Kentucky and Tennessee were largely unaffected by the war. As the population of Kentucky decreased with the departure of soldiers, so, too, the number of Methodists in Kentucky decreased for a time. It was later reported that Peter served as a chaplain to Andrew Jackson during the war. According to a newspaper article covering one of Peter's sermons, he was present with General Jackson during the Battle of New Orleans on January 8, 1815. (Jackson became the seventh president of the United States in 1829.) The article reads as follows:

> At the time of the last British War, just before Gen. Jackson fought his successful battle of New Orleans, a regiment of infantry camped near his [Peter's] residence in Christian County, Ky. The Chaplain was sick, and he was induced to take his place, and marched on the way to New Orleans. Gen. Jackson told the chaplains they must go in the front ranks of the battle; by their remonstrating, the general relented, but told them he wanted them to preach to his soldiers that no man would die till his time had come, and that they were as safe at the cannon's mouth as anywhere else. He refused to preach anything of the kind, because, as he stated it, it was a lie; but he promised to preach to them that the war was a justifiable one, and that they were engaged in a righteous cause. The general said that would do, and the minister told him it would have to do.[22]

[22] "Lecture by Rev. Peter Cartwright," *Bloomington Pantagraph*, June 4, 1868, 3:3; and *Chicago Times*, February 19, 1863, 3:1, quoted in Bray, *Peter Cartwright, Legendary Frontier Preacher*, 69.

This was not the only interaction Peter had with General Jackson. A few years later, the future president walked into a meeting where Peter was preaching.

> I then read my text: "What shall it profit a man if he gain the whole world and lose his own soul?" After reading my text I paused. At that moment I saw General Jackson walking up the aisle; he came to the middle post, and very gracefully leaned against it, and stood, as there were no vacant seats. Just then I felt some one pull my coat in the stand, and turning my head, my fastidious preacher, whispering a little loud, said: "General Jackson has come in; General Jackson has come in." I felt a flash of indignation run all over me like an electric shock, and facing about to my congregation, and purposely speaking out audibly, I said, "Who is General Jackson? If he don't get his soul converted, God will damn him as quick as he would a Guinea negro!"
>
> The preacher tucked his head down, and squatted low, and would, no doubt, have been thankful for leave of absence. The congregation, General Jackson and all, smiled, or laughed right out, all at the preacher's expense. When the congregation was dismissed, my city-stationed preacher stepped up to me, and very sternly said to me: "You are the strangest man I ever saw, and General Jackson will chastise you for your insolence before you leave the city." "Very clear of it," said I, "for General Jackson, I have no doubt, will applaud my course; and if he should undertake to chastise me, as Paddy said, 'There is two as can play at that game.'"
>
> General Jackson was staying at one of the Nashville hotels. Next morning, very early, my city preacher went down to the hotel to make an apology to General Jackson for my conduct in the pulpit the night before. Shortly after he had left, I passed by the hotel, and I met the general on the pavement; and before I approached him by several steps he smiled, and reached out his hand and said: "Mr. Cartwright, you are a man after my own heart. I am very

> much surprised at Mr. Mac, to think he would suppose that I would be offended at you. No, sir; I told him that I highly approved of your independence; that a minister of Jesus Christ ought to love everybody and fear no mortal man. I told Mr. Mac that if I had a few thousand such independent, fearless officers as you were, and a well-drilled army, I could take old England."
>
> General Jackson was certainly a very extraordinary man. He was, no doubt, in his prime of life, a very wicked man, but he always showed a great respect for the Christian religion, and the feelings of religious people, especially ministers of the Gospel.[23]

At this time, circuit riders in the West were lucky to make forty dollars a year, and lodging was often hard to come by. Their circuits could stretch as far as five hundred miles, and being away from friends and family most of the time must have been difficult. Temptations threatened to derail even the most devoted of ministers, and many succumbed to these temptations. Peter himself experienced at least one such temptation, when the sins of his youth called on him with great force and emotion. Read what he recorded and observe how he prevailed:

> Saturday night came on, and found me in a strange region of country, and in the hills, knobs, and spurs of the Cumberland Mountains. I greatly desired to stop on the approaching Sabbath, and spend it with a Christian people; but I was now in a region of country where there was no Gospel minister for many miles around, and where, as I learned, many of the scattered population had never heard a Gospel sermon in all their lives, and where the inhabitants knew no Sabbath only to hunt and visit, drink and dance. Thus lonesome and pensive, late in the evening, I hailed at a tolerably decent house, and the landlord kept entertainment. I rode up and asked for quarters. The gentleman said I could stay, but he was afraid I would not enjoy myself very much as a traveler, inasmuch as they had a party meeting

[23] Cartwright, *Autobiography*, 192–193.

there that night to have a little dance. I inquired how far it was to a decent house of entertainment on the road; he said seven miles. I told him if he would treat me civilly and feed my horse well, by his leave I would stay. He assured me I should be treated civilly. I dismounted and went in. The people collected, a large company. I saw there was not much drinking going on.

I quietly took my seat in one corner of the house, and the dance commenced. I sat quietly musing, a total stranger, and greatly desired to preach to this people. Finally, I concluded to spend the next day—Sabbath—there, and ask the privilege to preach to them. I had hardly settled this point in my mind, when a beautiful, ruddy [redheaded] young lady walked very gracefully up to me, dropped a handsome curtsey, and pleasantly, with winning smiles, invited me out to take a dance with her. I can hardly describe my thoughts or feelings on that occasion. However, in a moment I resolved on a desperate experiment. I rose as gracefully as I could; I will not say with some emotion, but with many emotions. The young lady moved to my right side; I grasped her right hand with my right hand, while she leaned her left arm on mine. In this position we walked on the floor. The whole company seemed pleased at this act of politeness in the young lady, shown to a stranger. The colored man, who was the fiddler, began to put his fiddle in the best order. I then spoke to the fiddler to hold a moment, and added that for several years I had not undertaken any matter of importance without first asking the blessing of God upon it, and I desired now to ask the blessing of God upon this beautiful young lady and the whole company, that had shown such an act of politeness to a total stranger.

Here I grasped the young lady's hand tightly, and said, "Let us all kneel down and pray," and then instantly dropped on my knees, and commenced praying with all the power of soul and body that I could command. The young lady tried to get loose from me, but I held her tight. Presently she fell on her knees. Some of the company kneeled, some stood, some fled, some sat still, all looked curious.

> The fiddler ran off into the kitchen, saying, "Lord a marcy, what de matter? what is dat mean?"
>
> While I prayed some wept, and wept out aloud, and some cried for mercy. I rose from my knees and commenced an exhortation, after which I sang a hymn. The young lady who invited me on the floor lay prostrate, crying earnestly for mercy. I exhorted again, I sang and prayed nearly all night. About fifteen of that company professed religion, and our meeting lasted next day and next night, and as many more were powerfully converted. I organized a society, took thirty-two into the Church, and sent them a preacher. My landlord was appointed leader, which post he held for many years. This was the commencement of a great and glorious revival of religion in that region of country, and several of the young men converted at this Methodist preacher dance became useful ministers of Jesus Christ.[24]

It is understandable that Peter would have been an attractive figure as a frontiersman. He was nearly six feet tall, and stood erect and composed. His thick, curly, black hair sat atop a large imposing head and a short, thick neck. His eyes were dark and piercing. He had a Roman nose, and he constantly wore a mirthful grin. His face was enormously theatrical: its expression was generally friendly but could turn stormy and menacing in an instant, a skill he used well in preaching. To these characteristics he added the air of a man in charge of the situation, a man born to rule. Combine that with his sharp wit and uncanny insightfulness, and he was an imposing, virile presence wherever he went.

Time for Change; Meddling in Politics

Peter remained in Kentucky until 1824, where he and his wife had five more children: three daughters (Cynthia, born on March 27, 1815; Wealthy M. Jane, born on August 9, 1819; and Sarah M., born on July 2, 1823) and two sons (Madison, born on July 4, 1817; and Valentine, born on May 19, 1821). Caroline M. and Arminda, their eighth and ninth children, would be born in Illinois on September 9, 1826, and October 3, 1828, respectively. As Eliza, now fourteen, was

[24] Cartwright, *Autobiography*, 206–209.

approaching marrying age on the frontier, Peter became concerned that his girls might marry into slave-owning families and thereby disgrace his antislavery stance. So he sold his land, and early in October 1824, he moved his family to Illinois.

Though the roads were much safer now, and Indian attacks posed less of a threat, traveling was still hazardous. Violent wind was partly responsible for the death of their daughter, Cynthia, as Peter recounted in his *Autobiography*:

> Just before we struck the prairies, the man that drove my team contrived to turn over the wagon, and was very near killing my oldest daughter [Eliza]. The sun was just going down; and by the time we righted up the wagon and reloaded, it was getting dark, and we had a difficult hill to descend, so we concluded to camp there for the night, almost in sight of two cabins containing families. I was almost exhausted reloading my wagon; the evening was warm, and my wife persuaded me not to stretch our tent that night; so I struck fire, kindled it at the root of a small, and, as I thought, sound, tree. We laid down and slept soundly.
>
> Just as day was appearing in the east, the tree at the root of which we had kindled a small fire fell, and it fell on our third daughter [Cynthia, who would have been nine years old], as direct on her, from her feet to her head, as it could fall; and I suppose she never breathed after. I heard the tree crack when it started to fall, and sprang, alarmed very much, and seized it before it struck the child; but it availed nothing. Although this was an awful calamity, yet God was kind to us; for if we had stretched our tent that night, we should have been obliged to lie down in another position, and in that event the tree would have fallen directly upon us, and we should all have been killed instead of one. The tree was sound outside to the thickness of the back of a carving knife, and then all the inside had a dry rot; but this we did not suspect.[25]

[25] Cartwright, *Autobiography*, 247–248.

On October 23, 1824, Peter and Frances buried Cynthia near present-day McLeansboro, Illinois. They set up their new homestead near Richland Creek in Illinois on November 15, and Peter named the area Pleasant Plains.

Peter Runs for Office against Abraham Lincoln

Now thirty-nine, Peter had become a formidable man to deal with, whether he was behind the pulpit, engaging in personal confrontations, or filling his role as a public figure. Though he had left slavery behind in Kentucky, he now embraced emancipation on an even larger scale. In addition to his circuit duties as a presiding elder and the responsibilities of running a farm, Peter ran for a two-year seat in the General Assembly of Illinois. He finished fourth of eleven men vying for three seats in 1826. He won a seat in 1828, lost in 1830, and won again in 1832, this time against a formidable opponent, Abraham Lincoln. Peter would run again in 1834, but he withdrew before the election, and thus Lincoln won his first public office. In 1835, Lincoln ran for a seat in the state senate but lost to Job Fletcher. Lincoln ran again for General Assembly in 1836, 1838, and 1840, and won—Peter was not an opponent in any of these elections. Neither Cartwright nor Lincoln would run for office again until the two vied for a U.S. Senate seat in 1846. Peter would find himself facing down another future president in one of his services, but this time not quite as successfully. As the story goes,

> during the campaign Lincoln went to a revival meeting where Cartwright was to preach. In the course of the meeting, Cartwright announced: "All who desire to lead a new life, to give their hearts to God and go to heaven, will stand." Quite a few stood up. Then the preacher raised his voice and roared: "All who do not wish to go to hell will stand." All stood up except Mr. Lincoln. Cartwright was quick to note the exception, and in solemn tones he said:
>
> "I observe that many responded to the first invitation to give their hearts to God and go to heaven, and I further observe that all of you save one indicated you did not wish

> to go to hell. The sole exception is Mr. Lincoln, who did not respond to either invitation. May I inquire of you, Mr. Lincoln, where you are going?"
>
> Lincoln rose slowly, the eyes of all upon him. "I came here," he said, "as a respectful listener. I did not know I was to be singled out by Brother Cartwright; I believe in treating religious matters with due solemnity. I admit that the questions propounded by Brother Cartwright are important. I did not feel called upon to answer as the rest did. Brother Cartwright asks me directly where I am going. I desire to reply with equal directness: I am going to Congress!"[26]

And so he did. He beat Cartwright by 1,511 votes.

In the course of the debates, Peter accused Lincoln of being an unbeliever, or a deist, at best. In a printed pamphlet, Lincoln retorted that while he was not a member of any church, he had "never denied the truth of the Scriptures."[27] This seemed to satisfy the populace, and the matter did Peter no good. In later years, Lincoln would confess to Congressman Henry C. Deming,

> When any church will inscribe over its altar, as its sole qualification for membership...the Saviour's condensed statement of both Law and Gospel, "Thou shalt love the Lord thy God with all thy heart, and with all thy soul, and with all thy mind, and thy neighbor as thyself," that church will I join with all my heart and all my soul.[28]

Lincoln's faith in Christ is a matter of public record—one has only to read the transcripts from his public speeches to notice the biblical influence. Perhaps he was more of a Calvinist, though, thinking the matter of his eternal salvation depended on God rather than on whether he stood or remained seated at a meeting. Despite the fact that these two "Kentucky boys" shared faith in God and stood

---

[26] Edgar DeWitt Jones, *Lincoln and the Preachers* (Salem, NH: Ayer Publishing, 1970), 44.

[27] Gordon Leidner, "Lincoln's Faith in God," *Great American History*, http://www.greatamericanhistory.net/lincolnsfaith.htm.

[28] John C. Bogle, "Reflections on the Importance of History—Milestones, Men, and a Moral Society," *Bogle Financial Markets Research Center*, http://www.vanguard.com/bogle_site/sp20061116.htm.

on the same side of the slavery issue, they seemed to agree on little else. Peter was ever the backwoodsman—he preferred the emotionally charged preaching of camp meetings to the stoic, sophisticated, progressive intellectualism he painted Lincoln as representing.

Peter's Preaching Style

Few examples of Peter's preaching style remain, but the best is probably "The Jocose[29] Preacher," a short narrative written about him from an eyewitness account of a camp meeting sometime in the 1830s.

The story begins by describing Peter's arrival at night to preach a sermon—he would have come in the morning, but his horse had fallen and been injured. He could have left the horse and walked, but in a note to the awaiting group, he had explained, "Horses have no souls to save, and therefore it is all the more the duty of Christians to take care of their bodies."[30] It was late on a beautiful summer evening when he finally arrived, and

> they knew not...what to think or make of the man. His figure was tall, burly, massive, and seemed even more gigantic than the reality from its crowning foliage of luxuriant coal black hair, wreathed into long, curling ringlets. Add a head that looked large as a half-bushel, beetling brows, and rough and craggy as fragmentary granite, irradiated at the base by eyes of dark fire, small and twinkling like diamonds in the sea—(they were diamonds of a soul shining in a measureless sea of humor,) a swarthy complexion, as if embrowned by the kisses of sunbeams, a fixedness of purpose in the expression of the mouth, with rich, rosy lips, always slightly parted as if wearing a perpetual and merry smile, and you have a life-like portrait of Peter Cartwright, the far-famed Methodist Residing Elder.[31]

---

[29] Means "with a playfully joking disposition."

[30] "Rev. Peter Cartwright, the Methodist Presiding Elder. A Genuine Portrait from 'Life in Illinois,'" *Southern and South-Western Sketches*, 6–7, quoted in Bray, *Peter Cartwright, Legendary Frontier Preacher*, 153.

[31] "Rev. Peter Cartwright, the Methodist Presiding Elder," 7–8, quoted in Bray, *Peter Cartwright, Legendary Frontier Preacher*, 153–154.

When the singing finished, a hush fell over the crowd. Taking his text from Mark 8:36, *"For what shall it profit a man, if he shall gain the whole world, and lose his own soul?"*—one of Peter's favorites—he began to preach. The eyewitness described his sermon as "transcendent eloquence." [32] Peter delivered a fifteen-minute conversational introduction that led into a half-hour satirical parable of the folly of a sinner. From here, he descended into a dramatic description of the horrors of hell itself, finally ascending to a triumphant picture of the joys of heaven awaiting those who turned to the Lord.

The audience was visibly moved. "Five hundred, many of them until that night infidels, rushed forward and prostrated themselves upon their knees. The meeting was continued for two weeks, and more than a thousand converts were added to the church." [33] Thus was the power of a Peter Cartwright sermon.

A Run-in with Joseph Smith

After escaping from prison in Independence, Missouri, in April 1839, Joseph Smith made his way into Illinois, and there, in a classic confrontation, ran into Peter Cartwright. Smith, founder of the Mormon Church, tried to befriend Cartwright as a fellow minister, but Peter would have none of it. In his *Autobiography*, Peter told of what happened when the two met:

> On a certain occasion I fell in with Joe Smith, and was formally and officially introduced to him in Springfield, then our county town. We soon fell into a free conversation on the subject of religion, and Mormonism in particular. I found him to be a very illiterate and impudent desperado in morals, but, at the same time, he had a vast fund of low cunning.
>
> In the first place, he made his onset on me by flattery, and he laid on the soft sodder thick and fast. He expressed great and almost unbounded pleasure in the high privilege of becoming acquainted with me, one of whom he had heard so many great and good things, and he had no doubt

---

[32] "Rev. Peter Cartwright, the Methodist Presiding Elder," 11, quoted in Bray, *Peter Cartwright, Legendary Frontier Preacher*, 154.

[33] Ibid.

I was one among God's noblest creatures, an honest man. He believed that among all the Churches in the world the Methodist was the nearest right, and that, as far as they went, they were right. But they had stopped short by not claiming the gift of tongues, of prophecy, and of miracles, and then quoted a batch of Scripture to prove his positions correct. Upon the whole, he did pretty well for clumsy Joe. I gave him rope, as the sailors say, and, indeed, I seemed to lay this flattering unction pleasurably to my soul.

"Indeed," said Joe, "if the Methodists would only advance a step or two further, they would take the world. We Latter-day Saints are Methodists, as far as they have gone, only we have advanced further, and if you would come in and go with us, we could sweep not only the Methodist Church, but all others, and you would be looked up to as one of the Lord's greatest prophets. You would be honored by countless thousands, and have of the good things of this world all that heart could wish."

I then began to inquire into some of the tenets of the Latter-day Saints. He explained, I criticised his explanations till, unfortunately, we got into high debate, and he cunningly concluded that his first bait would not take, for he plainly saw I was not to be flattered out of common sense and honesty. The next pass he made at me was to move upon my fears. He said that in all ages of the world the good and right way was evil spoken of, and that it was an awful thing to fight against God.

"Now," said he, "if you will go with me to Nauvoo, I will show you many living witnesses that will testify that they were, by the saints, cured of blindness, lameness, deafness, dumbness, and all the diseases that human flesh is heir to; and I will show you," said he, "that we have the gift of tongues, and can speak in unknown languages, and that the saints can drink any deadly poison, and it will not hurt them;" and closed by saying, "the idle stories you hear about us are nothing but sheer persecution."

I then gave him the following history of an encounter I had at a camp meeting in Morgan County, some time before, with some of his Mormons, and assured him I could prove all I said by thousands that were present.

The camp-meeting was numerously attended, and we had a good and gracious work of religion going on among the people. On Saturday there came some twenty or thirty Mormons to the meeting. During the intermission after the eleven o'clock sermon they collected in one corner of the encampment, and began to sing, and they sang well. As fast as the people rose from their dinners they drew up to hear the singing, and the scattering crowd drew up until a large company surrounded them. I was busy regulating matters connected with the meeting. At length, according, I have no doubt, to a preconcerted plan, an old lady Mormon began to shout, and after shouting a while she swooned away and fell into the arms of her husband. The old man proclaimed that his wife had gone into a trance, and that when she came to she would speak in an unknown tongue, and that he would interpret. This proclamation produced considerable excitement, and the multitude crowded thick around. Presently the old lady arose and began to speak in an unknown tongue, sure enough.

Just then my attention was called to the matter. I saw in one moment that the whole maneuver was intended to bring the Mormons into notice, and break up the good of our meeting. I advanced instantly toward the crowd, and asked the people to give way and let me in to this old lady, who was then being held in the arms of her husband. I came right up to them, and took hold of her arm, and ordered her peremptorily to hush that gibberish; that I would have no more of it; that it was presumptuous, and blasphemous nonsense. I stopped very suddenly her unknown tongue. She opened her eyes, took me by the hand, and said,

"My dear friend, I have a message directly from God to you."

I stopped her short, and said, "I will have none of your messages. If God can speak through no better medium than an old, hypocritical, lying woman, I will hear nothing of it." Her husband, who was to be the interpreter of her message, flew into a mighty rage, and said,

"Sir, this is my wife, and I will defend her at the risk of my life."

I replied, "Sir, this is my camp-meeting, and I will maintain the good order of it at the risk of my life. If this is your wife, take her off from here, and clear yourselves in five minutes, or I will have you under guard."

The old lady slipped out and was off quickly. The old man stayed a little, and began to pour a tirade of abuse on me. I stopped him short, and said, "Not another word of abuse from you, sir. I have no doubt you are an old thief, and if your back was examined, no doubt you carry the marks of the cowhide for your villainy." And sure enough, as if I had spoken by inspiration, he, in some of the old states, had been lashed to the whipping-post for stealing, and I tell you the old man began to think other persons had visions besides his wife, but he was very clear from wishing to interpret my unknown tongue. To cap the climax, a young gentleman stepped up and said he had no doubt all I said of this old man was true, and much more, for he had caught him stealing corn out of his father's crib. By this time, such was the old man's excitement that the great drops of sweat ran down his face, and he called out, "Don't crowd me, gentlemen; it is mighty warm."

Said I, "Open the way, gentlemen, and let him out." When the way was opened, I cried, "Now start, and don't show your face here again, nor one of the Mormons. If you do, you will get Lynch's law."

They all disappeared, and our meeting went on prosperously, a great many were converted to God, and the Church was much revived and built up in her holy faith.

My friend, Joe Smith, became very restive before I got through with my narrative; and when I closed, his wrath boiled over, and he cursed me in the name of his God, and said, "I will show you, sir, that I will raise up a government in these United States which will overturn the present government, and I will raise up a new religion that will overturn every other form of religion in this country!"

"Yes," said I, "Uncle Joe; but my Bible tells me the bloody and deceitful man shall not live out half his days;" and I expect the Lord will send the devil after you some of these days, and take you out of the way."

"No, sir," said he; "I shall live and prosper, while you will die in your sins."

"Well, sir," said I, "if you live and prosper, you must quit your stealing and abominable whoredoms!"

Thus we parted, to meet no more on earth; for in a few years after this, an outraged and deeply-injured people took the law into their own hands, and killed him, and drove the Mormons from the state.[34]

The No-nonsense Preacher

Despite his forays into politics, Peter remained a circuit preacher and participated regularly in camp meetings. As he got older, however, his tolerance for the hecklers and rowdies who tried to break up his meetings waned. In one particular camp meeting on the banks of the Cumberland River, a group tried to break up the meeting while Peter was preaching. In the midst of the sermon, one of the largest of the group came forward and shouted for Peter to "dry up!" Peter asked the crowd if they would give him a few moments. Taking off his jacket, he stepped down to face the ruffian. He proceeded to knock the man down, showering him with punches until he cried for mercy. Peter then said that he would not let him up until he repented. When the man did so, Peter sent him to the "Amen corner" to pray with others seeking salvation. He dusted off his shirt, remounted the pulpit, and put his jacket back on. Looking again at the audience, he said, "As I was saying brethren,"[35] and recommenced his sermon.

As the years progressed, camp meetings attracted all kinds of people, and soon carried a reputation for vice as much as for victory over it. Whisky sellers, card players, and carousers would hang around at the outskirts of the meetings to prey on the crowds. Some

---

[34] Cartwright, *Autobiography*, 342–347.

[35] Jones, *Lincoln and the Preachers,* 47.

said that there were more souls *conceived* at the camp meetings than there were *saved.* Peter was, of course, anxious to put a stop to such chicanery. At a camp meeting in 1841, Peter faced down a group of troublemakers who were actually supported by the local deputy sheriff.

> When we were called to the stand by the sound of the trumpet, I called the attention of the congregation to the absolute necessity of keeping good order. I stated that my father was a Revolutionary soldier, and fought for the liberties we enjoyed, and all the boon he had left me was liberty; and that, as the responsible officer of the camp-meeting, if the friends of order and the sworn officers of the law would give me backing, I would maintain order at the risk of my life. My lecture roused the friends of order, and they gave me their countenance and aid; but the whisky sellers and whisky drinkers, nothing daunted, commenced their deeds of darkness. Some were soon drunk, and interrupted our devotions very much. I then ordered several writs, and took into custody several of those whisky venders and drunken rowdies; but these rowdies rose in mob force, and rescued the whisky seller and his wagon and team from the officer of the law. The officer came running to me, and informed me of the rising of the mob, and that the whisky man was given up, and was making his escape; and it appeared to me he was very much scared. I told him to summon me and five other men that I named, and I would insure the re-taking of the transgressor, in spite of any mob. He did so. We rushed upon them and stopped the team. The man that had transgressed drew a weapon, and ordered us to stand off; that he would kill the first man that touched him: and as one of the men and myself that

Peter stepped down to face the ruffian, showering him with punches until he repented.

were summoned to take him rushed on him, he made a stroke at my companion with his weapon, but missed him. I then sprang upon him and caught him by the collar, and jerked him over the wagon bed, in which he was standing, among his barrels. He fell on all-fours. I jumped on him, and told him he was my prisoner, and that if he did not surrender I should hurt him. The deputy sheriff of the county, who was with the mob, and a combatant at that, ran up to me, and ordered me to let the prisoner go. I told him I should not. He said if I did not, he would knock me over. I told him if he struck to make a sure lick, for the next was mine. Our officer then commanded me to take the deputy sheriff, and I did so. He scuffled a little; but finding himself in rather close quarters, he surrendered.

We then took thirteen of the mob, the whisky seller, and the sheriff, and marched them off to the magistrate, to the tune of good order. They were fined by the justice of the peace; some paid their fine, some appealed to court. This appealing we liked well, because they then had to give security, and this secured the fine and costs, which some of them were not able to pay.

This somewhat checked them for a while, but they rallied again, and gave us trouble. There was one man, a turbulent fellow, who sold whisky about a quarter of a mile off. He had often interrupted us by selling whisky at our camp-meetings. He generally went armed with deadly weapons, to keep off officers. I sent the constable after him, but he had a musket well loaded, and would not be taken. He kept a drinking party round him nearly all night; however, toward morning they left him, and went off to sleep as best they could, and he lay down in his wagon, and went to sleep, with his loaded musket by his side.

Just as day dawned, I slipped over the creek and came up to his wagon. He was fast asleep. I reached over the wagon bed and gathered his gun and ammunition; then struck the wagon bed with the muzzle of the musket, and cried out, "Wake up! wake up!" He sprang to his feet, and felt for his gun. I said, "You are my prisoner; and if you resist, you are

> a dead man!" He begged me not to shoot, and said that he would surrender. I told him to get out of the wagon, and march before me to the camp ground; that I was going to have him tried for violating good order and the laws of his country. He began to beg most piteously, and said if I would only let him escape that time, he would gear up and go right away, and never do the like again. I told him to harness his team, and start. He did so. When he got ready to go, I poured out his powder, and fired off his musket and gave it to him; and he left us, and troubled us no more.[36]

Peter's Final Years

In 1856, Peter released his *Autobiography of Peter Cartwright, The Backwoods Preacher*, and the book became a best-seller in one of the greatest decades of American literature—a decade that produced such renowned works as Herman Melville's *Moby Dick*, Henry David Thoreau's *Walden*, Nathaniel Hawthorne's *The Scarlet Letter*, and Walt Whitman's *Leaves of Grass*. Peter's book is still popular today; it is a wonderful portrait of frontier life, the Kentucky camp meetings, and Peter's remarkable experiences of preaching and living in the Wild West of the early 1800s. It is hard to come away from reading his autobiography without feeling that Peter is indeed a legend from a time in America when the "West" was still *east* of the Mississippi River. This was not his only book, however; he also wrote *Fifty Years as a Residing Elder* (1871), among others.

Peter finally retired from circuit riding in 1869. Evidence suggests that Peter ended his days in senility, struggling to sell a piece of land to someone who thought he was only doing this because he had lost his mind. Before his prospective buyer could take legal action, however, Peter passed away at three o'clock in the afternoon on September 25, 1872, just a few weeks after his eighty-seventh birthday. The exact cause of his death is unknown.

Peter's long years as a circuit rider not only helped to establish Methodism as the way of revival in his time, but also contributed to the conversion of roughly ten thousand people. This figure says a good deal about a man who spent most of his time preaching to rural

[36] Cartwright, *Autobiography*, 377–381.

communities and small crowds. In his sixty-seven years as a minister, he preached almost fifteen thousand sermons. Peter Cartwright was a preacher to rival anything ever accomplished by Daniel Boone or Davy Crockett. With God's help, he won the West as no one else ever would.

Chapter Seven

★★★★★

Charles Finney

(1792–1875)

"The Father of Modern Revivalism"

"THE FATHER OF MODERN REVIVALISM"

Christian people, are you figuring round and round to get a little property, yet neglecting souls? Beware lest you ruin souls that can never live again! Do you say—I thought they knew it all? They reply to you, "I did not suppose you believed a word of it yourselves. You did not act as if you did. Are you going to heaven? Well, I am going down to hell! There is no help for me now. You will sometimes think of me then, as you shall see the smoke of my woe rising up darkly athwart the glorious heavens. After I have been there a long, long time, you will sometimes think that I, who once lived by your side, am there. O remember, you cannot pray for me then; but you will remember that once you might have warned and might have saved me."

—Charles G. Finney

On the eve of the Industrial Revolution in America, Charles Finney touched the United States and Western Europe as no single Christian had before. His ministry is credited with leading more than half a million people to salvation, and his methods and doctrine laid the foundation for revival services as we know them today. The power of the Holy Spirit worked mightily in him to transform the emerging culture of New England from impotent Calvinism into active and effective evangelism wherever he went. Finney's preaching catalyzed the Second Great Awakening, a movement that unified the United States at a critical time in its history—between the War of 1812 and the American Civil War. He may well be the most significant American evangelist of the nineteenth century, as well as one of the most important figures in American history during its first century as a nation. Finney may also have been the most innovative and anointed evangelist the world has ever seen.

A Refined Young Heathen

Charles Grandison Finney was born in Warren, Connecticut, on August 29, 1792—only a year after the death of John Wesley—the seventh child of Sylvester and Rebecca Finney. His name was pulled from the title of a novel by Samuel Richardson, *Sir Charles Grandison*, which tells the story of an English aristocrat.

Sylvester and Rebecca had had four daughters—Sarah, Dotia, Zenas, and Chloe—and two sons—Sylvester Jr. and Harry—before Charles was born. When Charles was about two years old, the family moved to Oneida County, New York, which, at the time, was a relative wilderness. Here, another son, George Washington Finney, was born in 1795, followed by Sylvester Rice Finney in 1802. Sylvester Jr. died about the time Sylvester Rice was born; sadly, Sylvester Rice died, too, in 1808.

Sylvester Sr. was a farmer who had fought in the colonial militia during the Revolutionary War. In all the years Charles lived with his family, he had little religious education. He never heard his father pray in the house; the first time he read the Bible, he was twenty-nine years old. Religious books were scarce among the households of the area, and there was no church. Not unlike many of their neighbors, Charles's parents professed no religion. Though Methodist circuit riders would speak in the local one-room schoolhouse from time to time, they were usually uneducated and rarely held their audience's attention. Western New York at this time had become known as the "Burned-over District," as it had seen so many preachers that the local population had grown immune to their preaching.

It was in this environment that Charles grew and was educated. By the time he was about fifteen or sixteen, he had learned enough to be the teacher of a one-room community schoolhouse. About this time, the Finneys moved again, to the wilderness skirting the shores of Henderson's Bay on Lake Ontario near Sackets Harbor, New York. It appeared Oneida County was becoming too "civilized" for Sylvester Finney.

Here, Charles Finney found a school looking for a master, and he accepted the post. Because of his love for music, the first thing he bought himself with his earnings was a cello. At six feet two inches, Charles was also an excellent athlete. His grandson later described this period of Charles's life as follows:

> When he was twenty he excelled every man and boy he met, in every species of toil or sport. No man could throw him; no man could knock his hat off; no man could run faster, jump farther, leap higher or throw a ball with greater force and precision.[1]

Charles's students adored him because he would participate in their sporting events and almost always championed the winning side. Since his family now lived by the water, Charles added rowing, swimming, and sailing to his list of skills. It was a clean, unfettered life for someone living on the frontiers—moral, but ignorant of God.

Off to Join the Navy

As the fledgling United States entered a second war with the British in 1812, Charles went to Sackets Harbor with the intention of enlisting in the navy, but when he arrived there, he heard more profanity than he had in his entire life. Also, the pretty, young prostitutes who accosted him did more to repel him than attract him. His grandson again related the story of one such encounter:

> He looked at her in wonder and when he comprehended the nature of her request, he was so overcome with pity for her...that his cheeks burned, and before he could check it he was shedding tears....She, moved to shame, wept too.[2]

It was an incident he would remember even fifty-five years later, when he spoke with anguish of his regret that he was not able to offer

---

[1] Basil Miller, *Charles Finney: He Prayed Down Revivals* (Grand Rapids, MI: Zondervan, 1951), 10.

[2] Ibid., 13.

the young woman God's grace since he himself did not know the Lord at the time.

Because this atmosphere so offended Charles, he chose not to join the navy, instead returning to Connecticut where he had been born. Eventually, he went to a town in New Jersey not far from New York City, where he resumed teaching in a schoolhouse and studying. He acquired a limited knowledge of Latin, Hebrew, and Greek, though he himself admitted, "I...never possessed so much knowledge of the ancient languages as to think myself capable of independently criticising our English translation of the Bible."[3] During these years, Charles returned twice to New England and also attended high school for a season. These were the first places he had lived where there were regular religious services, but Charles found the sermons dry and unmoving; they left "no impression whatever on my mind."[4] He also gave some thought to attending Yale College, but one of his teachers persuaded him that it would be a waste of his time. The teacher felt he could acquire the same knowledge of four years at Yale in just two years of independent study, and without the expense.

Charles the Lawyer

In 1818, Charles's parents persuaded him to enter the law office of Judge Benjamin Wright in Adams, New York, not far from their home near Lake Ontario, rather than move south to instruct at an academy with the same teacher who had dissuaded him from attending Yale. Though he had never attended law school, young Charles's mind took to the law profession with a passion.

It was in Adams that Charles met the Reverend George W. Gale, the pastor of the town's Presbyterian church. While Charles was not greatly moved by Gale's sermons, he spent a good deal of time discussing them with him. Charles was determined to make sense of what he heard, but the more he talked with Gale, the more questions formed in his mind. Gale found Charles rather well-informed about religion but hardened to it at the same time. When church members thought of making Charles a special subject of prayer for

[3] Charles Finney, *Memoirs of Charles Finney* (New York: A. S. Barnes and Company, 1876), 5.

[4] Ibid., 6.

his conversion, Gale advised against it; he thought it unlikely that Charles would ever be saved. Gale believed that no matter what he said to Charles, he would not be converted, for all he ever did was debate doctrine. Despite Gale's doubts, Charles faithfully attended a weekly prayer meeting that was held near the law offices. Whenever his legal work allowed enough time, he would go to listen to the prayers offered by those assembled. It was an experience that would affect him in much the same way as conversing with Gale did—again, Charles had generated more questions than answers.

Unanswered prayer troubled Charles and nearly drove him from Christianity.

As Charles studied the law, he began to notice how writers time and again quoted the Bible as an authority for many of the great principles of common law. This piqued his curiosity to the point that he went out and purchased his first Bible. Then, when he would come across legal texts that referred to Scripture passages, he would check the references and their biblical context. Though he didn't understand much of it, he found himself reading the Bible more and more, and with greater and greater interest.

The Word Starts Working

Finney described the impact of this practice on his soul:

> As I read my Bible and attended the prayer meetings, heard Mr. Gale preach, and conversed with him, with the elders of the church, and with others from time to time, I became restless. A little consideration convinced me that I was in no means in a state of mind to go to heaven if I should die. It seemed to me that there must be something in religion that was of infinite importance; and it was soon settled with me, that if the soul was immortal I needed a great change in my inward state to be prepared for happiness in heaven....The question, however, was of too much importance to allow me to rest in any uncertainty on the subject.[5]

[5] Finney, *Memoirs*, 8–9.

A major stumbling block fed his confusion, however: the issue that, as far as he could tell, no prayer offered at the weekly prayer meetings was ever answered. As he read the Bible, he came upon such passages as Luke 11:9–10: *"Ask, and it shall be given you; seek, and ye shall find; knock, and it shall be opened unto you. For every one that asketh receiveth; and he that seeketh findeth; and to him that knocketh it shall be opened."* He saw that God was more willing to give His Holy Spirit to those who asked Him to than parents were willing to give good things to their children. Yet week after week in these prayer meetings, he heard prayers offered up to heaven and saw nothing come back in return. The issue troubled his soul so much that it nearly drove him away from the Bible and Christianity.

In fact, as his frustration continued and became visible in the way he carried himself, the people who led the weekly meetings offered to pray for him. To these offers, he responded,

> I suppose I need to be prayed for, for I am conscious that I am a sinner; but I do not see that it will do any good for you to pray for me; for you are continually asking, but you do not receive. You have been praying for a revival of religion ever since I have been in Adams, and yet you have it not. You have been praying for the Holy Spirit to descend upon yourselves, and yet you complain of your leanness....You have prayed enough since I have attended these meetings to have prayed the devil out of Adams, if there was any virtue in your prayers. But here you are praying on, and complaining still.[6]

Despite the candor of his remarks, Charles didn't intend them to be insulting. They were merely an expression of his honest pursuit for real answers. Restlessness grew within him as he confronted the realization that he needed a Savior, but he could find no one who could tell him how to properly seek Him.

Calvinistic Barriers to God

One of the issues with which Charles struggled was the very one that had driven a wedge between George Whitefield and the Wesley

[6] Ibid., 10.

brothers. Despite what had happened during the First Great Awakening, New England churches—especially Presbyterian churches—remained staunchly Calvinistic. God's sovereignty was preached as supreme in all matters—especially salvation. Accordingly, those who were saved were the "elect" who had been "predestined" to receive salvation through the cross, so that Jesus' sacrifice covered their sin alone. Jesus died only for these elect, and no one else. Thus, no individual could know for certain whether he or she was saved; salvation depended on the will of God.

Everyone was still expected to live a holy life before a holy God, knowing that if they did not, they would provoke the wrath of God that Jonathan Edwards and those like him had so aptly described. They knew little, though, about responding to God's love and mercy. Their best hope was to live righteously before God the Father and inherit the salvation already ordained for them, or at least live the best life they could on earth before facing the hell they justly deserved. Salvation was a miracle that came only under God's sovereignty; it had nothing to do with human initiative.

When Charles struggled with the desire to know, with some degree of certainty, the state of his salvation, the Calvinists from whom he sought answers gave only doctrine. They knew how to pray, but they didn't think their prayers could have any effect on God's will—everything that was going to happen had been established to happen before the world began. In other words, they had no expectancy or faith that God would ever do what they were asking Him to do. They knew how to petition Him, but they didn't know how to receive from Him.

When Charles applied the same logic he used in preparing legal cases to what he read in the Bible, however, he saw that the Calvinists' basic failure was believing what was preached from the pulpit instead of believing what they read in the Bible. He saw that if God were a good and righteous judge, and if the Bible was His written Word and law to humanity, then either the Bible was a lie or the Calvinists were following a delusion. Once he concluded this, he knew he had only two choices: "accept Christ as presented in the Gospel, or pursue a worldly life."[7]

---

[7] Finney, *Memoirs*, 11.

Charles Finney

Is God a Lie?

On a Saturday evening in October 1821, twenty-nine-year-old Charles decided to settle the question of the future of his soul, once and for all. Either he would make his peace with God, or God was a lie and the Bible a fabrication. Since he found no answers in the church and no help from its membership, he knew his answers would be found in studying the Bible and seeking God in prayer. Although he was still required to spend long hours in the law office, Charles decided to try to put his work aside as much as possible until this issue was resolved.

The odd thing was that in the midst of this decision, he suddenly felt quite timid and ashamed when people saw him with a Bible or heard him praying. He had read his Bible openly at work when he first purchased it and had even left it lying open when others met with him, but now, whenever someone entered the office, he would throw a law book over his Bible to conceal it. Charles kept his Bible out of sight as much as he could. He also stopped up the keyhole to his office and whispered his prayers for fear that someone would hear him praying for the salvation of his soul. He spent Monday and Tuesday of that week in anguish; Tuesday night, he became virtually paralyzed with fear that he would die and go to hell because he couldn't find voice enough to cry out to God for His mercy.

On Wednesday morning, October 10, 1821, Charles prepared himself for work, still mulling these questions over in his mind. When he set out as he always did, a voice within confronted him suddenly, asking, "What are you waiting for? Did you not promise to give your heart to God? And what are you trying to do? Are you endeavoring to work out a righteousness of your own?"[8]

The answer to these questions came just as suddenly:

> Just at this point the whole question of Gospel salvation opened to my mind in a manner most marvelous to me at the time. I think I then saw, as clearly as I ever have in my life, the reality and fullness of the atonement of Christ. I saw that his work was a finished work; and that instead of having, or needing, any righteousness of my own to

[8] Ibid., 14.

> recommend me to God, I had to submit myself to the righteousness of God through Christ. Gospel salvation seemed to me to be an offer of something to be accepted; and that it was full and complete; and that all that was necessary on my part, was to get my own consent to give up my sins, and accept Christ. Salvation, it seemed to me, instead of being a thing to be wrought out, by my own works, was a thing to be found entirely in the Lord Jesus Christ, who presented himself before me as my God and my Saviour.
>
> Without being distinctly aware of it, I had stopped in the street right where the inward voice seemed to arrest me. How long I remained in that position, I cannot say. But after this distinct revelation had stood for some little time before my mind, the question seemed to be put, "Will you accept it now, to-day?" I replied, "Yes; I will accept it to-day, or I will die in the attempt."[9]

North of the village was a small forest where Charles would walk almost every day, provided the weather was fair. Instead of going to work, he headed away from the town, which would be filled with too many curious onlookers. He went to the forest, where he could drop to his knees and pray as loudly as he wanted. Still paranoid that someone might see him going into the woods, he snuck—not wanting to be seen—along under a fence until he was out of town before he made his way into the trees. He then went into the forest about a quarter of a mile, hiked over a small hill, and found a place where some trees had fallen together and formed a partially covered enclosure. Here, he decided, "I will give my heart to God, or I never will come down from there."[10] This exact phrase had run through his mind again and again since the time he had left the fence and entered the wood. He climbed into the enclosure within the fallen trees, knelt, and set his heart to pray.

The words still didn't come. He mumbled a little at a time but felt his words were heartless nonetheless. Each time he heard a rustle of leaves, he looked behind him, afraid that someone was watching. Inside he began to despair that somehow he had missed God's grace

---

[9] Finney, *Memoirs*, 14.

[10] Ibid., 15.

and that it was too late for him. He felt foolish, self-conscious, and discouraged, but he determined to stick to his vow—he would not leave that place unchanged.

Again, at a noise, he looked to see whether someone had followed him, and suddenly he saw his pride. He was more afraid that someone should see him than he was that he wasn't saved! He said to himself, "What!...such a degraded sinner as I am, on my knees confessing my sins to the great and holy God; and ashamed to have any human being, and sinner like myself, find me on my knees endeavoring to make my peace with my offended God!"[11] Suddenly, a Scripture passage came to his mind: *"Then shall ye...go and pray unto me, and I will hearken unto you.* [Then] *ye shall seek me, and find me, when ye shall search for me with all your heart"* (Jeremiah 29:12–13). Charles seized the message of these verses with all of his inner strength, crying out, "Lord, I take thee at thy word. Now thou knowest that I do search for thee with all my heart, and that I have come here to pray to thee; and thou hast promised to hear me."[12]

When Charles opened his heart, God filled it with promises from His Word.

Charles's Heart Opens

This finally allowed Charles to open his heart, and as he did so, God filled it with promises from His Word. Charles accepted each personally, as if it had been made to him alone, and he clung to them like a drowning man would cling to a branch or tree limb offered from the shore.

Soon, Charles found himself on his way back to town with no idea how long he had been in the woods, or when he had risen to his feet and begun walking back toward his office. He thought, "If I am ever converted, I will preach the Gospel." He then realized that the despair for his soul was completely gone—he had no conviction of sin in his heart. Still hesitant to believe he had truly been changed,

[11] Ibid., 16.

[12] Ibid.

he thought for a moment that perhaps the Spirit of God had left him altogether. He wondered whether he had grieved the Holy Spirit with his brashness of taking God at His Word in the way that he had; yet, at the same time, he could not get over the peace that now pervaded his soul and mind.

When he got back to town, he was surprised to find that it was dinnertime.[13] He went to eat, but finding that he had no appetite, he returned to the law office. Judge Wright had gone to his dinner, so he took down his viola and began to play and sing some hymns and sacred songs. As soon as he did, tears came to his eyes. It was as if his heart had turned to liquid within him. Every word filled him with emotion to the point that he finally put up his instrument and stopped singing.

Meeting Jesus Face-to-Face

That afternoon, the law office employees were occupied with moving all of the furniture and books from one office to another, so they worked hard and spoke little. Charles was still amazed by the peace within him, as well as by his inability to elicit any feelings of guilt or the anxiety for his soul that had possessed him in the past days and months. When it was finally dark and the office move was complete, Judge Wright bade Charles good night and went home. Charles described what happened at that moment:

> I had accompanied him to the door; and as I closed the door and turned around, my heart seemed to be liquid within me. All my feelings seemed to rise and flow out; and the utterance of my heart was, "I want to pour my whole soul out to God." The rising of my soul was so great that I rushed into the room back of the front office, to pray.
>
> There was no fire, and no light, in the room; nevertheless it appeared to me as if it were perfectly light. As I went in and shut the door after me, it seemed as if I met the Lord Jesus Christ face to face. It did not occur to me then, nor did it for some time afterward, that it was wholly a mental state. On the contrary it seemed to me that I saw him as I

[13] At this time in New England, it was the habit to eat the largest meal of the day (dinner) in the early afternoon and a lighter "supper" in the evening hours.

would see any other man. He said nothing, but looked at me in such a manner as to break me right down at his feet....I fell down at his feet and poured out my soul to him. I wept aloud like a child, and made such confessions as I could with my choked utterance. It seemed to me that I bathed his feet with my tears; and yet I had no distinct impression that I touched him, that I recollect.

I must have continued in this state for a good while; but my mind was too much absorbed with the interview to recollect anything that I said. But I know, as soon as my mind became calm enough to break off from the interview, I returned to the front office, and found that the fire that I had made of large wood was nearly burned out. But as I turned and was about to take a seat by the fire, I received a mighty baptism of the Holy Ghost. Without any expectation of it, without ever having the thought in my mind that there was any such thing for me, without any recollection that I had ever heard the thing mentioned by any person in the world, the Holy Spirit descended upon me in a manner that seemed to go through me, body and soul. I could feel the impression, like a wave of electricity, going through and through me. Indeed it seemed to come in waves and waves of liquid love; for I could not express it in any other way. It seemed like the very breath of God. I can recollect distinctly that it seemed to fan me, like immense wings.

No words can express the wonderful love that was shed abroad in my heart. I wept aloud with joy and love; and I do not know but I should say, I literally bellowed out the unutterable gushings of my heart. These waves came over me, and over me, and over me, one after the other, until I recollect I cried out, "I shall die if these waves continue to pass over me." I said, "Lord, I cannot bear any more"; yet I had no fear of death.[14]

For some time Charles sat in the midst of this experience, God's love rolling over him in wave after wave as the tears continued to flow from his eyes. It is likely that Charles's "unutterable gushings"

[14] Finney, *Memoirs*, 19–21.

were the beginning of a prayer language—a manifestation of speaking in tongues—that he could put no better description upon than this paraphrase of the words of Romans 8:26. At length one of the choir members from the church dropped by (despite his and his pastor's concerns for his salvation, Charles was the director of the choir) and asked what was wrong. At first, Charles could not find words to answer. "Are you in pain?" the man persisted. Charles replied, "No, but so happy that I cannot live."

A Great Presence and Holy Laughter

Still concerned, the man left the office and went to get one of the elders of their church whose shop was just across the street. When the two returned, the elder, whom Charles had always seen as a serious man, asked how he felt. When Charles started to explain, the Spirit of God overwhelmed the elder with convulsive laughter that sprang from the innermost parts of his soul, and he couldn't stop for some time. Coming from the presence of God in the room, this holy laughter confirmed Charles's testimony and poured into a staunch, religious man the true joy of the Holy Spirit.

Then, another friend of Charles, who had been struggling with his salvation in a similar way, stopped by. When he entered the room, saw the condition of the elder, and heard Charles explaining what he had experienced that day, he immediately fell to his knees, saying, "Do pray for me!"[15] The elder and the choir member knelt and prayed for him, and when they finished, Charles prayed for him. After this episode, they all returned to their homes.

Charles was still perplexed by what he had experienced. Why had the elder laughed as he did? Did he find his story preposterous? Did he think Charles was somehow deluded? He began to wonder again if he really had made his peace with God. After arriving home, he soon fell asleep but kept waking up throughout the night because of the love he felt welling up in his heart. He would begin to doubt again, the love would abate, and he would fall back to sleep—only to wake later from that love again overwhelming him from within. Finally, however, he fell asleep and slept until morning.

---

[15] Finney, *Memoirs*, 22.

Charles Finney

The Morning Light

In his *Memoirs*, Charles described his feelings as he awoke the next morning:

> When I awoke in the morning the sun had risen, and was pouring a clear light into my room. Words cannot express the impression that this sunlight made upon me. Instantly the baptism that I had received the night before, returned upon me in the same manner. I arose upon my knees in the bed and wept aloud with joy, and remained for some time too much overwhelmed with the baptism of the Spirit to do anything but pour out my soul to God. It seemed as if this morning's baptism was accompanied with a gentle reproof, and the Spirit seemed to say to me, "Will you doubt?" "Will you doubt?" I cried, "No! I will not doubt; I cannot doubt." He then cleared that subject up so much to my mind that it was in fact impossible for me to doubt that the Spirit of God had taken possession of my soul.[16]

In that instant, Charles fully understood what Paul meant in Romans 5:1, 5: *"Being justified by faith, we have peace with God through our Lord Jesus Christ...because the love of God is shed abroad in our hearts by the Holy Ghost which is given unto us."* It would become a foundational doctrine of his ministry that people were not elected or predestined by God to go to heaven but rather were justified by their own faith in accepting Jesus' sacrifice for their sin.

For Charles Finney, salvation had been an experience that wiped away all guilt and condemnation, and he expected the same experience could come to anyone else who sought it. His sense of the condemnation of sin had been washed away by the love *"shed abroad"* in his heart. He described it thusly: "Instead of feeling that I was sinning all the time, my heart was so full of love that it overflowed. My cup ran over with blessing and with love; and I could not feel that I was sinning against God. Nor could I recover the least sense of guilt for my past sins."[17]

[16] Ibid., 23.

[17] Ibid.

Charles finally rose, prepared for the day, went to the law office, and began his career as an evangelist. He first spoke with his employer, Judge Wright, who left the office greatly troubled by Charles's words. Later, though, he would be wonderfully converted as a result of their conversation. Charles had a case scheduled for ten o'clock that morning. When his client, who happened to be a deacon in the church, came in for his pre-trial appointment, he asked, "Mr. Finney, do you recollect that my cause is to be tried at ten o'clock this morning? I suppose you are ready?" Charles told him, "I have a retainer from the Lord Jesus Christ to plead his cause, I cannot plead yours." The deacon looked on in astonishment and asked, "What do you mean?" When Charles explained what had happened to him and said that he now intended to preach the Gospel rather than practice law, the deacon hung his head and walked out. He was so affected by Charles's words that he went directly to settle his case himself, then returned home to pray and rededicated his life to the Lord.[18]

Charles saw Scripture as the law book that governed the universe.

Charles Finney's conversion challenges us by the fact of the power that was released in his life simply by his being born again. If there was ever a person transformed through conversion, it was Charles Finney. Those around him immediately felt the power of God on his life—not because Charles was somehow special in his calling, but because he was uncompromising in praying for what God had promised in His Word. Charles Finney saw Scripture as the law book that governed the universe, and once he was convinced of something it promised, he wouldn't let go of it in prayer until he knew God had assured his heart it would be done on earth just as it had been decreed in heaven.

"I Don't Believe It!"

After the deacon had left, the law office became too quiet, and Charles ventured forth to find someone new to speak with for the

[18] Finney, *Memoirs*, 24–25.

sake of the Gospel. The Spirit of God made a lasting impression on the heart of every person he spoke with that day. The word spread, and soon the entire town was astir with the news of Charles's conversion. Many, including Rev. Gale, thought it was a hoax. People began to gather at the church to discuss it, and soon Charles found himself there as well. The place was packed. Since he seemed to be the principal point of discussion, Charles approached the pulpit and began telling everyone how he knew religion was from God and how his experience convinced him of that fact. The audience, for the most part, sat entranced. As soon as Charles was finished, Rev. Gale arose, greatly moved by what he had heard, and asked the congregation to forgive him for his unbelief. He confessed that he had been blocking the church's growth because of it and asked forgiveness for not believing that Charles could be saved.

Once Rev. Gale had finished repenting, he called on Charles to pray. As he did so, more hearts were touched. For the next several days, they had meetings every night. As Charles had been head of the choir and a leader among the young people, every member of the church except one was soon saved. Charles described it in this way: "The word of God had wonderful power; and I was every day surprised to find that a few words, spoken to an individual, would stick in his heart like an arrow."[19]

Charles's Anointing Starts to Spread

A short time later, Charles visited his parents in Henderson on Lake Ontario. Until this time, only his younger brother, George, had professed to have any kind of a relationship with God. On this trip, prayer was offered in his home for the first time in Charles's life, and he saw his parents come to the Lord. While at home, Charles also met with and spoke to others. The area experienced its own small revival during the next monthly prayer meeting of local Baptists and Congregationalists, even though it was George Finney, not Charles, who attended the meeting. Again, the work of the Lord spread in every direction. It seemed wherever Charles Finney went, the Holy Spirit touched lives in wonderful ways because of his submission to Christ.

[19] Ibid., 29.

In the following months, Charles took it upon himself to undergo training to be a Presbyterian minister. It was suggested that he attend Princeton for training, but Charles saw little fruit in the ministry of those trained at Princeton, so he opted instead to stay in Adams to be tutored by Rev. Gale and to study his library of religious books.

This training brought Charles head-to-head with the religious complacency that bound New England in his day. Had he attended Princeton, he would either have been converted to Calvinism or drummed out of ministry; however, under Rev. Gale's tutelage, he could meet doctrinal fallacies head-on. Rev. Gale did not spare Charles the education that he himself had completed, even though it conflicted at times with Charles's views—Rev. Gale was familiar with Charles and the good he had done in their community, so he accepted Charles's resistance without rejecting him as a pupil. In this way, Rev. Gale and Charles debated all of the recognized doctrines of the day. Before accepting anything Rev. Gale taught him, Charles ascertained that he had the witness of the Holy Spirit in his heart and proof from the Word of God. As a result, Charles never embraced Calvinism and "predestination" but took the view that each person held his own deciding "vote" regarding where he would spend eternity. As a result, Charles Finney would revolutionize evangelism in North America and Europe by actually calling people who attended his meetings to make a decision for Christ—a concept that never would have made sense according to strict Calvinistic thinking.

Charles would revolutionalize evangelism by calling people to make a decision for Christ.

Not only did Charles find Calvinist doctrine erroneous, but he also deemed many of the practices and teachings of the day empty. He clung tenaciously to prayer, a practice that proved to be his lifeline. As he described it,

> I used to spend a great deal of time in prayer; sometimes, I thought, literally praying "without ceasing." I also found it very profitable, and felt very much inclined to hold frequent days of private fasting. On those days I would seek

to be entirely alone with God, and would generally wander off into the woods, or get into the meeting house, or somewhere away entirely by myself.

Sometimes I would pursue a wrong course in fasting, and attempt to examine myself according to the ideas of self-examination then entertained by my minister and the church. I would try to look into my heart, in the sense of examining my feelings, and would turn my attention particularly to my motives, and the state of my mind. When I pursued this course, I found invariably that the day would close without any perceptible advance being made. Afterwards I saw clearly why this was so. Turning my attention, as I did, from the Lord Jesus Christ, and looking into myself, examining my motives and feelings, my feelings all subsided of course. But whenever I fasted, and let the Spirit take his own course with me, and gave myself up to let him lead and instruct me, I universally found it in the highest degree useful. I found I could not live without enjoying the presence of God; and if at any time a cloud came over me, I could not rest, I could not study, I could not attend to anything with the least satisfaction or benefit, until the medium was again cleared between my soul and God....

The Lord taught me, in those early days of my Christian experience, many very important truths in regard to the spirit of prayer.[20]

Praying for the Sick

Charles soon found that healing could follow this spirit of prayer. Not long after his conversion, the sister-in-law of Judge Wright became seriously ill; no one believed she would live through the night. Charles said, "It seemed to plant an arrow, as it were, in my heart. It came upon me in the sense of a burden that crushed me, the nature of which I could not at all understand; but with it came an intense desire to pray for that woman."[21] He went to the meetinghouse and began to pray but found few words, able only to "groan

[20] Finney, *Memoirs*, 35–36.

[21] Ibid., 36.

with groanings deep and loud."[22] It was an example of Romans 8:26: *"Likewise the Spirit also helpeth our infirmities: for we know not what we should pray for as we ought: but the Spirit itself maketh intercession for us with groanings which cannot be uttered."*

Charles went back and forth between the meetinghouse and his office that evening because he could find no peace in his heart that the woman would live. Finally, after his third trip back and forth, he felt a release that his prayer had been answered and that the woman would live and never die in her sins. The woman recovered and, soon after, she was converted and found hope for her future in Christ.

Charles also found that his arguments for God's truth were more and more difficult for people to resist the more he prayed. It didn't matter whether he debated Calvinists, nonbelievers, or Universalists—who believed that all would be saved because of Jesus' sacrifice—none could resist the truth as he preached it. He attributed this result to his having been baptized in the Holy Spirit—a baptism he renewed continually in prayer. In fact, he soon recognized that the ministers with whom he interacted lacked this "anointing," a lack he believed responsible for their apparent absence of fruit.

> When Christ commissioned his apostles to go and preach, he told them to abide at Jerusalem till they were endued with power from on high. This power, as everyone knows, was the baptism of the Holy Ghost poured out upon them on the day of Pentecost. This was an indispensable qualification for success in their ministry. I did not suppose then, nor do I now, that this baptism was simply the power to work miracles. The power to work miracles and the gift of tongues were given as signs to attest the reality of their divine commission. But the baptism itself was a divine illumination, filling them with faith, and love, with peace and power; so that their words were made sharp in the hearts of God's enemies, quick and powerful, like a two-edged sword. This is an indispensable qualification for preaching Christ to a sinful world. Without the direct teaching of the Holy Ghost, a man will never make much progress in preaching the Gospel. The fact is, unless he can preach the

[22] Finney, *Memoirs*, 36.

> Gospel as an experience, present religion to mankind as a matter of consciousness, his speculations and theories will come far short of preaching the Gospel.[23]

When the presbytery came to Adams to examine Charles for ordination in March 1824, his reputation and testimony preceded him, and they seemed to deliberately avoid asking questions that would bring out his disagreements with their doctrine. In the end, they voted unanimously to license him to minister.

Charles Marries

Charles did not desire to preach to an established church or regular congregation, so he took a six-month commission with a women's missionary society in Oneida County in upstate New York, and traveled to the town of Evans Mills to begin his ministry. He traveled back and forth between there and a German settlement in Antwerp, ministering regularly at both.

At the time, Charles was engaged to Lydia Andrews of Whitestown in Oneida County, and they married in October 1824 and traveled to Adams. Two days after the wedding, Charles went back to Evans Mills with the intention of returning about one week later to move the couple's home there. Lydia, meanwhile, would stay in Adams and get everything in order for the trip. Because the revival took off so quickly, however, Charles wouldn't return until early spring of 1825—some six months later. This delay was probably not the makings of a very good honeymoon.

Charles's preaching style was markedly different from that of his contemporaries, especially because it was influenced greatly by his legal training. He did not speak down to his audiences as if he were an authority to whom they needed to conform; rather, he preached as if they were the jury deciding a case—the case being the salvation of their own souls. While other ministers criticized his common speech, use of repetition, and illustrations of everyday occupations and events, these techniques were the same tools lawyers employed to elicit a desired verdict. The members of Charles's "juries" said, "Why, anyone could preach as you do. You just talk to the people. You talk as if you were as much at home as if you sat in the parlor,"

[23] Ibid., 55–56.

and, "It seems as if Mr. Finney had taken me alone and was conversing with me face to face."[24] Charles had no desire to impress or awe; he was looking for decisions for Christ and refused to deviate from that goal.

Preaching by Inspiration

In his first decade of ministry, he never preached from notes or prepared sermons but always took the text God presented in his heart and spoke on it as the Spirit of God led him. Speaking about this method, Charles said, "[I] first went among the people to learn their wants. Then in light of the Holy Spirit I take the subject that I think will meet their present necessities....I pray much over the subject and then go pour it out to the people." Charles would put the Word in his heart and keep his prayer life full, and the Holy Spirit would give him the words when he stepped before an audience. As he put it, "If I do not preach from inspiration, I don't know how I did preach."[25]

When his style was criticized by more educated ministers, Charles answered matter-of-factly,

> Show me a more excellent way. Show me the fruits of your ministry; and if they so far exceed mine as to give me evidence that you have found a more excellent way, I will adopt your views. But do not expect me to abandon my own views and practices, and adopt yours, when you yourself cannot deny that, whatever errors I may have fallen into, or whatever imperfections there may be in my preaching, in style, and in everything else, yet the results justify my methods....I intend to improve all I can; but I never can adopt your manner of preaching the Gospel, until I have higher evidence that you are right and I am wrong.[26]

Charles's preaching also received a great deal of attention because he proclaimed that his listeners could find peace with God and assurance of their salvation by prevailing in prayer, something that truly rocked the boat of traditional Calvinists. He held people

---

[24] Finney, *Memoirs*, 92.

[25] Miller, *Charles Finney: He Prayed Down Revivals*, 33–34.

[26] Finney, *Memoirs*, 83.

accountable for their own salvation. When he was getting little response from those at Evans Mills, he called them directly to the primary question he wanted to hold before them:

> You admit that what I preach is the Gospel. You profess to believe it. Now will you receive it? Do you mean to receive it, or do you intend to reject it? You must have some mind about it. And now I have a right to take it for granted, inasmuch as you admit that I have preached the truth, that you acknowledge your obligation at once to become Christians.[27]

When they refused to rise to their feet in response to this call, he said,

> Then you are committed. You have taken your stand. You have rejected Christ and his Gospel; and ye are witnesses one against the other, and God is witness against you all. This is explicit, and you may remember as long as you live, that you have thus publicly committed yourselves against the Saviour and said, "We will not have this man, Jesus Christ, to reign over us."...
>
> I am sorry for you; and will preach to you once more, the Lord willing, to-morrow night.[28]

The next night, he started his sermon thusly: "Say ye to the righteous that it shall be well with him; for they shall eat the fruit of their doings. Woe to the wicked! It shall be ill with him; for the reward of his hands shall be given him."[29]

At the end of the sermon, a woman in the back of the audience fell, slain by the Spirit, and her friends held her up. Thinking she had suffered a fainting spell, Charles went to check on her and discovered she had been struck dumb. The woman lay speechless for sixteen hours. When she finally spoke again, she admitted she thought she had been saved before, but when she had been presented with the true righteousness of God, she realized her salvation was not complete. Her realization caused several others in her church to rethink their standing with Christ.

---

[27] Ibid., 62–63.

[28] Ibid., 63–64.

[29] Ibid., 65.

Another time, Charles was called to the bedside of a woman ailing from consumption.[30] Her husband was a Universalist and had indoctrinated her to be one, as well; but upon hearing Charles's words and prayers, she rejected Universalism and accepted Jesus Christ as her Lord and Savior. Her husband was so incensed that he took his gun to Charles's next meeting planning to kill him. In the middle of the sermon, the man began to sink down in his seat, groaning and crying out that he was sinking down to hell. After the meeting, the man's friends helped him home. As Charles was walking down the street the next day, this man went to meet him. He practically leaped in greeting him, taking Charles up in his arms and spinning him around in the air! All opposition to the Gospel had gone out of him, and he began seeking his peace with God.

Meeting the Prayer Warrior

It was also in Evans Mills that Charles again met Daniel Nash for the second time, a minister he had first encountered when he was examined to be licensed. At that time, his impression of Nash, better known as "Father Nash," was rather unfavorable; he had felt Nash was in somewhat of a backslidden state. Charles learned, however, that since they had last met, Nash had been infected with an eye disease that had left him lying in a dark room, unable to read or write. Because of his ailments, Nash had given himself almost entirely to prayer; eventually, he had emerged from the sickness physically healed and spiritually transformed into a man of intercessory prayer. He was far from the man whose acquaintance Charles had made earlier.

When Nash arrived in Evans Mills, he had "a praying list," as he called it, with the names of people for whom he felt called to pray every day, often several times a day. As Charles and Nash began to pray together in meetings, Charles was deeply moved by the power of Nash's prayers and the magnitude of his faith.

A Bar Becomes a Prayer Chapel

When Nash learned of a bar owner who was causing a good deal of trouble for the Christians in the community, he wrote the man's

[30] A deterioration of internal tissues, usually tuberculosis.

name down on his list as a "hard case." The bar owner was known to accost those he knew to be Christians with the most abusive and foul language. His bar had a reputation for entertaining people who engaged in drunkenness and profane revelry. A few days later, Nash pressed on, being called to another area to pray.

Not long afterward, this "hard case" showed up at one of Charles's meetings. His appearance caused considerable commotion, but as he caused no trouble when he entered, Charles left him alone, though he felt obliged to keep an eye on him throughout the service. As the meeting progressed, Charles sensed that the man was uneasy; he fidgeted constantly in his seat. Finally, he arose and asked if he could speak. When Charles gave him permission to do so, he poured himself out in brokenhearted repentance before those who had gathered. It was incredibly moving for everyone there, and many whose hearts had been hardened against what Charles had been preaching found themselves broken before God as well. Within a short time, the man made his peace with God and closed his bar to the debauchery that had formerly been prevalent in it. For the remainder of the time that Finney spent in this town, a prayer meeting took place virtually every night in this bar.

Nash's ministry had been nothing special up to this point. He was born on November 27, 1775, and took his first pastorate in Lowville Township in 1816, just short of his fortieth birthday. During his first year there, a revival broke out that saw seventy people come to the Lord, but convoluted church politics slowed things down and resulted in a church split. On September 25, 1822, Nash was voted out of office and replaced by a younger minister, although he was still asked to speak at that church from time to time. When he returned to speak, a second revival broke out. Two hundred people were converted—a sizeable number for a community of only two thousand—but Nash was not recalled to leadership in the congregation. This rejection took its toll on Nash, and it was during this downtrodden time that Charles had first met him as a member of his examination team.

After meeting again at Evans Mills, Charles and Nash decided to work together, as the Lord was leading them in similar directions. They determined to make the unchurched their primary focus. As Nash stated in a letter,

> When Mr. Finney and I began our race, we had no thought of going amongst ministers. Our highest ambition was to go where there was neither minister or reformation and try to look up the lost sheep, for whom no man cared. We began and the Lord prospered....We go into no man's parish unless called....We have room enough to work and work enough to do.[31]

Prayer Paves the Way

They established a pattern of ministry: Nash would go into an area three to four weeks ahead of Charles to prepare the ground for his arrival and even set up his speaking engagements. Sometimes Nash would go alone; at other times, he would travel with someone he knew well—most often Abel Clary; sometimes he would come together with a few local people to pray. Rarely were more than three people involved in this advance prayer movement. While the revivals were happening, Nash rarely attended the meetings; instead, he would stay in a house nearby and continue praying as the services took place.

Following Evans Mills, Nash preceded Charles to the town of Gouverneur, New York, where Charles's next speaking appointments were planned. As the meetings began to gain steam, a group of young men from a neighboring church began to oppose the move of God happening through Charles's meetings. Feeling that prayer was the only way to overcome this opposition, Nash and Charles entered a grove of trees and prayed until they felt they had gained the victory. In his *Memoirs*, Charles described what happened as a result of this prayer time:

> The next Sabbath, after preaching morning and afternoon myself—for I did the preaching altogether, and Brother Nash gave himself up almost continually to prayer—we met at five o'clock in the church, for a prayer meeting. The meeting house was filled. Near the close of the meeting, Brother Nash arose, and addressed that company of young

[31] Paul Reno, *Daniel Nash: Prevailing Prince of Prayer* (Asheville, NC: Revival Literature, 1989), 7.

> men who had joined hand in hand to resist the revival. I believe they were all there, and they sat braced up against the Spirit of God. It was too solemn for them really to make ridicule of what they heard and saw; and yet their brazen-facedness and stiff-neckedness were apparent to everybody.
>
> Brother Nash addressed them very earnestly, and pointed out the guilt and danger of the course they were taking. Toward the close of his address, he waxed exceeding warm, and said to them, "Now, mark me, young men! God will break your ranks in less than one week, either by converting some of you, or by sending some of you to hell. He will do this as certainly as the Lord is my God!" He was standing where he brought his hand down on the top of the pew before him, so as to make it thoroughly jar. He sat immediately down, dropped his head, and groaned with pain.
>
> The house was as still as death, and most of the people held down their heads. I could see that the young men were agitated. For myself, I regretted that Brother Nash had gone so far. He had committed himself, that God would either take the life of some of them, and send them to hell, or convert some of them, within a week. However on Tuesday morning of the same week, the leader of these young men came to me, in the greatest distress of mind. He was all prepared to submit; and as soon as I came to press him he broke down like a child, confessed, and manifestly gave himself to Christ. Then he said, "What shall I do, Mr. Finney?" I replied, "Go immediately to all your young companions, and pray with them, and exhort them at once to turn to the Lord." He did so; and before the week was out, nearly if not all of that class of young men, were hoping in Christ.[32]

For the next seven years until his death, Nash became a key part of every revival Charles Finney led. Together, they learned a great deal about "praying down revival." Nash was not timid in prayer—it was said his prayers could sometimes be heard up to half a mile away, though some attributed this to his poor hearing.

[32] Finney, *Memoirs*, 122–123.

Revival in the "Burned-over District"

Between 1825 and 1827, Charles itinerated throughout other parts of western New York, speaking wherever he could in frontier towns and community halls. This region had earned the nickname of the "burned-over district"—few could generate any excitement about religion anywhere in the region since it had been traveled by so many circuit preachers. Then, from December 1827 until June 1829, Charles traveled and ministered in Delaware and Pennsylvania. On June 8, 1828, while Charles was leading a revival in Philadelphia, his first child, Helen Clarissa Finney, was born. Charles took his wife, Lydia, and his daughter back to Lydia's family in western New York, then preached his way back to Philadelphia. He wouldn't return to New York to see them until June of the following year.

After Philadelphia, Charles ministered in New York City from October 1829 until May 1830. These revivals were marked with events similar to those that had marked his time in Evans Mills, nearby Antwerp, and elsewhere, and Finney attracted increased attention from the press and from churches throughout New England.

Charles's revivals benefited greatly from the industrialization and urbanization of his day. For example, the Erie Canal, finished in 1825, connected Lake Erie near Buffalo to the Hudson River at Albany, and thus the Atlantic Ocean and New York City were connected to any of the communities that could access the Great Lakes. As a result, the towns along the canal became centers of industry to which workers flocked from the rural communities throughout the region. As water transport was much cheaper than transporting goods by wagon (railways weren't built in New York before 1829), these population centers flourished and became hubs of enterprise. Thus, by speaking in places such as Utica, Troy, Rochester, and New York City, Charles was able to touch the hearts of larger crowds and youth who had left their families for jobs in the larger towns and cities. As a result, his revivals spread like wildfire and his fame grew more rapidly.

Charles Finney's fame earned him some enemies as well. Established ministers such as Lyman Beecher (father of Harriet Beecher Stowe, author of *Uncle Tom's Cabin*) and Asahel Nettleton saw his practices as unrefined, barbaric, and manipulative. They dealt harsh criticism to the "new measures" Charles used—the adoption of the Methodists' "anxious seat" as seen in the camp meetings (marking off a bench or area in the front of a meeting hall for those "anxious" about their salvation to come and dwell in prayer), nightly instead of weekly meetings (called "protracted meetings"), allowing women to pray in mixed-gender prayer meetings, as well as the use of common speech and slang in his sermons. Many saw these measures as too aggressive and felt Charles was more interested in conquering territory than winning souls.

At one point, Beecher challenged, "Finney, I know your plan, and you know I do; you mean to come to Connecticut, and carry a streak of fire to Boston. But if you attempt it, as the Lord liveth, I'll meet you at the state line and call out the artillerymen and fight every inch of the way to Boston and then I'll fight you there."[33]

Prayer warrior Daniel Nash became a key part of every revival that Charles led.

Others took up Nettleton and Beecher's cause. Many of the stories about Charles's practices were exaggerated, and false reports were printed in the newspapers. They made Charles out to be a harsh inquisitor of his audiences rather than a man pleading passionately for their souls. He was also accused of being a flagrant self-promoter who whipped crowds into emotional frenzies in order to manipulate them and draw larger and larger audiences. People who opposed Charles claimed his meetings ran to unreasonable hours, his prayers were irreverent, and his language was coarse. Those who attended his meetings, however, knew that the Spirit of God did mighty things wherever Charles Finney went.

For example, in 1826, Charles spoke at the schoolhouse in New York Mills, a community skirting Utica. His brother-in-law, a superintendent in a local cotton factory, invited him there to speak; he felt the Word would have a powerful effect among the young people.

---

[33] Miller, *Charles Finney: He Prayed Down Revivals*, 65.

The next morning, Charles took a tour of the factory, and he wrote about the experience in his memoirs:

> One of them [a young girl], was trying to mend a broken thread, and I observed that her hands trembled so that she could not mend it. I approached slowly, looking on each side at the machinery, as I passed; but observed that this girl grew more and more agitated, and could not proceed with her work. When I came within eight or ten feet of her, I looked solemnly at her. She observed it, and was quite overcome, and sunk down, and burst into tears. The impression caught almost like powder [exploding], and in a few moments nearly the whole room was in tears. The feeling spread throughout the factory....The owner of the establishment was present, and seeing the state of things, he said to the superintendent, "Stop the mill, and let the people attend to religion; for it is more important that our souls should be saved than that this factory run."... The revival went through the mill with astonishing power, and in the course of a few days nearly all in the mill were hopefully converted.[34]

Portrait of Charles Finney

The Reverend John Frost, a local Presbyterian minister, estimated that three thousand people had been saved in the region; eight months later, every one was still a faithful, active church member.

Ever Relying on the Spirit of Prayer

In Auburn, New York, in 1826, Charles was confronted with so much opposition that many of the churches to the east began closing their doors to him. Newspapers included reports of excesses in his meetings. Of this time, Nash wrote,

---

[34] Finney, *Memoirs*, 183–184.

> The work of God moves forward in power, in some places against dreadful opposition. Mr. Finney and I have both been hanged and burned in effigy. We have frequently been disturbed in our religious meetings. Sometimes the opposers make a noise in the house of God; sometimes they gather round the house and stone it, and discharge guns. There is almost as much writing, intrigue, and lying, and reporting of lies, as there would be if we were on the eve of a presidential election. Oh, what a world! How much it hates the truth! How unwilling to be saved! But I think the work will go on.[35]

Charles again took the matter to prayer:

> I said nothing publicly, or as I recollect privately, to anybody on the subject; but gave myself to prayer. I looked to God with great earnestness day after day, to be directed; asking him to show me the path of duty, and give me grace to ride out the storm....
>
> The Lord showed me as in a vision of what was before me. He drew so near to me, while I was engaged in prayer, that my flesh literally trembled on my bones. I shook from head to foot, under a full sense of the presence God. At first, and for some time, it seemed more like being on the top of Sinai, amidst its full thunderings, than in the presence of the cross of Christ.
>
> Never in my life, that I recollect, was I so awed and humbled before God as then. Nevertheless, instead of feeling like fleeing, I seemed drawn nearer and nearer to God—seemed to draw nearer and nearer to that Presence that filled me with such an unutterable awe and trembling. After a season of great humiliation before him, there came a great lifting up. God assured me that he would be with me and uphold me; that no opposition should prevail against me; that I had nothing to do, in regard to all this matter, but to keep about my work, and wait for the salvation of God.[36]

---

[35] Reno, *Daniel Nash: Prevailing Prince of Prayer*, 13.

[36] Finney, *Memoirs*, 193.

Such prayer became a key not only in facing opposition, but also in everything else Charles faced, especially in "praying down revival." While most people thought of revivals only as moves of God, who, in His sovereignty, poured out His Spirit (another instance where the ministers of the day used God's sovereignty as an excuse for their lack of effective ministry), Charles believed that human beings could set the stage for revival through prayer, fasting, and holding God accountable to His promises in the Bible. Charles wrote about this spirit of prayer as it affected him during the revival at De Kalb in upstate New York:

> I found myself so much exercised, and so borne down with the weight of immortal souls, that I was constrained to pray without ceasing. Some of my experiences, indeed, alarmed me. A spirit of importunity sometimes came upon me so that I would say to God that He had made a promise to answer prayer, and I could not, and would not, be denied. I felt so certain that He would hear me, and that faithfulness to his promises, and to himself, rendered it impossible that he should not hear and answer, that frequently I found myself saying to him, "I hope thou dost not think that I can be denied. I come with thy faithful promises in my hand, and I cannot be denied." I cannot tell how absurd unbelief looked to me, and how certain it was, in my mind, that God would answer prayer—those prayers that, from day to day, and from hour to hour, I found myself offering in such agony and faith. I had no idea of the shape the answer would take, the locality in which the prayers would be answered, or the exact time of the answer. My impression was that the answer was near, even at the door; and I felt myself strengthened in the divine life, put on the harness for a mighty conflict with the powers of darkness, and expected soon to see a far more powerful outpouring of the Spirit of God, in that new country where I had been laboring.[37]

Oswald J. Smith explained why this kind of prayer was so important to Charles's ministry:

---

[37] Finney, *Memoirs*, 142–143.

> He always preached with the expectation of seeing the Holy Spirit suddenly outpoured. Until this happened little or nothing was accomplished. But the moment the Spirit fell upon the people, Finney had nothing else to do but point them to the Lamb of God. Thus he lived and wrought for years in an atmosphere of revival.[38]

Charles and his wife went on to minister in several places from October 1829 until May 1830, ending in New York City, where their second child and first son, Charles Beman Finney, was born on March 28.

100,000 Saved

A major breakthrough, and the greatest outpouring of his life, came when Charles held a revival in Rochester, New York, starting in September 1830. Rochester was the fastest-growing American city in the 1820s. The town was founded in 1811, when fifteen people settled along the Genesee River to take advantage of the waterfalls to power their mills. In 1823, the city had grown to a population of twenty-five hundred, and the aqueduct connecting the Erie Canal to the Genesee River was completed, connecting the farmers of western New York with New York City and the Atlantic Ocean.

It seemed that the town became a thriving commercial center overnight. Farmers would take their grains there, receive cash payment from the mills, and then shop for necessities in Rochester's marketplaces before returning home. As a result, more than half of the adult men in Rochester were skilled artisans, and many professional people, such as county-seat lawyers and physicians, settled there.

By 1830, Rochester had almost quadrupled to nearly ten thousand residents, making the town about a tenth of the size of Philadelphia. During the months when Charles spoke there, nearly the entire population was converted; roughly one hundred thousand people in the region came to the Lord.[39] The revival touched communities as far as a hundred miles away. Lyman Beecher, Charles's harsh critic in his early years, would eventually call Charles's work

[38] Reno, *Daniel Nash: Prevailing Prince of Prayer*, 15.

[39] Finney, *Memoirs*, 301.

in Rochester "the greatest work of God, and the greatest revival of religion, that the world has ever seen, in so short a time. One hundred thousand…were reported as having connected themselves with churches….This…is unparalleled in the history of the church, and the progress of religion."[40]

It was recorded that as many as 85 percent of Charles's converts remained Christians years later. It was all that Cane Ridge had been, with fewer excesses, but multiplied several times over—and it was in an urban area striving to become a cultural center rather than at a rural gathering of farmers and pioneers.

Charles was initially invited to Rochester to fill the pulpit for the Third Presbyterian Church, whose pastor had just been called to lead the First Presbyterian Church in New York City. Helping to initiate this move was one of the church elders, Josiah Bissell. Bissell was a wealthy businessman who owned the Pioneer Stage Line, famous throughout the East for not operating its coaches on Sundays. Bissell was a generous man who helped significantly to finance the construction of both the Second and Third Presbyterian Churches in Rochester.

Before accepting the call to Rochester, however, Charles looked into the spiritual atmosphere of the town to determine whether it was ripe for revival. He learned that there was disagreement among the Christians of the town. It appears Bissell had seen the Second Presbyterian Church pastor, the Reverend William James, riding in one of the Sunday coaches of another stage line. Bissell, who apparently thought his wealth and social position gave him a say in everything, had already entered into conflict with James about the day-to-day affairs of the church. This was the last straw

A camp meeting in 1829

Library of Congress, 96510018

[40] Finney, *Memoirs*, 300–301.

for Bissell, and he persuaded the members of the congregation to request James's dismissal. Dr. Joseph Penney, pastor of the First Presbyterian Church of Rochester, came to James's defense, provoking Bissell to complain to the presbytery[41] about Penney's interference. Thus, the rift between the churches began.

After praying about the matter and seeking advice from those around him, Charles concluded that Rochester was an unpromising invitation. He determined to turn it down, but God had other ideas. When Charles was alone that night and about to retire, he came to the realization that his logic had been faulty: "Certainly you are needed at Rochester all the more because of these difficulties. Do you shun the field because there are so many things that need to be corrected, because there is so much that is wrong? But if all was right, you would not be needed."[42] He determined at once to answer the invitation.

Between September 1830 and March 1831, Charles preached several nights each week and three times each Sunday. Penney came to one of Charles's first services, and their spirits were immediately knit together by the Holy Spirit. Penney then invited Charles to speak at the First Presbyterian Church, and as the revival began to take hold, Bissell and Penney soon resolved their difference in the spirit of Christian unity that overpowered Rochester and the surrounding communities, including Ogden, Brockport, Penfield, and Clarkson.

It was a revival that touched all social classes—from civic and business leaders to schoolteachers, from physicians and shopkeepers to farmers and migrant workers. Many businesses closed so that employees could attend the meetings, and women from the church went door-to-door, praying for people and inviting them to come to the evening service. Bars closed for lack of patrons. Crime rates dropped dramatically and stayed low for years, even as the population grew. At one point, the teenagers in the local high school were so distraught about the condition of their souls that they paid no attention to their lessons, so the director invited Charles to come and speak. Nearly the entire student body was saved, including the director, who had originally thought it was a ploy by the students to get

---

[41] The presbytery is a local council that oversees the churches of a region in Presbyterian Church governance.

[42] Finney, *Memoirs*, 142–143.

out of their work. Forty of the students went on to become ministers. The society in and around Rochester was transformed and became distinctly Christian. One could not go out into the streets or into a bank or shop and not overhear a discussion about religion. As one student, Charles P. Bush, who later became a leading pastor in New York City, put it,

> The whole community was stirred. Religion was the topic of conversation, in the house, in the shop, in the office and on the street. The only theater in the city was converted into a livery stable; the only circus into a soap and candle factory. Grog shops were closed; the Sabbath was honored; the sanctuaries were thronged with happy worshippers; a new impulse was given to every philanthropic enterprise; the fountains of benevolence where opened, and men lived to good.[43]

Again, Charles felt that prayer played a major part in the work of the revival. He wrote that "the key which unlocked the Heavens in this revival was the prayer of [Abel] Clary, Father Nash, and other unnamed folk who laid themselves prostrate before God's throne and besought Him for a divine outpouring."[44] When Charles heard that Clary was in town, he remarked, "I have not seen him at any of our meetings." The man who told him of Clary's attendance responded, "No...he cannot go to meetings, he says. He prays nearly all the time, day and night, and in such an agony of mind that I do not know what to make of it. Sometimes he cannot even stand on his knees, but will lie prostrate on the floor, and groan and pray in a manner that quite astounds me." Charles replied, "I understand it; please keep still. It will all come out right; he will surely prevail."[45] He knew what this spirit of prayer was doing and he knew better than to do anything to interfere with it.

Of this kind of fervent prayer, Charles said,

> I have never seen a person sweat blood, but I do know a person who prayed until his nose bled. And people have

[43] V. Raymond Edman, *Finney Lives On* (Minneapolis: Bethany House Publishers, 1971), 68, quoted in Hyatt, *2000 Years of Charismatic History*, 137.

[44] Reno, *Daniel Nash: Prevailing Prince of Prayer*, 12.

[45] Finney, *Memoirs*, 297.

> prayed until drenched with sweat, even in the coldest winter. Some have prayed for hours until their strength was exhausted from the labor of their minds. Such prayers reached out and took hold of God.[46]

Rochester became the first place where Charles really began using the "anxious bench"—a precursor to the altar calls used widely today. Prior to this, Charles had had "anxious meetings"—gatherings following the main evening service, often held the next morning, where those anxious about the state of their souls could come to inquire more earnestly and personally about the conversion of their souls. In Rochester, however, Charles found people needed no "working up" to salvation but were immediately ready to embrace it once it was presented to them. Rather than waiting, he sectioned off a front part of the meetinghouse so that people could come forward to pray for their salvation as soon as he invited them. As he put it,

> I had found also that something was needed, to make the impression on them that they were expected at once to give up their hearts; something that would call them to act, and act as publicly before the world, as they had in their sins; something that would commit them publicly to the service of Christ. When I had called them simply to stand up in the public congregation, I found that this had a very good effect; and so far as it went, it answered the purpose for which it was intended. But after all, I had felt that for some time, that something more was necessary to bring them out from among the masses of the ungodly, to a public renunciation of their sinful ways, and a public committal of themselves to God.[47]

The Rochester revival would prove to be the height of the Second Great Awakening and a spark to light the fuse of a national revival that ran like wildfire throughout the United States in 1831. A host of evangelists, including Beecher himself, took up the torch from Rochester, and the rolls of membership swelled in churches everywhere—Presbyterian, Methodist, Baptist, Episcopalian, Congregational,

---

[46] Charles Finney, "Prevailing Prayer," *Lectures on Revival* (Minneapolis: Bethany House Publishers, 1988), 43.

[47] Finney, *Memoirs*, 288–289.

and others alike. New England churches grew by one-third in 1831 alone. Following the Rochester revival, criticism of Charles and his methods all but evaporated.

The National Revival of 1831 brought greater unity to the United States, where the common talk of the day centered on religion. Day-to-day chores and business hours revolved around church gatherings and prayer meetings. Churches became the community centers of the day. Protestantism became a glue that bound together American hearts through prayer, and the Protestant work ethic became synonymous with prosperity, growing communities, and Yankee ingenuity.

It is also important to note that Father Nash died at the age of fifty-six near the end of that year, on December 20, 1831. Less than four months later, Charles would give up his itinerant ministry to take a position as a pastor.

Pastoring in New York City

The heavy preaching load of the Rochester revival took its toll on Charles. Doctors believed that he had consumption, and they prescribed rest. Several thought he would die. Having heard this before, Charles informed them that they were mistaken—he was merely overtired, and all he needed was a little rest.

By the spring of 1831, Charles felt his work in Rochester was done. He had accepted an invitation to speak at Union College in Schenectady, New York, and began making his way there by coach. The going was tough, however, and in three days he had traveled only as far as Auburn, a distance of roughly sixty miles. Before continuing on his way, he received a written request to stay and preach in Auburn. The request had been signed by a large number of town leaders, many of whom had formerly opposed his ministry. Charles would stay and minister six weeks, and many years later, a historian of the First Presbyterian Church of Auburn recorded,

> He was then at the prime of life and at the height of his fame. As a preacher...he was without rival. The glance of his full sharp eye and the tones of his commanding voice were in keeping with the sterner aspects of truth, which he never failed to present with searching discrimination and

> powerful effect....Mr. Finney preached in no other pulpit than this, but the results were by no means limited to this congregation. Many, who ascribed their conversion to his instrumentality, united with other churches in the village and vicinity; and now, after a generation has passed, and with it the prejudice of the time, there can be no question of the service then rendered to the cause of vital religion.[48]

From Auburn, Charles would press on to Buffalo, New York; Providence, Rhode Island; and eventually, Boston, Massachusetts. His opposition had softened so much by this time that he even held meetings together with his former critic, Lyman Beecher.

On March 7, 1832, the Finneys' third child, Frederick Norton Finney, was born, and Charles and his wife decided that the traveling evangelist's life was not conducive to raising a family. As Charles put it, "I had become fatigued, as I had labored about ten years as an evangelist, without anything more than a few days or weeks of rest, during the whole period."[49] These factors, among others, led him to take the pastorate of the Chatham Street Chapel (also known as the Second Free Presbyterian Church) in New York City. He left Boston and began his pastorate in New York in April 1832.

A group of benefactors, including businessman and abolitionist Lewis Tappan, paid to have the Chatham Street Theatre refurbished into a church. Upon the building's completion, Charles spoke to crowds of fifteen hundred to two thousand—sizeable audiences even for New York City. From May to June of that year, he preached seventy consecutive evenings. Charles purposed not to take members from other churches but to reach the unsaved. He instructed his church members

> to scatter themselves over the whole house, and to keep their eyes open, in regard to any that were seriously affected under preaching, and if possible, to detain them after preaching, for conversation and prayer. They were true to

[48] Charles Howley, *The History of the Presbyterian Church, Auburn, New York* (Auburn: Daily Advertiser and Weekly Journal Stoan Book Print, 1876), 49–51, quoted in Lewis Drummond, *A Fresh Look at the Life and Ministry of Charles G. Finney* (Minneapolis: Bethany House Publishers, 1985), 146–147.

[49] Finney, *Memoirs*, 318.

> their teaching, and were on the lookout at every meeting to see, with whom the Word of God was taking effect; and they had faith enough to dismiss their fears, and to speak to any whom they saw to be affected by the Word. In this way the conversion of a great many souls was secured. They would invite them into those rooms, and there we could converse and pray with them, and thus gather up the results of every sermon.[50]

He and his congregation did this with such success that another church was soon planted out of new members from Chatham Street.

By midsummer, a cholera epidemic hit New York City; while many fled, Charles stayed to minister to his flock. However, at his installation service on September 28, Charles took ill with a fever that proved to be cholera. Though he survived the disease, the treatments were so harsh that he was unable to resume his preaching until the spring of 1833. In January 1834, taking a break due to the fatigue of work and the toll of the cholera and its treatment, Charles left for six months on a sea voyage to try to recover his strength. His trip took him to the Mediterranean Sea and the islands of Malta and Sicily. He recorded in his *Memoirs*,

> On my homeward passage my mind became exceedingly exercised on the question of revivals. I feared that they would decline throughout the country. I feared that the opposition that had been made to them, had grieved the Holy Spirit. My own health, it appeared to me, had nearly or quite broken down; and I knew of no other evangelist that would take the field, and aid pastors in revival work. This view of the subject distressed me so much that one day I found myself unable to rest. My soul was in an utter agony. I spent almost the entire day in prayer in my stateroom, or walking the deck in intense agony, in view of the state of things. In fact I felt crushed with the burden that was on my soul. There was no one on board to whom I could open my mind, or say a word.

---

[50] Finney, *Memoirs*, 322.

> It was the spirit of prayer that was upon me; that which I had often before experienced in kind, but perhaps never before to such a degree, for so long a time. I besought the Lord to go on with His work, and to provide Himself with such instrumentalities as were necessary. It was a long summer day, in the early part of July. After a day of unspeakable wrestling and agony in my soul, just at night, the subject cleared up to my mind. The Spirit led me to believe that all would come out right, and that God had yet a work for me to do; that I might be at rest; that the Lord would go forward with His work and give me strength to take any part in it that He desired. But I had not the least idea what the course of His providence would be.[51]

Taking a Stand for Social Justice

Upon returning to New York, Charles found that the issue of slavery had captured the consciences of many there. Those opposed to slavery included Lewis Tappan and his brother, Arthur, who had founded the New York City Antislavery Society, later the American Antislavery Society, in that same year. Earlier, the Tappan brothers had urged Charles to allow African Americans to attend service at the Chatham Street Chapel, and he had agreed, even though whites and blacks sat in different sections.

Charles routinely denounced slavery from the pulpit, even going so far as to refuse Communion to slave owners. As a result of his stance and that of the Tappan brothers—both primary financiers of the new Broadway Tabernacle that was nearing completion as Charles's next church—a pro-slavery mob set fire to the building in protest, burning the roof off. The Tappan brothers ordered construction to recommence at once, and the building was finished in 1836. Charles had had significant input into the building's design. It had a circular sanctuary with the pulpit in the center, and it accommodated twenty-four hundred people. With two levels, it resembled two amphitheaters pushed together, and the sound carried remarkably well.

---

[51] Ibid., 328–329.

The *New York Evangelist*, a newspaper started by a group brave enough to publish responses to Finney's critics, took up the abolitionist cause and subsequently lost subscribers. By this time, the Reverend Joshua Leavitt was the newspaper's editor. He went to Charles for help, and Charles told him he would pray about it. After considering it for a day or two, Charles suggested that he could preach a series of lectures on revival, and that the *Evangelist* could reprint them. Leavitt was pleased, and printing the lectures had the desired effect: readers subscribed to the *Evangelist* at a rate faster than that at which he had lost them. In this series of lectures, Charles taught that revival was not a miracle but a matter of human beings calling on God and obediently following the leadership of the Holy Spirit. Once again, Charles shook the Calvinist foundations of New England orthodoxy and people's reliance on the sovereignty of God as an excuse for their own backslidden conditions.

Broadway Tabernacle temperance activists set fire to Communion wine.

Mary Evans Picture Library

Once these lectures were published in the newspaper, they were compiled in a book entitled *Finney's Lectures on Revival*, and the book sold almost as quickly as it could be printed. Copies were published and translated as needed in the U.S., Canada, England, Scotland, Wales, France, Germany, and elsewhere in Europe. Many people read the book and were converted as a result. Charles's impact on the communities of New England and New York was now spreading around the world. He saw this success as part of the answer to his prayers while at sea—God was using him even more mightily than before.

Charles Becomes a Professor

Revival continued to flow whenever Charles spoke in New York through the end of 1834 and into the winter of 1835. As a result, he was suddenly faced with a large number of young men who wanted to go into the ministry but had no proper place to be educated and ordained according to the Gospel as Charles Finney preached it.

Soon, the requests for Charles to teach theology grew numerous enough that he agreed and began a lecture series.

Around this time, there was a controversy at Lane Seminary in Cincinnati, Ohio, that would soon take Charles's career as a theology instructor a step further. The seminary was composed largely of converted young people from New York's "Burned-over District" who firmly believed that owning slaves was a sin. Many of Lane Seminary's trustees owned slaves themselves, however, and they tried to silence the students. Asa Mahan, a trustee, took up the students' cause, and when the students left to start a new college in Oberlin, Ohio, Mahan left with them. He became the first president of Oberlin College, and the students requested Charles Finney as their professor of theology. When the Tappan brothers offered to finance the professorship of Charles and seven others, he agreed to teach at Oberlin in the summer and return and pastor in New York City in the winter. The Finneys' first summer in Oberlin was in 1835.

Charles accepted the position at Oberlin on several conditions, one of which was that African-American students were to receive the same treatment as white students—there would be no discrimination or segregation based on color or gender. Oberlin was even a station for the Underground Railroad, helping slaves escape the South to find freedom in Canada. While Oberlin's African-American population never exceeded 5 percent, it was still a symbol of all that abolitionists hoped for—a place of freedom, regardless of racial differences. Charles also believed strongly in the education of women, since they were the primary educators of children, and Oberlin created a women's department.

Oberlin College opened its doors to one hundred students when Charles began teaching there, and by 1840, five hundred students were enrolled. By the time Charles became the president of Oberlin in 1851, the college had more than one thousand students. Mary Jane Patterson, whose parents had been slaves, graduated from Oberlin in 1862 as the first African-American woman in the United States—probably in the world—to receive a bachelor's degree.[52] She went on to become the principal of the first "preparatory high school

[52] "God's College and Radical Change," *Christian History* 7, no. 4 [Issue 20] (1988): 27.

for colored youth" in Washington, D.C. After Charles's death, U.S. President James Garfield affirmed to the student body of Oberlin "that no college in the land had more effectively touched the nerve centers of the national life and thought and ennobled them than did this institution to which Charles Finney devoted so many years of Christian service."[53]

A Change in Denominations

When an inconsistency arose in the rulings of the local presbytery concerning the discipling of transferring members, Charles took issue with the presbytery's lack of precedence—something that deeply offended his sense of justice from his days as a lawyer when precedence was as important as legislation. He decided to withdraw from the denomination. This was no easy decision for a man who had been a Presbyterian since the start of his ministry, but he felt he must continue to answer God's call with a clear conscience and a pure heart. Thus, it was decided that Chatham Street Chapel would become a Congregational church and would occupy the new Tabernacle on Broadway that had been under construction for some time. On March 13, 1836, Charles resigned his pastorate of the Second Free Presbyterian Church and transferred his ordination to the Congregational church. He held a few more meetings at Chatham Street Chapel until the Broadway Tabernacle was finished; the first meeting in the Tabernacle was held on Sunday, April 10. That evening, Charles was installed as the Tabernacle's pastor.[54]

Moving to Oberlin

Charles split his years between Oberlin and New York City from the summer of 1835 until April 6, 1837, when he resigned as pastor of the Tabernacle and moved permanently to Oberlin. In that same year, the Finneys' fourth child, Julia Finney, was born on March 16. The previous year, when James Shipherd resigned as pastor of the Oberlin church due to ill health, Charles was asked to step in temporarily. With the Finneys moving to Oberlin to live year-round, this

---

[53] Miller, *Charles Finney: He Prayed Down Revivals*, 96–97.

[54] Keith J. Hardman, *Charles Grandison Finney: 1792–1875* (Grand Rapids, MI: Baker Book House, 1987), 311, 313.

temporary pastorate became permanent in May 1837. Charles could now teach during the week and preach every Sunday. His primary calling would always be that of an evangelist—it was something from which he could never stray too far. The church prospered under his leadership, as did the university; the First Church of Oberlin grew so rapidly that, in 1844, another church that could seat two thousand people was completed for Charles. This church would be the largest building west of the Appalachian Mountains for many years to come.

Still a revivalist at heart, Charles now established himself as a social reformer, as well. Since Rochester, he had learned that the Gospel could not only change hearts—if given the chance, it could transform society. Besides the abolitionist cause, Charles's work at Oberlin would touch other social reforms, such as the temperance movement, Sabbath keeping, and the participation of women in the church. Charles always put the winning of souls first and foremost, however—a message not all of his students at Oberlin took to heart. Many who later attended Oberlin lost their way, getting caught up only with causes they supported and thereby missing God's perfect will for their lives in the process. Their rebellious nature overpowered their love and faithfulness.

Charles remained mostly in Oberlin until 1842, when he returned to Boston, Providence, New York City, and Rochester to hold meetings. God had not yet finished using him, and revival again sprang up everywhere he preached. He now had formulaic methods: "The measures were simply preaching the Gospel, and abundant prayer, in private, in social circles, and in public prayer meetings; much stress being always laid upon prayer as an essential means of promoting the revival."[55] When Charles Finney was joined by those around him in prayer, God certainly answered.

A Deeper Baptism of the Holy Spirit

During his first years in Oberlin, Charles was troubled by the fact that some of those who had been converted during his revivals had since backslidden, or fallen away, from the faith. He began to think that Christians needed a deeper conversion, or "second blessing" beyond conversion, if they were going to live wholly sanctified

[55] Finney, *Memoirs*, 363.

lives on this earth. He came to believe that a further work of the Holy Spirit would allow Christians to live in holiness, thereby following Jesus' exhortation in His Sermon on the Mount in Matthew 5:48 to *"be ye perfect."* This belief would bring more criticism on Oberlin, an institution that many people came to see as a den of extremists—chief among them, Charles and Mahan. The Second Blessing was a theme that Charles developed in his lectures at Oberlin, which would eventually be published as the two-volume *Lectures on Systematic Theology.* Charles would not experience anything along these lines in his own life, however, until the winter of 1843–1844.

In the fall of 1843, Charles was invited to Boston again, and he answered the call. Boston had been seduced by Universalism and Unitarianism to the point that Charles found many people in the following spiritual condition:

> The mass of the people in Boston, are more unsettled in their religious convictions, than in any other place that I have ever labored in....It is extremely difficult to make religious truths lodge in their minds, because the influence of Unitarian teaching has been, to lead them to call in question all the principal doctrines of the Bible. Their system is one of denials. Their theology is negative. They deny almost everything, and affirm almost nothing. In such a field, error finds the ears of the people open; and the most irrational views, on religious subjects, come to be held by a great many people.[56]

Charles went on to describe the change that occurred within him as he prayed over the problems in Boston and how to address them. (This passage is somewhat lengthy, but the insight herein is so deep I felt it better served to present it in Finney's own words.)

> During this winter, the Lord gave my own soul a very thorough overhauling, and a fresh baptism of his Spirit.... My mind was greatly drawn out in prayer, for a long time; as indeed it always has been, when I have labored in Boston.... This winter, in particular, my mind was exceedingly exercised on the question of personal holiness; and in respect to

[56] Finney, *Memoirs*, 372.

the state of the church, their want of power with God; the weakness of the orthodox churches in Boston, the weakness of their faith, and their want of power in the midst of such a community. The fact that they were making little or no progress in overcoming the errors of the city, greatly affected my mind.

I gave myself to a great deal of prayer. After my evening services, I would retire as early as I well could; but rose at four o'clock in the morning, because I could sleep no longer, and immediately went to the study, and engaged in prayer....I frequently continued from the time I arose, at four o'clock, till the gong called to breakfast, at eight o'clock. My days were spent, so far as I could get time, in searching the Scriptures. I read nothing else, all that winter, but my Bible; and a great deal of it seemed new to me. Again the Lord took me, as it were, from Genesis to Revelation....The whole Scripture seemed to me all ablaze with light, and not only light, but it seemed as if God's Word was instinct with the very life of God....

I labored that winter mostly for a revival of religion among Christians. The Lord prepared me to do so, by the great work He wrought in my own soul....

In this place, there is a larger number of persons, by far, that understand me, and devour that class of truths, than I have found elsewhere; but even here, the majority of professors of religion, do not understandingly embrace those truths. They do not object, they do not oppose; and so far as they understand, they are convinced. But as a matter of experience, they are ignorant of the power of the highest and most precious truths of the Gospel of salvation, in Christ Jesus....

I felt very confident that, unless the foundations could be relayed in some sense, and that unless the Christians in Boston took on a higher type of Christian living, they never could prevail against Unitarianism. I knew that the orthodox ministers had been preaching orthodoxy, as opposed to Unitarianism, for many years; and that all that could be accomplished by discussion, had been accomplished. But

> I felt that what Unitarians needed, was to see Christians live out the pure Gospel of Christ. They needed to hear them say, and prove what they said by their lives, that Jesus Christ was a divine Savior, and able to save them from all sin. Their professions of faith in Christ, did not accord with their experiences. They could not say that they found Christ in their experience, what they preached Him to be. There is needed the testimony of God's living witnesses, the testimony of experience, to convince the Unitarians; and mere reasonings and arguments, however conclusive, will never overcome their errors and their prejudices.
>
> The orthodox churches there, are too formal; they are in bondage to certain ways; they are afraid of measures, afraid to launch forth in all freedom, in the use of means to save souls. They have always seemed to me, to be in bondage in their prayers, in so much that what I call the spirit of prayer, I have seldom witnessed in Boston. The ministers and deacons of the churches, though good men, are afraid of what the Unitarians will say, if, in their measures to promote religion, they launch out in such a way as to wake the people up. Everything must be done in a certain way. The Holy Spirit is grieved by their yielding to such a bondage.
>
> I have labored in Boston in five powerful revivals of religion; and I must express it as my sincere conviction, that the greatest difficulty in the way of overcoming Unitarianism, and all the forms of error there, is the timidity of Christians and churches.[57]

Charles's Most Challenging Setback

Back in Oberlin, Lydia Finney had grown more and more frail, something that was not helped by the pregnancy and birth of her fifth child, Sarah Finney, in 1841. Sarah fell deathly ill early in 1843 and died on March 9. The Finneys' sixth and final child, Delia Finney, was born in 1844 but would live only eight years, dying from illness on September 1, 1852.

[57] Finney, *Memoirs*, 373–374, 380, 384.

Lydia had supported Charles faithfully throughout her adult life and contributed a good deal to his ministry. Being the wife of Charles Finney couldn't have been easy for someone as humble and retiring as Lydia, but she stood the test well, even during her husband's months-long absences. She was the model of what Charles thought women should be—faithful in prayer and diligent to see to the education and salvation of their children. On her deathbed, Lydia summoned her children to her side and prayed one last time with each of them, only weeks before she passed away. She then told her husband that "her work was done with and for them. She had had her last prayer meeting with them and had said all she had to say. She had given them her last advice."[58] Lydia Finney died on December 17, 1847, and her death was one of the lowest points in Charles's life. Had it not been for the deep blessing he had experienced in Boston, he might not have endured her loss.

Charles was left with five children: Helen, nineteen, who had married an Oberlin professor, William Cochran; Charles, seventeen; Fredrick, fifteen; Julia, thirteen; and Delia, who was three at the time. The burden of work for his revivals and the busyness of his teaching schedule made it difficult if not impossible for Charles to remain a single parent. It was a tough decision to remarry, but on November 13, 1848, Asa Mahan, then president of Oberlin College, officiated at the marriage of Charles and Elizabeth Ford Atkinson, a widow from Rochester. She and her late husband, William Atkinson, had been ardent supporters of Charles after the 1830 revival in Rochester. Elizabeth had lost her husband and two daughters to an epidemic of typhoid fever in 1843. Though the marriage of Charles and Elizabeth may have been more of a matter of convenience than of love, Elizabeth proved an able mother to Charles's children, and Charles came to love and admire her over time as she became a positive influence on his ministry and family throughout their years together.

Finney's Final Years

Acceding to many requests, Charles and his wife traveled to Great Britain in the fall of 1849 to minister there. Charles again

[58] Charles G. Finney, "Last Sickness and Death of Mrs. Finney," *Oberlin Evangelist*, January 5, 1848, http://www.gospeltruth.net/1848OE/48_lets_art/480105_art_mrs_finney.htm.

found success with the methods he had come to rely on in the United States, and Elizabeth found success holding meetings for women—a greater empowerment of women's involvement in ministry was started under her husband's leadership.

In 1851, Charles became the president of Oberlin College, but he continued to travel and lead revivals as his duties would allow him. Between 1851 and 1857, he would travel and preach in Boston, Massachusetts; New York City; Hartford, Connecticut; and Rochester, New York. In 1859, he returned to England and pushed north to preach in Scotland. It was this last trip to the British Isles that taxed his health to its limits; after returning to the United States in 1860 at the beginning of the Civil War, Charles would not leave Oberlin again. On November 27, 1863, Elizabeth passed away. The following year, Charles married for the third time. His new wife, Rebecca Allen Rayl, was the assistant principal of Oberlin's women's department.

Though he continued to teach and preach in Oberlin for the rest of his days, Charles resigned from his position as college president in 1866. At the request of friends and colleagues, he would finish his *Memoirs* in 1868, even though they wouldn't be published until a year after his death.

Two weeks short of his eighty-third birthday, Charles Finney passed away as the first hints of autumn hung in the morning air of August 16, 1875.

A Legacy of a Nation Revived

Charles Finney's life spanned nearly the entire first century of U.S. presidents—from George Washington to Ulysses S. Grant—and no single individual had more influence in the United States' coming to be considered "A Christian Nation" at the beginning of the twentieth century. Finney's revivals sparked the Second Great Awakening and unified the country around the Bible and the power of prayer, while his moral stances for social justice laid the foundations for everything from abolition to temperance to the civil rights movement. His teachings on Christian perfectionism inspired the holiness movement of the latter half of the nineteenth century—a movement that laid the groundwork for the Pentecostal and charismatic movements in the twentieth century. Finney's evangelistic style and methods are still used in revivals throughout the world today. These include prayer meetings before and during the event, nightly meetings for weeks at a time, altar calls, and pushing for decisions before listeners leave the auditorium—aspects that influenced everyone from Dwight L. Moody to Billy Graham. Finney's example in lifestyle, ministry, and doctrine has yielded much that is good in American Christianity today. We will need more people like Charles Finney if the church is to impact our world in the twenty-first century as God is calling us to do in the decades to come.

Chapter Eight

☆☆☆☆☆

Dwight L. Moody

(1837–1899)

"The Greatest Layman"

"The Greatest Layman"

The world has yet to see what God can do with and for and through and in and by the man who is fully and wholly consecrated to Him....I will try my utmost to be that man.

Why don't you turn your life over to Christ? He can do more with it than you can.

—Dwight L. Moody

Of all the revivalists discussed in this book, none did so much with so little as Dwight L. Moody. Nor would any of them vault so quickly from obscurity to international fame. Moody was also unique in that his success as an evangelist would start in a nation that was not his own. He would go from being a simple, uneducated layman—never having more than a fourth-grade education—to starting a college, Moody Bible Institute; establishing two major publishing companies, Moody Press and Fleming H. Revell; and preaching to more people than anyone except Billy Sunday and Billy Graham. Moody himself said, "If God calls a man to work, He will be with him in that work, and he will succeed no matter what the obstacles may be." Moody proved this truth in his own life through dogged determination, God's anointing to preach, and the combined power of prayer and publicity, to create revival.

In his lifetime, he would see the greatest setbacks of any of the revivalists—the Civil War nearly tore his nation in two; he nearly drowned at sea; he would see the fruits of his labor burn to the ground. Yet, even with these adversities, D. L. Moody would become the most influential American evangelist of the nineteenth century.

No Father and Eight Brothers and Sisters

The sixth child of Edwin and Betsy Moody, Dwight Lyman Moody was born on February 7, 1837, in Northfield, Massachusetts. In the next four years, his parents would have three more children, the last two a set of twins. Tragically, on the morning of May 28, 1841, Edwin Moody would experience a deep pain in his side while working, return home at midday only to have it grow worse, and collapse in front of his wife, dying before either of them could understand the severity of his condition. Betsy was eight months pregnant with the twins when her husband died.

The Moodys were not a wealthy family. Edwin had been a brick and stone mason, and their property was under mortgage when he died. Dower rights—the laws that kept creditors from seizing the homes and livelihoods of new widows—protected Betsy's right to the house. But upon her husband's death, creditors descended on the property and took their horse, buggy, cow, and everything else of value, except for Edwin's masonry tools and a calf that Betsy and her oldest son, Isaiah, managed to conceal before the creditors arrived. The creditors even took the pile of firewood and kindling in their shed. Even so, Betsy was responsible for the mortgage payments—a tough time for a mother of seven with two more on the way in a month. With the help of her brothers and some neighbors, and with a pile of determination and Yankee grit, Betsy would retain the homestead and keep her family together. Of this accomplishment, Dwight later revealed in a sermon about the Good Samaritan,

> It brings the tears to my eyes every time I think of it. My father died before I can remember. There was a large family of us. The little twins came after his death—nine of us in all. He died bankrupt, and the creditors came in and took everything as far as the law allowed. We had a hard struggle. Thank God for my mother! She never lost hope. She told me some years later after that she kept bright and sunny

> all through the day and cried herself to sleep at night. We didn't know that as it would have broken our hearts.[1]

It was cold the morning after the creditors came, and the family awoke to a dark hearth, but Betsy's brothers soon changed that. In Dwight's own words, even though he was only about four at the time,

> I remember just as vividly as if it were yesterday, how I heard the sound of chips flying, and I knew some one was chopping wood in our wood-shed, and that we should soon have a fire. I shall never forget Uncle Cyrus coming with what seemed to me the biggest pile of wood I ever saw in my life.[2]

Another person who stepped in to help the family was the Reverend Oliver Everett, a pastor of the Northfield Unitarian Church. Reverend Everett was an unusual Unitarian in that, according to biographer W. H. Daniels, "he believed in the Bible as the inspired word of God, [and] in Jesus Christ as the savior."[3] In the next eighteen months, the entire Moody family would become members of the church, and Rev. Everett supplied for the family materially and in person when neither Betsy's brothers nor her neighbors could. He encouraged her to keep the family together when others suggested dividing the children among various homes. Rev. Everett also urged his flock to comb the suburbs of Northfield and invite stray children to Sunday school. Years later, when Dwight was running a Sunday school of his own in Chicago, he would use the same tactic to fill his classrooms. Unfortunately, Rev. Everett would eventually be replaced by a younger minister who had been educated in the worst traditions of the rationalistic school, and the family quickly lost interest in attending his services.

---

[1] Charles F. Goss, *Echoes from the Pulpit and Platform* (Hartford, CT: A. D. Worthington, 1900), 490–495, quoted in Lyle W. Dorsett, *A Passion for Souls: The Life of D. L. Moody* (Chicago: Moody Press, 1997), 34.

[2] William R. Moody, *The Life of Dwight L. Moody* (New York: Fleming H. Revell Company, 1900), 20.

[3] W. H. Daniels, *D. L. Moody and His Work* (Hartford, CT: American Publishing Company, 1875), 5.

Dwight's pain in losing his father was later compounded when his oldest brother, Isaiah, left the house without a word when Dwight was seven. Isaiah was fifteen at the time, and no one would see or hear from him again for thirteen years. Dwight's feelings of abandonment and neglect must have been intense. When Dwight was ten, he began spending the winters away from home helping other families with their chores in exchange for room and board. The first winter, he had gotten so homesick that he nearly returned home. But one day, walking with his brother, Luther, Dwight chanced upon an old man who took away his homesickness with a story that would impact his life forever. Dwight described the incident as follows:

> And the old man put his trembling hand on my head and looked down upon me. He got hold of my heart, and as he held my hand he told me that God had an only Son in Heaven, and that He loved this world so much He died for it. He went on talking about Heaven, and told how the Father loved me, and how my father on earth was lifted up, and how I had a Saviour up there, and he told me that story of the Cross in about five minutes. Then he put his hand in his pocket, and he gave me a brand new cent. I had never seen such a bright and beautiful cent before, and I almost thought it was gold. He put it in my hand, and I never felt as I did then before or since. That act of kindness took the "homesickness" out of me. I felt that from that hour that I had a friend. I thought that man was God, almost.[4]

Dwight did not respond decisively to the Gospel at this time, but his heart was surely touched.

For the next seven years, if Betsy Moody and her children were in close enough proximity to one another, she gathered her children to attend church and eat Sunday dinner together. These times spent with his mother, brothers, and sisters would provide precious memories for Dwight.

The whole of Dwight's formal education was complete by the time he was ten, and it spanned a period of less than four years.

[4] Goss, *Echoes from the Pulpit and Platform*, 490–495, quoted in Dorsett, *Passion for Souls*, 35.

Afterward, he was deemed fit to work to support himself and contribute to his family's finances. At seventeen, he decided it was time to strike out on his own. So, in April 1854, he headed to Boston to see what he could make of himself.

A Little Fish in a Big Pond

Samuel and Lemuel Holton, two of Dwight's uncles who had taken such good care of the Moody family over the years, had left the Northfield area a few years earlier for Boston, where they had two prosperous shoe and boot stores. Young Dwight decided to follow them to the big city. For a teenager who had never seen a town more populous than one thousand, Boston's population of 150,000 must have been daunting. The 1850s were a time of rapid change in the United States. At the beginning of the decade, there were a mere 8,571 miles of railroad in the U.S., but by 1860, there were nearly 30,000. The railroad had reached only as far as Northfield in 1848, and stories of what lay at the other end of the track must have beckoned to Dwight. He spent the only money he had on a train ticket to Boston. It was an inauspicious beginning for a man who would one day be known around the world.

Dwight was a direct young man with a stubborn streak that put him at odds with others.

By all accounts, Dwight was a self-assured, direct young man with a stubborn streak that tended to put him at odds with others. Fearing that Dwight's brashness and lack of refinement would only get him into trouble, his uncle Samuel had advised him to avoid Boston. Nevertheless, Dwight showed up on his doorstep only four months after this warning, hoping to stay with him and work in his store. When his uncle did not make an immediate offer, Dwight boasted about plans to find a job on his own, and left. Turning his back proved more of a challenge than he had expected, however. Several days later, he showed up at his uncle Lemuel's, where he announced he would walk to New York to find work. Lemuel asked Dwight whether he had asked his uncle Samuel for work, knowing Samuel to be in a better position than he to give Dwight a job. When Dwight said that he had not, and that his other uncle "knows I am looking for a place, and he may help or not, just as he pleases,"[5] Lemuel advised him to show a little humility, be willing to be governed by his elders, and go ask. Dwight, cap in hand, was soon back at his uncle Samuel's, who told him,

> Dwight, I am afraid if you come in here you will want to run the store yourself. Now, my men here want to do their work as I want it done. If you want to come in here and do the best you can and do it right, and if you'll be willing to ask when ever you don't know, and if you promise to go to church and Sunday-school, and if you will not go anywhere that you wouldn't want your mother to know about, we'll see how we can get along. You can have till Monday to think it over.[6]

But Dwight didn't need that much time. He agreed on the spot, and he went to work for his uncle straightaway as a sales clerk. His uncle also found him a room to rent from some Christians, showed him a place where he could get his meals, and pointed him to the Mount Vernon Congregational Church.

In the next few years, Dwight grew up quickly, enjoying the opportunities to attend lectures and ball games, meet people of various ethnic backgrounds, and check out books at the local Young Men's Christian Association (YMCA), where he had become a member. In three months, he became his uncle's best salesman and was soon prosperous enough to buy new shoes for his mother and siblings back home.

He also became the family provider. His extended family—uncles, aunts, and cousins—welcomed Dwight as part of their immediate family, which provided a healthy support system for him. Following his uncle's instructions, he also attended Mount Vernon Church, but services interested him little; it was not uncommon to find him sleeping through the sermons, fatigued from the long hours he worked.

---

[5] Dorsett, *Passion for Souls*, 43.

[6] Moody, *Life of Dwight L. Moody*, 37.

Moody Meets Jesus

Dwight's Sunday school class was run by Edward Kimball, a devout middle-aged man who took some interest in the eighteen-year-old shoe clerk. On Saturday, May 21, 1855, Edward felt compelled to check on the state of Dwight's soul rather than do his daily devotions. Along the way, however, he had second thoughts about the impulse, and by the time he reached the shoe store, he had all but talked himself out of it. He was afraid of embarrassing Dwight in front of his fellow associates or of being a mere nuisance while he tried to work. A wary Edward walked right past the store, but he soon returned, entered, and proceeded with his errand. He found Dwight alone in the back of the store, wrapping and shelving shoes.

Dwight had a solid admiration for Edward Kimball because of his kindness displayed on the first day of class. He had asked his students to open to the book of John, and Dwight, unfamiliar with the Holy Book, began searching through it, page by page. Seeing this, Edward saved his student embarrassment by handing Dwight his own Bible, which was open to the correct spot, in exchange for the one Dwight had been using.

Dwight later remembered this of Kimball's visit to the shoe store:

> I used to attend a Sunday school class, and one day I recollect my teacher came around behind the counter of the shop I was at work in, and put his hand upon my shoulder, and talked to me about Christ and my soul. I had not felt that I had a soul till then. I said to myself, "This is a very strange thing. Here is a man who never saw me till lately, and he is weeping over my sins, and I never shed a tear about them." But I understand it now, and know what it is to have a passion for men's souls and weep over their sins. I don't remember what he said, but I can feel the power of that man's hand on my shoulder to-night. It was not long after that I was brought into the Kingdom of God.[7]

---

[7] J. Wilbur Chapman, *The Life and Work of Dwight Lyman Moody* (Philadelphia: American Bible House, 1900), http://www.biblebelievers.com/moody/05.html.

Forty years after Kimball's visit, Dwight would speak of how his life had changed after coming to Christ:

> I remember the morning on which I came out of my room after I had first trusted Christ. I thought the old sun shone a good deal brighter than it ever had before—I thought that it was just smiling upon me; and as I walked out upon Boston Common and heard the birds singing in the trees I thought they were all singing a song to me. Do you know, I fell in love with the birds. I had never cared for them before. It seemed to me that I was in love with all creation. I had not a bitter feeling against any man, and I was ready to take all men to my heart. If a man has not the love of God shed abroad in his heart, he has never been regenerated. If you hear a person get up in the prayer-meeting and he begins to find fault with every body, you may doubt whether his is a genuine conversion; it may be counterfeit. It has not the right ring, because the impulse of a converted soul is to love, and not to be getting up and complaining of every one else and finding fault.[8]

Dwight Denied Church Membership

Three and a half weeks later, on Wednesday, May 16, 1855, Dwight sought membership at the Mount Vernon Congregational Church. He testified that he had been saved, but since he knew too little of the tenets of their faith, he was rejected by the deacons who interviewed him. For example, when asked, "What has Christ done for you, and for us all, that especially entitles Him to our love and obedience?" Dwight replied, "I think He has done a great deal for us all, but I don't know of anything He has done in particular."[9] Despite the fact that Edward Kimball was on the panel of interviewers, they felt that Dwight's testimony lacked solid evidence of his conversion. Dwight's application for membership was deferred, and he was put under the mentorship of Edward Kimball and two other deacons.

Kimball and the two deacons encouraged and coached Dwight

---

[8] Moody, *Life of Dwight L. Moody*, 42.

[9] Ibid., 44.

for his next interview, scheduled for nearly a year later. The minutes of this interview read as follows:

> No. 1,131. March 12, 1856. Mr. Moody thinks he has made some progress since he was here before at least in knowledge. Has maintained his habits of prayer and reading the Bible. Believes God will hear his prayers, and reads the Bible. Is fully determined to adhere to the cause of Christ always. Feels that it would be very bad if he should join the church and then turn. Must repent and ask forgiveness, for Christ's sake. Will never give up his hope, or love Christ less, whether admitted to the church or not. His prevailing intention is to give up his will to God.[10]

This time, even though little seemed to have changed in his life since the first interview, Dwight's willingness to remain under the mentorship of Kimball and the two deacons, paired with his sincere desire to repent, swayed the group in his favor, and Dwight was admitted as a Congregationalist. He would sign the church registry on May 3. Dwight would later testify frequently, "I was born of the flesh in 1837. I was born of the Spirit in 1856."[11] According to Dwight's son, in *The Life of Dwight L. Moody*,

> The action of the examining committee in refusing admission to young Moody on this occasion has been criticised by others, but the wisdom of the decision was always felt by Mr. Moody himself, who in later years laid great emphasis upon a young convert's being ready to give a reason for the hope that was in him.[12]

Heading West: Dwight Moves to Chicago

Around this time, Dwight had a falling out with his uncle for a reason no one in the family could truly discern. When his cousin, Frank Holton, told him he was going West, Dwight decided to join him until he found a place to settle.

---

[10] Moody, *Life of Dwight L. Moody*, 44.

[11] Ibid., 555.

[12] Ibid., 44.

When Dwight returned from his trip, his strong, impulsive personality began to resurface. He was outspoken during prayer meetings at church; he tried to lead and teach when others felt he should be listening and learning from those more experienced in the faith. Finally, the elders and deacons told him he needed to sit quietly and all but barred him from speaking in these meetings. Yet Dwight's zeal was irrepressible, so he soon developed a reputation as a troublemaker in the eyes of the church leaders.

The young D. L. Moody
Roberts Liardon Archives

Dwight's future in his uncle Samuel Holton's shoe selling business also looked dim. His coworkers found him to be more and more of a nuisance. Even though Dwight was a successful salesman, he was still brash in asserting opinions, and he lacked tact when dealing with other people. Dwight later confided to a friend that he "felt like a caged bird. The settled and finished condition of everything around him was a constant constraint. There seemed to be no room for him anywhere."[13] Dwight found Boston too small and stifling, oddly enough. Betsy Moody believed that the solution for her son would be for him to return home and assume leadership of the family, but home was an even more confining environment than the city of Boston. That fall, Dwight acted on impulse and moved west to Chicago without even a word to his mother.

Chicago offered Dwight the opportunities and elbow room he was looking for. It was a burgeoning city in 1850: the population was 29,963; by the end of the decade, it had nearly quadrupled—to more than 112,000. It became the shipping center for the rapidly growing

[13] Daniels, *D. L. Moody and His Work*, 27.

Western grain belt—both by water and by rail—and immigrants from Europe were moving there in droves to meet the demands for workmen. Of course, like any young city full of young people far removed from the moral jurisdiction of their families, Chicago was also rife with saloons, brothels, and gambling dens. That the young Dwight sought out a church and prayer meeting within the first week of arriving in Chicago—not falling prey to any of the popular vices—is evidence that his conversion was more authentic than the deacons at Mount Vernon had recognized.

Dwight also found his faith to be a boon for business—his integrity and friendliness made a great combination for salesmanship. Within two days of his arrival in Chicago, Dwight had secured another job selling shoes through yet another Holton uncle, Calvin. Young Dwight set his eyes on saving $100,000—an ambitious amount in a time when few workers earned more than a dollar a day in wages. One of Dwight's new employers said of him, "His ambition made him anxious to lay up money. His personal habits were exact and economical. As a salesman he was...[a] zealous and tireless worker."[14] Dwight soon proved that he could earn the same amount in a week in Chicago that he could in a month in Boston. Chicago also offered great opportunities for loaning money and profiting from real estate, two other enterprises in which Dwight began to speculate rather successfully. By 1860, Dwight would amass between $7,000 and $12,000 toward his goal, while also giving generously to his family back home. Yet something besides the desire to earn money burned within him—the desire to save souls. Dwight was convinced that Jesus was the answer to everything that plagued the human heart, and he felt he was called to apply that cure to as many hearts as he could.

Dwight's Rent-a-Pew

Dwight transferred his membership from Mount Vernon to Chicago's Plymouth Congregational Church, where, because of his growing affluence, he rented a pew of his own. Dwight took a different view of pew rentals than most, however—he did this not for prestige but because it was now his pew to fill every Sunday!

---

[14] Daniels, *D. L. Moody and His Work*, 28–29.

According to his son's biography,

> He would hail young men on the street corners, or visit their boarding-houses, or even call them out of saloons to share his pew. Whether the novelty of the invitation or the irresistible earnestness and cordiality of the young man induced a large number to attend, the object was at any rate attained, and before long he was renting four pews, which he filled every Sunday with his strangely assorted guests.[15]

One church did not seem sufficient for Dwight. Before long, he was attending meetings at three churches: Plymouth Congregational Church, the First Methodist Episcopal Church, and the First Baptist Church. Every evening after work, Dwight would find a prayer meeting to attend. It was at the First Baptist Church that he would meet "Mother" H. Phillips, who would take him under her wing as a spiritual son, as well as Emma Revell, the future Mrs. Dwight Moody. By 1857, Dwight was rooming and taking meals at Mother Phillips's house, and every meeting together became a chance for her to encourage him in prayer and solidify his faith. She also taught him the importance of Bible study and Scripture memorization, as well as ministering to children and discipling converts. A revival of sorts broke out in Chicago in 1858, and Mother Phillips was near its epicenter. Urban missions began to spring up to reach the derelicts of the city, most of whom were alcoholics, opium addicts, or prostitutes.

Just as Mother Phillips was Dwight's spiritual mother, J. B. Stillson was his spiritual father. Stillson worked among the sailors along the Chicago River, and when he met Dwight, the two found kindred spirits in one another. Stillson would take him to minister in places women dared not go. It was Stillson who loaned Dwight a copy of George Mueller's *A Life of Trust*, a book that would influence him significantly for years to come.

Yet, for all of this spiritual mentoring, Dwight's faith was still young and rather legalistic. For him, Christianity was more about what not to do than what to do; it emphasized the Ten Commandments and the taboos of drinking, dancing, and card playing over

[15] Moody, *Life of Dwight L. Moody*, 47.

the Sermon on the Mount and the law of love. His zeal was irrepressible, but its focus was not always correct. One time after a prayer meeting, he came upon two friends playing an innocent game of checkers, and he acted as if he were Jesus among the moneychangers. He seized the board, dashed it to pieces, and dropped to his knees in prayer—presumably on behalf of his friends stuck in such idle pursuits, not for his own self-righteousness and uncontrolled anger. It would be some time before he came to the conviction that it was God's goodness, not His wrath, that leads people to repentance. When his tenacity came under the anointing of the Holy Spirit later in his life, together they would prove an explosive mixture for revival wherever he ministered.

Dwight's First Congregation: Little Rascals

While missions and Sunday schools were popping up all over Chicago, Dwight noted a void. No one was reaching out to the children who were orphaned or who lived in homes broken by alcoholism or poverty. As these children tended to be unruly and difficult to handle in a standard sit-and-listen Sunday school environment, they were expelled more than pursued directly. However, Dwight's heart went out to them, and he decided to act on his empathy.

Dwight started a Sunday school in "The Sands," the worst slum of Chicago, an area that many referred to as "Little Hell." The Sands was inhabited mostly by single-parent families, and it was not uncommon for the single parent to be an alcohol or opium addict. The children who lived there were more likely to be sent to work to earn a living for their families than to attend school. They were also frequently abused—physically and sexually—malnourished, and exposed to constant vice, filth, and disease. While the word in Chicago was to avoid The Sands, Dwight followed his impulses and rented a vacant saloon in the heart of the area, where he established a "Sabbath School." Children would sit on the floor and listen to Dwight preach from his "pulpit": an old, discarded barrel. An early visitor described the scene:

> When I came to the little old shanty and entered the door, the first thing I saw by the light of the few candles, was

> a man standing up, holding in his arms a Negro boy, to whom he was trying to read the story of the Prodigal Son. A great many words the reader could not make out and was obliged to skip. My thought was, "If the Lord can ever use such an instrument as that for His honour and glory it will astonish me!" When the meeting was over, Mr. Moody said to me, "I have got only one talent. I have no education, but I love the Lord Jesus Christ, and I want to do something for Him." I have watched him since, and have come to know him thoroughly, and for consistent walk and conversation I have never met a man equal to him.[16]

Touching the lives of these "Little Arabs," as they were not so affectionately called, become Dwight's passion, and he was willing to throw convention out the window to do it. Probably remembering the shiny penny he had been given by the old man when he was ten, Dwight loaded his pockets with pennies and pieces of maple sugar candy to offer children in exchange for coming to his school. Dwight would join in their games, teaching them to follow the rules and to understand the power of teamwork. He learned to alternate five minutes of listening time with five minutes of playtime—five minutes that looked more like a bar brawl than a game of tag. Dwight also seemed to believe the old adage, "Music calms the savage beast," and so he followed this playtime with five minutes of music before returning to the lesson. This would go on for roughly two hours, until the meetings were called to a close.

Dwight paid attention to orphans and misfortunate children as no one else did.

Because he was willing to pay attention to these children as no one else did, however, the school attracted more and more students, and the urchins gradually tolerated longer periods of teaching and singing between periods of roughhousing. Dwight earned the nickname "Crazy Moody" for his efforts. After all, why would anyone

[16] Chapman, *Life and Work of Dwight Lyman Moody*, http://www.biblebelievers.com/moody/06.html.

D. L. Moody and John Farwell pose with their first Sunday school class, "Moody's Bodyguard," at North Market Hall in Chicago, Illinois.
Library of Congress, 03372

in his right mind set up a Sunday school in Little Hell? Yet Dwight reveled in the chaos. These little hellions were as dear to him as if they were his own children. The first summer, in a fit of inspiration, Dwight told fourteen boys he would give them new suits of clothing for Christmas if they showed good behavior and regular attendance at the meetings. All but one met the challenge. Charles Dickens, author of *Oliver Twist*, could not have generated a better list of characters to live with the Artful Dodger than this lot of Dwight's, who went by the names Red Eye, Smikes, Madden the Butcher, Jackey Candles, Giberick, Billy Blucannon, Darby the Cob[b]ler, Butcher Lilray, Greenhorn, Indian, Black Stove Pipe, Old Man, and Rag-breeches Cadet. The group well could have been the model for the later movie serial, *The Little Rascals*, and it was unusual in its time for its racial diversity—it included African-American and Native

American members. Dwight posed for two pictures with the boys after he had given them their new clothes. One of them, pictured on the previous page, was captioned, "Will it pay?" The group became known as "Moody's Bodyguard," and Dwight used it for years as an example of what could be done in the poorest of neighborhoods if people were simply willing to put forth the effort.

Sometime in 1858, Dwight was asked to speak to one of the adult Sunday school classes about his work in The Sands. His inspired speech won him a new helper at the mission: Miss Emma Charlotte Revell. Emma and Dwight would grow closer, not only because of their work at the Sunday school, but also because Emma volunteered to tutor Dwight for one hour each day. Under her instruction, Dwight's spelling and overall comportment became more refined and presentable, though his pronunciation still required work.

From the Methodists, Dwight won another compatriot who would serve faithfully with him for many years to come: John V. Farwell. Farwell's six-foot-four-inch frame cut an impressive figure with the children, giving him an immediate air of authority. When Dwight later opened a second Sunday school in the North Market area, Dwight had Farwell attend one of the meetings, at which he gave him the podium momentarily near the end. After venturing a few words, he heard "himself nominated by Moody as superintendent of the North Market Mission Sunday School! Before he had time to object, the school had elected him with a deafening hurrah."[17]

President Lincoln Comes to See Dwight's Work

By 1860, the Sabbath schools had grown to roughly 1,500 participants a week under Dwight's leadership. President-elect Abraham Lincoln even visited the school on his first visit to Chicago after the election in November to recognize the good work the school was doing. Lincoln had said that he would attend only if he was not asked to speak. Farwell agreed to this condition, but Moody's impetuousness would not be repressed. When it appeared that the President-elect was preparing to leave, Moody announced, "If Mr. Lincoln desires to

[17] Daniels, *D. L. Moody and His Work*, 40–41.

say a word, as he goes out, of course all ears will be open." Lincoln walked to the center of the room as if ready to decline the offer, but "he suddenly stopped, and made a most appropriate Sunday School address, in which he referred to his own humble origin."[18]

His final words to the group were, "With close attention to your teachers, and hard work to put into practice what you learn from them, some one of you may also become president of the United States in due time like myself, as you have had better opportunities than I have had."[19] A few months later, when President Lincoln called for 75,000 volunteers to save the Union, seventy-five who had heard him that day were among the first to enlist.

Stepping Out into Full-time Ministry

As the Civil War erupted, Dwight entered into a struggle of his own. He now felt the call to leave business in order to dedicate himself to full-time ministry. Years later, he would speak of this time and other times when he felt God was calling him to do more:

> Whenever God has been calling me to higher service, there has always been a conflict with my will. I have fought against it, but God's will has been done instead of mine. When I came to Jesus Christ, I had a terrible battle to surrender my will, and to take God's will. When I gave up business, I had another battle for three months; I fought against it. It was a terrible battle. But oh! how many times I have thanked God that I gave up my will and took God's will.[20]

When the battle was won and Dwight had decided to go into full-time mission work, he did so quickly and quietly. He gave notice at work and informed his landlady that he would be moving out. He began living as meagerly as possible to make his savings go as far as possible, keeping his sparse living conditions secret so that no one might pity him. When Farwell learned that Dwight slept on some

[18] John V. Farwell, *Early Recollections of D. L. Moody* (Chicago: Winona Publishing Company, 1907), quoted in Dorsett, *Passion for Souls*, 74.

[19] Ibid.

[20] Joseph B. Bowles, *Moody the Evangelist: A Character Sketch with Original Sayings* (Chicago: Moody Bible Institute, 1926), 17.

chairs he had pushed together at the local YMCA, where he was also doing some janitorial work, he vowed his friend would never want for support again—as long as he was able to provide it. Dwight feared that his extremism and lack of income might have repelled Emma Revell, but they did just the opposite. She "promised to cast her lot with his,"[21] which warmed his heart greatly, as he had gradually fallen for Emma and hoped to make her his wife one day.

Stepping out as he did was all the more remarkable for the twenty-four-year-old Dwight, because in doing so, he sought no ordination or pulpit other than the ministry he had already established in The Sands. In fact, in all his years of ministry, he would never be ordained. He was not looking for a full-time position in a church that could pay his bills. His seminary training would consist of hearing the Bible taught wherever he could and approaching various ministers he respected to ask, again and again, "What does this mean?" and "How do you interpret this verse?" He was ever eager and humble to seek out help where he could from ministers more experienced than he.

In his heart, Dwight determined to serve wherever he could, and among the first places where he identified a need was the local Young Men's Christian Association (YMCA). The organization quickly named him its city missionary and librarian, and allowed him to be its unofficial custodian and administrator. Though the organization had no money with which to compensate him for his work—he would not have accepted the money anyway—it did lend Dwight a new level of credibility when, in 1861, it adopted his Sabbath School and his North Market Hall Mission as part of its outreaches. The YMCA also provided Dwight with a place to sleep, saving him precious rent money that he would have had to draw from his now dwindling savings.

Civil War

While Dwight was going though these initial adjustments to full-time ministry, the United States was undergoing significant changes as well. Abraham Lincoln had drawn a line in the sand by being elected on a platform of forbidding any new territory from becoming a

[21] Moody, *Life of Dwight L. Moody*, 76.

slave state. Even before he even took the oath of office, seven states seceded from the Union. This series of secessions was quickly followed by four more shortly after his inauguration. There was talk of a diplomatic settlement, but when the newly formed Confederacy attacked Fort Sumter on April 12, 1861, the executive response from President Lincoln was to put down the rebellion. Lincoln called for 75,000 three-month volunteers, hoping that the show of force would put a quick end to the insurrection. Instead, four additional states that had been wavering over secession decided to go through with it. The Confederacy prepared to fight its own war for independence against the "invading" North. Each side thought that it could earn a quick victory, and no one was prepared for the brutality and long duration of the fight the United States had before it.

The Civil War gave Dwight a crash course in the practices of mass evangelism.

The state of Illinois quickly answered President Lincoln's call for soldiers. The YMCA helped to facilitate mobilization. It hosted large meetings and rallies to raise the money needed for supplies such as horses, food, and equipment. From these meetings, five companies of roughly 150 men each assembled. These companies joined together with other companies formed by the Board of Trade and Mercantile Association as the 72nd Illinois Volunteer Regiment, and they were stationed at Camp Douglas, which had been thrown together quickly just three miles north of Chicago. Dwight, along with B. F. Jacobs and John Farwell, were put in charge of the YMCA's efforts to minister to the spiritual needs of these soldiers. Dwight ordered 3,500 hymnals to be printed with the American flag on the cover to distribute to the soldiers, and he set out to establish a YMCA tent for every regiment gathered. Every day, Dwight held between eight and ten services for the soldiers, and the association handed out thousands of tracts and religious literature. This would be Dwight's first organizational success, as he recruited 150 people to run these tents and minister to the soldiers of Camp Douglas. Hundreds were converted, and numbers several times greater than that rededicated their lives to Christ.

At this time, the volunteers' biggest fear was that the war would be over before they had a chance to fight. A confident 30,000 soldiers descended from around Washington, D.C., toward Richmond, Virginia, in July 1861, and many thought that this would be the end of the Confederacy. In the initial hours of the battle, the Union troops pushed forward until they met the reinforcements of General Thomas J. Jackson, who stopped the North's forces so abruptly that he earned the nickname "Stonewall." The Union lines were broken, and when a retreat was sounded, the battle turned into a rout for the South. This first Battle of Bull Run immediately changed the complexion of the war—it showed President Lincoln and his army commanders that their forces required better training and leadership, and it boosted the confidence of the Southerners, who felt that the Union had neither the ability nor the resolve to defeat them.

Moody on the Battlefields

The YMCAs decided to coordinate their efforts in a Christian Commission dedicated to ministering to the Union soldiers. Dwight was selected as the Chicago delegate. He would be the first official delegate of thousands sent to minister to the troops. His first post was in October 1861 in Kentucky, where he raised money to fund the building of a wood-framed chapel, all the while managing his missions work in Chicago and his work at Camp Douglas. By 1862, General Ulysses S. Grant was setting up a major Union stronghold in Cairo, Illinois, at the junction of the Ohio and Mississippi rivers, with plans to both protect the state's vital railways from Confederate attack and launch Union attacks down the Mississippi to cut the South in half. Early in the war, the Commission had recognized Cairo as another important outreach, and Dwight assumed leadership for turning it into a command post for the Commission, as well.

He was getting a crash course in the practices of mass evangelism—an outreach that quickly added ministering to the sick, wounded, and dying. Soon, as a detachment of Confederate soldiers was put under lock and key at Camp Douglas, Dwight added ministering to the prisoners of war to his to-do list. He would travel to the front lines nine different times with General Grant's forces to minister in the makeshift hospitals there. Years later, Dwight would be among the first Northerners to enter Richmond when it fell to the Union forces. Somehow, in the midst of all of this, he still found the time to marry Emma on August 28, 1862. Before the Civil War drew to an end, Dwight and Emma would also have their first child—a daughter, named Emma after her mother and grandmother—born on October 24, 1864.

The war was also a hands-on training ground for tapping into the power of prayer. One night, in the wake of a battle that had left the field pockmarked with craters and casualties, it was up to the Christian workers to search for the living among those who had been left on the battlefield. Hundreds of wounded soldiers, hungry and thirsty, were left in their care. They located a stream from which to draw water, but no food was to be found. The band of Christians knelt and asked God to provide bread, but many of them later admitted that they had prayed without much hope of an answer. Even so, as the sun rose the next morning, a wagon pulled into view—packed to the roof with loaves of bread. The driver told the following story:

> When I went to bed last night, I knew the army was gone and I could not sleep for thinking of the poor fellows who were wounded and would have to stay behind. Something seemed to whisper in my ear, "What will those poor fellows do for something to eat?" I could not get rid of this voice.[22]

Unable to get back to sleep, the man had awakened his wife and asked her to begin baking as much bread as possible. He went and prepared his wagon, calling on his neighbors to gather more food. He told the workers, "Some hours later when I reached home my wagon was full, but my wife succeeded in piling her baking on top, and then I hastened to bring the bread to the boys, feeling just as if I was being sent by our Lord Himself."[23]

Ministry to the Wounded and Dying

It must have been a heart-wrenching time for Dwight, not yet twenty-five, as he had to minister time and again at the bedsides of

[22] Dorsett, *Passion for Souls*, 95.

[23] Ibid., 96.

those near death. In a sermon years later, he would tell the following story of one deathbed account:

> After the battle of Pittsburgh Landing I was in a hospital at Murfreesboro. In the middle of the night I was aroused and told that a man in one of the wards wanted to see me. I went to him and he called me "chaplain"—I was not the chaplain—and said he wanted me to help him die. And I said, "I would take you right up in my arms and carry you into the kingdom of God if I could; but I cannot do it. I cannot help you die!" And he said, "Who can?" I said, "The Lord Jesus Christ can—He came for that purpose." He shook his head, and said, "He cannot save me; I have sinned all my life." And I said, "But He came to save sinners." I thought of his mother in the north, and I was sure that she was anxious that he should die in peace; so I resolved I would stay with him. I prayed two or three times, and repeated all the promises I could; for it was evident that in a few hours he would be gone.
>
> I said I wanted to read him a conversation that Christ had with a man who was anxious about his soul. I turned to the third chapter of John. His eyes were riveted on me; and when I came to the 14th and 15th verses—the passage before us—he caught up the words, "As Moses lifted up the serpent in the wilderness, even so must the Son of Man be lifted up; that whosoever believeth in Him should not perish, but have eternal life." He stopped me and said, "Is that there?" I said "Yes." He asked me to read it again; and I did so. He leaned his elbows on the cot, and clasping his hands together, said, "That's good; won't you read it again?" I read it the third time; and then went on with the rest of the chapter. When I had finished, his eyes were closed, his hands were folded, and there was a smile on his face. Oh, how it was lit up! What a change had come over it! I saw his lips quivering, and leaning over him I heard in a faint whisper, "As Moses lifted up the serpent in the wilderness, even so must the Son of Man be lifted up; that whosoever believeth in Him should not perish, but have eternal life." He opened his eyes and said, "That's enough;

> don't read any more." He lingered a few hours, pillowing his head on those two verses; and then went up in one of Christ's chariots to take his seat in the Kingdom of God.[24]

During the war, the work in Chicago had continued to thrive. Dwight's first Sunday school students were growing into adulthood, and as the missions flourished, other adults began attending as well. While Dwight had always tried his best to get along with the pastors in town and to feed his Sunday school children into their churches, his converts never really felt comfortable or welcome in these more established, traditional worship services. So, as the war was drawing to a close, on December 30, 1864, the Illinois Street Mission Sunday school became the Illinois Street Church, an independent evangelical church with an assertive outreach program. The Congregationalists offered to ordain Dwight; he felt unqualified, and declined, holding true to his desire to remain impartial to—and equally friendly with—all denominations.

The Civil War created a pressing mind-set in Dwight that would never leave him. While the War Between the States came to a bloody conclusion in 1865, the war against the forces of darkness for the souls of men would not. Dwight seemed to apply wartime urgency to all of his preaching endeavors thereafter, treating each engagement as if it were the last time he would be able to preach the Gospel to someone, and doing everything in his power to see that the people received it then and there. He also developed a rather practical view of the essentials of the gospel message—a view to which he would cling for the remainder of his ministry. Salvation was the doctrine around which every denomination could rally, and this concept gave him an ecumenical key to working among churches wherever he went. He also learned that he needed no formal training or title to be effective in his work for God, and for the rest of his ministry, he was constantly reminding people that his name was "Mr. Moody," not "Reverend."

When the Civil War came to an end, America entered the period of Reconstruction (technically spanning from 1865 to 1877) and the period of economic growth and social reform that would be dubbed

---

[24] Dwight L. Moody, *The Way to God and How to Find It*, http://www.whatsaiththe-scripture.com/Voice/Moody.The.Way.to.GOD.html.

the Gilded Age (from 1865 to 1893). This time of economic growth was a second industrial age for the United States, as the country put itself back together after the war and expanded westward. It was also a time of tremendous immigration, and cities nationwide grew rapidly. Based on Andrew Carnegie's book of the same name, the "gospel of wealth" became predominant, as many entrepreneurs flourishing in industry felt compelled to make charitable and philanthropic contributions to their communities. In this atmosphere, organizations such as the YMCA greatly benefited because of their focus on reaching the poor.

The war had also revealed the YMCA to be an ecumenical organization that could be trusted with leadership, and through Dwight's efforts, the Chicago YMCA was distinguished among all the YMCAs in the U.S. Soon, Dwight would become the president of the Chicago YMCA, a position he would hold from 1865 to 1870. This was a platform of influence and respectability. Chicago itself would experience a "Golden Age of Religion" under Dwight's influence within five years after the war's end.

The First Trip to England

In 1867, Emma Revell Moody was in poor health—she suffered from asthma and had trouble keeping up with her husband, who was ministering at a maddening pace. The couple decided to take a cruise to England so that Emma could rest and recover, as well as visit relatives in England whom she had not seen since her immigration to the United States eighteen years earlier. Dwight also wanted to make time to meet with Sir George Williams, founder of the YMCA, who lived in London. In addition, he hoped to meet George Mueller, whose testimony had so inspired him, and to hear Charles Haddon Spurgeon preach. The Moodys also planned to attend an international Sunday school convention being held in London. All of these plans eased Dwight's conscience enough that he was able to leave his work in Chicago in the capable hands of others. He and his wife left three-year-old Emma in the care of Dwight's mother in Northfield, Illinois.

With his characteristically uncouth yet honest candor, Dwight made an immediate impression on the English in his first public address. He was asked to come forward at the Sunday-school convention to give a word about his work in America, and according to one witness,

> the vice-chairman announced that they were glad to welcome their "American cousin, the Reverend Mr. Moody, of Chicago," who would now move a vote of thanks to the noble Earl who had presided on this occasion. With refreshing frankness and an utter disregard for conventionalities and mere compliments, Mr. Moody burst upon the audience with the bold announcement:
>
> "The chairman has made two mistakes. To begin with, I'm not the 'Reverend' Mr. Moody at all. I'm plain Dwight L. Moody, a Sabbath-school worker. And then I'm not your 'American cousin'! By the grace of God I'm your brother, who is interested with you in our Father's work for His children.
>
> "And now about this vote of thanks to 'the noble Earl' for being our chairman this evening. I don't see why we should thank him, any more than he should thank us. When at one time they offered to thank our Mr. Lincoln for presiding over a meeting in Illinois, he stopped it. He said he'd tried to do his duty, and they'd tried to do theirs. He thought it was an even thing all round."
>
> That opening fairly took the breath away from Mr. Moody's hearers. Such talk could not be gauged by any standard. Its novelty was delightful, and Mr. Moody carried his English hearers from that time on.[25]

The Moodys would spend four and a half months in the British Isles, and, as was usual for Dwight, they accomplished everything that they had set out to do. He managed to hear Charles Spurgeon speak on several occasions, and even met with him, leaving with high hopes of getting Spurgeon to come to America to preach.

The Moodys also traveled to Bristol to meet with George Mueller, of whom Dwight wrote to Farwell, "He has 1,150 children in his house but never asks a man for a cent of money to support them. He

---

[25] Moody, *Life of Dwight L. Moody*, 132.

calls on God and God sends the money to him. It is wonderful to see what God can do with a man of prayer."[26]

Dwight was also greatly influenced by Mueller's doctrinal leanings. Mueller was part of the Plymouth Brethren church, which had an immovable commitment to the integrity and inspiration of the Scriptures. The Plymouth Brethren preached conversion as a powerful, life-altering event, and they believed in the premillennial return of Christ. Dwight would cling to these two doctrines in later ministry. It may be that these Brethren had an impact on him similar to the Moravians' impact on John Wesley. More than any other group's doctrine, theirs seemed to form the cornerstone of Dwight's theology.

Emma Revell Moody
Roberts Liardon Archives

For his part, Dwight would make an equally significant impact on England. A sixteen-year-old John Kenneth MacKenzie heard Dwight speak in Bristol on May 10; he would go on to become a famous medical missionary to China. While in Liverpool, Dwight would inspire the Reverend Charles Garrett to open an inexpensive restaurant as an alternative to the town's bars and brothels. Another man started a noonday prayer meeting in London, modeled after that of the Chicago YMCA, and he would lead it for the next forty-one years.

Dwight would also inspire a young pickpocket-turned-preacher, Henry Moorehouse, to leave England to hear him speak in Ireland. Reaching no higher than Dwight's shoulder, this "boy preacher" was only a few years younger than Dwight, and he convinced the Moodys to invite him to speak in Chicago, were he ever to visit America. Little did they know at the time how providential this meeting would be for Dwight's ministry.

On July 1, a farewell reception was arranged for the Moodys at London's Aldersgate YMCA. At this event, one of the speakers said of Dwight,

[26] Dorsett, *Passion for Souls*, 135.

> Few men who have visited a foreign shore have endeared themselves to so many hearts in so short a time, or with an unknown name and without letters of commendation won their way so deeply into the affections of a multitude of Christian brethren as had Mr. Moody. Few had ever heard of him before, but having talked with him or heard him speak of Jesus, asked for no other warrant to yield him a large measure of their love.[27]

Dwight was given a gold watch to remember his trip and an envelope containing a good-sized honorarium.

The Moodys soon left for home, thinking fondly of this wonderful adventure they never expected to repeat. It was a trip that had influenced Dwight immeasurably, for it came at a time when he was very open to learning more about God and how to minister to others. He little suspected that his education from this trip was far from over, much less that he would return in just a few years to be an even greater blessing to the United Kingdom than it had been to him.

Moorehouse's John 3:16 Sermons

Several weeks after returning to Chicago, Dwight received a letter from Harry Moorehouse to say that he was stateside, and asking whether the invitation to speak was still standing. Dwight answered casually, thinking he would never hear from him again. But he did. Much to the chagrin of Dwight's staff members, who were suspicious of the outsider, Dwight agreed to let him speak a few weeks later, while he would be out of town. Moorehouse spoke on but one text each of the two nights that Dwight was away: John 3:16: *"For God so loved the world, that he gave his only begotten Son, that whosoever believeth in him should not perish, but have everlasting life."* When Dwight returned, he heard this testimony of what had happened:

> When I got back Saturday morning I was anxious to know how he got on. The first thing I said to my wife when I got in the house was, "How is the young Englishman coming along? How do the people like him?"

[27] Moody, *Life of Dwight L. Moody*, 136.

"They like him very much."

"Did you hear him?"

"Yes."

"Well, did you like him?"

"Yes, I liked him very much. He has preached two sermons from that verse of John, *'For God so loved the world, that He gave His only begotten Son, that whosoever believeth in Him should not perish, but have everlasting life,'* and I think you will like him, although he preaches a little differently from you."

"How is that?"

"Well, he tells the worst sinners that God loves them."

"Then," said I, "he is wrong."

"I think you will agree with him when you hear him," said she, "because he backs up everything he says with the Bible."

Sunday came, and as I went to the church I noticed that every one brought his Bible. The morning address was to Christians. I had never heard anything quite like it. He gave chapter and verse to prove every statement he made. When night came the church was packed. "Now, beloved friends," said the preacher, "if you will turn to the third chapter of John and the sixteenth verse, you will find my text." He preached the most extraordinary sermon from that verse. He did not divide the text into secondly and thirdly and fourthly; he just took the whole verse, and then went through the Bible from Genesis to Revelation to prove that in all ages God loved the world. God had sent prophets and patriarchs and holy men to warn us, and then He sent His Son, and after they killed Him, He sent the Holy Ghost. I never knew up to that time that God loved us so much. This heart of mine began to thaw out; I could not keep back the tears. It was like news from a far country: I just drank it in. So did the crowded congregation. I tell you there is one thing that draws above everything else in this world, and that is *love*. A man that has no one to love him, no mother, no wife, no children, no brother, no sister, belongs to the class that commits suicide.

> It's pretty hard to get a crowd out in Chicago on a Monday night, but the people came. They brought their Bibles, and Moorehouse began, "Beloved friends, if you will turn to the third chapter of John, and the sixteenth verse, you will find my text," and again he showed on another line, from Genesis to Revelation, that God loved us. He could turn to almost any part of the Bible and prove it. Well, I thought that was better than the other one; he struck a higher note than ever, and it was sweet to my soul to hear it. He just beat that truth down into my heart, and I have never doubted it since. I used to preach that God was behind the sinner with a double-edged sword ready to hew him down. I have got done with that. I preach now that God is behind him with love, and he is running away from the God of love.[28]

In the end, Harry Moorehouse spoke for seven consecutive nights on John 3:16. And every night, the truth of this passage and Moorehouse's message struck a deeper cord in Dwight's heart. He would experience a total transformation in his life and the way he preached.

Dwight and Emma would have two more children—both sons—in the coming years. William Revell Moody was born on March 25, 1869, in Chicago, and their youngest, Paul, would be born during Dwight's extended Baltimore campaign, more than a decade later, on April 11, 1879. The Baltimore campaign would be an interim in which Dwight's ministry would again drastically change—yet he required one more important element before that would happen.

Empowered by the Spirit of God

While the concept of transformation by the love of God was perhaps the most important revelation of God's truth to Dwight, it was not everything he needed to be the evangelist he would become in a few short years. Dwight still operated largely on his own strength of will, skill with people, and seemingly unquenchable ambition to increase whatever he set his hand to. Emma watched as her husband drove himself in his pursuits—dogged by an ever present feeling of

---

[28] Moody, *Life of Dwight L. Moody*, 138–139.

inadequacy—to provide for his family, expand the influence of the Chicago YMCA, and reach a world filled with people who needed to hear the Gospel of Jesus Christ.

Yet, all along, God had been trying to reach Dwight to let him know where his true power would come from—a message of His love that He tried to convey to humankind throughout the entire Bible: the importance of God's Spirit living within and empowering His children. Dwight just needed to put the pieces together.

Years later, he would describe how this puzzle started coming together for him, and how first pieces had appeared soon after he was saved:

> I remember once when I was first converted I spoke in a Sabbath school, and there seemed to be a great deal of interest, and quite a number rose for prayer, and I remember I went out quite rejoiced; but an old man followed me out. I have never seen him since. I never had seen him before, and don't even know his name—but he caught hold of my hand and gave me a little bit of advice. I didn't know what he meant at the time, but he said: "Young man, when you speak again, honor the Holy Ghost." I was hastening off to another church to speak, and all the way over it kept ringing in my ears—"Honor the Holy Ghost." And I said to myself, "I wonder what the old man means."[29]

Years later, Dwight would have a similar experience with two women at a series of encounters he found equally perplexing. Each time he spoke with them, they would tell him, "We are praying for you." One night when he was especially weary, he lost his patience with them and pointedly asked, "Why are you praying for me? Why don't you pray for the unsaved?" They told him, "We are praying that you may get the power." Since Dwight asked no further questions, they said nothing more of this but stayed resolute in their quest. In the fall of 1871, Moody crossed paths with these two women again; this time, he asked more pointedly about what they had meant.

[29] M. Laird Simons, *Holding the Fort: comprising sermons and addresses at the Great Revival meetings conducted by Moody and Sankey...lives and labors of Dwight L. Moody, Ira D. Sankey, and P. P. Bliss* (Norwich, CT: Henry Bill Publishing Co., 1877), quoted in "Dwight Lyman Moody," Christian Biography Resources, http://www.wholesomewords.org/biography/biomoody.html.

According to R. A. Torrey, the first superintendent of Moody Bible Institute, to whom Dwight later recounted these events, "They told him about the definite baptism with the Holy Ghost. Then he asked that he might pray with them and not they merely pray for him."[30] Thus, they agreed to meet in Farwell Hall (a YMCA building named after Dwight's friend, John V. Farwell) every Friday afternoon for prayer.

Dwight learned that the leader of the two women was Sarah Cooke, a devout Methodist who had moved with her husband to Chicago in 1868 and had received a burden from the Lord that Dwight might be baptized with the Holy Spirit and with fire. In the following weeks, they met on Fridays, as planned, whenever Dwight had the time to attend. And on Friday, October 6, 1871, they seemed to have a breakthrough. Cooke would later write, "At every meeting each of us prayed aloud in turn, but at this meeting Mr. Moody's agony was so great that he rolled on the floor and in the midst of many tears and groans cried to God to be baptized with the Holy Ghost and fire."[31] Dwight, however, reported that he left this meeting unchanged. He felt near his breaking point.

The Great Chicago Fire

Things would get worse before they would get better. That Sunday night, October 8, a fire burned roughly four square miles of Chicago, destroying the Illinois Street Church where Moody presided, a newly constructed YMCA building, for which Dwight had only recently finished raising funds, and the Moody home. The family moved in with Emma's sister, and Dwight hit the road again to start raising new capital to rebuild the destroyed edifices.

It was some months later, while walking the streets of New York, that Dwight finally experienced the breakthrough for which he and Sarah Cooke had been praying together. It was shortly before his second and most important trip to England. R. A. Torrey had this to say about this significant advance in Dwight's life:

---

30 R. A. Torrey, *Why God Used D. L. Moody*, sermon delivered in 1923 (Murfreesboro, TN: Sword of the Lord Publishers), http://www.whatsaiththescripture.com/Voice/Why.God.Used.D.L.Moody.html.

31 Sarah A. Cooke, *The Handmaiden of the Lord, or Wayside Sketches* (Chicago: T. B. Arnold, 1896), 362.

> Not long after, one day on his way to England, he was walking up Wall Street in New York; (Mr. Moody very seldom told this and I almost hesitate to tell it) and in the midst of the bustle and hurry of that city his prayer was answered; the power of God fell upon him as he walked up the street and he had to hurry off to the house of a friend and ask that he might have a room by himself, and in that room he stayed alone for hours; and the Holy Ghost came upon him, filling his soul with such joy that at last he had to ask God to withhold His hand, lest he die on the spot from very joy. He went out from that place with the power of the Holy Ghost upon him, and when he got to London (partly through the prayers of a bedridden saint in Mr. Lessey's church), the power of God wrought through him mightily in North London, and hundreds were added to the churches; and that was what led to his being invited over to the wonderful campaign that followed in later years.[32]

Dwight described the experience in this way:

> I was crying all the time that God would fill me with His Spirit. Well, one day, in the city of New York—oh, what a day!—I cannot describe it, I seldom refer to it; it is almost too sacred an experience to name. Paul had an experience of which he never spoke for fourteen years. I can only say that God revealed Himself to me, and I had such an experience of His love that I had to ask Him to stay His hand. I went to preaching again. The sermons were not different; I did not present any new truths, and yet hundreds were converted. I would not now be placed back where I was before that blessed experience if you should give me all the world—it would be as the small dust of the balance.[33]

The experience heightened Dwight's hunger for the knowledge of God and the guidance of the Holy Spirit. So, for a time, he and Emma moved their family back to his mother's home in Northfield to distance themselves from the demands and busyness of the bustling city, believing that this would enable them to hear the Holy

[32] Torrey, *Why God Used D. L. Moody.*

[33] Moody, *Life of Dwight L. Moody*, 149.

Spirit's direction more clearly. As a result, Dwight felt an unquenchable desire to return to England. He felt he needed to sit again at the feet of the teachers he had met there. However, it appeared that God had different plans.

D. L. Moody's Great Awakening

Dwight set sail for London in June 1872 and slipped quietly into the country. In no time, he found some meetings to attend, and he would sit in the back to take notes. Thus began his religious retreat. Then, one night at a prayer meeting at the Old Bailey—the building that formerly housed London's central criminal court—the Reverend John Lessey saw Dwight and begged him to speak at his church the following Sunday. Reluctantly, Dwight agreed. That particular Sunday morning passed uneventfully, but Sunday night was a different story altogether.

> At the next service, which was at half-past six in the evening, it seemed, while he was preaching, as if the very atmosphere was charged with the Spirit of God. There came a hush upon all the people, and a quick response to his words, though he had not been much in prayer that day, and could not understand it.
>
> When he had finished preaching he asked all who would like to become Christians to rise, that he might pray for them. People rose all over the house until it seemed as if the whole audience was getting up.
>
> Mr. Moody said to himself: "These people don't understand me. They don't know what I mean when I ask them to rise." He had never seen such results before, and did not know what to make of it, so he put the test again.
>
> "Now," he said, "all of you who want to become Christians just step into the inquiry-room."
>
> They went in, and crowded the room so that they had to take in extra chairs to seat them all. The minister was surprised, and so was Mr. Moody. Neither had expected such a blessing. They had not realized that God can save by hundreds and thousands as well as by ones and twos.
>
> When Mr. Moody again asked those that really wanted to become Christians to rise, the whole audience got up. He

did not even then know what to do, so he told all who were really in earnest to meet the pastor there the next night.

The next day he went over to Dublin, but on Tuesday morning received a despatch urging him to return, saying there were more inquirers on Monday than on Sunday. He went back and held meetings for ten days, and four hundred were taken into that church.[34]

The Cause of Revival

Dwight was no less perplexed than other people by these results, but he later found out what had caused the revival. It appeared that there were two sisters who belonged to this church, and one of them was bedridden with illness. One day, while feeling sorry for herself, it occurred to her that if she could do nothing else, she could at least pray. So, day and night, she began a vigil of praying for revival in her church. Then one day, she came across a newspaper article about a meeting Dwight had organized in the United States, and she was so impressed by what she read that she kept the article under her pillow and began praying that God would send him across the sea to preach at their church.

Then that Sunday morning, the healthy sister came home to ask her sister,

> "Whom do you think preached this morning?"
>
> She suggested the names of several with whom her pastor was in the habit of exchanging.
>
> Finally her sister told her, "It was Mr. Moody, from America."
>
> "I know what that means," cried the sick woman; "God has heard my prayers!"[35]

Years later, G. Campbell Morgan met this woman, Marianne Adlard, when he took over the pastorate of Lessey's New Court Congregational Church. In Morgan's book, *The Practice of Prayer,* he told her side of the story:

> When in 1901 I was leaving England for America I went to see her. She said to me, "I want you to reach that birthday

[34] Moody, *Life of Dwight L. Moody,* 152–153.

[35] Ibid., 153–154.

> book." I did so and turning to February 5 I saw in the handwriting I knew so well, "D. L. Moody, Psalm xci." Then Marianne Adlard said to me, "He wrote that for me when he came to see me in 1872, and I prayed for him every day until he went home." Continuing, she said, "Now, will you write your name on your birthday page, and let me pray for you until either you or I go home." I shall never forget writing my name in that book. To me the room was full of the Presence. I have often thought of that hour in the rush of my busy life, in the place of toil and strain, and even yet by God's good grace I know that Marianne Adlard is praying for me, and it is for this reason that to her in sincere love and admiration I have dedicated this book. There are the labourers of force in the fields of God. It is the heroes and heroines who are out of sight, and who labour in prayer, who make it possible for those who are in sight to do their work and win. The force of it to such as are called upon to exercise the ministry can never be measured.[36]

Dwight sensed that God wanted him to do more in England than just take notes. When he received similar results after preaching at Chelsea Chapel at the invitation of an Anglican priest, he concluded that God did want him to minister in Great Britain, but he also felt he should do so properly. So, he decided to return to the United States, find a singer to accompany him, solicit support for an extended campaign, collect his family, and return to Great Britain as quickly as he could. But before he could even book a ticket home, money to cover his expenses had already been volunteered from Dublin, as well as from a wealthy Methodist in Newcastle-upon-Tyne.

Another confirmation came before he returned to the U.S. When Dwight attended a conference sponsored by the Reverend William Pennefather at Mildmay Park in northern London, he immediately felt at home, and he sensed a kindred spirit in Pennefather during his opening sermon. Pennefather then convinced Dwight to speak, and again the reception was phenomenal. In response, Pennefather

---

[36] G. Campbell Morgan, *The Practice of Prayer* (London: Hodder and Stoughton, 1906), 124–127.

announced from the podium, "Mr. Moody was one for whom God had prepared a great work," and those prophetic words would be fulfilled in the months to come.

Just before his return to the States, Dwight struck a deal in Dublin. He agreed to purchase tracts and booklets for the price of the paper they were printed on, ordered thousands of them, arranged for their free transport to Chicago, and then made preparations for their reception and purchase as soon as he arrived stateside again, in September 1872. He had Chicago Yokefellows set up racks to display the tracts in passenger depots and hotels. On each rack was a sign indicating that the tracts were complimentary. Dwight then wrote to forty businessmen, asking them each to give $25 to cover the cost of the project, which was $1,000. The Yokefellows would then check the racks three times a week and replenish them as needed.

Dwight had also been inspired by William Pennefather's training program, which created deaconesses for the Church of England who would serve the community under the auspices of the Church. Upon his return to the States, Dwight wanted to create an institution that would do something similar, and he soon found just the person to lead it. A former college professor, Emma Dryer had been healed miraculously of typhoid fever and an eye disorder, and she felt called to the ministry. While Dwight never believed in divine healing as Dryer did, he was thrilled by her premillennialist teachings—she believed that Jesus would return before the millennium, rather than in the midst of it or afterward, to reign on the earth. Many people still believe this today. Dwight also knew that she had leadership abilities, given her positions as head of the Chicago Women's Aid Society and superintendent of the Women's Auxiliary of the YMCA. Dwight convinced her to start a school to train women in home and foreign missions and evangelistic work. This school would eventually welcome male students, as well. It was the beginning of what would become the Moody Bible Institute.

Dwight Finds a Psalmist

Dwight now set himself to the matter of finding a singer to accompany him back to England. He approached two men, Philip Phillips and P. P. Bliss, but both were unable to commit. So Dwight turned to Ira D. Sankey, his song leader in Chicago, and asked him. He had not wanted to do this, as he felt Ira was too important to his congregation in Chicago, but his skills as a soloist and song leader were unparalleled. Dwight had met Ira at a conference in Indianapolis in 1871, just before his previous trip to Great Britain. Ira had come to hear Dwight speak, but instead, when Ira had stepped in to lead a song at the request of one of his other Pennsylvania delegates, it was Ira who had impressed Dwight. Dwight knew the importance of a good song leader and how difficult it was to find one, so when the two were introduced, Dwight used the full force of his persuasive skills as a salesman to convince Ira to come to Chicago to work with him.

D. L. Moody and his psalmist, Ira Sankey
Roberts Liardon Archives

> At the close of the service Mr. Sankey was introduced by his friend, and was immediately recognized by Moody as the leader of the singing. A few inquiries regarding Mr. Sankey's family ties and occupation followed; then the evangelist announced in his determined fashion, "Well, you'll have to give that up! You are the man I have been looking for, and I want you to come to Chicago and help me in my work."[37]

According to Sankey's autobiography, when he told Dwight that he could not join him, Dwight retorted, "You must; I have been looking for you for the last eight years."[38]

Sankey was unsure at first, and the fact that he had started a promising career with the Treasury Department did little to help. Once he had the chance to visit with Dwight and Emma in Chicago and see the work they were doing there, however, he was convinced that it was his calling. So when Dwight asked him to come with him

[37] Moody, *Life of Dwight L. Moody*, 125.

[38] Ira Sankey, *My Life and the Story of Gospel Hymns* (New York: Harper, 1907), 19, quoted in Dorsett, *Passion for Souls*, 175.

to England to minister there for eight to ten months, he agreed. The Moody and Sankey families boarded a ship for Liverpool on June 7, 1873.

The British Revival

Ten days later, Liverpool welcomed them with stunning news. Pennefather, the man who had promised support from Dublin, and the Methodist supporter from Newcastle-upon-Tyne had both died. The entirety of Dwight's promised income had evaporated before he had even left the U.S. The two families set to prayer. Ira and Fanny Sankey found accommodations with Harry Moorehouse in Manchester, and the Moodys and their children stayed with Emma's sister in London. Hearing of their arrival, George Bennett, head of the YMCA in York, invited Dwight to speak there. When Dwight told Ira about the invitation, he said, "Here is a door which is partly open, and we will go there and begin our work."[39]

What happened next was phenomenal. Dwight and Ira had arrived in Great Britain without anyone to meet them at the dock, yet in two years, they would depart to the fanfare of the world. The work in York started slowly—only fifty people attended the first meeting, and six came to the prayer meeting the first midday—but interest grew quickly as local pastors began to throw their support to the thirty-six-year-old evangelist. Dwight's to-the-point, American style and anointing from God struck a cord with the British public, who were accustomed to sermons that sounded more like history lessons or philosophy lectures. As a rule, Dwight also limited his preaching to half an hour or less, believing it was better to leave an audience wanting more than to overstay his welcome. As one listener put it,

> He is a master in his work: he aims at one thing, viz.; getting people to consider their state before God, and he brings everything to bear on the one object—to accept Jesus, as offered to us in the Gospel. From this aim he is never for a moment diverted. His simplest illustrations, his most touching stories, his most pathetic appeals, his gentlest persuasiveness, his most passionate declamation, his most direct home thrusts, his (almost unfair) reference to people and

[39] Sankey, *My Life*, 38–39, quoted in Dorsett, *Passion for Souls*, 177.

> places, all are used, and unsparingly, unfearingly, used, for the one purpose of touching the heart, that Jesus and the Father may come in and abide there.[40]

Dwight's preaching style, honed in the slums of Chicago to hold the attention of the most uneducated, grabbed the hearts of even the most educated. He loved to tell stories, and he told them well. His illustrations of biblical truths were always concise and to the point. One minister who had heard Dwight speak several times summed up his appeal in this way:

> He had learned to preach simply,—let us rather say he had not learned to preach otherwise; and in the unaffected language of nature, uncorrupted by the fastidious culture of the schools, he spoke face to face with men; and they heard him. Sprightly and vivacious, with a touch of humor as well as pathos, direct and pointed in his appeals, urging to an immediate decision, and feeling his dependence of the Spirit of God, he compelled all classes to acknowledge that he was a man of power. And yet God gave him the grace to be humble; not to think of himself more highly than he ought to think, but to feel that he was himself nothing and that God was all.[41]

In York, roughly two hundred people joined the churches as a result of Dwight and Ira's meetings, and Baptist pastor Arthur A. Rees invited them to come to Sunderland. There, churches began to overflow, and to avoid the appearance of favoring one denomination over another, the meetings were moved to a public hall. As Dwight began to draw more attention, closer scrutiny was applied, and criticism of his motives began to arise among people who had never met him or attended one of his meetings.

Newcastle Burns Bright

Things wouldn't really start to take off, though, until Dwight and Ira arrived in Newcastle:

---

[40] Jane MacKinnon, "Journal of Mrs. Jane MacKinnon," 61, 95, Yale Archives, quoted in Dorsett, *Passion for Souls*, 185.

[41] Arthur T. Pierson, *Evangelistic Work in Principle and Practice* (New York: Baker and Taylor, 1887), 253, quoted in Dorsett, *Passion for Souls*, 185.

At Newcastle the fire was kindled which was to mightily move Great Britain. Ministerial opposition was overcome, five of the principal chapels of the town being offered for the services. Mr. Moody accepted the use of the Rye Hill Baptist Chapel, a large edifice, and within a fortnight crowds were turned away for want of room. All the neighbouring towns and villages felt the spiritual impulse, and in response to requests hundreds of meetings were held outside the city by multiplying assistants of the evangelist.

Mr. Moody, in order to prevent the exclusion of the unconverted by the crowds of Christians who attended the meetings, now began to divide his congregations into classes, giving tickets of admission to the various services. Meetings for merchants were held in the Assembly Hall; meetings for mechanics were held at the Tyne Theatre, and in each instance the size of the crowds usually necessitated three or four overflow meetings.

The name and residence of every inquirer was made a matter of record, and in order that assistants in the inquiry room should be more fitted to the purpose, tickets were issued to clergymen and other men of practical experience in Christian work, that they might help in the great work of leading souls to Christ. At first most of the conversions were among the educated classes, but afterward the work became more general. The noon prayer meetings which had been commenced previous to the arrival of Mr. Moody, by way of preparation had grown to remarkable proportions, while Mr. Moody's afternoon Bible readings drew even from the ranks of busy merchants and professional men. Two whole-day meetings or conferences were held....

As a result of this month's work, hundreds of converts were received into the churches, and the whole North of England was aroused. Scores of Christian workers were sent out to carry the good tidings to the remoter districts, and the stimulus to the various churches proved unprecedented.[42]

[42] Chapman, *Life and Work of Dwight Lyman Moody*, http://www.biblebelievers.com/moody/10.html.

Next, Dwight ministered in Edinburgh, where three thousand members were added to the churches, and by the beginning of 1854, he was in Dundee, then Glasgow. They had scheduled meetings in the Botanical Gardens, which could accommodate between five and six thousand, but a few nights into the "campaign"—a term Dwight had picked up from his time with Ulysses S. Grant during the Civil War—he couldn't get through the crowd to enter the auditorium. Undaunted, Dwight preached from the top of his carriage—there were more people outside the Botanical Gardens than inside, anyway! The crowd numbered an estimated twenty to thirty thousand people. One witness later wrote,

> We thought of the days of Whitefield, of such a scene as that mentioned in his life, when, in 1753 at Glasgow, twenty thousand souls hung on his lips as he bade them farewell. Here there were thirty thousand eager hearers, for by this time the thousands within the Crystal Palace had come out, though their numbers quietly melting into the main body did not make a very perceptible addition to the crowd; and many onlookers who knew something of such gatherings were inclined to estimate the number much higher.[43]

The tour would continue on to Ireland, then return to England in November 1874, to continually overflowing crowds.

A Formula That Worked

Soon after the campaigns began, Dwight deduced a formula for the meetings that would make up the campaign. Those attending prayer meetings held at noon would pray over the concerns and souls of those who would attend that evening. Not long into the revival, the attendance at these noontime meetings grew into the thousands. Following the prayer meeting, a "question-drawer" meeting would be held. People were asked to write their questions on sheets of paper, which were collected and addressed at random from the podium by Dwight and at least two other pastors. Then, after a break for lunch and a bit of a rest, a Bible reading meeting would take place, where portions of Scripture were read and then explained. These were the

[43] Moody, *Life of Dwight L. Moody*, 199.

most popular of the afternoon meetings. As they grew larger, several of these meetings would be held at one time in order to give proper attention to everyone in attendance. Dwight circulated among these concurrent meetings, putting in an appearance at each one. All of these meetings always started and ended exactly on time. Evening services would then follow as scheduled.

Dwight also started something quite novel for his day: children's services. Echoing his work among the youth in The Sands, Dwight started meetings for children and created even more techniques to preach the Gospel to children in particular. Among these techniques was the *Wordless Book*—a large booklet with four leaves of black (sin), red (blood of Christ), white (cleansing from sin), and gold (heaven)—which he used as a prop while asking his audience a series of questions leading them to understand their need for a Savior. Many of these meetings resulted in permanent Sunday schools being established as the locals answered Dwight's challenge to reach the youth of their communities.

Another change Dwight implemented was exchanging Finney's "anxious seat" for the "inquiry room." He felt that the anxious seat put the penitent on display and was abused by those who were more interested in making a spectacle of themselves than in pursuing salvation. Instead, those "inquiring" about salvation would be taken aside to another room, where they met with counselors who would answer their questions as best they could from Scripture and pray with them. This seemed, however, to take the "fear and trembling" out of conversion. The struggle for assurance within a person's heart that he or she was saved no longer seemed necessary. Salvation became more an assurance of the words of the counselor than a revelation of the heart. In addition, with the tight focus on conversion, there seemed little room for other works of the Spirit. There was no more "crying out for the touch of God," but rather, quiet prayers away from the crowds. Thus, Dwight's meetings would never see the manifestations of the Spirit that happened at Cane Ridge or in the meetings of John Wesley, or even those that took place as William Booth ministered at roughly this same time, elsewhere in London.

In 1875, Dwight and Ira returned to London for the final months of the campaign. When asked to come, Dwight said, "You will need to raise £5,000 for expenses of halls, advertising, etc." The reply came almost immediately: "We have £10,000 already." The city was divided into four quarters, and each was addressed individually. A portable hall was created that could hold five to six thousand people. The final service was held on July 12, 1875. In London alone, the evangelists had conducted 285 meetings and addressed 2,500,000 people.[44]

In his closing address, Dwight finished with this appeal:

> For two years and three weeks we have been trying to labor for Christ among you, and now it is time to close. This is the last time I shall have the privilege of preaching the Gospel in this country at this time. I want to say that these have been the best years of my life. I have sought to bring Christ before you and to tell you of His beauty. It is true I have done it with stammering tongue. I have never spoken of Him as I would like to. I have done the best I could, and at this closing hour I want once more to press Him upon your acceptance. I do not want to close this meeting until I see you all in the ark of refuge. How many are willing to stand up before God to-night and say by that act that they will join us in our journey to Heaven? You that are willing to take Christ now, will you not rise?[45]

At that, many did stand, and Dwight was able to escape the podium with the emphasis on God rather than in celebration of all that had taken place as a result of his ministry in the British Isles over a period of twenty-five months.

One author summed up Dwight's effects on Great Britain in this way:

> Lecky, the historian, calmly and dispassionately asserts that the evangelistic labors of John Wesley and his co-workers, by lifting the moral tone of the common people, saved England from a revolution. Mr. Moody may not have served as an instrument for the accomplishment of so deep an economic purpose, but it is certain that the regenerating springs of spiritual life, which God used him to draw from

[44] Chapman, *Life and Work of Dwight Lyman Moody*, http://www.biblebelievers.com/moody/10.html.

[45] Moody, *Life of Dwight L. Moody*, 247.

> the rock of indifference, refreshed and revived a people fast tending to religious numbness. And nothing is so dangerous as this apathetic numbness; it has done more to hinder the progress of salvation than all the active forces of the devil put together.
>
> I am not prepared to deny that many who were awakened or converted during Mr. Moody's labours in Great Britain went back to their former walks soon after the immediate presence of the evangelists ceased to be felt; nor will I deny that much of the work inspired by his efforts crystallised into conventional and narrow forms; but I believe from the bottom of my heart that the movement blessed Britain as she had not before been blessed for one hundred years, and I know that tens of thousands of persons became better men and women for the effect of Mr. Moody's words upon them. Through this man God led men to read their Bibles, to live honestly, to rid themselves of besetting sins, and to place their faith in Christ as a personal Saviour.[46]

The Moodys and Sankeys would head back to New York on August 4. When they arrived there on August 14, the change was evident. They were no longer simple Christian missionaries serving their Lord in whatever capacity they felt led; rather, they were now international celebrities, welcomed back to America with the fanfare usually reserved for the rich or famous.

Dwight's Strengths

In the years to come, Dwight would prove that he could hold meetings as no one else had in the history of the world. For most, a lack of education limits what a person can do, but it seemed the opposite with Dwight—he was not limited to conventional thinking, and therefore thought to do things in a way no one else ever had. It seems that the word *cannot* was never part of his experience. In the years to come, he would master his use of the press to promote his meetings. Many of the ministries of the day criticized this tactic, but he obtained results none of them ever would. He embraced new

[46] Chapman, *Life and Work of Dwight Lyman Moody*, http://www.biblebelievers.com/moody/10.html.

opportunities rather than worrying that they would dilute his focus, and organizations and schools emerged from Chicago to Northfield with the Moody imprint on them. His schools would never be held back for lack of credentials in the same way that not being ordained never kept him from becoming a minister. It would not keep the crowds away, either.

Dwight Moody had a drive that few other men possessed. There was no questioning his passion to see people come to Christ. Wherever he preached, he attracted the curious, and many of them left as believers. No detail seemed too small to merit his attention or to increase the effectiveness of his campaigns—a trait the Billy Graham Evangelistic Association would fully adopt. Prayer was ever a foundation of these campaigns as well. The noon-hour prayer meetings remained an important part of all of his campaigns.

Phenomenal testimonies followed of how people came to the Lord after hearing Dwight preach. Here are two such stories:

> One great feature of Mr. Moody's work had always been the singing, the wisdom of which may be seen in the following: While he was holding services in the Monument Street M. E. Church, a man addicted to drink and with no thought of God attended one of the meetings. He was much impressed with the singing, particularly with one hymn, "Come, O, Come to Me." He heard the announcement for the day meetings, and he determined to attend. As he entered the church Mr. Bliss was singing the hymn above mentioned. The man bought a hymn book that he might read the hymn for himself, and testified that he had no peace. Finally he burned the book, but he could not burn the impression that had been made by the Spirit. He then drank the harder, but could not drown the impression. Time passed on; one night he wandered into the Methodist Church, and as he did so he heard them singing again, "Come, O, Come to Me," and there that night he obeyed the call and accepted Christ. The hymn was number eighty-eight (88) in *Gospel Hymns*, No. 3. Mr. Moody always spoke of him after that as No. 88.
>
> During the meetings at Broadway M. E. Church, a pickpocket entered the meeting for the purpose of relieving some

> one of his gold watch, which he was not long in doing; after procuring his prize, he started to leave the church but was unable to do so, for those who were in had to remain, and those who were out could not get in; he was therefore led to listen, was much impressed with the sermon, and stayed for the inquiry meeting, where he accepted Christ as his personal Saviour. The next day the door bell of the parsonage was rung, and when the servant answered, she found no one, but tied to the knob of the door was a package. This when opened was found to contain a gold watch and chain, and with it a note stating the facts, and asking that it be returned to the owner, which was done. The repentant thief gave his name and address, but asked that he might be forgiven, as God had forgiven him.[47]

Perhaps Dwight's greatest year of was 1876—America's Centennial. In January of that year, 210 meetings attended by more than a million people were held in Philadelphia's Pennsylvania Freight Depot. In New York, Dwight rented the Hippodrome, which had formerly housed the Barnum Circus. They filled the 14,000-seat building to overflowing for ten consecutive weeks. Years later, in 1883, when Barnum's Circus finished at Madison Square Garden, Dwight secured that venue for a series of meetings.

Dwight preaches in New York's Hippodrome in 1876.
Roberts Liardon Archives

In the following decades, Dwight's meetings would continue to touch hearts. Back in England in the spring of 1884, Dwight was speaking in London when a young medical student named Wilfred Thomason Grenfell slipped in at the back of one of his meetings. He

[47] Chapman, *Life and Work of Dwight Lyman Moody*, http://www.biblebelievers.com/moody/11.html.

was a student at Queens College, Oxford, and came from a well-to-do family. As he entered, he heard a man praying in a rather sanctimonious tone, and he was ready to turn on his heels and leave, seeing nothing about this meeting that appeared different. Yet, at that moment, according to Grenfell, "a vivacious person jumped up and shouted: 'Let us sing a hymn while our brother finishes his prayer.'" He was astounded, as "unconventionality, common sense, or humor in anything 'religious' was new to me." When he found out that it was the man who would speak that evening, he decided to stay and hear him out. Dwight preached that night about a life of service being the call of every Christian, stating, "Why don't you turn your life over to Christ? He can do more with it than you can." As he left the meeting, Grenfell took one of Dwight's *How to Read the Bible* booklets and later studied it. Eventually, he ended up spending forty years in Labrador, Canada, building clinics and hospitals, as well as attending to the physical and spiritual needs of the Native Americans, Eskimos, and whites.[48]

Just a few years before this instance, Dwight spoke at Cambridge and similarly inspired seven young athletes there to become missionaries under Hudson Taylor in China. They were known as the "Cambridge Seven" and included C. T. Studd, M. Beauchamp, S. P. Smith, A. T. Polhill-Turner, D. E. Hoste, C. H. Polhill-Turner, and W. W. Cassels.

"The Boat Is Sinking"

In 1892, after ministering again in Great Britain, a fatigued Dwight finally saw a physician about his health. The doctor told him that his heart was weakening from the strain of his hectic schedule, and if he wanted to live much longer, he would need to slow his pace. As Dwight boarded the *Spree*, which would take him home, he was already making plans for how he might let up a good deal in his work, but his voyage home would change that.

> I was on the steamer *Spree*, and when the announcement was made that the steamer was sinking, and we were there in a helpless condition in mid-ocean, no one on earth knows

[48] See Wilfred Grenfell, *A Labrador Doctor* (Boston: Pilgrim Press, 1927); *Forty Years for Labrador* (Boston: Houghton Mifflin, 1932); and *What Christ Means to Me* (London: Pilgrim Press, 1927), 21–27.

> what I passed through as I thought that my work was finished, and that I should never again have the privilege of preaching the Gospel of the Son of God. And on that dark night, the first night of the accident, I made a vow that if God would spare my life and bring me back to America, I would come to Chicago, and at the World's Fair preach the Gospel with all the power that He would give me.[49]

On the third morning of the voyage, the *Spree*'s drift shaft shattered, sending two large fragments through the hull. The ship was taking in water so quickly that the pumps could not expel it at a sufficient rate. For two days, it drifted on seas so rough that the lifeboats capsized almost as soon as they were dropped into the water. On the second evening, Dwight started prayer services, at which he read from Psalms 91 and 107:20–31. The ship's bow was high in the air, and the stern was sinking deeper as the sun went down. The passengers and crew sat in total darkness—the generators were out—and the captain announced that all was lost. He was mistaken, however, and Dwight's prayers for rescue were answered. The Canadian freighter, *Lake Huron*, happened upon them and towed the *Spree* back to Ireland. All 750 people on board were saved.

Dwight kept his word. He would preach at the World's Fair with all the force God would give him. Having come so close to forfeiting his life at sea, he viewed all of his remaining days as bonuses. He would give them all to the Lord without complaint. When other ministers threatened to boycott the World's Fair because it was scheduled to be open on Sundays, Dwight just planned more services. He said, "Let us open so many preaching places and present the Gospel so attractively that the people will want to come and hear it."[50] The fair provided another great opportunity to preach the Gospel. In his closing remarks, Dwight noted,

> We have to-day everything to encourage us, and nothing to discourage us. This has been by far the best week we have had. The Gospel has through this agency been brought to 150,000 people during the week. I have never seen greater eagerness to hear the word of God. The largest halls are

[49] Moody, *Life of Dwight L. Moody*, 410, 413.

[50] Ibid., 413.

too small for the crowds that come to many of the services. One night, for instance, on my way to the Fair Grounds, I beheld one of the most beautiful sights I have ever seen on earth. It was a wonderful display of fireworks and illuminations, tens of thousands of people gazing on the scene. It seemed useless to expect any one to come away from that scene and sit down in a tabernacle to hear the Gospel; but the house was filled, and we had a blessed meeting. The following nights though cold and rainy, with a damp, uncomfortable room, the people crowded in until every inch of space was occupied. I thank God that I am living in Chicago to-day; these have been the happiest moments of my life; what a work He has given us to-day; what encouragements He has given us; how He has blessed us. Perhaps never in your life will some of you have an opportunity to do as much for Christ as now.[51]

Dwight and Emma Moody with two granddaughters
Roberts Liardon Archives

Dwight's final campaign would begin on November 12, 1899, in Kansas City, Missouri. His last sermon would be on November 16, after which he would retire, exhausted, and hear his physician's charge to get more rest. He returned to Northfield by train, but would not recover; nor would he see the twentieth century. According to his son's biography, on Dwight's last day,

about six o'clock he quieted down, and soon fell into a natural sleep, from which he awoke in about an hour. Suddenly

[51] Chapman, *Life and Work of Dwight Lyman Moody*, http://www.biblebelievers.com/moody/17.html.

> he was heard speaking in slow and measured words. He was saying: "Earth recedes; Heaven opens before me." The first impulse was to try to arouse him from what appeared to be a dream. "No, this is no dream, Will," he replied. "It is beautiful. It is like a trance. If this is death, it is sweet. There is no valley here. God is calling me, and I must go."[52]

Following this vision, he had time to call his family to him and speak with them awhile. Then, quieting, he fell asleep—and never woke up. The date was December 22, 1899. Dwight was only sixty-three. Emma survived him, and she died four years later, in 1903.

Of his own death, Dwight had stated earlier,

> Some day you will read in the papers that D. L. Moody, of East Northfield, is dead. Don't you believe a word of it! At that moment I shall be more alive than I am now. I shall have gone up higher, that is all out of this old clay tenement into a house that is immortal; a body that death cannot touch, that sin cannot taint, a body fashioned like unto His glorious body. I was born of the flesh in 1837. I was born of the Spirit in 1856. That which is born of the flesh may die. That which is born of the Spirit will live forever.[53]

One of Dwight's critics may have best summed up his life when he admitted,

> In his rage to save souls he traveled more than a million miles, addressed more than a hundred million people, and personally prayed and pleaded with seven hundred and fifty thousand sinners. All in all, it is very probable, as his admirers claim, that he reduced the population of hell by a million souls.[54]

Dwight's ministry and name traveled even farther than he did, as this story published in *The Youth's Companion* illustrates:

---

[52] Moody, *Life of Dwight L. Moody*, 552.

[53] Ibid., 554–555.

[54] Robert L. Dufus, "The Hound of Heaven," *American Mercury* 5, April 1925, 424–425, quoted in Gamaliel Bradford, *D. L. Moody: A Worker in Souls* (Garden City, NJ: Doubleday, Doran, and Company, 1928), 16, quoted in Dorsett, *Passion for Souls*, 21.

> A young missionary far in the interior of China received for baptism a little child. The name given was Moo Dee, so unusual a combination that the minister asked its origin. "I have heard of your man of God, Moo Dee," was the reply. "In our dialect *Moo* means 'love,' and *Dee*, 'God.' I would have my child, too, love God." Mr. Moody knew no Chinese, but his name alone told in that language the secret of his life.[55]

Dwight would have been quite happy knowing hell would be that much less populous for his having lived. It is a worthy goal for us all.

[55] Moody, *Life of Dwight L. Moody*, 529.

Chapter Nine

William & Catherine Booth

(1829–1890) (1829–1912)

"Through Blood and Fire"

"Through Blood and Fire"

The chief danger of the twentieth century will be religion without the Holy Ghost, Christianity without Christ, forgiveness without repentance, salvation without regeneration, politics without God, and Heaven without Hell.

—William Booth

We want men who are set on soul-saving; who are not ashamed to let every one know that this is the one aim and object of their life and that they make everything secondary to this.

—Catherine Booth

In the mid-1800s, England was in the first decades of the Industrial Revolution, a time etched into our minds by authors such as Charles Dickens, in his stories *Oliver Twist* and *A Christmas Carol*, among others. The power of industrial efficiency had driven many middle-class craftsmen into the streets as paupers. Factory conditions were often untenable, child labor was rampant, and England might have been well on her way to a civil war between the classes—reminiscent of the French Revolution—had it not been for the sweep of revival and social reform initiated by William and Catherine Booth. In a matter of a few decades, the movement they began went from transforming England with renewed hope to encircling the globe with new missions. The Salvation Army undertook to seek out each nation's distressed, indebted, and discontented, and to bring them the transforming grace of Jesus Christ. It became a movement—an army of "Salvationists"—determined to set captives free through the blood of the Lamb and the fire of the Holy Spirit.

"Willful Will"

William Booth was born on April 10, 1829, in Nottingham (in central England), the only son of Samuel and Mary Booth. He and his three sisters grew up in their parents' redbrick terrace home in Sneinton, a small village that was eventually swallowed by Nottingham, a burgeoning hub of industry. Samuel had started working as a nail-maker, but the occupation soon became obsolete as the Industrial Revolution raged on. So, he became an architect, and, for some time, he was successful building houses in cities and towns that grew to overflowing.

The Booth family professed membership in the Church of England, but William's father rarely darkened the doorstep of a chapel. It was a time in England when the Church relegated those who could not afford the fees for pew rentals to the rear galleries, segregating rich and poor in much the same way that the races were segregated for so many years in the American South.

Mary Booth was Samuel's second wife. His first, Sarah Lockitt, had died of unspecified causes on January 13, 1819, at the age of fifty-three. Samuel and Sarah had had at least one son together, William Adcock (or Hadcock), but he died of consumption at the age of twenty-four. Our William—the one would go on to found the Salvation Army—was named after this deceased stepbrother he never knew.

Samuel met Mary Moss during the summer of his son's death, and after a short courtship, they married on November 2, 1824. Samuel, still an aspiring businessman, was nearing fifty, and Mary was thirty-three. The reason for a short courtship was likely that this was a marriage of convenience. Samuel was seeking comfort and hoping to secure an heir as he grew older, and Mary did not want to end up a spinster. Together, Samuel and Mary had five children: Henry, born January 6, 1826 (died January 6, 1828); Ann, birth date unknown, but baptized April 1, 1827; William, born April 10, 1829; Emma, born January 21, 1831, who would be an invalid her entire life; and Mary, born September 16, 1832.

For William and his sisters, life was much more comfortable than it was for most. Unlike many other children, they did not have to toil twelve hours a day in the factories to help put bread on the table and coal in the fireplace. William began attending the academy of Nottingham at the age of six, quickly becoming a standout among his peers for his strength of will, leadership abilities, and impulsive chicanery. These traits earned him the nicknames "Willful Will" and "Wellington," after the Duke of Wellington, who was famous for his military victories, most notably his defeat of Napoleon at Waterloo. William earned this latter title because he was a master at sport. As with the young Charles Finney, if you wanted to win, then you made sure Booth was on your team—and, if possible, your captain.

Despite affluent appearances, though, Samuel Booth's fortune was all but gone by the time William was born. Throughout William's early years, the Booths managed to keep up the air of being propertied, but poor business decisions resulted in bankruptcy. Thirteen-year-old William was pulled out of school and sent to be an apprentice for a pawnbroker named Francis Eames. William's father passed away a little more than a year later, on September 23, 1843. On his deathbed, he repented for his former lack of faithfulness to God; he made his peace with his Creator in the moments before he met Him face-to-face.

Young William was a quick study and soon became an efficient pawnbroker, but watching family after family sell its treasures to make ends meet started to wear on him. He soon began to view pawnbroking as a vulture of a profession and came to hate it. Some people would sell their "Sunday best," earn enough to buy it back on Saturday, and then sell these garments again on Monday morning. They went to great expense to look good for one day. It didn't take William long to learn that trinkets and fancy clothes went first, family heirlooms and furniture next, and wedding rings last.

Poverty in England increased dramatically throughout William's childhood and early teenage years. Failed crops, rising taxes, and heavy corn levies designed to protect the income of wealthy landowners transformed Nottingham from a farming center into a stocking-weaving mill town. Workers riots were not uncommon. Prostitution and crime were rampant, as people did whatever they felt they needed to do to survive. Times were hard: the machine slowly replaced the plow, and factory-made products gradually put ordinary craftsmen and artisans out of work. Industry had no regulation to protect workers, nor did it evince any conscience—eroding the middle class, it made man just another cog in the production lines, literate and illiterate alike.

"A Soul Dies Every Minute!"

After his father died and he assumed headship of the household responsibilities, fifteen-year-old William began to search for new meaning in his life. This search led him frequently to the Broad Street Wesleyan Chapel, where, late one evening, he heard a minister by the name of Isaac Marsden. The minister's warning, "A soul dies every minute!" haunted William for some time. Marsden had thundered at the stunned congregation, and the words sank deeply into William's heart. Though he didn't give his life to Christ that night, in the following days, he would come under a deep conviction of his need for repentance.

Unlike the other Generals of revival in this book, William Booth could not ascribe a specific date to his conversion. It was not many days after this, however, that he signed on as a Methodist and gave his life over to saving those "souls dying every minute"—something he would strive to do for the next six decades. As personal sins came to mind, he would repent and made restitution, if possible. There was the matter of a silver pencil case he had wrested from some friends through trickery. Though he had to swallow a good bit of pride to face them, he returned it. In the coming days, William reached a certainty that he belonged to God. Years later, he would describe his sense of certainty in this way:

> My brethren, if you have salvation you are sure of it. Not because...you have heard it preached. Not because you have read with your eyes, or heard read by others in that wonderful book, the wonderful story of the love of God to you. Not because you have seen with your eyes transformations of character wrought by the power of the Holy Ghost; changes as marvelous, as miraculous, as divine, as any that ever took place in apostolic or any other days. These things may

> have led up to it. But these things, wonderful as they may be, have not power to make you sure of your part and lot in the matter of salvation. Flesh and blood has not revealed this to you, but God Himself, by His Spirit has made this known.[1]

William started attending every service and Bible class he could at the Wesleyan chapel, filling himself as much as possible with the Word and fire of God. While others were assembling in the streets to riot or preach social reform, William was seeking God. With his talents and his enthusiasm, William easily might have become a successful politician or a revolutionary, had God not reached him first; but because God did get to him first, he would do more to reform the social ills of his nation than any other person in the nineteenth century.

Another Catherine the Great Is Born

Some three months before William's birth, Catherine Mumford was born on January 17, 1829, in Ashbourne, Derbyshire, the only daughter of John and Sarah Mumford. The Mumfords also had four sons, but only one of them lived beyond childhood. Catherine's mother, Sarah, was a devout believer from her youth. She and John had met at the local Methodist chapel.

Catherine was a sickly child, and she was fragile and unwell for her entire life. Yet there burned within her something that rendered such frailty rather unimportant: a compassion and intensity of feeling unparalleled in anyone but her future husband. Catherine was anything but an unhappy child. Constant illness kept her indoors most of the time, but because of this, she grew to love books—and treasured no book above the Bible. Her mother so prized God's truth that she allowed no novels or other fiction books into their household; she saw them as foolish and a waste of time. Catherine had learned to read by the age of three, and she would often stand on a stool to read aloud from the family Bible while her mother worked around the house, listening. By the time Catherine was twelve, she had read the Bible eight times from cover to cover—and out loud.

---

[1] William Booth, *The Salvationist*, January 1879, quoted in Cyril Barnes, ed., *The Founder Speaks Again* (London: Salvationist Publishing and Supplies, 1960), 47.

In 1834, Catherine's father moved the family back to his native Boston in Lincolnshire, England. Catherine was about five years old at the time, and she would spend most of her childhood here. The family hoped the sea air would benefit the children's health.

Catherine was not a girl marked with indifference. Again, the weakness of her health never hampered the passion in her heart, much less her intolerance for cruelty of any kind. She always defended the unfortunate and weak. One time, while riding in a carriage, she saw a boy beating a donkey with a hammer. Infuriated, she burst forth from the carriage, overtook the boy, confiscated his hammer, and sent him home with his ears still burning from her rebukes. She then dropped to the ground in a faint and had to be carried home.

The weakness of Catherine's health never hampered the passion in her heart.

Another time, when a nine-year-old Catherine was playing outside, rolling a hoop down the street, she was interrupted by a mob coming toward her. A constable was half marching, half dragging a drunken man down the sidewalk, and the mob had gathered to jeer and mock him along the way. In the face of this cruelty, Catherine immediately took pity upon him. Even though her home was an active outpost of the Temperance Society, Catherine's heart could not condemn the man; she could not stand such treatment of someone so disoriented. So, she marched into the midst of the crowd, right up to the face of the drunkard. Everyone was caught off guard by the boldness of such a small creature, and they stopped dead in their tracks. Catherine came nose-to-nose with the man, smelling the foulness of his breath and searching his eyes for some hint of humanity behind their empty stare. Then, taking him by the hand, she turned and began to lead him in the same direction the crowd had been taking him. The man's steps became steadier, and the policeman no longer had to tug at him, but walked alongside, merely holding his arm to steady him.

Thus, Catherine and the policeman took the man to the lockup, and the crowd lost interest in their taunts. The scene was reminiscent of the biblical account of the accusers of the woman caught in adultery had lost interest when Jesus confronted them. (See John 8:2–11.)

When Catherine heard about the plight of the poor in other countries, she gave up sugar and other luxuries; the money thus spared was sent to missionary societies instead.

At the age of twelve, Catherine was finally deemed strong enough to attend school and she took to it with a scholar's eagerness. Even at this young age, Catherine's love for the truth was so strong that her teachers quickly learned to take her version of any story as the most objective and accurate one. Because of her fine organizational and leadership skills, she was appointed class monitor. She fell in love with history and geography almost instantly, desiring to visit foreign lands and experience new cultures. Mathematics took a bit longer for her to appreciate, but once she could make sense of it, she added it to her competencies.

Unfortunately, when Catherine was fourteen, she was diagnosed with a severe curvature of the spine, and had to withdraw from school. The only remedy was to lie flat for three months while her body healed itself. For most children her age, such a treatment would have been akin to solitary confinement, but Catherine had a welcome occupation—she returned to her beloved books. Although her body was inactive, her mind was not. She focused on church history and theology, devouring the writings of such revivalists as John Wesley and Charles Finney, as well as those of John Newton, who penned the lines of the hymn "Amazing Grace." While she grasped the logic of each theologian's arguments, she was struck by the fact that they didn't always agree. She became perplexed by the question of how to determine who was correct, or more precisely, how to discern the truth so that she could live by it. Years later, she would describe her struggle in this way:

> When I was fourteen years old I rejected all theories about God and religion which contradicted my innate conceptions of right and wrong. I said, "No, I will never believe any theory which represents that a course of procedure is good and benevolent in God, which in man would be despicable and contemptible. I cannot receive it." I could not then put it into this language, but I remember distinctly the feelings of my soul. I said, "No, all that there is

> in me akin to goodness and truth God has put there, and I will never believe that what God has put in me contradicts what He has put into this book. There must be a mistake somewhere," and thank God, I came to the Scriptures for myself, which I recommend you to do. Don't imagine that the repugnant views of the character of God which have been forced upon you by professed theologians will form any excuse for your rejections of His book or of the Divine authority of it in the great day of account. God will say, "Had you not the light for yourself?"[2]

In other words, she clung deeply to the truth of 1 John 2:27:

> *But the anointing* [of the Holy Spirit] *which ye have received of him abideth in you, and ye need not that any man teach you: but as the same anointing teacheth you of all things, and is truth, and is no lie, and even as it hath taught you, ye shall abide in him.*

Her guides would be Scripture and the hand of the Holy Spirit upon her heart, whose job it was to bring her to Jesus and His teachings.

Before long, Catherine's back responded favorably to sustained rest, and her period of confinement ended. In 1844, her family moved to London, and Catherine recommenced her schooling. She still had a voracious appetite for knowledge and study, but in the next few years, she would face one of the biggest questions of her life: *How could she know that she was saved?*

"How Do I Know If I Am Saved?"

Catherine could not accept the idea that she had simply been saved all of her life, and she determined to know in her heart that she had been truly converted. When she returned to school, her internal passion for righteousness at times turned to impatience and anger. While she never did anything rash—at least, outwardly—inwardly, these powerful emotions convinced her that sin still controlled her heart. She knew that a converted person would not have such a seed of corruption within her but would be spiritually born again. Though she might sin mistakenly on the outside, the root of sin within her

[2] W. T. Stead, *Mrs. Booth* (London: James Nisbet and Co., 1900), 27–28.

would be gone. Catherine determined to pluck sin from her life so that she could know that she was dead to it and alive to God, following Paul's exhortation in Romans 6:11 to *"reckon ye also yourselves to be dead indeed unto sin, but alive unto God through Jesus Christ our Lord."* For her, only the gift of faith could bring her to true conversion. As she later recalled,

> About this time I passed through a great controversy of soul. Although I was conscious of having given myself up fully to God from my earliest years, and although I was anxious to serve Him and often realized deep enjoyment in prayer, nevertheless, I had not the positive assurance that my sins were forgiven, and that I had experienced the actual change of heart about which I had read and heard so much. I was determined to leave the question no longer in doubt, but to get it definitely settled, cost what it might. For six weeks I prayed and struggled on, but obtained no satisfaction. True, my past life had been outwardly blameless. Both in public and in private I had made use of the means of grace, and up to the very limit of my strength, and often beyond the bounds of discretion, my zeal had carried me. Still, so far as this was concerned, I realised the truth of the words:
>
> Could my zeal no respite know,
> Could my tears forever flow—
> These for sins could not atone;
> Thou must save, and Thou alone.
>
> I knew, moreover, that "the heart is deceitful above all things, and desperately wicked" [Jeremiah 17:9]. I was terribly afraid of being self-deceived. I remembered, too, the occasional outbursts of temper when I was at school. Neither could I call to mind any particular place or time when I had definitely stepped out upon the promises, and had claimed the immediate forgiveness of my sins, receiving the witness of the Holy Spirit that I had become a child of God and an heir of heaven.
>
> It seemed to me unreasonable to suppose that I could be saved and yet not know it. At any rate I could not permit

> myself to remain longer in doubt regarding the matter. If in the past I had acted up to the light I had received, it was evident that I was now getting new light, and unless I obeyed it I realized that my soul would fall into condemnation. Ah, how many hundreds have I since met who have spent years in doubt and perplexity because, after consecrating themselves fully to God, they dare not venture out upon the promises and believe!
>
> I can never forget the agony I passed through. I used to pace my room till two o'clock in the morning, and when, utterly exhausted, I lay down at length to sleep, I would place my Bible and hymnbook under my pillow, praying that I might wake up with the assurance of salvation.[3]

This pattern continued for some time, until, on the evening of June 14, 1846, she again prayed as she let her head fall to her pillow, "Father, may it be that I awake tomorrow to an assurance of Your forgiveness of my sin."[4] And the next day, she did just that. When her eyes opened, she sat up in bed and recovered her Bible and hymnal from under her pillow. As she did so, the hymnal fell open and her eyes were drawn to a verse penned by Charles Wesley:

My God, I am Thine,
What a comfort Divine,
What a blessing, to know that my
Jesus is mine![5]

Light shot through her soul. Months of struggle were answered in an instant. Her heart was changed, and Jesus, not guilt, flooded her spirit. She later recalled,

> Scores of times I had read and sung these words, but now they came home to my inmost soul with a force and illumination they had never before possessed. It was as

[3] Fredrick de Lautour Booth-Tucker, *The Life of Catherine Booth: The Mother of the Salvation Army*, vol. 1 (London: Salvationist Publishing and Supplies, Ltd., 1924 [3rd printing]), 36–37.

[4] Trevor Yaxley, *William and Catherine: The Life and Legacy of the Booths, Founders of the Salvation Army: A New Biography* (Minneapolis, MN: Bethany House Publishers, 2003), 40.

[5] *The Methodist Hymn Book* (London: Novello and Co., 1933), Hymn 406.

> impossible for me to doubt as it had before been for me to exercise faith. Previously not all the promises in the Bible could induce me to believe; now not all the devils in hell could persuade me to doubt. I no longer hoped I was saved, I was certain of it. The assurance of my salvation seemed to flood and fill my soul. I jumped out of bed, and without waiting to dress, ran into my mother's room and told her what had happened.[6]

As an affirmation that she now belonged to God, she registered for membership at the Brixton Wesleyan Methodist Church, something she had refused to do until she had the assurance of her salvation. A few months later, in September 1846, Catherine fell ill again, this time with consumption. Though her body ached and she was often delirious with fever, the knowledge of her salvation brought her comfort. Her doctors feared that she might contract tuberculosis. She was confined again to her home throughout the winter, and in May, when she was well enough to travel, she moved in with her aunt, who lived in Brighton, near the sea. She hoped that the salty air would do her some good. When she felt strong enough, she started attending services at the local Wesleyan chapel.

Changing Times, Dead Churches

Although Methodism was on the rise in the United States due to the efforts of the likes of Peter Cartwright, the movement was sinking into the mire of bureaucracy in Great Britain. It seemed that Methodism was no longer about the power of God that appeared as John Wesley or George Whitefield spoke, but that it had become more about regulation and governance. Circuit ministers were so overrun with paperwork that they hardly had time to preach. Methodists' memberships were also submitted to an annual review to ensure that members remained in good standing with the society. Calls for reform and a return to the original principles of the founders began in the 1840s, but by the conference in 1850, leaders of the reform were singled out as troublemakers and expelled. Methodism had strayed from unleashing the power of God to convert souls and focused instead on controlling the members and keeping the coffers filled.

[6] Stead, *Mrs. Booth*, 38.

The Wesleys were probably wringing their hands in heaven, as Methodism was doomed never to regain its former power to transform lives through the preaching of the Word and the presence of God.

Though they had yet to meet, both William and Catherine fell afoul of the mainline Methodists, and they ended up with the reformers. Catherine, passionate as ever about injustice, would not be silenced about the gross unfairness of expelling these godly leaders. When her membership came up for review, her class leader withheld her ticket of readmittance. In effect, Catherine was excommunicated from the body that had been her spiritual sanctuary since the time she was born, and in being expelled, she lost many of her mentors and close personal friendships.

William Booth addresses a multicultural crowd.

Mary Evans Picture Library

William offended the Methodists in a different way. His exuberance at his own salvation had not yet worn off, and the haunting statement "A soul dies every minute!" still seemed to pound in his ears. Two years after his conversion, he went to a meeting where James Caughey was speaking. The Irish-American's style was such that he seemed to breathe purifying fear with each word, and William was captivated. That night, he rededicated himself to his Lord and Savior, deciding to become a soulwinner like Caughey. William rose from his knees at the end of the service with the conviction that "God shall have all there was of William Booth."[7]

William was convinced that if he planned to save the souls of the poor, he could not afford to wait for them to come to him. He persuaded his good friend, Will Sansom, to preach with him in the streets. The two headed for "The Bottoms," the worst of Nottingham's slums. Young Booth cut an impressive figure standing atop a barrel or a chair to address his audiences. He was tall, with deep grey eyes, black hair, and a high, prominent nose. William's appeals did not go unanswered, but he needed a significant breakthrough if

[7] Richard Collier, *The General Next to God* (London: Collins, 1965), 189.

he was going to get the people of this neighborhood to follow him into a church—a building where they had been unwelcome for so long. That breakthrough was not long in coming.

He and Will went to Kid Street to preach, and, unfamiliar with the area, set up camp right in front of the home of a notorious, rowdy drunkard known as Besom Jack. The two sang a hymn, and William stood on a chair and began to address the crowd. "Friends," he cried,

> I want to put a few straight questions to your soul....Have any of you got a child at home without shoes to its feet? Are your wives sitting now in dark houses waiting for you to return without money? Are you going away from here...to spend on drink, money that your wives need for food?[8]

Suddenly, the front door of the house behind them burst open, and Besom Jack made straight for the pair of preachers. Just as he was coming within reach, William's gaze met him straight in the eyes, and he said, "Jack, God loves your wife, and so did you once." Jack stopped dead in his tracks—the words had struck a nerve. "Can you remember how much you loved her and cherished her when you first met?" Jack's eyes were fixed on the ground before William's feet. He nodded slowly. "Well, Jack, God loves you with a love like that, with a love far deeper and greater than that."

The crowd was hanging on every word. Jack finally looked up. "Me?"

"Yes, Jack, you." William stepped down from his chair and took Jack by the arm. "Come, Jack, kneel down here and tell the Lord you love him too, and ask him to forgive you." Jack did just that.[9]

William knew that these new converts needed much more than just to be saved. He knew that they needed teaching so that they could grow enough to take care of their own faith. So, the next Sunday, the two Wills headed for The Bottoms again, gathered a crowd, and marched them all to the Wesleyan chapel. They burst into the church in the middle of a service, just following the fourth hymn, and seated their "catch" in the front rows—the best seats in the house. William enjoyed the service immensely, but at the end,

---

[8] Collier, *General Next to God*, 23–24.

[9] Ibid.

the Reverend Samuel Dunn came down not to congratulate William, but to reprimand him.

Rev. Dunn directed William's gaze to a row of seats tucked away behind a partition in the back of the chapel, out of sight—and virtually out of earshot of the preaching—and pointed to the obscure side door that provided access to these seats. Rev. Dunn told William that the front rows in which he had seated his "guests" were reserved for those who could contribute to the cause of Methodism—the poor, he said, were to enter through the side door and sit in the back seats. They were, by all means, welcome to attend every service, but they were to stay out of the way and were not to interfere with the other parishioners' enjoyment of the service. William accepted the rebuke humbly, but this snobbery was the beginning of the end of William's association with the Methodists.

The Young Methodist Preacher

Even though he was only seventeen, William was placed on the schedule of circuit preachers' speaking engagements. He began speaking at the Broad Street Chapel, as well as in other villages around Nottingham. Keeping up his open-air meetings, he continued to develop as a preacher over the next few years.

When he was nineteen, he finished his apprenticeship at the pawnshop and was informed that he needed to find a job elsewhere, as Mr. Eames could no longer afford to employ him. For the next year, he looked for another job in Nottingham; finding nothing, he decided to move to London. Times were hard there, too, but he eventually found a position in a small pawnshop. Not only could he make a small wage, but he could also live above the pawnshop.

In his free time, he began attending the Methodist Chapel in Walworth, and he soon found himself registered there as a preacher. His circuit's presiding elder gave him little encouragement, and when William realized that he was finding more converts by canvassing the streets than by preaching in the chapels, he asked to be removed from the preaching rotation so that he could spend the little time he had to preach in the open air. The presiding elder grew even more suspicious and assumed that he was conspiring with the reformers, so he withheld William's ticket of membership the next time it came up for renewal. William's heart for reaching the poor with God's salvation had resulted in his eviction from the Methodist Church, just as Catherine's refusal to be quieted had resulted in her own eviction. This dismissal must have pained William greatly, for he had always believed that "there was one God, and John Wesley was His prophet."[10]

William may have been rejected, but he was not alone. Among the Methodists was a wealthy shoe factory owner, Edward Rabbits, and though the local Methodist elder did not prize William's ministry, Edward did. In the controversy between the Methodist mainliners and the reformers, Edward had sided with the reformers and lost his membership. When he heard that William also had been kicked out of the Methodist Church, he invited him to join the reformers and preach under their banner. Having nowhere else to go, William accepted his offer.

In the coming months, Edward Rabbits came to appreciate William's calling even more. One night, when hosting William for dinner, Edward told him that he would provide twenty shillings a week as his salary—for at least three months—if he would quit his pawnbroking job to preach full time. William was startled, but the fact was that he had been dreaming for months of doing this very thing. He heartily agreed to Edward's proposal. Within a short time, William had left his employment, found new lodging, and set out to save the world as a revivalist.

A Romance Made in Heaven

Sometime in early 1852, William was invited to a tea party at the home of Edward Rabbits. He felt that declining to attend would be remiss, even though he was not fond of such social gatherings. At the party, William was introduced to a number of other reformers, including a small, delicate, dark-haired young woman with smiling eyes. He immediately recognized her as the woman he had met after addressing a gathering of reformers at the Binfield Road Chapel in Clapham. Her name was Catherine Mumford. By way of entertainment, William was asked to present a dramatic poem about a grog-seller—a thoroughly pro-temperance subject. Not everyone present

[10] Stead, *Mrs. Booth*, 61.

subscribed to this stance, however, and as he reached the end of the poem, William received some rebuffs from the audience. But before he could defend himself, the young woman stepped forward and presented one of the best arguments for banning alcohol that he had ever heard. Obviously, there was much more behind those shining eyes than he had initially perceived.

William Booth and Catherine Mumford were destined to meet again at a church service a few weeks later, on April 9, 1852, which was Good Friday. It was also the day before William's twenty-third birthday. At the service, they spoke together briefly, and then partway through the service, Catherine felt ill and decided to return home. If William was disappointed to see her go, his sorrow must have turned to joy when Edward requested that he escort her home to Brixton. It would be a carriage ride to change both of their lives.

Their conversation progressed rapidly from small talk to sharing their hopes and dreams with one another. Catherine would later write of their ride together,

> That little journey will never be forgotten by either of us....We struck in at once in such wonderful harmony of view and aim and feeling on various matters that passed rapidly before us, that it seemed as though we had intimately known and loved each other for years and suddenly, after some temporary absence, had been brought together again. Before we reached my home we both...felt as though we had been made for each other....
>
> It was curious, too, that both of us had an idea of what we should require in the companion with whom we allied ourselves for life; if ever such alliance should take place... and here we were, thrown together in this unexpected fashion, matching those preconceived characters, even as though we had been made to order! We felt that henceforth the current of our lives must flow together.[11]

When they arrived at her house, Catherine invited William in so that they could continue their conversation. Inside, Catherine's mother joined them, and they were caught up in the conversation

[11] Catherine Booth, "Reminiscences," quoted in Catherine Bramwell-Booth, *Catherine Booth* (London: Hodder and Stoughton, 1970), 58–60.

until it was too late for William to go home—it was too late to call a carriage, and too far to walk. Mrs. Mumford set him up in a spare room, and though William left early the next morning, he was back before evening to visit with them again—as he would be nearly every day in the weeks to come.

In some respects, William and Catherine were like fire and ice—William was the bold and often overzealous evangelist; Catherine, the quiet scholar with a well-reasoned theology—but together, they became a powerful force for God. William was the spirit; Catherine, the word. William was the liberator of souls, and Catherine was the administrator, making sure that those who were set free stayed free, found their callings, and carried on with God. William was the flamboyant leader; Catherine, the manager who structured day-to-day activities.

The more William prayed for God to remove his attraction to Catherine, the more he wanted to spend the rest of his life with her.

William was surprised by his sudden affection, fearing that it might distract him from his soul-winning efforts. He actually prayed that God would take it away, but God would do just the opposite. The more William prayed, the more he realized that he wanted to spend the rest of his life with Catherine. The couple discussed the matter a great deal, knowing the folly of rushing into anything, but as they spoke together, prayed together, and pined for each other when apart, they felt sure God had created them for each other. So, on May 15, 1852, just a little more than a month after their carriage ride, having secured their parents' blessings, William and Catherine were engaged to be married. Sometime that same month, Catherine recorded her feelings for William in a letter. "My dearest William," she wrote,

> I fancy I see a look of surprise...at the reception of this after such a recent visit. You will think it unnecessary and so it is....The evening is beautifully serene and tranquil according sweetly with the feelings of my soul, the whirlwind is

> past....All is well. I feel it is right and my soul praises God for the satisfying conviction. Most gladly does my soul respond to your invitation to give myself afresh to Him and to strive to link myself closer to you, by rising more into the likeness of my Lord; the nearer our assimilation to Jesus, the more perfect and heavenly our union. Our hearts are now indeed one, so one that disunion would be more bitter than death....The thought of our walking through life together perfectly united, together enjoying its sunshine and battling with its storms, by softest sympathy sharing every smile and every tear, and with thorough unanimity performing all its momentous duties, is to me exquisite happiness, the highest earthly bliss I desire....We have acknowledged God from the beginning, we have sought His will... and we do now love Him more for the love we bear each other....You are always present in my thoughts. Believe me, dear William, as ever your own loving Kate.[12]

While many couples have long courtships and short engagements, William and Catherine would have just the opposite. During the next three years, William would venture forth to secure them a future and a steady income, and to establish his ministry to the point that it could sustain them both. By the time they were engaged, William was halfway through the three months of support that Edward Rabbits had pledged, so he turned his full attention to the remaining month and a half. Edward had already gotten William's name onto several of the reformers' preaching plans, so William set out to preach wherever he was welcome.

As fast and furious as William and Catherine's courtship had been, their engagement would be a time during which their love would grow and develop—a process that is recorded line after line in their letters to one another over the next few years. This long "written" engagement also offered them the unique opportunity to address many issues and differences of opinion. It seemed more difficult for them to carry on any harsh arguments through written correspondence, and they worked through many issues other couples

[12] Catherine Mumford, letter to William Booth, May 1852, quoted in Bramwell-Booth, *Catherine Booth,* 66–67.

do not deal with until several years into their marriages. Letter by letter, they came together on difficult points of theology, child-rearing, evangelism, and other matters, building a foundation not only for their life together, but also for their future ministry together.

Perhaps the most significant difference of opinion discussed in their correspondence related to the issue of gender equality. As Catherine put it in a letter,

> I am ready to admit that in the majority of cases the training of women has made her man's inferior...but that *naturally* she is in any respect, except in physical strength and courage, inferior to man I cannot see cause to believe, and I am sure no one can prove it from the *Word of God*.[13]

William's response was guarded, but he soon came around to be as avid a supporter of women in the ministry as Catherine:

> Thy remarks on woman's position I will read again before I answer....I would not stop a woman preaching on any account. I would not encourage one to begin. You should preach if you felt moved thereto; felt equal to the task. I would not stay you if I had the power to do so. Although I should not like it. I am for the world's salvation; I will quarrel with no means that promises help.[14]

William among the Churches

In the following weeks, William found the reformers, for all their zeal, to be disorganized and fraught with many of the same problems as the Methodists. So, William and Catherine decided that they would not renew Edward's generous support. This left William without any income at all, but Catherine spoke only words of encouragement concerning their dreams. She was confident that God would provide.

The coming months were not easy, however. William threw his hat in with the Congregationalists. He and Catherine began attending the Stockwell Congregational Church, led by the Reverend Dr.

[13] Catherine Mumford, letter to William Booth, 9 April 1855, British Library Microfilm 64802.

[14] William Booth, letter to Catherine Mumford, 12 April 1855, quoted in Bramwell-Booth, *Catherine Booth*, 121–122.

David Thomas. Yet William could not reconcile his beliefs with their Calvinist theology, and although the open door looked at first to be free of doctrinal stipulations, it was not. William looked to invest himself elsewhere.

He soon found himself selling most of his furniture in order to survive. In the end, he returned for a stint with the reformers when Edward Rabbits arranged for him to take charge of a small group of churches in the Spaulding district. This provided William with a salary of eighty pounds a year—ten shillings a week—a raise from the support Edward had originally provided. William took charge of these churches in November 1852.

This new position commenced the first period of a long-distance relationship for William and Catherine; and while they agreed to write once every week, they started sending and receiving letters once daily. Catherine might start a letter in the morning, add some lines after lunch and tea, and then include some more thoughts before she had to hand it over to the postman that evening. Each of her letters averaged about two thousand words.

Before six months had passed, William returned to London for a time to visit with Catherine. During this visit, he was offered a position with the newly organized Methodist New Connexion, another group that had formed in hopes of returning to the values and practices of their original founder. The Reverend Dr. William Cooke offered to take William under his tutelage and prepare him for the ministry. At first, William refused, but when his year in Spaulding was up, he accepted Rev. Cooke's offer. Again, William proved that he was not the scholar, but the first time that he spoke at the Brunswick Chapel, fifteen people were converted. William's unorthodox preaching techniques confounded his teacher, but he couldn't argue with the results.

At the New Connexion Conference in June 1854, Rev. Cooke nominated William to be the superintendent of a large London circuit, but twenty-five-year-old William felt he was still too young for such a position. They decided on a compromise: William was appointed the resident minister of a new chapel on Packington Street in Islington, another part of London, under the guidance of an older minister. Demand for his preaching grew, however, and he soon began traveling and holding revival campaigns as much as he was ministering at Packington Street. At the next Conference in 1855, William would be released from his duties at Packington Street and appointed as a full-time traveling minister for the New Connexion. Feeling he had finally achieved a proper level of support, he and Catherine were married on June 16, 1855.

Catherine traveled with William for the first time on their honeymoon—a speaking engagement on the Isles of Wright and Jersey. Catherine found herself both taxed and amazed by the pace of William's schedule. She stayed home during his next trip, hoping to recover so that she could accompany him on the next one.

In the following years, the Booths found themselves moving frequently to accommodate William's preaching schedule. William was becoming more and more effective as an evangelist. Initially, there were handfuls of conversions at each set of meetings; then, there were dozens, and finally hundreds! In February 1856, a month of meetings yielded 640 converts. Then, at a six-week meeting that ended in December, William saw 740 people converted. On March 8 of that year, the Booths' first child was born. They named him William Bramwell.

Troubles with the Religious Dead

William was too preoccupied with his revival work to attend the New Connexion Conference in 1857, and he was stunned when he heard what had happened there. His license as a traveling evangelist had been revoked. His detractors claimed that his meetings were too chaotic, his manner of speaking was too unorthodox, and he saved so many people, that it was all the local pastors could do to manage the horde of new believers. As one minister put it, "He is taking the cream and leaving the skimmed milk for others."[15] William had been demoted by four votes. He was assigned to the run-down mill town of Brighouse in Yorkshire—the least promising district—for the next year.

Brighouse did, however, prove to have some advantages for the Booths, and it was also a good training ground for future ministry. They set up a home for the first time, and they not only could bring people to salvation, but also could work to establish these believers

[15] Collier, *General Next to God*, 33.

in their new faith. After the birth of their second son, Ballington, on July 28, 1857, William urged Catherine to begin teaching a Bible class at the church. She became a leader among the female church members. At the next Conference, in May 1858, William was again denied the right to return to fieldwork, and was requested to work one more year in a circuit. He agreed. Having been with the New Connexion for four years, he had completed his probationary period, and he was ordained a minister of the denomination. William and Catherine thus moved to Gateshead, where Catherine had an interesting experience that would shape much of the work ahead of them with the Salvation Army:

> One Sabbath I was passing down a narrow, thickly populated street on my way to chapel, anticipating an evening's enjoyment for myself and hoping to see some anxious ones brought into the kingdom, when I chanced to look up at the thick rows of small windows above me, where numbers of women were sitting, peering through at the passers by, or listlessly gossiping with each other.
>
> It was suggested to my mind with great power, "Would you not be doing more service and acting more like your Redeemer, by turning into some of those houses, speaking to these careless sinners, and inviting them to the service, than by going to enjoy it yourself?" I was startled; it was a new thought, and while I was reasoning about it, the same inaudible interrogator demanded, "What efforts do Christians put forth, answerable to the command, 'compel them to come in, that My house may be filled?'"
>
> This was accompanied by a light and unction which I know to be Divine. I felt greatly agitated. I felt verily guilty. I knew that I had never thus labored to bring lost sinners to Christ; and, trembling with a sense of my utter weakness, I stood still for a moment, looked up to heaven, and said, "Lord, if Thou wilt help me, I will try," and without stopping further to confer with flesh and blood, turned back and commenced my work.
>
> I spoke first to a group of women sitting on a doorstep; and what that cffort cost mc, words cannot dcscribc; but thc

Spirit helped my infirmities, and secured for me a patient and respectful hearing with a promise from some of them to attend the house of God. This much encouraged me; I began to taste the joy which lies hidden under the Cross, and to realize, in some faint degree, that it is more blessed to give than to receive....I went on to the next group who were standing at the entrance of a low, dirty court. Here again I was received kindly and promises were given. No rude repulse, no bitter ridicule, were allowed to shake my newfound confidence, or chill my feeble zeal. I began to realize that my Master's feet were behind; nay, before me, smoothing my path and preparing my way.

This blessed assurance so increased my courage and enkindled my hope that I ventured to knock at the door of the next house, and when it was opened to go in, and speak to the inmates of Jesus, death, judgement, and eternity. The man, who appeared to be one of the better class of mechanics, seemed to be much interested and affected by my words, and promised with his wife to attend the revival services which were being held at the chapel.

With a heart full of gratitude and eyes full of tears, I was thinking where I should go next, when I observed a woman standing on an adjoining doorstep with a jug in her hand. My divine teacher said, "Speak to that woman." Satan suggested, "Perhaps she is intoxicated" but after a momentary struggle I introduced myself to her by saying, "Are the people out who live on this floor?" observing that the lower part of the house was closed. "Yes," she said, "they are gone to chapel." I thought I perceived a weary sadness in her voice and manner. I said, "Oh, I am so glad to hear that; how is it that you are not gone to a place of worship?" "Me," she said, looking down upon her forlorn appearance; "I can't go to chapel, I am kept at home by a drunken husband. I have to stop with him to keep him from the public house, and I have just been fetching him some drink." I expressed my sorrow for her, and asked if I might come in and see her husband. "No," she said, "he is drunk;

you could do nothing with him now." I replied, "I do not mind his being drunk, if you will let me come in; I am not afraid; he will not hurt me." "Well," said the woman, "you can come in if you like; but he will only abuse you." I said, "Never mind that," and followed her up the stairs.

I felt strong now in the Lord and in the power of His might, and as safe as a babe in the arms of its mother. I realized that I was in the path of obedience, and I feared no evil.

The woman led me to a small room on the first floor, where I found a fine, intelligent man, about forty, sitting almost double in a chair, with a jug by his side, out of which he had been drinking. I leaned on my Heavenly Guide for strength and wisdom, love and power, and He gave me all I needed. He silenced the demon, strong drink, and quickened the man's perceptions to receive my words. As I began to talk to him, with my heart full of sympathy, he gradually raised himself in his chair, and listened with a surprised and half-vacant stare. I spoke to him of his present deplorable condition, of the folly and wickedness of his course, of the interest of his wife and children, until he was fully aroused from the stupor in which I found him. I read to him the parable of the Prodigal Son, while the tears ran down his face like rain. I then prayed with him as the Spirit gave me utterance, and left, promising to call the next day with a pledge-book, which he agreed to sign.

I now felt that my work was done. Exhausted in body but happy in soul, I wended my way to the sanctuary, just in time for the conclusion of the service and to lend a helping hand in the prayer meeting.

On the following day I visited this man again. He signed the pledge, and listened attentively to all I said. Full of hope I left him, to find another similarly lost and fallen. From that time I commenced a systematic course of house-to house visitation, devoting two evenings per week to the work. The Lord so blessed my efforts that in a few weeks I succeeded in getting ten drunkards to abandon their

> soul-destroying habits, and to meet me once a week for reading the Scriptures and for prayer.[16]

On September 18, 1858, the Booths' third child—a daughter, Little Catherine—was born. She quickly earned the nickname "Kate." That year, they saw their congregation in Gateshead swell from thirty-nine members to three hundred, and the chapel was dubbed "The Converting Shop" by the community because of the impact it was having. When reassignment came up the next year, the promise from the previous year of returning to revival work had not even been recorded in the minutes! William was reassigned to Gateshead to consolidate the work he was doing there as district superintendent.

William was not one to be pigeonholed, however. If he was to remain in leadership at Gateshead, then he would be in charge of his own revival work in the area. He began a series of revival meetings and called for a day of prayer and fasting. Then, he sponsored a ten-week campaign of intercessory prayer by writing the names of the most notorious sinners in the area on scraps of paper, which he distributed randomly to participants in the campaign. They would hold daily revival meetings and canvass the neighborhoods, going door-to-door to pass out flyers and personally invite people to come.

During the time that she spent flat on her back as a teenager, Catherine had become well-versed in Charles Finney's *Lectures on Revival*, and she and her husband began to use Finney's principles in their campaign. William also reinstituted the open-air meetings he had begun in his teens. People would gather in a public place to sing, he would speak briefly, and then they would form a procession and walk to the chapel, inviting any interested passersby to follow. Almost everyone who had been targeted with intercessory prayer attended at least one of the meetings and was converted.

It was a marvelous time; however, Catherine's frailty again made her sick, so the work slowed as she recovered. During this time, Catherine happened upon a pamphlet by the Reverend Arthur Ross attacking the right of women to preach. Indignant, Catherine decided to write her own pamphlet in response. She finished the

[16] Stead, *Mrs. Booth*, 152–155.

pamphlet just prior to the birth of their fourth child, Emma Moss Booth, who was born on January 8, 1860.

"My Dear Wife Wishes to Speak"

Up to this point, though Catherine was a staunch advocate of women teaching and preaching from the pulpit, she had refused to do so herself. William had always encouraged her, but she was happy to stay in the background and hide behind her shyness. Then, on Sunday, May 27, 1860, a mass outdoor meeting had to be moved to the chapel due to inclement weather, so roughly a thousand people gathered in the chapel to hear William speak. As Catherine sat in the audience with young Bramwell, the Holy Spirit spoke to her heart, "Now, if you were to go and testify, you know I would bless it to your own soul as well as to the souls of the people."

"Yes, Lord," she responded, "I believe Thou wouldst, but I cannot do it."

Another thought occurred to her, but she immediately recognized its sinister source: "Besides, you are not prepared to speak. You will look like a fool and have nothing to say."

Catherine grew indignant at this taunt. "Ah! This is the point. I have never yet been willing to be a fool for Christ. Now I will be one." Catherine leapt to her feet and mounted the stage, where her husband was just drawing his message to a close. William crossed the stage to help her, thinking that something was wrong. Catherine simply told him, "I want to say a word."

William was caught a bit off guard, but inwardly, he was pleased. Turning to the congregation, he stated, "My dear wife wishes to speak," and relinquished the stage to her. He found a seat, interested to hear what she had to say.[17]

Catherine gathered herself and addressed the audience, saying,

> I daresay many of you have been looking upon me as a very devoted woman, and one who has been living faithfully to God, but I have come to know that I have been living in disobedience, and to that extent I have brought darkness and leanness into my soul; but I promised the Lord three or

[17] Ibid., 152–155.

four months ago, and I dare not disobey. I have come to tell you this and to promise the Lord that I will be obedient to the Heavenly vision."[18]

With great humility, she confessed her sin of disobeying God in His promptings for her to speak in public, and she urged everyone to obey God's promptings in his own heart. When she had finished, William gained her consent and announced, "Tonight, my wife will be the preacher!"[19]

"My dear wife wishes to speak."

The Salvation Army Archives

Thirty minutes later in the Booth household, Ballington and Kate Booth, too young to attend the service, were chasing the maid around the kitchen table and crying with joy, "The mistress has spoken! The mistress has spoken!"[20] The significance of this breakthrough seemed evident to every member of the family. That night, the chapel was filled to overflowing. Catherine based her sermon on Ephesians 5:18: *"Be filled with the Spirit."* Her fame spread quickly, and within a matter of months, there was a greater demand to hear her speak than there was for her husband!

Striking Out on Their Own

At the New Connexion Conference of 1861, William felt he finally had to make a stand for what his heart was telling him he

[18] Stead, *Mrs. Booth*, 152–155.

[19] Bramwell-Booth, *Catherine Booth*, 158.

[20] Ibid., 159.

must do: return to full-time revival work. The Connexion did not see eye to eye with him on this, however, so after several weeks of careful consideration and prayer, and despite his lack of alternative income, William submitted his resignation to the New Connexion. This was a difficult decision for a father with four children at home and no foreseeable means to support them. It would also forever sever the Booths' formal connection with anything Methodist.

Now with no home, the Booths moved their belongings and their children to Catherine's parents' home in Brixton. When a minister in Cornwall who had been converted at one of William's earlier meetings asked him to lead a revival, he and Catherine accepted, even though they knew the minister had no money to offer them. They planned to be in Cornwall for six weeks.

But God had a different plan. Eighteen months and seven thousand converts later, the Booths were still in Cornwall. Fishermen were known to have rowed ten miles across stormy seas just to attend their meetings. "Business is no longer carried out," one local noted. "The shopkeepers and their customers are all busily engaged in the Booth meetings."[21] As their ministry had picked up with no end in sight, the Booths arranged for their children to join them in Cornwall. It was there that their fifth child, Herbert Howard, was born, on August 26, 1862.

In early 1863, the Booths were invited to speak in Cardiff, Wales, but they had a hard time finding a venue large enough to accommodate the crowds they drew. Most of the churches were shutting their doors to them as if they were outlaws, but Catherine managed to find a circus tent to rent, and the meetings went on as planned. It was the first time they would use a secular facility, but it would be far from the last. For the next two years the Booths continued to travel and minister throughout the country. After their sixth child, Marian, was born on May 4, 1864, Catherine started her own revival services, which were highly successful. The novelty of "The Woman Preacher" drew considerable numbers, and she began receiving requests to minister in some of the more traditional churches that had shut William out.

The time spent apart weighed heavily on the couple, however, and in 1865, they moved to London and established a home in

[21] Collier, *General Next to God*, 36.

Hammersmith. With William shut out of all but the smallest of churches, they survived for a time primarily on money earned from Catherine's speaking.

The London they returned to was not the same one that they had left. It was far darker and sootier than it had been before. William's compassion for the poor again gripped his heart. The sight of one lifeless face put him back in the pawnshop, bartering for family heirlooms that were buying a few more weeks' worth of food for another incomeless family. One writer described East London as "a squalid labyrinth, with half a million people, 290 to an acre....Every fifth house was a gin shop, and most had special steps to help even the tiniest [children] reach the counter."[22]

William Booth preaches at a large tent gathering.

The Salvation Army Archives

Returning from a meeting one night early in July of that year, William came upon a small crowd gathered in the street outside of the Blind Beggar pub. A man was ministering there, and as he finished, he asked if anyone in the group wanted to share a testimony or a word of Scripture. William didn't have to be asked twice. Within minutes, his preaching had captivated those gathered there, and William felt like a teenager again, standing on a chair ministering in front of Besom Jack's house. The organizers of this meeting, the East London Special Services Committee, were so impressed by

[22] Norman H. Murdoch, "The General," *Christian History* 9, no. 2 [Issue 26] (1990): 6.

William's command of his audience that, within a few days, they offered him a temporary position as the head of their work. Despite initial reluctance, William agreed, and on July 2, 1865, he began a series of meetings in a dilapidated tent located a stone's throw from the slums of Whitechapel Road. These meetings would continue for six weeks.

While William would bring many hearts to the Lord, he soon found he had lost his own heart to East London. He had no steady income, but seeing the jobless crowds milling about in front of the Blind Beggar's pub told him he would never be without work. These people would be his work! They needed salvation—not only from their spiritual depravity, but also from their physical depravity. Though he had no idea how he would pay for it, he wrote the following mission statement and appeal for funds:

> We have no very definite plans. We shall be guided by the Holy Spirit. At present we desire to be able to hold consecutive services for the purpose of bringing souls to Christ in different localities of the East of London every night all the year round. We propose holding these meetings in halls, theatres, chapels, tents, the open-air and elsewhere as the way may be opened or we seem likely to attain the end we have in view. We purpose to watch over and visit personally those brought to Christ, either guiding them to communion with adjacent and sympathetic churches or ourselves nursing them and training them to active labor. In order to carry on this work we propose to establish a Christian Revival Association....We shall also require some central building in which to hold our more private meetings, and in which to preach the Gospel when not engaged in special work elsewhere.[23]

The following week, a wealthy manufacturer sent William the first one-hundred-pound check that would come in to support this work. More money followed. God was faithful, as always. This was the beginning of the work that would become the Salvation Army, initially known as the East London Christian Mission.

---

[23] Robert Sandall, *The History of the Salvation Army, vol. 1, 1865 1878* (London: Thomas Nelson, 1947), 42.

The East London Christian Mission

Over the next few years, the Booths' work was ever changing. Within the first year, most of the people who had started the work with them had left, for one reason or another—usually because they disliked William's preaching style, his uncompromising stance on an issue, the chaos that characterized his meetings, or the poor conditions of their working environment. Since the Booths had no permanent building, they rented facilities of all sorts for their meetings—from dance halls to livery stables. One time, they even held a meeting in the back of a pigeon shop. These spaces were often uncomfortably crowded for their clientele, and some people would leave because of the constant odors of gin and tobacco. But by the summer of 1866, William had gathered a group of about five dozen faithful people who would help to continue the work of the mission.

However staunch William was about his doctrine, he was just the opposite when it came to his methods. Given his aim of saving the lost, there were few things he wasn't willing to try. In one meeting at which the crowd seemed to have little interest in his preaching, he decided to turn the floor over to a Gypsy hawker who had recently been saved. Almost as soon as this man started to give his testimony, the crowd was transformed and seemed to hang on his every word. From that day forward, testimonies from new converts were given at almost every meeting. William also started to delegate responsibility to new converts at each meeting. He found their enthusiasm to be contagious, and as they served at each gathering, prospective converts became even more receptive to the gospel message. It later became a saying in the Army that William preached some of his best sermons through the lips of other men. "He never monopolized the meetings. He made others help him—they were as much theirs, as his. This helped to make them attractive as well as effective."[24]

Bands and Bar Tunes

One day, a man and his three sons offered to be William's bodyguards, and they just happened to have brought their brass instruments with them. They offered to play, and William agreed. When he saw the crowd's favorable reception of the music, he decided to

---

[24] Bramwell Booth, *Our First Captain* (London: Salvationist Publishing, n.d.), 10.

make such "bands" a regular part of the outdoor meetings. Hearing a catchy bar tune, William thought that the devil should not have all of the best music, so he told his musicians to learn to play the popular songs but to rewrite the lyrics to honor God. These tunes surely surprised many a drunkard—imagine someone singing a song in his evening revelries, only to hear it the next day inviting him to make his peace with God and forsake the drink that had been ruining him!

William had initially hoped that the mission would be primarily for evangelism—bringing people to Christ, then funneling them into churches for further growth and maturation. Finding a church home for every convert soon proved impractical, however. Many who were saved would refuse to attend church; those who went to church were often unwelcome there; and, since William had no help from the outside, he needed to put the new converts to work for the mission to keep up with the ever increasing number of conversions. The mission started Bible classes, and it also sent people to visit the new converts within one week of their conversions. These visitors would check on the new converts, pray with them, and try to get them involved in the work of the mission. They also taught the converts how to pray and intercede for the lost. William sent them out two by two to invite people to the meetings, distribute flyers advertising various events, and pray for those who needed help and deliverance. These visits infused new converts with a sense of purpose and the drive they had lacked before they were saved. Their enthusiasm greatly enhanced the work already being done.

William portrayed playing the accordion.

Mary Evans Picture Library

The American Civil War caused a drop in demand for English products, and unemployment increased. A cholera epidemic in 1866 spread like wildfire through east London, killing more than eight thousand people. For every two steps the mission moved forward, it felt as if it was three steps back. "Quit" wasn't in the Booths' vocabulary, though, and the mission continued on. Throughout their trials, William kept exhorting his people to pray:

> Bring more faith into your praying....Do not be content with merely telling God about your wants, or expressing your desires, or even in reminding yourself of His ability and willingness to supply your needs, but take hold of His word, and believe that He does, there and then, if it be His blessed will, give you the things for which you ask.[25]

He also once wrote,

> You must pray with your might....That does not mean saying your prayers, or sitting gazing about in church or chapel, with eyes wide open, while someone else says them for you. It means fervent, effectual, untiring wrestling with God. It means that grappling with Omnipotence, that clinging to Him, following Him about, so to speak, day and night, as the widow did to the unjust judge, with agonizing pleadings and arguments and entreaties, until the answer comes and the end is gained. This kind of prayer be sure the devil and the world and your own indolent, unbelieving nature will oppose. They will pour water on this flame. They will ply you with suggestions and difficulties. They will ask you how you can expect that the plans and purposes and feelings of God can be altered by your prayers. They will talk about impossibilities and predict failures; but, if you mean to succeed, you must shut your ears and eyes to all but what God has said, and hold Him to His own word: and you cannot do this in any sleepy mood; you cannot be a prevailing Israel unless you wrestle as Jacob wrestled, regardless of time aught else, save obtaining the blessing sought—that is, you must pray with your might.[26]

Eight-hour prayer meetings—some taking place throughout the night—were not uncommon. Prayer was a cornerstone of everything that they did.

---

[25] William Booth, *Faith-Healing* (London: Salvationist Publishing and Supplies, 1902), 7.

[26] William Booth, *The Christian Mission Magazine*, January 1870, quoted in Barnes, ed., *Founder Speaks Again*, 76.

During this time, the Booths' seventh and eighth children were born. Evangeline Cory was born on Christmas Day of 1865, and Lucy Milward was born on April 28, 1867. The Booth household was never short of helping hands for the work to be done!

The Hungry Must Be Fed

It didn't take long for William and Catherine to realize that it was easy for growling stomachs to drown out the preaching of the Gospel, and with unemployment still on the rise, many people needed as much physical help as they needed spiritual help. Thus, the Salvation Army soup kitchen was born.

Feeding the hungry would stretch the mission's finances more than anything had before, and William was constantly coming up with new schemes to keep the mission afloat. Ever since the beginning of their work, however, William and Catherine had never excised their own salary from the mission's money. They had always raised their personal support separately; every cent that they received for the mission went to the work of the mission.

At one point, William appointed Bramwell, by this time a teenager, to head his Food-for-the-Million shops. Every morning, Bramwell would awake faithfully at three o'clock to trudge four miles down to the Covent Garden Markets, where he would ask for discarded vegetables and purchase bags of soup bones. The program was supposed to provide a meal of bread and soup for the cost of sixpence, but because of corrupt managers, huge numbers of hungry people to feed, and young Bramwell's inexperience with leadership, these shops soon went bankrupt. They were eventually closed, and the soup kitchen was sold.

William did not view these social outreaches as being any less important than reaching people's souls. To him, the soup kitchens and other such outreaches were part of living out the Gospel. As he would later try to sum it up,

> Our social operations are the natural outcome of Salvationism, or, I might say, of Christianity as instituted, described, proclaimed, and exemplified in the life, teaching, and sacrifice of Jesus Christ. Social work, in the spirit

> and practice which it has assumed with us, has harmonized with my own personal ideas of true religion from the hour I promised obedience to the commands of God....All this time, nevertheless, I felt, and often keenly felt, that there surely must be some way by which, without any evil consequences, I could legitimately fulfil the cravings of my own heart, as well as comply with the commands of my Lord, who had expressly told me that I was to feed the hungry, clothe the naked, care for the sick, and visit the prisoners. For a long time, however, I failed to see how this work could be done in any organized or extensive manner.
>
> Gradually, however, the way opened, and opened largely as a result of our determination to make the godless crowds hear the message of salvation. In the very earliest days of the Army, therefore, in order to reach the people whom we could not reach by any other means, we gave the hungry wretches a meal, and then talked to them about God and eternity. Then came the gradual unfolding of our social methods.[27]

William quickly learned that handouts could easily erode the recipients' self-respect. As the mission's social charity efforts grew, they found it best to allow each beneficiary to either pay a small fee for the services or work to earn enough to pay for food and lodging.

By 1870, the mission's influence had reached beyond the limits of east London. Other missions had already been started in Croydon, in South London, and Edinburgh, Scotland. The East London Christian Mission now had about eight thousand members, so they bought a large building on Whitechapel Road, where they opened a soup kitchen, several classrooms, a large meeting hall, and a bookstore.

William became gravely ill for the next two years, so Catherine stepped in to run the mission. It was a trying time, and many of the individual posts suffered with Catherine being stretched, both at home and in running the mission. While she was extremely organized, she had not the force of will of her husband, nor his air of command. When William had regained his health and returned in

---

[27] Sandall, *History of the Salvation Army, vol. 3, 1883–1953*, xiii.

1872, however, he took the reigns back into his own hands, and the organization began to grow again.

In 1873, William and Catherine agreed to add a ninth child to their family when a dying woman requested that young Bramwell take care of her child. Not fully realizing the responsibility involved, Bramwell had agreed, and when the woman died, he asked his mother and father for guidance. They agreed to adopt the child, and they let their daughter Emma take care of him. Thus was Harry added to their family. He would grow up to be the Salvation Army's first medical worker in India, where he would serve for thirty years. He died in India in 1919 and was posthumously awarded the Victoria Cross for his service to the Crown.

The Mission Becomes an Army

The Christian Mission (as it was now called, having dropped the "East London" from its name as the work moved beyond those borders) continued to grow by leaps and bounds over the next several years. Then, in May 1878, as William was putting the final touches on an annual report, something seemed amiss. The header on the title page read, "The Christian Mission under the superintendence of the Rev. William Booth is a Volunteer Army recruited from amongst the multitudes who are without God and without hope in the world."[28]

Puzzling over this sentence, William called in Bramwell and his assistant, George Scott Railton, to look it over with him. Railton read it out loud, and when Bramwell commented on the term "Volunteer Army," his father grabbed Railton's pen from him, crossed out *Volunteer* and wrote in the word *Salvation*. Seeing this change, Railton and Bramwell declared together, "Thank God for that!" The name "Salvation Army" had struck a chord with all three men. Over the next few months, the Christian Mission changed its name to the Salvation Army, adopting military titles, hierarchy, uniforms, and a "war against the forces of darkness" mentality. The newsletter's name was even changed to the *War Cry*.

The following year, "General" Booth described the organization and its plan of attack with these words:

[28] Collier, *General Next to God*, 56.

> We are a salvation people—this is our specialty—getting people saved and keeping them saved, and then getting somebody else saved....Look at this. Clear your vision. Halt, stand still and afresh and more fully apprehend and comprehend your calling. You are to be a worker together with God for the salvation of your fellow men. What is the business of your life? Not merely to save your soul and make yourself meet for Paradise?...No, you are to be a redeemer, a savior, a copy of Jesus Christ Himself. So consecrate every awakened power to the great end of saving them.
>
> Rescue the perishing. There they are all around you everywhere, crowds upon crowds, multitudes. Be skilful. Improve yourself. Study your business.
>
> Be self-sacrificing. Remember the Master. What you lose for His sake, and for the sake of the poor souls for whom He died, you shall find again. Stick to it. Having put your hand to the salvation plough, don't look behind you.[29]

The General's First Command

The instructions for signing up for "The Army" were now clear. "Make your will, pack your box, kiss your girl, be ready in a week"[30] became the General's first command to every new recruit. In the last six months of 1878, the number of mission stations grew from fifty to eighty-one, and the number of evangelists from eighty-eight to one hundred twenty-seven. By 1884, the Army had more than 900 members, and roughly 260 of those were overseas—some as far away as America, Canada, and Australia. By the organization's twentieth anniversary in 1885, there were 802 corps members in England alone, and 520 overseas in ten different nations.

As the Army grew larger and more popular, opposition grew as well. Bar and brothel owners who were losing business because of the Army hired thugs to attack their outdoor meetings and beat the musicians and speakers with clubs. The rowdies in Oldham grew so

[29] William Booth, *The Salvationist*, January 1879, quoted in Barnes, ed., *Founder Speaks Again*, 45, 48.

[30] Collier, *General Next to God*, 47.

bold that they called themselves "The Skeleton Army" in mockery. Their flags bore the image of a skull and crossbones. Another group that called itself "The Sheffield Blades" attracted more than a thousand members.

General William Booth

The Salvation Army Archives

Once, they tried to stop an Army parade in which the General himself was traveling. They attacked with clubs, rocks, and rotten food, but the Salvationists refused to fight back. The General called for them to stay near the carriage, and they complied. One lieutenant was struck between the eyes and hit so forcefully in the back of the head that he had to be held on his horse all the way to the meeting. When the group arrived, he slid off his horse and said, "I hope they'll get saved,"[31] before falling into a coma.

The Army members who were already gathered at the meetinghouse were shocked by the newcomers' broken instruments and bloodied, battered appearances. General Booth's remark was, "Now's the time to get your photo taken."[32] This was war, after all, and the Salvationists wore their cuts and bruises like medals. When local officials turned against the Army and prosecuted them for such things as "public prayer," the Salvationists replied by protesting the fines as unjust, refusing to pay them, and gladly going to jail when arrested. They saw opposition as a sign that they were doing true apostolic work, and the harder they were pressed, the more determined they grew to spread the Gospel!

Stories of bravery abounded. One example, entitled simply, "The Lass from the Army," follows:

> She was a Salvation Army lass, and her lot was a hard one. Working from seven in the morning till six o'clock at

---

[31] Ibid., 92.

[32] Ibid., 93.

night, weaving hair-cloth, was dull and poorly paid work, but in addition she had to bear the constant and thoughtless gibes of her fellow-workers. One Autumn morning a spark from a bonfire on some adjoining allotment gardens entered an open window, alighted on a heap of loose hair, and the next minute the place was ablaze. A rush for safety of the work-girls followed.

"Is everybody down?" asked the foreman. His question was answered by one of the weavers, who holding up a key, shrieked, "My God! I locked Lizzie Summers in the 'piece shed' for a joke not a minute ago!" The "piece shed" was a room to be reached only through the burning building, through which it seemed impossible to make way. Girls and men were standing aghast and helpless, when two figures stumbled through the smoke, which poured from the weaving-room. One was seen to be Lizzie Summers; the other was, for the time, unrecognizable. It was The Salvation Army lass. She had stayed behind, burnt, blistered, and half-suffocated, to batter down the door in order to liberate and save the life of her coarsest-tongued tormentor.[33]

Unconventional Conventions

The meetings of the Salvation Army often flowed with manifestations of the Holy Spirit, similar to what was witnessed with earlier revivalists, and they were anything but conventional. On Wednesday, May 21, 1879, the *Newcastle Daily Chronicle* printed the following article about one such meeting:

> The people present, taken as a whole, were the roughest lot I have seen at any of these meetings....Taking a policeman into my confidence, I asked him if he knew any of these young men. "Know any of them?" he said. "Why, I know them all. This one is from Newcastle; the other sitting near him is one of the worst roughs we have"; and so he went on, with a description almost as long as the catalogue of ships in Homer. There was a fair sprinkling of women amongst the audience, too; and most of these were young

[33] William Booth, *The Seven Spirits* (London: The Salvation Army, 1985), 91–92.

ones, who did not appear to have been much troubled, previously, with thoughts about religion. I went to the meeting at about two o'clock [a.m.]. It had then been going on for some two or three hours; but so far it was very orderly and cool. There was a long, low platform in the middle of the room, round which the "Hallelujah Lasses," the "Converted Sweep," the "Hallelujah Giant," and other notabilities concerned with the movement were seated....

Singing was followed by what is called "Witnessing," various officers of the Salvation Army narrating their experience of "what the Lord had done for them." About half an hour was occupied in this wise; and, but for the ordinary interjections of enthusiasm, the time passed quietly enough. It would have been impossible to guess at what followed....

The General requested his audience to sit still and sing when the "witnessing" was concluded. He gave out these lines:—

I need Thee every hour, Most gracious Lord!
No tender voice like Thine can peace afford.
I need Thee, oh I need Thee: Every hour I need Thee,
Oh, bless me now, my Savior! I come to Thee.

The words were taken up by the whole audience; the chorus was rolled out to a rattling tune, and was no sooner finished than it was commenced again with additional vigor. This chorus might have been sung perhaps a dozen times when there was a shrill scream, a bustle round the platform, and a general rise of the audience. Seats were mounted; hands were raised in the air; the singing was mingled with loud "Hallelujahs," bursts of vociferous prayer, shouting, and hysterical laughter.

To add to the confusion four of the forms fell backwards, and threw their occupants into a common heap on the floor....Sinners were creeping to the penitent form; the Salvation Army was rejoicing; fully one third of those present acted as if they were more or less insane....

Several figures are bent double near the platform, groaning and wringing their hands. The "Hallelujah Lasses" have surrounded them; the tall figure of the proprietor of the "Hallelujah Fiddle" gyrates around them; the sweep is dancing and shouting "Glory be to God"; and the "General" is smiling placidly and twiddling his thumbs....

As may be seen from what I have written, until penitents "throw themselves at the feet of Jesus," as it is called, a meeting of the Salvation Army is a tolerably sane affair. The fat is at once in the fire, however, when penitents come forward....Half-a-dozen crop-headed youths—boys they are, indeed—are praying vociferously, with their faces towards me. Did I say praying? I only suppose they were. It was vociferous shouting, with closed eyes. Their bodies sway to and fro; their hands are lifted, and brought down again with a thump on the form; they contort themselves as if they were in acute agony. The hymn resounds high above their prayers;...everybody is carrying on a separate service on his own account.

Meanwhile the "lasses" are busy with the work of conversion. It proceeds by stages, with a separate hymn for each. The final stage is reached with the singing of "I do believe, I will believe, that Jesus died for me." The process being thus rendered complete, the converts retire to their seats with red faces. Let us follow one of them. He is a broad-faced, shock-headed youth, of about twenty. A few minutes since, he was foaming out of a well-developed mouth. Now he is dancing about the floor, shouting "hallelujah" and wringing the hands of all those who will yield their arm to him....He has in fact been converted....

Here...was an extraordinary effect produced without anything that can be called preaching. It was the singing that appeared to be most powerful....After more singing, there was another rush to the penitent form, another repetition of the same hymns, of the same gesticulations, of the same frantic prayers. But a quite new interest was added. I watched the proceedings for some time from my point of vantage on a back form; and then struggled through the crowd to get a look at the penitents. They had fainted away. Here lay a woman in a dead swoon, with six "Hallelujah lasses" singing round her, and not one of them trying to bring her round even by so much as sprinkling water on her face. On the other side of the platform was a man lying at full length, his limbs twitching, his lips foaming, totally unregarded....

I appealed to the "Hallelujah Giant." The General had stated on Monday that he was not a quack doctor, but a real doctor. It struck me as peculiar that he should sit there singing under such circumstances, and I said, "Really, cannot you do something to bring these people round?" "My good man," he replied, "won't you sit down? They will come round all right." They may have done so—both their recovery and their conversion may have been complete—but it was hard to stay there and witness so much of what looked like gross inhumanity. When I came away people were swooning all over the place. I had to step over a man in a fit in order to get to the door.

When I reached the street and the pure air it was a fresh, gray morning...."Is this a common sort of thing here?" I asked of the policeman outside. "Very," he said, "but it has reduced our charge sheet, and I haven't had a case for two months." I didn't ask him if it was as good for the persons who took part in such "services" as it was for the charge sheet. Neither he nor I could properly answer that question.[34]

Need Found—Need Met!

Whenever the Salvation Army saw a need, they found a way to answer it. Women rescued from prostitution needed somewhere to go, so homes were started for them. The same happened for those recently released from prison. The Army would open "labour bureaus" in 1888 to help the unemployed find work—some twenty-three years before the British government thought to start such social services! These offices would place 69,000 people into jobs during the first seven years of operation.

[34] A Special Correspondent, "The Salvation Army III: An All Night Meeting," *Newcastle Daily Chronicle*, Wednesday, 21 May 1879, http://www.vision.pwp.blueyonder.co.uk/revival/hlndciii.html.

The Salvation Army also opened the first missing person's bureau to help families find their loved ones; England was a country where more than 9,000 people went missing each year. William and Catherine also wanted to find a way to provide legal services for the poor and to start a Poor Man's Bank that could give loans to help unemployed entrepreneurs start businesses. Whenever they discovered a need, they did their best to fill it; when they faced a wrong, they would spare no expense in righting it. It was an attitude that would bring them continually into Satan's crosshairs.

The Armstrong Case: The Army Fights Sex Trafficking

In 1885, the legal age of consent in Britain was thirteen. Although slavery had been abolished throughout the Empire in 1833 through the efforts of William Wilberforce and others, young girls needing work often got duped into coming to London as housemaids or factory workers, only to find their place of employment to be a brothel. They were then trapped within stone-walled compounds with little means of escape until their spirits were broken enough to do their new employers' bidding. To enforce their compliance, they were often raped repeatedly, and the guilt of having been violated was used against them to keep them in check.

When a victim of this system showed up on the doorsteps of the Salvation Army headquarters one day and told her story to Bramwell, everyone found it hard to believe, at first. But further investigation showed her story to be true, and the Salvation Army took on a new enemy: the white slavers and sex-trade profiteers of London.

As was too often the case, the brothels seemed to have more friends in high places than the Army had, and closing down prostitution was a low priority for the local police departments. If any brothel owner was tried on such accounts, plea bargains were often struck, and the owners got away with only minor fines. The system was corrupt, and the only way to turn it around was for there to be a huge public outcry against the kidnapping and abuse of these young women. The age of consent needed to be raised to protect the younger, more naïve girls from the sex traders' tricks and wiles. When Bramwell went to the Home Secretary about this issue, he reintroduced a bill to raise the age of consent to sixteen, but it was immediately blocked in the House of Commons. One speaker on the floor even argued that the age of consent should be dropped to ten!

Still determined to break the silence, Bramwell convinced William T. Stead, editor of the *Pall Mall Gazette,* to investigate the case and publish the facts. What they uncovered was a complicated network of duping, drugging, and shanghaiing thousands of girls, most of whom were under the age of sixteen. Clients would often give a description of the girl they wanted, and then pay to have a "fresh girl"—a young virgin—delivered to them. Some girls were shipped out of the country in coffins—nailed shut, with air holes drilled into them—to serve in the state-controlled brothels of mainland Europe. Many who regained consciousness mid-trip actually died of terror as they tried to claw their way out. Kidnappers would even dress as nuns to fool the young girls—a ploy they found particularly effective in Ireland. The magnitude of the conspiracy was unimaginable. It was an industry worth more than eight million pounds a year—roughly $929 million today!

The Salvation Army opened the first missing person's bureau to help families find loved ones.

To learn more about sex trafficking, Stead posed as a client, and a young Salvation Army lass allowed herself to be captured as his mistress. Stead would visit her regularly to hear what she had learned on the inside and endured in her kidnapping. She made a serious mistake, however—the brothel mistress discovered her Salvation Army badge sewn into the folds of her dress.

Plans were made immediately to ship her off to Europe, and she was locked in the attic to await deportation. More afraid of being shipped overseas than dying, she jumped out of the attic window to escape. When she landed, she sprained her ankle, fainted, and fell to the ground, unconscious. As providence would have it, her fiancé, another young Army officer, decided that he had had enough of this ruse, and he had organized a group of young officers to storm the brothel and rescue his beloved. As the group made its way through the compound gates, they found the girl, lying on the ground, just moments after she had landed. Her fiancé scooped her up and took her home, never having to cross the threshold of the brothel. The girl healed quickly and came through the ordeal largely unharmed.

Stead's evidence was exhaustive and compelling, but he still needed more. It was necessary to be able to track at least one girl who had responded to an employment advertisement in the newspaper and ended up in a brothel. Stead would need to document every step to allow no room for denying the evidence. Plus, writing the story from the perspective of a victim and filling in the details was the surest route to the hearts and minds of the population.

The hope was that this exposé would provoke a public outcry that would blow the cover off this unseemly trade and change the law. After all, Stead had discovered that some of the most respected men in the community—doctors, politicians, royalty, and even clergymen—were among the brothel clients! If such influential men were complicit in the cover-up, the only way to change things would be to incite a massive public backlash.

When Stead shared his plan with William and Catherine, they gave him their full support. They also decided that while Stead and Bramwell were putting their plan into effect, the Army would introduce the issue in a "Purity Crusade" to prime the pumps of public opinion. They would also write to the queen and prime minister, asking them again to reintroduce the bill to raise the age of consent and urging them to demand that it receive an honest hearing. At one meeting, Catherine spoke about the issue:

> I question whether any face has burned with fiercer shame than mine....Three years ago a committee of the House of Lords sat to consider these very things and they recommended improved legislation for the protection of young girls... and yet nothing has been done. I would like to ask those responsible for this state of things how many thousands of innocent victims have been sacrificed during those three years?...They have found time to legislate on the preservation of game, and the diseases of cattle!...Time to legislate for British interests in far-off corners of the earth, surely they might have found time to legislate for the protection of the children of their own country!...The wretches

> who cater for the child-destroying monsters perfectly well know the present state of the law....Hence their anxiety to get children who are turned thirteen even if only by a day![35]

Stead spoke with a lawyer to ensure that he would not be breaking any laws in the pursuit of his plan, and the lawyer assured him that without criminal intent, there would be no crime. Stead thus outlined his intentions, which he also presented to the archbishop of Canterbury, the head of the Roman Catholic Church of England, and the bishop of London—three witnesses whose integrity could not be questioned.

One of the Salvation Army officers, Rebecca Jarrett, had participated in the trade of kidnapping girls before she turned her life around and joined the Army. Stead approached her to enlist her aid in the plan. At first, she wanted nothing to do with any part of her old life, but Stead soon convinced her that it was her duty to try to save those whom she had previously condemned to a life of prostitution. She contacted some of her old acquaintances and got the ball rolling.

On June 2, 1885, posing as a rich merchant's wife in search of a housemaid, Rebecca was introduced to a thirteen-year-old girl named Eliza Armstrong. Rebecca warned Eliza's mother that the housemaid angle was a ruse, and that her daughter was destined to be some man's toy. An alcoholic, she didn't care; she just wanted to take the money and return to her drinking. Eliza, fully taken in, was excited at the prospect of living in a new home and earning her own money. Her mother relinquished her for a mere pound.

Again acting the part of the client, Stead waited in a room he had rented at a brothel. Eliza was brought in, and after they had chatted together for awhile, Stead left her to sleep. Later, as would have been the custom, he returned as a real client would. He was hoping that she would still be asleep, so that he could enter the room and leave again without disturbing her, but she awoke when he came in, crying and pleading to be taken home. Rebecca returned and calmed her, then told her the truth of the entire affair and apologized

---

[35] Catherine Booth, *The War Cry*, 1 August 1885, quoted in Bramwell-Booth, *Catherine Booth*, 330.

for the trickery. Within twenty-four hours, Eliza was escorted away, sent to stay with Salvationists in France for safekeeping. Stead had his story.

A Newspaper Reports the Truth

On Monday, July 6, 1885, the *Pall Mall Gazette* published the first of four articles in a series entitled "The Maiden Tribute of Modern Babylon." Eliza was referred to as "Lilly" in the article for her protection, but the story was no less compelling. It was frank and factual, leaving no sordid stone unturned. The paper sold out almost immediately, and London seemed in a panic. Politicians were soon calling for Stead's head, labeling the material pornographic and, therefore, illegal. Several newsboys were arrested for selling the paper the next day. Brothel owners hired hooligans to storm the *Gazette* building and destroy the presses. Stead appealed to William for help, and he instantly replied, "Tell Mr. Stead that we'll throw open this building for the sake of his paper. We'll do everything in our power to help him."[36]

The next day, the Salvation Army headquarters looked like a giant newsstand, and Army cadets walked the streets of London, selling the papers. Catherine spoke at Exeter Hall and produced testimony after testimony from the Army's own archives of stories confirming Stead's article. One of the stories was of a rich merchant who had made arrangements for a girl, and just such a girl was enticed away from her Sunday school lessons and kept at a brothel to await him. Imagine the man's shock when he entered the room with the worst of intentions to find his own daughter was the one kidnapped to be his victim!

The Booths presented a petition that called for the following:

- Protection for children, boys and girls, to the end of their seventeenth year
- The procuring of young persons for immoral purposes to be made a criminal act
- Magistrates to be given the power to order entry into a house where it is believed underage girls may be detained against their will

---

[36] Collier, *General Next to God*, 122.

- Equality for men and women in the law—that it be made an offence for men to solicit women[37].

In the next seventeen days, the Booths collected 393,000 signatures for the petition, which they represented to the House of Commons on Thursday, July 30, 1885. The scrolls of names stretched for more than two and a half miles. On August 14, the House of Commons amended the criminal code to raise the age of consent to sixteen years, and other commonwealth countries, such as Australia and Canada—as well as parts of the United States—followed suit.

Despite this victory, the fight was not yet over, unfortunately. The Armstrongs soon realized that "Lilly" was indeed their own Eliza, and likely seeing a chance for some profit, filed charges against Stead and the Booths for kidnapping. Eliza's father had not consented to the "sale" of his child, and his entire case would build on this important fact. An extradition warrant was issued, and Mr. Armstrong went to France to recover his daughter. She was home again with her family by August 24, even though she had begged to stay with the Salvationists. Everyone involved with Eliza's removal from her mother was asked to stand trial. The brothel owners and sex traffickers collected mobs to stand outside the courthouse and call for "justice" on the Booths. For the next few weeks, the trial would occupy the public's attention as much as the O. J. Simpson trial did in the 1990s. The hope was to ruin the Salvation Army, once and for all.

Blatantly favored by the judge, the prosecution pulled every trick in the book to condemn the Booths. In the end, the Booths were acquitted; only Stead and Rebecca were found guilty. Stead and Rebecca were sentenced to three and six months of hard labor, respectively, which they both endured with the support of the Army by their side. After his release, Stead discovered that the Armstrongs had never actually married, and, therefore, Mr. Armstrong was not a legal guardian of Eliza. This fact would have caused the case to be thrown out, had it been presented in court.

While Stead had been on trial, a young girl who was dying had asked that her only remaining shilling be donated to the editor's defense. He was handed the shilling on his release from prison,

[37] Yaxley, *William and Catherine: The Life and Legacy of the Booths*, 206.

and he kept it with him until the day he died. He wrote that it was "the shilling which I most prize of all the pieces of money in my possession."[38] Stead donated his prison uniform to the Army on the anniversary of his conviction, and he remained a friend of the Army for many years to come. He died on April 14, 1912, a passenger who didn't survive the sinking of the Titanic.

Instead of destroying the Salvation Army, as it was intended to, the trial had made it a household name as an institution dedicated to doing the right thing, no matter what. The work of the Army would now grow faster than ever.

Catherine's Final Years

In February 1888, Catherine was diagnosed with malignant breast cancer, and despite her family's pleas, she refused surgery. The risks seemed too great, and she was concerned that her heart would not be able to withstand the strain of the operating table. Her health deteriorated quickly, and her bed became a makeshift office where she could attend meetings without having to get up and go anywhere.

With Catherine confined to her sitting room, William decided to spend more time with her, and he finally began working on a book that he had been considering writing for some time. It would be titled *In the Darkest England and the Way Out*, and it presented a systematic plan for helping England's impoverished. He held up what he called the "cab horse"[39] standard: every human being should be entitled to the same things a cab horse had—namely, food, shelter, and a job. If a cab horse faltered along its way, people treated it, if necessary, and got it back on its feet. Shouldn't the same be done for our fellow human beings who fall on hard times? William's plan had three parts:

1) The City Colony: an institution in the cities to supply short-term help to the needy with the goal of catching those who slip and getting them right back on their

[38] Estelle W. Stead, *My Father: Personal and Spiritual Reminiscences* (London, 1913), quoted in Owen Mulpetre, "The 'Maiden Tribute of Modern Babylon': W. T. Stead and the Making of a Scandal," The W. T. Stead Resource Site, http://www.attackingthedevil.co.uk/worksabout/babylon.php.

[39] The horses that drew the cabs and carriages of the day.

feet again. Those who could be reinstated into society would be; those who needed retraining or more help could be passed on to the next phase.

2) The Farm Colony: Those who could not find work in the cities could be moved to a farm in the countryside where they could be reeducated, as needed, into new trades and instructed in spiritual matters to give them the strength to become self-supporting again. The farm would also be away from the call of such vices as alcohol and gambling. If this wasn't sufficient, after they were retrained, they could be given a new beginning in the next phase.
3) The Colony across the Sea: At this time, the British colonies in South Africa, East Africa, Australia, and Canada were still open for settlement. Once people were retrained at a farm colony, if they couldn't find work in England, then the colony across the sea could give them a new start in a new country.

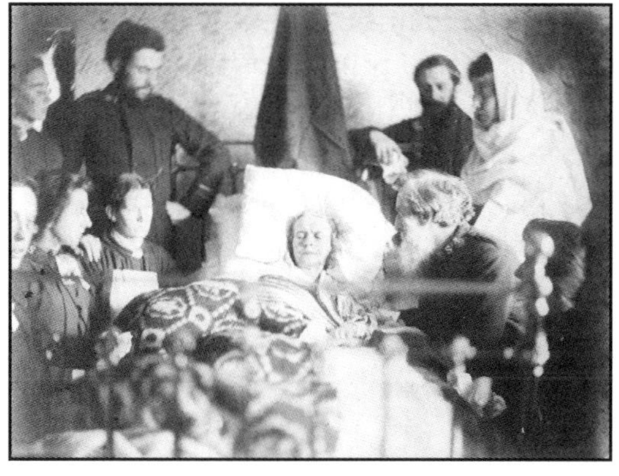

Catherine Booth on her deathbed, her husband at her side

The Salvation Army Archives

Catherine was enthusiastic about the project, and again with the help of Stead, the two of them began piecing the book together.

The condition of Catherine's health continued to deteriorate rapidly. By October 1889, she was almost completely confined to bed. The doctors offered her narcotic drugs to ease her pain, but she refused them as long as she could; she wanted to experience life without the haze of painkillers. She wasn't expected to live to see the New Year, but she made a recovery, and in January 1890 seemed stronger. William and his family cherished every minute with her until her last.

In September 1890, Catherine, William, and Stead put the finishing touches on the *Darkest England* manuscript. It was a triumphant finish—but a conclusion that also seemed to signify the finish line for Catherine's life. Her strength was nearly gone by October 2, and her family gathered around to see her depart this life for her eternal home. She breathed her last on October 4, 1890.

Catherine's funeral service was held on October 13, and more than 36,000 people came. The next day, a parade of four thousand Salvationists escorted her body to its final resting place in Abney Park Cemetery. In remembrance of her, William addressed those who had gathered at the cemetery:

> My beloved Comrades and Friends:
>
> You will readily understand that I find it a difficulty to talk to you this afternoon. To begin with, I could not be willing to talk without an attempt to make you hear, and sorrow doesn't feel like shouting.
>
> Yet I have come riding through these, I suppose, hundreds of thousands of people this afternoon, who have bared their heads and who have blessed me in the name of the Lord at almost every resolution of the carriage wheels. My mind has been full of two feelings, which alternate—one is uppermost one moment, and the other the next—and yet which blend and amalgamate with each other; and these are the feeling of sorrow and the feeling of gratitude.
>
> Those who know me—and I don't think I am very difficult to understand—and those who knew my darling, my beloved, will, I am sure, understand how it is that my heart should be rent with sorrow.
>
> If you had had a tree that had grown up in your garden, under your window, which for forty years had been your shadow from the burning sun, whose flowers had been the adornment and beauty of your life, whose fruit had been almost the stay of your existence, and the gardener had come along and swung his glittering axe and cut it down before your eyes, I think you would feel as though you had a blank—it might not be a big one—but a little blank in your life!

If you had had a servant, who for all this long time had served you without fee or reward, who had ministered, for very love, to your health and comfort, and who had suddenly passed away, you would miss that servant!

If you had had a counselor who, in hours—continually occurring—of perplexity and amazement, had ever advised you, and seldom advised wrong; whose advice you had followed and seldom had reason to regret it; and the counselor, while you are still in the same intricate mazes of your existence, had passed away, you would miss that counselor!

If you had had a friend who had understood your very nature, the rise and fall of your feelings, the bent of your thoughts and the purpose of your existence; a friend whose communion had ever been pleasant—the most pleasant of all other friends—to whom you had ever turned with satisfaction, and your friend had been taken away, you would feel some sorrow at the loss!

If you had had a mother for your children, who had cradled and nursed and trained them for the service of the living God, in which you most delighted—a mother, indeed, who had never ceased to bear their sorrows on her heart, and who had been ever willing to pour forth that heart's blood in order to nourish them, and that darling mother had been taken from your side, you would feel it a sorrow!

If you had had a wife, a sweet love of a wife, who for forty years had never given you real cause for grief; a wife who had stood with you side by side in the battle's front, who had been a comrade to you, ever willing to interpose herself between you and the enemy, and ever the strongest when the battle was fiercest, and your beloved one had fallen before your eyes, I am sure there would have been some excuse for sorrow!

Well, my comrades, you can roll all these qualities into one personality, and what would be lost in each I have lost in all. There has been taken away from me the delight of my eyes, the inspiration of my soul, and we are about to lay all that remains of her in the grave. I have been looking right at the bottom of it here, and calculating how soon they may bring and lay me alongside of her, and my cry to God has been that every remaining hour of my life may make me readier to come and join her in death, to go and embrace her in life in the Eternal City!

And yet, my comrades, my heart is full of gratitude too that swells and makes me forget my sorrow, that the long valley of the shadow of death has been trodden, and that out of the dark tunnel she has emerged into the light of day. Death came to her with all its terrors, brandishing his heart before her for two long years and nine months. Again and again she went down to the river's edge to receive her last thrust, as she thought, but ever coming back to life again. Thank God, she will see him no more—she is more than conqueror over the last enemy!

Death came to take her away from her loved employment. She loved the fight! Her great sorrow to the last moment was: "I cannot be with you when the clouds lower, when friends turn and leave you, and sorrows come sweeping over you; I shall no longer be there to put my arms round you and cheer you on!"

But she went away to help us! She promised me many a time that what she could do for us in the Eternal City should be done! The valley to her was a dark one in having to tear her heart away from so many whom she loved so well. Again and again she said, "The roots of my affections are very deep." But they had to be torn up. One after another she gave us up; she made the surrender with many loving words of counsel, and left us to her Lord.

This afternoon my heart has been full of gratitude because her soul is now with Jesus. She had a great capacity for suffering and a great capacity for you, and her heart is full of joy this afternoon.

My heart has also been full of gratitude because God lent me for so long a season such a treasure. I have been thinking, if I had to point out her three qualities to you here, they would be: First, she was good. She was washed in the Blood of the Lamb. To the last moment her cry was, "A sinner saved by grace." She was a thorough hater of shams, hypocrisies, and make-believes.

Second, she was love. Her whole soul was full of tender, deep compassion. I was thinking this morning that she suffered more in her lifetime through her compassion for poor dumb animals than some suffer for the wide, wide world of sinning, sorrowing mortals! Oh, how she loved, how she compassioned, how she pitied the suffering poor! How she longed to put her arms round the sorrowful and help them!

Lastly, she was a warrior. She liked the fight. She was not one who said to others, "Go!" but "Here, let *me* go!" And when there was the necessity she cried, "I *will* go." I never knew her flinch until her poor body compelled her to lie aside....

I am going to meet her again. I have never turned from her these forty years for any journeyings on my mission of mercy but I have longed to get back, and have counted the weeks, days, and hours, which should take me again to her side. When she has gone away from me it has been just the same. And now she has gone away for the last time. What then is there left for me to do? Not to count the weeks, the days, and the hours which shall bring me again into her sweet company, seeing that I know not what will be on the morrow, nor what an hour may bring forth. My work plainly is to fill up the weeks, the days, and the hours and cheer my poor heart as I go along with the thought that when I have served Christ and my generation according to the will of God—which I vow this afternoon I will, to the last drop of my blood—then I trust that she will bid me welcome to the skies, as He bade her. God bless you all.[40]

The War of the Matches

With all of the business of the Salvation Army before him, William had little time to mourn. Shortly after Catherine's passing,

[40] Roger J. Green, *Catherine Booth* (Crowborough, UK: Monarch, 1997), 294–297.

Darkest England was released and became an instant best-seller. William Booth was the man talked about most in all of England. Supporters began sending donations to help fund William's plan. Other people criticized him anew for what they cited as the folly and inadequacies of his schemes. He was never one to heed critics' remarks, though, and he maintained focus on what had been his aim since the beginning: the salvation of souls.

During their research for *Darkest England*, one of the ills the Booths had come across had to do with the manufacture of "strike anywhere" matches. The workers in the match factories were mostly women and children—some as young as eight—who worked sixteen-hour days with no breaks for meals. They were paid a shilling a day. Even worse, however, was that the chemicals used to make these matches were extremely toxic, and with poor ventilation in the factories, the workers had no protection from these gases. After extended exposure, workers began to get toothaches and what was called "flossy jaw"—the rotting away of the jawbone due to exposure to the yellow phosphorous. Though the manufacturers recognized these risks, they refused to do anything to help or protect

William, late in life

The Salvation Army Archives

In response, the Salvation Army decided to go into the matchmaking business itself in order to produce matches under safer working conditions. Their factory was well lit and properly ventilated, the workers' wages were nearly double those in the "strike anywhere" match factories, and they made sure to give the workers regular breaks every day. Also, instead of the harmful yellow phosphorous, they used red phosphorous. They produced matches with "safety tips," which would strike only on the box, but the quality of the working conditions enabled them to produce as many as six million matches a year.

Because these matches were nearly two times as expensive as the "strike anywhere" matches, the Army launched an advertising campaign to make people aware of the dangers of their competitors' products. They invited the press to tour their factory and took them to the homes of people who had worked in competitors' factories. These people stank of rotting flesh—the effects of the yellow phosphorous—and when they snuffed out their gaslights, the glow of the phosphorous was visible on their hands and teeth. Salvationists across the nation went into local shops to tell the proprietors of the dangers of "strike anywhere" matches, urging them to carry only the Army's "Lights in Darkest England" matches. Public opinion slowly turned the Salvationists' way, and the government eventually enforced higher work standards in all of the factories. By the turn of the century, the largest match manufacturer in England had stopped using yellow phosphorous altogether. The Army's match factory closed down soon after—it was no longer needed, and it had never been a financial success—but it had accomplished what the Army had set out to do.

As for the rest of the *Darkest England* plan, the Army received enough money to purchase eight hundred acres near Hadleigh, where they established a farm colony. That was about as far as the *Darkest England* plan grew, however, for want of adequate capital. Many parts of the plan were eventually implemented by various other nations and governments that could more easily collect the finances necessary (through taxation) to carry out the strategies. William was ahead of his time by at least a decade.

Finishing Strong

William grew restless at home with Catherine gone. He had little to keep him in the home office, having passed most of his responsibilities on to Bramwell and other officers, so he began traveling and speaking again. The Army now extended around the world, and checking up on his troops required William to travel extensively—by train, car, and ship. The last two and a half decades of his life were spent on the road—visiting stations, encouraging the troops, and preaching the Gospel wherever he could.

William died on August 20, 1912, having outlasted his wife, many of his friends, and even one of his children. More that 150,000 people filed past his casket to pay their respects before his funeral on August 27. Forty thousand people attended the service. Among those in attendance was Queen Mary, who had decided at the last minute to attend, and, fittingly enough, had to sit with the commoners. She ended up sitting next to a woman whom the Army had saved from prostitution. This woman told the queen, "He cared for the likes of us."[41] The next day, ten thousand Salvationists and forty Salvation Army bands marched in the procession to Abney Park Cemetery, where William's body was laid to rest beside Catherine's.

William had left the Generalship of the Army—an organization with 15,945 officers in fifty-eight nations at the time of his death—to Bramwell. In his life, William had traveled more than five million miles and preached some sixty thousand sermons. Charles Spurgeon said of the Army, "If the Salvation Army were wiped out of London, five thousand extra policemen could not fill its place in the repression of crime and disorder."[42] Booker T. Washington said, "I have always had the greatest respect for the work of the Salvation Army, especially because I have noted that it draws no color line in religion."[43] Josiah Strong, who became the founder of the Social Gospel movement in the United States, said, "Probably during no one hundred years in the history of the world have there been saved so many thieves, gamblers, drunkards, and prostitutes as during the past quarter century through the heroic faith and labors of the Salvation Army."[44]

Forty thousand people attended William Booth's funeral service.

The Salvation Army Archives

The legacy of William and Catherine Booth, the Salvation Army is the largest charitable organization in the world, with twenty-five thousand officers in

[41] Collier, *General Next to God*, 223.

[42] Kevin A. Miller, "Fashionable or Forceful?" *Christian History* 9, no. 2 [Issue 26] (1990): 2.

[43] Ibid.

[44] Ibid.

ninety-one countries. Today, it sadly lacks the fire for evangelism that it had in the General's day. Yet the Booths' passion to love people with the love of God is still touching lives, nearly one hundred and fifty years after the first sermon was preached for the East London Christian Mission. The Salvation Army reaches more that 2.5 million people each year through its ten thousand centers worldwide, continuing to fulfill Jesus' admonition in Matthew 25:35–40:

> *For I was an hungered, and ye gave me meat: I was thirsty, and ye gave me drink: I was a stranger, and ye took me in: naked, and ye clothed me: I was sick, and ye visited me: I was in prison, and ye came unto me. Then shall the righteous answer him, saying, Lord, when saw we thee an hungered, and fed thee? or thirsty, and gave thee drink? When saw we thee a stranger, and took thee in? or naked, and clothed thee? Or when saw we thee sick, or in prison, and came unto thee? And the King shall answer and say unto them, Verily I say unto you, Inasmuch as ye have done it unto one of the least of these my brethren, ye have done it unto me.*

William Booth's casket is carried out of the Salvation Army headquarters the day of his funeral.

Mary Evans Picture Library

Chapter Ten

★★★★★

Billy Graham

(1918–)

"Evangelist to the World"

"Evangelist to the World"

My one purpose in life is to help people find a personal relationship with God, which, I believe, comes through knowing Christ.

—Billy Graham

If God blessed the twentieth century with technological advancements in order that more people might hear the Gospel preached, then no one picked up that challenge better than Billy Graham. Billy's calling as an evangelist would transcend ministry in the church to a place on the world stage equal in influence to that of presidents and prime ministers. He would find a simple formula for preaching the Gospel of Jesus Christ so that thousands and millions could hear it and respond in one sitting: the crusade. People could accept Jesus as their personal Savior whether they attended a crusade, watched one on television, heard it on the radio, read about it in a book, caught its message in a film or video, or even downloaded it as a Webcast via the Internet. No single person has touched so many for the name of Christ in the history of the world; and when it comes to Christianity, there are few names known more widely today than that of Billy Graham.

When Life Was Simpler

William Franklin Graham Jr. was born on November 7, 1918, on a dairy farm outside Charlotte, North Carolina, where his grandfather had first built a log cabin after the Civil War. It was four days before the armistice of World War I, and a year after the Communist Revolution in Russia—two events that would ultimately spark the Cold War. Billy was born to William Franklin Graham and Morrow Coffey Graham. His maternal grandmother had been a Presbyterian, and she had raised her children devotedly. When she died, "Billy Frank," as the evangelist was then called, was still in elementary school, as was his sister Catherine. They were pulled out of school the day their grandmother passed away and were told that she went home happily. Just before she died, she had sat up in bed almost laughing, and said, "I see Jesus. He has His arms outstretched toward me. And there's Ben! [Her husband.] He had both of his eyes and both of his legs."[1] Ben had fought in the Civil War, and during the Battle of Gettysburg, he had lost a leg and an eye from some shrapnel fire. The story took on the weight of a family legend.

Billy grew to adolescence in the midst of the Great Depression. His father had lost $4,000 of lifetime savings in the bank runs on the day the stock market crashed, but because the Grahams lived on a farm, they could make do. They barely survived as the price of milk fell to five cents a quart, but Billy's father's dry sense of humor kept everyone in good spirits, and the family endured together. Despite hardships, the Grahams were still the first in their neighborhood to have a radio in their car.

As a boy, Billy grew to love baseball, though he was really only good enough to make the team and sit on the bench. His fielding was solid, but he was a left-handed batter whose hitting record was not extremely lustrous. Because of his height and a good glove, he generally played first base. When he was five, his father had taken him to hear the professional baseball player-turned-evangelist, Billy Sunday, but Billy Frank was too young for the evangelist to make much of an impression on him. All he really remembered of the service was that his father had dryly told him he needed to sit quietly or the preacher might call out his name and have him arrested. It took him a few years to figure out that his father had been joking.

His parents were devout in many ways. On the first day of their marriage, they had established an altar in their home and dedicated themselves to daily Bible reading. Billy's father, raised as a Methodist, had been a strong supporter of Prohibition. The day that the

---

[1] Billy Graham, *Just As I Am: The Autobiography of Billy Graham* (San Francisco: HarperSanFrancisco, 1997), 4. Insert added.

movement was repealed in 1933, he brought home some beer and took Billy and his sister into the kitchen, where he forced them to drink it—all of it—until they were ready to vomit. "From now on," he said, "whenever any of your friends try to get you to drink alcohol, just tell them you've already tasted it and you don't like it. That's all the reason you need to give."[2] It wasn't exactly an argument from Scripture, but it was effective. Billy would be a teetotaler his entire life.

About the time that Billy's sister Jean was born, his father had an accident that nearly killed him. He had approached a friend working with a table saw, and when his friend turned slightly to hear him, a piece of wood got caught by the blade and was flung out of control at Billy's father, smashing his jaw and cutting him severely along the side of the head. He was rushed to the hospital but lost a good deal of blood along the way. Friends and family turned to prayer, and for a few days, things looked grim. He soon stabilized, however, and underwent plastic surgery to reconstruct his face.

Deeply grateful for this answer to prayer, William Graham Sr. couldn't refuse when a group of local businessmen asked to use part of his land for an all-day prayer meeting. When a farmhand asked Billy who these men were, he answered, "I guess they're just some fanatics that have talked Daddy into using the place."[3] Years later, he would learn that someone at that prayer meeting had prayed "that out of Charlotte [North Carolina] the Lord would raise up someone to preach the Gospel to the ends of the earth."[4]

"I Like a *Fighter*"

Dr. Mordecai Ham began a revival in Charlotte when Billy was fifteen, but he had no desire whatsoever to go; he turned down every invitation for the first month of Ham's meetings. His attitude would change, however, after Ham voiced some accusations about a house of immorality near Central High School in Charlotte. He claimed that some students were frequenting the house every day during their lunch hour, stating that he had affidavits to prove it. The story

[2] Graham, *Just As I Am*, 17.

[3] Ibid., 24.

[4] Ibid. Insert added.

made the *Charlotte News.* Offended by the accusations, a group of students from the school pledged to march on Ham's next meeting and protest in front of the podium. Some had even threatened to pull him from the podium to teach him a lesson.

The day of the scheduled protest, a friend of Billy's asked, "Why don't you come out and hear our fighting preacher?"[5]

"Is he a *fighter*?" Billy responded. "I like a *fighter*." So he agreed to go. That night, Billy found himself awestruck—not as much by what Ham said as by the power behind it. As he put it in his autobiography, "I was hearing another voice, as was often said of Dwight L. Moody when he preached: the voice of the Holy Spirit."[6]

From that night on, Billy was at every one of Ham's meetings that he could attend. Ham preached the first sermon that Billy had ever heard about hell, and it was the first time Billy had considered it as anything other than a swear word. Over the course of these meetings, Billy became convicted that he was rebellious and sinful, but he was confused about how to respond. He had been baptized as an infant in the Presbyterian Church, learned the Shorter Catechism by heart, and been confirmed in the Associated Reformed Presbyterian Church before the elders and the pastor, but these no longer seemed adequate qualifications. He had previously believed himself to be anything but a wicked person—morally upstanding, an excellent citizen, and even the vice president of his youth group. Yet when Ham fixed his gaze on him, he knew in his heart that none of this was enough. He gradually realized that what Ham was getting at was the fact that a person could come to know Jesus personally, and the more he talked of it, the more Billy realized he did not really know Jesus at all.

Then, one night shortly after Billy's sixteenth birthday, Ham extended an invitation at the end of his sermon, quoting Romans 5:8: *"But God commendeth his love toward us, in that, while we were yet sinners, Christ died for us."* On the last verse of the second song that played while people were coming forward, Billy responded to the invitation and walked to the front of the stage with some three hundred or so other people. In *Just As I Am*, Billy described how he felt standing among the crowd:

---

[5] Ibid.

[6] Ibid.

> My heart sank when I looked over at the lady standing next to me with tears running down her cheeks. I was not crying. I did not feel any special emotion of any kind just then. Maybe, I thought, I was not supposed to be there. Maybe my good intentions to be a real Christian wouldn't last. Wondering if I was just making a fool of myself, I almost turned around and went back to my seat.
>
> As I stood in front of the platform, a tailor named J. D. Prevatt, who was a friend of our family with a deep love for souls, stepped up beside me weeping....In his heavy European accent, he explained God's plan for my salvation in a simple way. That explanation was addressed to my own mental understanding. It did not necessarily answer every question I had at the moment—and it certainly did not anticipate every question that would come to me in the months and years ahead—but it set forth simply the facts I needed to know in order to become God's child.
>
> ...Now came the moment to commit myself to Christ. Intellectually, I accepted Christ to the extent that I acknowledged what I knew about Him to be true. That was mental assent. Emotionally, I felt that I wanted to love Him in return for His loving me. But the final issue was whether I would turn myself over to His rule in my life.[7]

As Billy described this night to biographer William Martin in *A Prophet with Honor*,

> I didn't have any tears, I didn't have any emotion, I didn't hear any thunder, there was no lightning....But right there, I made my decision for Christ. It was simple as that, and as conclusive.[8]

College and Ordination

Billy hadn't given much thought to college until the time to enroll was nearly upon him. He had always assumed in the back of his mind that he would attend the University of South Carolina.

---

[7] Graham, *Just As I Am*, 29–30.

[8] William Martin, *A Prophet with Honor: The Billy Graham Story* (New York: William Morrow and Company, 1991), 64.

But when Dr. Bob Jones came to speak at his high school, and Billy discovered that a few of his friends were planning to go to the school Jones had named after himself, he decided to attend Bob Jones College (Bob Jones University, since 1947), as well.

The summer before he started college, Billy joined another friend selling Fuller brushes door-to-door to make some money. Despite the difficulty of this work, Billy found he could earn as much as $50 to $75 a week—a respectable sum for a young man in 1936. He learned to pray as he walked up to each home, preparing to present his wares. He also looked for opportunities to share his faith in Christ, but he found this to be a hit-and-miss process, as he was still learning to discern the leading of the Holy Spirit.

That fall, he enrolled at Bob Jones College but found the institution socially stringent and the classes difficult. Dating was strictly monitored and required a chaperone. Outside of registered times, boys could not talk with their girlfriends, and during dates, they were not allowed to hold hands or even sit on the same couch with one another. "Free time" conversations with members of the opposite sex had to be limited to fifteen minutes. The classroom was also a stringent environment. Questions were rarely tolerated, and when they were, it was only for the purpose of clarifying a point, not to discuss different interpretations or opinions of the material being taught. Jones's interpretations of doctrines and Scripture determined the subject matter—everything else was off topic.

When Billy came down with the flu, he was persuaded to leave the stifling structure of Bob Jones College for sunny skies and less rigid training at the Florida Bible Institute in Tampa. Billy transferred, but not before Jones warned him that taking such a step would be disastrous. Jones told him that if he left, "at best, all you could amount to would be a poor country Baptist preacher somewhere out in the sticks."[9] Billy went anyway—the draw of sunshine, golf, and dating more freely was more than this prophecy of doom could overcome.

In Florida, Billy met Emily Cavanaugh, a pretty classmate whom he began dating and soon decided he would marry. When she confided in him that she was in love with another student who was a

---

[9] Nancy Gibbs and Richard N. Ostling, "God's Billy Pulpit," *Time*, November 15, 1993, http://www.time.com/time/magazine/article/0,9171,979573,00.html.

better preacher than Billy, however, he was perplexed. According to Billy's brother Melvin, "She wanted to marry a man who was going to amount to something."[10] This led to a good deal of soul-searching for Billy about God's will for his life and how he could achieve it. He felt called to be a minister, but also felt he was inadequate, and he spent hours walking around campus at night, praying to convince God that he was better qualified to do something else.

As he searched his heart, however, he found that his preaching was improving, and that his invitations for people to receive Christ were seeing more and more responses. So, on another night spent walking around a golf course in Tampa in 1938, Billy decided to give in to what he felt was inevitably established in his heart—that he must be a minister of the Gospel. He knelt on one of the greens, where he spread himself face down in prayer. "O God," he prayed, sobbing. "If you want me to serve You, I will."[11]

Later that year, Billy was convinced that his infant baptism with the Presbyterians was not enough, so he allowed a Baptist minister to baptize him by immersion. Early in 1939, he was ordained as a Southern Baptist minister.

When one of the ordaining ministers started probing him about his theology, Billy grew impatient, and, hoping to put an end to the questioning, said, "Brother, you've heard me preach around these parts, and you've seen how the Lord has seen fit to bless. I'm not an expert on theology, but you know what I believe and how I preach, and that should be enough to satisfy you."[12] The man chuckled, as did some of the others, and they decided that it was. He had no further questions for Billy.

An Evangelist in Training

With his baptism settled, Billy started practicing his sermons and polishing his voice, of which Bob Jones had said, "You have a voice that pulls....God can use that voice of yours. He can use it mightily." [13] He practiced his sermons standing in old sheds or

[10] Gibbs and Ostling, "God's Billy Pulpit."

[11] Graham, *Just As I Am*, 53.

[12] Ibid., 57.

[13] Gibbs and Ostling, "God's Billy Pulpit."

sitting in a canoe on the middle of a lake, where he would preach to the fish. The summer after he was ordained, he preached a two-week evangelistic series at Welaka Baptist Church, a fishing village on the St. John River. During the day, he would walk the streets of the town, praying and preaching to the cracks in the sidewalk. Following that, he was asked to preach for six weeks at the Tampa Gospel Tabernacle while the pastor took some time off. When the sanctuary was empty on Saturdays, he would go in and preach to the seats. It was like having his own church.

Sharing his faith was a hit-and-miss process for Billy, who was still learning to discern the Holy Spirit's leading.

There was a certain genuineness about Billy to which his audiences were drawn. He had a simple, honest, Southern-gentlemanly way about him that made him appeal to both rich and poor, and like many young evangelists, he filled his sermons with sincere emotional tugs on the heart, even if all the facts of what he was preaching didn't line up exactly. To his credit, Billy never really saw himself as a theologian, and throughout his life, he wished he had done more reading and studying. He also found, though, that if he stuck to the basics and preached sincerely, people gave their hearts to the Lord.

In May 1940, Billy graduated from Florida Bible Institute. It was a tradition that just before the commencement ceremony, one of the class members was asked to read a "prophecy" that he or she prayed over and composed at the Class Night. That year, the reading came close to being prophetic indeed, for the woman who was chosen read,

> Each time God had a chosen human instrument to shine forth His light in the darkness. Men like Luther, John and Charles Wesley, Moody, and others were ordinary men, but men who heard the voice of God. Their surrounding conditions were as black as night, but they had God. "If God is for us, who can be against us?" (Romans 8:31). It has been said that Luther revolutionized the world. It was not

> he, but Christ working through him. The time is ripe for another Luther, Wesley, Moody, _______. There is room for another name in this list. There is a challenge facing us.[14]

Wheaton and Ruth

During Billy's last year at Florida Bible Institute, a lawyer from Chicago named Paul Fischer heard him preach and offered to pay for his first year at Wheaton College in the Chicago area if he would enroll there. After a little hemming and hawing, mostly over concern that Wheaton would not admit him once they saw his high school grades, Billy applied and was accepted. Neither Bob Jones College nor Florida Bible Institute had been accredited, so Billy was now on his first step to receiving a college diploma from an accredited institution. Fortunately for him, Wheaton accepted many of his courses at Florida Bible Institute as credits, and he was able to enter as a second semester freshman.

Then, in December 1941, Japan attacked Pearl Harbor and America entered World War II. Billy's first instinct was to volunteer for service, but as a minister, his next was to sign on as a chaplain. In pursuing this course, he needed to finish his degree, which kept him at Wheaton.

Remaining at Wheaton, Billy met Ruth Bell. She was born in China, where her parents had been missionaries, and she had spent most of her first seventeen years in Asia. She had attended high school in Pyongyang, now part of North Korea. Billy was immediately taken with her hazel eyes and attractive figure. Despite the fact that she wanted to be a missionary to Tibet, Billy started dating her, and within a few months, he proposed. Ruth decided to take time to consider his proposal before responding, and when her sister came down with tuberculosis, she dropped out of Wheaton for a while to care for her.

On his way to preach one night, Billy received a letter from Ruth announcing that she would marry him. In the following pages, she proceeded to explain why. Billy read her letter again and again after arriving at the church, then got into the pulpit and preached

---

[14] Graham, *Just As I Am*, 59–60.

up a storm. When he finished, the pastor turned to him and asked, "Do you know what you just said?" A little caught off guard, Billy answered honestly, "No." "I'm not sure the people did either!" the pastor responded. [15]

Billy and Ruth agreed to wait until after graduation to get married. They graduated in the same year and were married later that summer, on Friday, August 13, 1943.

Soon after their wedding, Billy took over the pastorate of the Village Church in Western Springs, Illinois. The church had fewer than a hundred members, only fifty of whom typically attended each service. All that had been constructed of this church was the basement, so that is where they met. Since it was still wartime, Ruth thought of the basement as an air raid shelter. By the turn of 1944, however, church attendance had doubled to more than one hundred people each week. Billy was still hoping to become a chaplain, but with the war winding down, opportunities would take him in a different direction.

Radio Ministry Starts

A local minister featured regularly on the radio called Billy one day and offered him a radio show he had planned but had no time to record. Billy approached his congregation with the idea, and at first, they thought that it would cost too much. But when a way was provided to pay for it, they agreed. It would prove another turning point for Billy's ministry—that booming voice of his sounded great on the radio. As the program grew in popularity, Billy got more calls to do evangelistic outreaches in other areas. Soon, however, this put a strain on his congregation—they felt as if they were paying a full-time salary for a part-time pastor.

Near the end of the war, a bout of mumps silenced Billy's hopes of being a chaplain, once and for all. He was asked to be the first employee and organizer of a budding ministry—Youth for Christ, International. After much prayer, he took the position, resigned from his church, and was granted a discharge from the chaplaincy corps. Billy became a full-time evangelist, preaching wherever Youth for Christ could secure a venue. Billy felt like a traveling salesman

[15] Ibid., 75.

again; only, this time, he carried his Bible instead of a suitcase of brushes. The organization grew rapidly in post-war America, and Billy's enthusiasm for the Gospel caught on wherever he went. Then, on September 21, 1945, the Grahams' first child, Virginia Leftwich, nicknamed "Gigi," was born.

Billy earned the nickname "God's machine gun" because of his rapid-fire delivery and seemingly boundless energy on the stage. Some people called the Youth for Christ rallies "Christian vaudeville," as their events would feature everything from bands to quiz shows to performing animals and emcees with light-up bow ties. Nevertheless, these meetings grew in popularity—as many as a million kids across the nation might attend a Youth for Christ meeting on a given week.[16]

"You've Spoken of Something I Don't Have"

In the spring of 1946, Billy and the Youth for Christ team traveled to Europe to launch the ministry there. It was Billy's first trip overseas, and after a rough start on a military base that wanted showgirls rather than a revival meeting, things started to improve. Billy enjoyed the life of an evangelist, and his sincerity and energy continued to serve him well, despite the cultural differences that made it difficult for him to adjust to Europe.

In October 1946, Billy heard a minister by the name of Stephen Olford when he ministered at Hildenborough Hall in Kent. Olford's text was Ephesians 5:18: *"Be not drunk with wine, wherein is excess; but be filled with the Spirit."* Hearing this message, Billy began a struggle to obtain the infilling of the Holy Spirit and His anointing on his ministry. At the end of the service, Billy approached Olford and asked, "Mr. Olford, I just wanted to ask you one question: Why didn't you give an invitation? I would have been the first one to come forward. You've spoken of something I don't have. I want the fullness of the Holy Spirit in my life too."[17]

---

[16] Gibbs and Ostling, "God's Billy Pulpit."

[17] Sherwood Eliot Wirt, *Billy: A Personal Look at Billy Graham, the World's Best-loved Evangelist* (Wheaton, IL: Crossway Books, 1997), 28.

Of meeting Olford, Billy said, "I was seeking for more of God in my life, and I felt that here was a man who could help me. He had a dynamic, a thrill, an exhilaration about him I wanted to capture."[18]

Billy and Olford agreed to meet shortly thereafter in Wales, near where Billy was scheduled to preach. They spent a day studying the Scriptures together, after which Billy prayed, "Lord, I don't want to go on without knowing this anointing You've given my brother."[19] Billy didn't receive this blessing, however, for his sermon that night was ordinary, and "not the Welsh kind of preaching,"[20] a phrase that was perhaps left over from the days of Evan Roberts and the Welsh Revival.

Billy was called "God's machine gun" for his rapid-fire delivery and boundless energy.

The two men met again the next day, and Olford began teaching about being filled with the Holy Spirit, and how one had to be broken as Paul was, when he proclaimed himself "crucified with Christ," before he could receive this infilling. He taught Billy that "where the Spirit is truly Lord over the life, there is liberty, there is release—the sublime freedom of complete submission of oneself in a continuous state of surrender to the indwelling of God's Holy Spirit." Billy's response was, "Stephen, I see it. That's what I want."

About mid-afternoon, the two men knelt together to pray. Olford described what happened as they prayed: "All heaven broke loose in that dreary little room. It was like Jacob laying hold of God and crying, 'Lord, I will not let Thee go except Thou bless me.'" Billy described how he exclaimed after the prayer, "My heart is so flooded with the Holy Spirit!...I have it! I'm filled. I'm filled. This is the turning point of my life. This will revolutionize my ministry."[21]

The effects were immediate. According to Olford, "That night

[18] John Pollack, *Billy Graham* (London: Hodder and Stoughton, 1966), 62, quoted in Wirt, *Billy: A Personal Look at Billy Graham*, 28.

[19] Wirt, *Billy: A Personal Look at Billy Graham*, 29.

[20] Ibid.

[21] Ibid.

Billy was to speak at a large Baptist church nearby. When he rose to preach, he was a man absolutely anointed....The Welsh listeners jammed the aisles. There was chaos. Practically the entire audience rushed forward." Olford told his father that evening, "Dad, something has happened to Billy Graham. The world is going to hear from this man. He is going to make his mark in history."[22]

Billy Graham and the Holy Spirit

Thus began a tenuous link between Billy Graham and what is known as the "infilling," or "baptism," of the Holy Spirit. Billy has admitted that he's never spoken in tongues—though he also said he believed this to be a wonderful experience for those who have—but it is difficult, if not impossible, to link his success throughout his six decades as an evangelist merely to his "pulling" voice and tall, lanky Southern charm. Billy Graham is not a charismatic Christian, and it is interesting to note that he never mentioned this incident with Stephen Olford in his own autobiography, *Just As I Am*, instead leaving the story for other biographers to reveal.

At the same time, Billy did not shy away from charismatics any more than he did politicians, such as Bill and Hillary Rodham Clinton, who were unpopular with the evangelical world as a whole. Billy called Oral Roberts a "longtime friend" in his autobiography,[23] and he was the chief speaker at the dedication for Oral Roberts University in 1967. Many believe it was Billy who legitimized Oral's ministry by inviting him to his podium in 1950 and allowing him to give the opening prayer. David Harrell described the incident in this way in his book *Oral Roberts: An American Life*:

> As they left their Portland hotel to catch a taxi to the crusade, Billy was just leaving. The ever-gracious Graham grabbed Oral's hand and requested that he and Evelyn ride with him. Oral demurred, but Billy insisted: inside the taxi he told Oral that he expected him to sit on the platform and lead the evening prayer. Oral protested: "Billy you can't afford to have me pray." As they rode, Billy told Oral

---

[22] Letter from Stephen Olford, 9 May 1996, quoted in Wirt, *Billy: A Personal Look at Billy Graham*, 29–30.

[23] Graham, *Just As I Am*, 563.

> that he and Cliff Barrows had visited a Roberts campaign in Florida a few months before, slipping in and out unnoticed, and they had been blessed by it. He also revealed that his wife's sister had experienced a healing in a pentecostal setting; he was not ashamed to be identified with Oral Roberts. Oral offered the evening prayer, and that evening, after he and Evelyn returned to the hotel coffee shop, Billy and Ruth Graham insisted that they join them for a snack.
>
> The meeting had been brief, casual, and mostly unplanned. But for Oral it was loaded with meaning. His appearance on Graham's platform was unprecedented recognition for a pentecostal to receive from an evangelical ministry—especially from Billy Graham. Graham's personal kindness, his glad and wholesome embrace of a fellow Christian, placed Oral momentarily in a larger, more respectable, world than he had ever imagined he could be a part of. He had glimpsed a vision which Graham would open to him more clearly sixteen years later.[24]

The prayer experience with Olford seems as close as Billy ever came to being filled with the Holy Spirit, as a charismatic would define it. If Billy was truly seeking the baptism of the Holy Spirit, perhaps it was in the limited sense that evangelicals seem to use when they read Ephesians 5:18—*"And be ye not drunk with wine, wherein is excess; but be filled with the Spirit"*—for the fruit of the Spirit, but not for the gifts. On the other hand, they may define the gifts as something much less than they truly are—something more like spiritual instincts than manifestations of the power of God as were illustrated in the lives of Jesus and the apostles. Billy seems to have sought the power of God only to preach. He sought God to be an anointed evangelist, and, by all indications, God answered that prayer. But there Billy seems to have drawn the line. He wanted enough of God to fulfill his calling, but maybe not so much that things would get out of control. He wanted to see people moved to come forward to answer his altar calls, but seeing manifestations of the Spirit like those witnessed in the ministries of John Wesley and Charles Finney,

---

[24] David Harrell, *Oral Roberts: An American Life* (Bloomington: Indiana University Press, 1985), 179.

and at the Kentucky Camp Meetings, may have been too much for him, as it seems to have been for most twentieth-century American Christians.

Evangelicalism had departed significantly from the way it began under John Wesley, who released salvation from the deterministic clutches of Calvinism. The great revelation that sparked evangelicalism was that it was the individual's choice whether or not to be saved, even though that salvation still had to be worked out with fear and trembling (see Philippians 2:12) and could not occur without the work of the Holy Spirit. Now, under evangelists such as Moody and Graham, the individual's decision became an all-important factor.

Billy's Campaigns Begin

The following year, 1947, Billy returned to tour in the United States. He began focusing his "campaigns"—as he called them then, borrowing D. L. Moody's term—on specific cities. That year, these campaigns would be in Grand Rapids, Michigan, and Charlotte, North Carolina. In 1948, Billy's campaigns would be in Augusta, Georgia, and Modesto, California.

Sometime in 1947, Billy was also asked to speak at Northwestern Schools in Minneapolis, Minnesota, where the president of the schools, Dr. W. B. Riley, took him aside to tell him he felt Billy was to be the next president of the college. Billy was shocked, of course, being only in his late twenties, though he thought this might be something for distant years ahead. But Riley was eighty-six years old and in poor health. On December 5, 1947, he breathed his last, and even though Billy had no higher degree than his undergraduate diploma and had graduated just four years earlier, the board of directors respected the late president's wishes and offered him the presidency of Northwestern Schools. Despite his misgivings, Billy accepted the interim position, hoping that it would be a short one.

A Billy Graham campaign program

It didn't take Billy long to realize that he had stepped into a hornets' nest. The institution, having just completed construction of a new administrative building, was out of money. Billy had no dearth of ideas about how to fix the school's financial straits, but he did lack the experience and patience to see them through. He wanted to make major changes overnight, much to the discomfort of many of the board members. He also still spent most of his time on the road, evangelizing. Billy obviously had the leadership potential to turn things around at Northwestern, but would he give the school the attention it required?

In the following years, Billy would make a great figurehead as an absentee president, but the college was left to limp along as best it could on its own. Billy did, however, add fund-raising for the university to his evangelistic objectives, and this seemed to help considerably. Money began to roll in, and soon the financial situation had improved enough to raise salaries at the school to a more adequate wage. Despite the rough spots, when Billy tried to resign in 1950, the board refused his resignation.

In the meantime, the Grahams had added two new members to their family. Anne Morrow Graham was born in May 1948, and Ruth Bell Graham, whom they nicknamed "Bunny," was born in December 1950.

Does the Bible Have Errors in It?

Around this time, Billy had a new struggle that he needed to settle before he could hone the message that would be so powerful in the years to come. Charles Templeton, a fellow evangelist he had met while first working with Youth for Christ, had encouraged Billy to continue his education, in hopes that it would improve his preaching. Now, as the president of a Bible college, it seemed fitting for him to follow his friend's advice and work toward a Ph.D. For his part, Templeton had resigned as a pastor in Toronto and enrolled at Princeton Theological Seminary. He and Billy had grown close in a rather short span of time, and as Templeton began to struggle with some theological issues related to what he was learning, particularly concerning the authority and accuracy of the Bible, Billy could identify with his feelings. Over the years, Billy had broadened his reading, as well, and had added the pioneers of neo-orthodoxy, Karl Barth and Reinhold Niebuhr, to his list. It didn't take long for their writings to force him to start questioning many of the beliefs he had held since boyhood. He never doubted the central message of the Gospel itself, or the deity of Christ, but confusion about other major issues soon crept in. So Billy decided to devote more time to these subjects, particularly the inspiration and inerrancy of the Word of God.

Reading the works of theologians and scholars on both sides of the issue, Billy grew only more confused. He knew, however, that Paul had written, *"All scripture is given by inspiration of God, and is profitable for doctrine, for reproof, for correction, for instruction in righteousness"* (2 Timothy 3:16), Peter had written, *"For the prophecy came not in old time by the will of man: but holy men of God spake as they were moved by the Holy Ghost"* (2 Peter 1:21), and even Jesus Himself had said, *"Heaven and earth shall pass away, but my words shall not pass away"* (Matthew 24:35). But were the Scriptures truly *inspired*—were they "God-breathed" writings?

The subject came to a head in a series of conversations with Charles Templeton. Templeton's studies of philosophy and anthropology had led him to a willingness to read the Bible as metaphor rather than as literal truth.[25] Graham found he couldn't address all of the issues with which Charles presented him, but he still felt that he had to hold to the accuracy of the Bible, and to interpret it literally, if he was to be faithful to God and to his calling. Templeton told him that such a position was fifty years out of date, making the case that, "People no longer accept the Bible as being inspired the way you do. Your faith is too simple. Your language is out of date. You're going to have to learn the new jargon if you're going to be successful in your ministry."[26]

At a conference about this same time, Billy met Henrietta Mears, the director of religious education at the First Presbyterian Church of Hollywood. Although she was just as educated about modern thought on the Bible as Charles Templeton, her enthusiasm for Jesus

---

[25] Gibbs and Ostling, "God's Billy Pulpit."

[26] Nancy Gibbs and Michael Duffy, "Why Christopher Hitchens Is Wrong about Billy Graham," *Time*, September 18, 2007, http://www.time.com/time/nation/article/0,8599,1662757,00.html.

was very different. She had every confidence in the integrity of the written Scriptures, and her compassion for her students was like nothing Billy had ever experienced. In comparison, Templeton's passion seemed only for intellectualism. Billy saw the choices on road ahead of him mapped out by these two people.

Billy responded to Charles, as honestly as he could, "Chuck, look, I haven't a good enough mind to settle these questions.... The finest minds in the world have looked and come down on both sides....I don't have the time, the inclination, or the set of mind to pursue them. I found that if I say 'The Bible says' and 'God says,' I get results. I have decided I'm not going to wrestle with these questions any longer."[27]

Templeton told him that such an attitude was paramount to intellectual suicide, but Billy was resolute. Either he would believe the Bible and what had gotten him to where he was at the moment, or he would leave the ministry. After all, "it was not too late to be a dairy farmer."[28] He had no room to be double-minded about it. Either the Bible was the Word of God, or it was not.[29]

Still wrestling with these thoughts, Billy took a late-night walk in the San Bernardino Mountains, determined to put an end to this debate. It was a beautiful night, and the moon was out. He dropped to his knees, opened his Bible before him on a tree stump, and prayed,

> Oh God! There are many things in this book I do not understand. There are many problems with it for which I have no solution. There are many seeming contradictions. There are some areas in it that do not seem to correlate with modern science. I can't answer some of the philosophical and psychological questions Chuck and the others are raising....
>
> Father, I am going to accept this as Thy Word—*by faith!* I'm going to allow faith to go beyond my intellectual questions and doubts, and I will believe this is Your inspired Word.[30]

---

[27] Gibbs and Ostling, "God's Billy Pulpit."

[28] Gibbs and Duffy, "Why Christopher Hitchens Is Wrong about Billy Graham."

[29] Gibbs and Ostling, "God's Billy Pulpit."

[30] Graham, *Just As I Am*, 139.

When he arose from his knees, he sensed the power of God's presence for the first time in months. The battle in his spirit was over.

In the years to come, Reinhold Niebuhr himself would accuse Billy of preaching too simplistically. He felt the state of the human condition was far more complex than the way Billy spoke of it, and that his answers were far too limited in scope.[31] As for Templeton, he wrote in his *Memoir*,

> I disagree with him [Billy] profoundly on his view of Christianity and think that much of what he says in the pulpit is puerile nonsense. But there is no feigning in him: he believes what he believes...with an invincible innocence. He is the only mass evangelist I would trust. And I miss him.[32]

Launching the Crusades

Following this decision, Billy faced the crusade that would prove to be the launching pad of a ministry that would continue for decades to come. In 1949, he had four campaigns scheduled in Miami, Florida; Baltimore, Maryland; Altoona, Pennsylvania; and Los Angeles, California. It would be at the final crusade in Los Angeles that Billy would first grab the attention of the entire nation, if not the world.

An organization called Christ for Greater Los Angeles had invited Billy to speak at its next revival, which was set to start the last week in September and run for three weeks. Billy agreed—with a few conditions. First, he wanted to invite a broader base of churches to participate, so that as many different denominations as possible would be included. Second, he asked that $7,000 to $25,000 be raised in order to advertise and promote the event. Third, he wanted a larger tent—one that could seat more than 5,000 people. His campaign experience had taught him that crowds usually grew as the meetings continued. Billy had adopted many of the revival techniques of D. L. Moody, and he felt these things would be necessary if this revival was to be a success.

---

[31] Gibbs and Duffy, "Why Christopher Hitchens Is Wrong about Billy Graham."

[32] Charles Templeton, *An Anecdotal Memoir*, http://www.templetons.com/charles/memoir/evang-graham.html.

Up until that point, revivalists considered a campaign successful if they were speaking to 2,000 people and fifty of them came forward at the invitation.

Billy felt that success in Los Angeles, media magnet that it was, could send shock waves around the world. He didn't want the organizers to set their expectations too low. But many people thought that he was being egotistical, and that the money he requested was simply too much. Some people even alleged that he was asking for so much money in order to keep some for himself. Billy's leadership abilities prevailed, however, and he convinced enough of the committee members to embrace his bigger vision and to get the ball rolling.

Billy determined to accept the Bible as God's Word by faith.

On the eve of the campaign, the revival looked as if it would fizzle; the media seemed apathetic about covering the event, and organizers wondered whether they would get any coverage at all. The advance press conference was poorly attended, and it didn't produce one line of copy in the local papers. No information was printed, with the exception of the ads the committee had purchased to print in the church sections.

Billy pushed on, though. He had accepted an invitation to speak to a group of Hollywood celebrities in Beverly Hills, and when he went there, he met Stuart Hamlin, who had a popular local radio program sponsored by a tobacco company. He told Billy that he might invite him on his show, and that if he did, he could fill his tent. Billy thought he was joking, but he expressed his gratitude for the thought.

A team was set up to bathe the event in prayer. Every member of the team prayed whenever he could, and forty or fifty of them would get together to pray before attending the event each evening. They would sit in the front, and afterward, they would pray with those who came forward.

The meetings began as planned. While initial crowds averaged about three thousand people (and about four thousand on Sunday afternoons), the tent was never filled. Also, Billy found he was speaking to audiences that were already saved rather than non-Christians, so the numbers of those answering the altar calls were scant. As they approached the final week and found that they had met their budget, some thought it might be worth extending the meetings for a short time. Billy turned the matter over to prayer.

Once the meetings had started, Stuart Hamlin proved good to his word; he invited Billy onto his radio show. Billy knew that some committee members would be upset with his appearing on the show because of its connection with Hollywood, but he also felt that if he was going to get sinners to come to his tent, then he had to find a way to invite them directly. Stuart's enthusiasm bubbled over the radio as he told his audience to "go down to Billy Graham's tent and hear the preaching."[33] Billy was even more surprised when Stuart announced that he himself was planning to attend. Stuart did attend, but what he experienced was different from the mere entertainment he had expected. His heart struggled with what Billy said at the campaign, and, angered, he walked out of the meetings repeatedly. He kept coming back, however, and in the end, it would be Stuart's wrestling with repentance that would turn the event around.

Billy and some of the others decided to follow the example of Gideon and set out a fleece, asking God for a sign to tell them whether they should extend the campaign. Stuart ended up providing that sign. At 4:30 a.m., the morning after they had put out the fleece, Stuart called Billy to say that he was in the lobby and needed to see him right away. Billy woke Ruth, who went to pray in the next room with Grady and Wilma Wilson. Once Billy was dressed, Stuart and his wife, Suzy, who had been praying for him for some time, came to the room. Stuart and Billy talked for awhile, then prayed together, and Stuart gave his heart to the Lord. At the service the next evening, he came forward in response to the altar call. From his response, Billy and the committee saw that the work of the campaign was not yet finished, so they decided to extend it. They had not yet decided for how long, though.

"Puff Graham"

The first week of the extended campaign, Stuart delivered his testimony over the radio, and interest began to build. Billy and

[33] Graham, *Just As I Am*, 147.

his team put out another fleece to determine whether to extend the campaign again, and the answer came at the meeting the next night. When they showed up, the place was crawling with reporters and photographers—the first of any press they had seen. When Billy asked one reporter about the media's newfound curiosity, he responded, "You've just been kissed by William Randolph Hearst." Somehow, Hearst, the cantankerous newspaper mogul known for using his press's power to make things happen, had heard that Graham was a red, white, and blue patriot calling for spiritual renewal. Hearst decided that Graham had a message that the nation needed to hear, so he sent a simple, two-word telegram to his editors: "Puff Graham."[34] It would change Billy's outreach forever.

The next morning's headline story in the *Los Angeles Examiner* was about the campaign, as was the headline story in the evening's *Los Angeles Herald Express*, both Hearst papers. The story spread to New York, Chicago, San Francisco, and Detroit, and then competitors' papers. The committee again had their sign that the campaign should continue, and the larger tent Billy had requested was soon filled to overflowing.

On November 14, *Time* even covered the Los Angeles campaign. The article touted Billy as America's next great revivalist:

> "We are standing on the verge of a great national revival," says Evangelist Billy Graham, "an oldfashioned, heaven-sent, Holy Ghost revival that will sweep the nation...In the words of Joel: 'Put in the sickle while the harvest is ripe.'"
>
> This week, in a big circus tent ("the largest revival tent in history") in downtown Los Angeles, Evangelist Graham seemed to be wielding the revival sickle as no one since Billy Sunday had wielded it. Sponsored and financed by businessmen, ministers and such groups as Christian Endeavor, Youth for Christ, and the Gideons, 31-year-old Billy Graham arrived in September to conduct a four-week revival.
>
> S.R.O. Graham's sponsors, combined under the namc "Christ for Greater Los Angeles," expected him to hold

[34] Gibbs and Ostling, "God's Billy Pulpit."

> meetings for only four weeks. But this week he had already overstayed his original engagement by two weeks, and was drawing bigger crowds every night. Some 250,000 had crowded to hear him (the tent holds 6,280 but the standees fan out into the street), and nearly every prominent minister in Los Angeles had put in an appearance on Billy Graham's crowded platform....
>
> Blond, trumpet-lunged North Carolinian William Franklin Graham Jr., a Southern Baptist minister who is also president of the Northwestern Schools in Minneapolis, dominates his huge audience from the moment he strides onstage to the strains of Send the Great Revival in My Soul. His lapel microphone which gives added volume to his deep, cavernous voice, allows him to pace the platform as he talks, rising to his toes to drive home a point, clenching his fists, stabbing his finger at the sky and straining to get his words to the furthermost corners of the tent.[35]

In *Just As I Am*, Billy explained that despite the increased press coverage, what happened next could not be explained by the headlines. After all, it is God who changes hearts. Testimonies began to roll in very similar to Stuart Hamlin's. One night, a technician who was on trial for wiretapping for the mob came forward and was saved, giving Billy the rare opportunity to meet with an actual mob boss, Mickey Cohen, and preach the Gospel to him. The next morning's newspaper headline, which was a surprise to those who had done everything they could to keep the meeting secret, again put Billy in the spotlight: "Wiretapper in Confession as Evangelist Tries to Save Cohen."

The tent had to be doubled in size to try to accommodate the crowds, and three thousand seats were added. Every day, the newspapers covered the campaign—whether or not they were owned by Hearst. As had happened with earlier revivals, the event had now become a curiosity as well as a religious meeting, and people started coming for all kinds of reasons. One time, in the middle of the night, a watchman was awakened by someone rattling the chains at the

---

[35] "Sickle for the Harvest," *Time*, November 14, 1949, http://www.time.com/time/magazine/article/0,9171,934304,00.html.

gate. He investigated and found a man who said that he had come to find Jesus, so the watchman, a pastor helping with the campaign during a leave of absence from his church, prayed with him on the spot for salvation.

This one-on-one praying became a trend throughout the rest of the campaign—people would often walk solo or in pairs, hours after the service had ended, looking for someone to pray with them. The sermons seemed secondary to the atmosphere of the Holy Spirit working on hearts. One night, a man came directly from a bar to the meetings. He walked straight down the aisle in the middle of the sermon, asking for someone to pray with him. When Billy asked Grady Wilson to take him to the auxiliary prayer tent, scores of others followed, even though the invitation had yet to be extended.

Soon, the revival started to appear in the newsreels, which were still big in the cinemas at that time. Billy's face was beginning to receive national recognition.

By the end of the fifth week, the intense nightly meetings were starting to take their toll. Billy was out of sermons to preach, and he had to work between six and eight hours each day to prepare new ones. Because of his increased notoriety, he was continually asked to speak three or four times each day at civic gatherings, churches, school assemblies, interviews, and evangelistic parties at the mansions of the rich and famous before he even got to the tent for the evening service. After the service, prayer workers and staff would stay until every individual who had come forward had talked and prayed with someone. Billy had to ask others to step in and preach so that he had time to rest and prepare new sermons. Even so, the committee didn't feel the release to end the meetings for another eight weeks.

The meetings did not end because the numbers were dwindling, either. For the final Sunday afternoon service, more than eleven thousand people lined up two hours early to get in, and the tent was again filled to overflowing. Thousands were left outside, unable to fit under the tent, but they packed in as close as they could in attempts to overhear Billy's preaching. In the course of the eight weeks, hundreds of thousands had come to hear him, and thousands had answered the altar calls—82 percent of whom had never been church members before. Thousands of others had come forward to recommit their lives to Christ.

Something else unexpected had happened. Billy Graham was now a celebrity recognized the nation over.

Campaign Overflow

Had the Los Angeles campaign been a flash in the pan? Obviously not. When Billy traveled on to Boston, the campaign drew the largest crowd of any event in that city on New Year's Eve. The campaign was moved to the thirteen-thousand-seat Boston Garden because the extra room was necessary, but thousands of people were still turned away. Billy's organizational skills were being honed and expanded, as each meeting raised new challenges and fresh obstacles to overcome through training and prayer before the next event. Billy and his staff streamlined the process of handling such large crowds and managing the logistics of evangelistic outreach, turning their recruits into an organizational machine disciplined enough to handle the numbers of attendees and converts alike.

In the spring of 1950, Billy had the rare opportunity to repeat something that George Whitefield once did: preach in Boston Common. Though Billy's crowd was more than two times the size of Whitefield's—fifty thousand—he paid tribute to his forebear by using the same sermon title, "Shall God Reign in New England?"

A major campaign in Portland, Oregon, later that year presented a new problem. The money that came in for the event was far more than was needed for the crusade. Billy told his audience that he would put the money toward radio broadcasts, but where would he keep it? He didn't want to put it in a personal account in his name, and thereby make it subject to income taxes. The solution came when he, Grady Wilson, and Cliff Barrows established the Billy Graham Evangelistic Association (BGEA) as a non-profit umbrella to handle their outreaches.

At thirty-two, Billy was the most famous Christian in America. He had the chance to be involved in a number of different projects all at once. In the next several years, he began working in the film industry to produce movies aimed at drawing young people to Christ. His radio show, *The Hour of Decision*, was taking off. He outlined the structure for the magazine that would become *Christianity Today*, and he would eventually become involved in television.

As Billy's popularity grew and his revivals expanded, press coverage turned more critical. Billy and his team had established safeguards by agreeing that none of them would ever be alone in a room with a woman who was not his wife, and they would have members of their staff sweep hotel rooms and meeting rooms to make sure that no one was hiding there, hoping to trap them with "compromising" photos. This nearly happened at least once—a woman and a cameraman were planted in a room—and had reportedly happened to other notable ministers.

Billy Graham addresses a crowd at London's Wembley Stadium during a 1954 crusade.

Time & Life Pictures/Getty Images

Then, in Atlanta, it was revealed to the press that Billy and Cliff Barrows's love offering at the end of the meetings exceeded the annual salary of most of the local ministers. Billy and Ruth decided to give about a third of the money away, and Billy had the BGEA put him on salary so that similar issues would never arise again. His leadership team also decided always to keep the association's books open to keep people from asking questions about how they spent the money that they received during crusades. These books would be audited regularly. When other ministries crashed or were called into question in the mid-1980s for succumbing to one of the three major temptations of ministry—falling for "girls, gold, or glory"—Billy Graham and his organization came through unscathed because they always stuck to their high standards of integrity and financial transparency.

In 1952, Northwestern would finally accept Billy's resignation as president; by this time, it was obvious that he was too busy running his crusades to continue even as a figurehead for the school. Billy's family would continue to grow, as well. The Grahams' two daughters were joined by two sons: William Franklin Graham III—called "Franklin" by the family—on July 14, 1952, and Nelson Edman—"Ned"—in May 1958. Today, both sons work in the ministry, and Franklin assumed leadership after his father's final crusade in 2005. Yet the Billy Graham Evangelistic Association did more than just survive. Billy broke ground that no one else could. In 1977, he was the first to speak beyond the Iron Curtain and hold a crusade in Hungary. In 1992, he gave a Bible and one of his books, *Peace with God*, to President Kim Il Sung of North Korea, one of the most anti-Christian nations on the face of the earth. Billy's instinct to keep things simple and take the Gospel wherever he was invited, without regard to politics or public opinion, allowed him to go places few others ever have.

A Pastor to Presidents

On July 14, 1950, Billy made his first visit to the White House—one that would prove far from his best. Through the influence of some supporters in Congress, Billy went to meet with President Harry Truman, though Truman seemed reluctant to meet with him. War had broken out with North Korea on June 25, just a few days after the appointment had been set.

Grady Wilson, Cliff Barrows, and Jerry Beavan accompanied him. Truman was cordial, though he appeared unsure whether he should receive these men as ministers or as the entertainers they looked like in their cream-colored suits. Billy told him about his recent successes with revivals in Los Angeles and Boston, and reminded him that he had called upon the president to proclaim a national day of repentance and prayer for peace in April, hoping to avoid war as the news was released that the Soviets were stockpiling nuclear weapons. Truman nodded in recognition. Graham then asked him about his religious background. "Well, I try to live by the Sermon on the Mount and the Golden Rule," the President answered.

"It takes more than that, Mr. President. It's faith in Christ and His death on the Cross that you need," Billy replied.

Truman stood as if to dismiss them in response, so Billy asked if they could pray with him before they left. "It can't do any harm," Truman responded. So Billy put his arm around the president's shoulder and they all prayed.[36]

Once outside, Billy and his team were immediately swarmed by the press. Unprepared for the onslaught, Billy made the mistake of telling the reporters everything that had happened in the Oval Office, an indiscretion that would ban him from the White House for the rest of Truman's presidency. Later on, Billy learned that Truman saw him as nothing more than a publicity hound. Truman would issue a statement about the campaign planned for Washington in 1951: "At Key West the President said very decisively that he did not wish to endorse Billy Graham's Washington revival meeting and particularly he said he did not want to receive him at the White House. You remember what a show of himself Billy Graham made last time he was here. The President does not want it repeated."[37]

Billy learned his lesson and proved he would never again abuse the confidence of a president. He became a confidant of every president for the next five and a half decades. He met with each of them, Eisenhower through George W. Bush—eleven presidents in all—and because of this, George H. W. Bush called him "America's pastor."

Things had changed so rapidly for Billy in the early 1950s that within a year of being dismissed by Truman, he found himself writing Dwight Eisenhower and encouraging him to run for president. It was an odd place for him—as a Southerner and a Baptist, Billy was basically a Democrat by birth—but at this time, Eisenhower had yet to declare a party affiliation. When he finally put himself forward as a candidate for the Republican nomination for president, however, Billy didn't waver in his secret support. When Eisenhower asked for Billy to help him work a more religious slant into his speeches, Billy gladly volunteered some Scripture verses he thought might help. He cautioned him, however, that he could not issue a statement supporting him, as he didn't want his platform for the Gospel to be misused for politics. Eisenhower applauded him for his integrity in the matter.

---

[36] Graham, *Just As I Am*, xx–xxi.

[37] Ibid.

Billy remained friends with "Ike" throughout his presidency, even if he could never bring himself to call the president that nickname. It was always "Mr. President" in the White House, and it had been "General" before. Yet Billy soon learned his value to men whose friends and associates usually wanted something from them.

By 1955, Eisenhower was asking Billy how he could know that he was saved. It is interesting that Billy said of this, "I didn't feel that I could answer his question as well as others could have."[38]

It seems doubtful that John Wesley, Charles Finney, or even Peter Cartwright would have come up short on that one. Each of their conversion experiences greatly influenced their teachings on how people could know they were saved. Billy had more thorough answers for President John F. Kennedy when he asked how the world would end.[39] Is this a telling fact for a generation of believers who today can spend years studying the book of Revelation, yet finish a course on the gifts of the Spirit in one lesson?

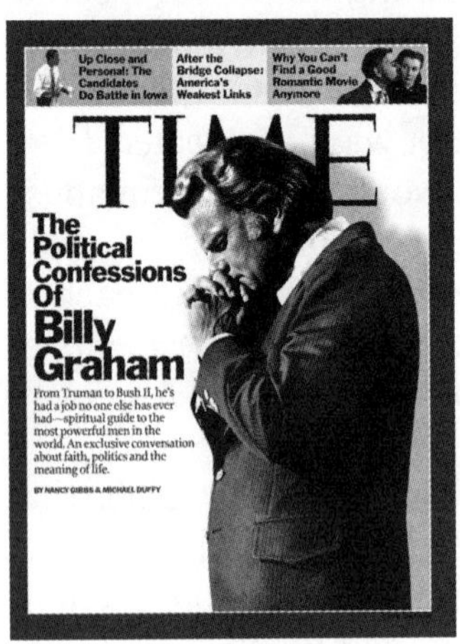

Cover of Time *magazine, August 20, 2007.*

Time & Life Pictures/ Getty Images

Billy soon learned that he needed to minister to U.S. presidents as he would minister to any other person. He was not there to convince them of anything other than to care for the destiny of their souls—and to prove that they needed to love those who opposed them as much as they loved their most ardent supporters. Because Billy was such a popular figure, highly respected and well regarded by evangelicals across the nation, many people equated his willingness to befriend presidents and pray with them with an endorsement of them. In 1981, after years of experience with this, and even some appalling failures, he advised, "Evangelicals can't be closely identified with any particular

---

[38] Nancy Gibbs and Michael Duffy, "Billy Graham, Pastor in Chief," *Time*, August 9, 2007, http://www.time.com/time/magazine/article/0,9171,1651625,00.html.

[39] Gibbs and Duffy, "Billy Graham, Pastor in Chief."

party or person. We have to stand in the middle, to preach to all the people, right and left. I haven't been faithful to my own advice in the past. I will in the future."[40]

This was rarely an issue for evangelicals when they favored the president, but when Bill Clinton won the presidency in 1992 and Billy still visited him in the White House, many people said that he had turned traitor to his faith. Billy had known the Clintons for years, however, and would not refuse a chance to influence them toward Christ or pray with them, no matter what anyone said. In 1989, while Billy was in Little Rock, Arkansas, Hillary Rodham Clinton invited him to lunch. His only stipulation was, "'I don't eat with beautiful women alone,'...so they met in a hotel dining room and talked for a couple of hours."[41]

Years later, he said of Bill Clinton, "When he left the presidency, he should have become an evangelist, because he has all of the gifts," and then added, "and he could leave his wife to run the country."[42] This angered many members of the Religious Right, who saw it as an endorsement of Hillary for the presidency. Franklin Graham later came forward to clarify that the comment was meant as a joke, but this did little to ease criticism. Democrats hadn't liked it much better when Billy still visited with President Richard Nixon after his resignation. Nixon had such respect for Billy that he had actually "offered him the ambassadorship to Israel at a meeting with Golda Meir. 'I said the Mideast would blow up if I went over there,' Graham recalls. 'Golda then reached under the table and squeezed my hand. She was greatly relieved.'"[43]

President Gerald Ford once said, "Billy came to the White House to give me the kind of reassurance that was important in decisions and challenges at home and abroad....Whenever you were with Billy, you had a special feeling that he was there to give you help and guidance in meeting your problems."[44] At an event honoring Billy in May 2007, President Bill Clinton said of him, "When he prays with

---

[40] Ibid.

[41] Gibbs and Ostling, "God's Billy Pulpit."

[42] Nancy Gibbs and Michael Duffy, *The Preacher and the Presidents* (New York: Center Street, 2007), 340.

[43] Gibbs and Ostling, "God's Billy Pulpit."

[44] Ibid.

you in the Oval Office or upstairs at the White House, you feel he is praying for you. Not for the President." At the same event, President Jimmy Carter said, "I'm just one of tens of millions of people whose spiritual life has been shaped by Billy Graham."[45] As a young man, Carter had actually worked at one of Billy's crusades in Georgia.

President Lyndon Johnson voiced his concern to Billy that he might die in office. He had watched a president's death throw the country into turmoil when Kennedy was assassinated, and this was a legacy he himself did not want to leave. It seems Johnson may have confided in Graham about this more than anyone else. "I've already had one heart attack," he told Billy in 1967. "I don't think [running again] is fair to the people or to my party." He even asked Billy to do his funeral, telling him that he didn't want anything fancy for it. "I want you to look in those cameras and just tell 'em what Christianity is all about. Tell 'em how they can be sure they can go to heaven. I want you to preach the Gospel." Then, he added, "Somewhere in there, you tell 'em a few things I did for this country."[46] It was Johnson who called on Billy the most—during LBJ's presidency, Billy visited the White House more than twenty times.

It seems that the nation's First Families considered Billy as close to them when they faced death as he was to them in life. Billy was the first one Nancy Reagan called outside of the family to tell that Ronald had passed away. He has presided over many of their funerals, the latest being Gerald R. Ford's in January 2007; he did Lady Bird Johnson's a few months later, in July.

Billy was also invited to eleven different inaugurations, and he delivered the opening prayer at most of them.[47]

When U.S. presidents wanted to pray, they usually called Billy. Just before the Gulf War started in 1991, Billy spent the night in the White House by the side of President Bush and his wife, Barbara.

---

[45] Nancy Gibbs and Michael Duffy, "Billy Graham: 'A Spiritual Gift to All,'" *Time*, May 31, 2007, http://www.time.com/time/nation/article/0,8599,1627139,00.html.

[46] Gibbs and Duffy, "Billy Graham, Pastor in Chief."

[47] "Presidential Inaugural Prayers and Sermons of Billy and Franklin Graham," Wheaton College Billy Graham Archives, http://www.wheaton.edu/bgc/archives/inaugural01.htm.

Again, critics thought that his presence with them signified his endorsement of the war, but Billy said he was merely there to support the Bushes in a time of difficulty. This made sense, as Billy was a faithful friend of the Bushes. In 1985, he had taken a long walk on the beach with the President's son, George W., that set the then forty-year-old oilman on the path to salvation. On the eve of his eighty-ninth birthday in October 2007, Billy was a guest for lunch at the White House with George W., just a short time after Ruth Graham's death. The President just wanted to offer his prayers and encouragement to the man whose personal church, more than any other building, might well have been the White House.

The Final Crusade

The Billy Graham Evangelistic Association planned Billy's final crusade for June 24–26, 2005. It was held at Flushing Meadows-Corona Park in Queens, New York. By this time, they had organizing mass revivals down to a science, but it was no less difficult. The first step was to find a list of the churches within a fifty-mile radius of New York City, but no such list existed. Never ones to be frustrated, they created a list that included some twelve thousand churches. Every one of these churches was contacted and its members were invited to attend. Of these churches, 1,424 agreed to participate, representing eighty different denominations—from Adventist churches to the Vineyard churches, and even one calling itself Hebrew Pentecostal. It was the greatest number of

Billy stands at the pulpit at his final crusade.

Billy Graham Evangelistic Association

participating churches in the history of the Billy Graham crusades. Leaders and congregation members from these churches were then invited to attend forty-three different seminars on every aspect of the crusade, from soliciting donations to reaching the neighborhoods of their city with invitations. Applications were reviewed as the crusade planners selected six thousand volunteer counselors to meet with those people who would come forward during the crusade. These volunteers didn't even include the ushering staff, which alone had five tiers to its organizational chart.

As with every one of Billy's crusades, prayer was the foundation of the event. More than 35,000 people were on a monthly mailing list so that they could be notified about individual requests, as well as be encouraged to pray for the event overall. More than seventy thousand chairs were set up, and facilities were erected to translate the message into thirteen different languages—including Tamil, Hungarian, and Arabic—simultaneously. The cost of the revival was estimated at $6.8 million, even with all of the volunteer work.[48]

When Billy was asked some years earlier about being the last of the big-time evangelists, he could only comment, "After D. L. Moody was finished, they said that same thing,...and after Billy Sunday they said the same thing, and after I'm finished they'll say the same thing. But God will raise up different ones who will do it far better than me." [49] Oh, that some of us could be those ones!

Six Decades Spreading the Name of Jesus

Billy Graham has preached in person to nearly 215 million people in more than 185 countries and territories—an unprecedented number. Millions more people have been reached through television, video, film, literature, and Webcasts. In his 417 crusades, more than 3.2 million people have come forward in response to his altar calls. This is not counting the millions of others who have responded to his books, television broadcasts, or other media he has used to spread the Gospel. In April 1996, the Billy Graham Evangelical Association

---

[48] Andy Newman, "Mounting a Billy Graham Crusade Takes Prayers, Mailings, and Many, Many Chairs," *New York Times*, June 23, 2005, http://www.nytimes.com/2005/06/23/nyregion/23crusade.html.

[49] Gibbs and Ostling, "God's Billy Pulpit."

sponsored a rebroadcast of one of Billy's sermons to an audience of around 2.5 billion in forty-eight languages and 160 countries—a remarkable feat, as it represented a truly global simulcast.[50]

Billy and his son, Franklin, at a Billy Graham rally on June 12, 2003, in Oklahoma City, Oklahoma

Getty Images

As I write these words, eighty-nine-year-old Billy is all but retired from ministry, and he battles Parkinson's disease, the same disease that removed his "good friend," Ronald Reagan, from public appearances. Billy still gave a remarkably lucid interview for the book *The Preacher and the Presidents,* which was released in August 2007. Though not involved in the day-to-day affairs of his ministry, he is still consulted from time to time by his son, Franklin, who has taken over the reigns of the Billy Graham Evangelistic Association. Billy's wife of sixty-three years, Ruth, died on June 14, 2007, at the age of eighty-seven. Ruth's body is buried next to the Billy Graham Library in Charlotte, North Carolina, where Billy will one day be laid to rest beside her. He now lives in Montreat, North Carolina, in the house his wife had built as a retreat from the public, not far from where he was born. Billy's legacy will live on through his organization and his sons, with his place secured as one of the greatest evangelists of all time.

---

[50] See "William (Billy) F. Graham," Billy Graham Evangelistic Association Web site, http://www.billygraham.org/MediaRelations_Bios.asp?id=0; Newman, "Mounting a Billy Graham Crusade Takes Prayers, Mailings, and Many, Many Chairs," and David Aikman, *Great Souls: Six Who Changed a Century* (Lanham, MD: Lexington Books, 2003), 4.

Conclusion

John Wesley to Billy Graham: Evangelicalism from Its Beginnings until Today

Evangelicalism was effectively birthed when John Wesley was able to pry salvation from the hands of Calvinist predestination and return it to the individuals who would seek and accept what Jesus did on the cross as all that was necessary to be right with God. When the likes of John Wesley, George Whitefield, Charles Finney, William and Catherine Booth, or Billy Graham took this message and combined it with the presence of God, revival erupted to transform communities and nations. Thus, evangelicalism was not just the birthplace of the Methodist, Baptist, and Congregationalist movements, or of others who rejected the doctrine of predestination, but it was also the birthplace of the Pentecostal and charismatic movements, both of which have embraced God's presence and power, as they were exemplified in the lives of these Generals of God.

In the final analysis, it seems that evangelicalism today has shifted from a spiritual to a political emphasis. While we still largely focus on the work of evangelism, we have laid aside the power of God for the more easily controlled power of a conservative voting block. We seem to have forgotten that it was revivalism that changed nations and righted social injustices during the past three centuries—not the power of democracy or the right to vote alone. It seems that evangelical Christianity has lost much of its relevance to societies because it tends to focus more on changing laws than changing hearts.

Revivalists such as John Wesley, George Whitefield, Charles Finney, and William and Catherine Booth transformed communities and nations by preaching the Gospel. These revivalists righted social ills through grassroots efforts and door-to-door ministry. Where they saw needs, they reached out to meet them, offering a hand to help people get back on their feet and the power of the Gospel to change their lives and establish their livelihoods. They changed the spiritual climate of the communities they touched by seeking God's power in prayer, and by preaching Jesus and the power of what He accomplished on the cross. When Jesus became the topic of conversation in these communities, it mattered little what the law of the land said—morality was determined by people who were seeking to please God, not follow legislative measures.

In contrast to this, twentieth-century conversion became more a matter of one answering an altar call than one laboring in prayer until sensing confirmation in one's heart of having been saved by Christ. "Coming forward" replaced Finney's "anxious benches." Knowledge of one's salvation came from a pat on the back from a prayer worker instead of a personal conviction or revelation that had been pursued hotly. If Christianity today seems impotent, perhaps it is because we have lost what the early revivalists knew—that salvation must be worked out *"with fear and trembling"* (Philippians 2:12).

We need a return to the great revelation that God's Generals knew so well—that Jesus is the only way to remedy social ills and permanently change people's lives. When Jesus is presented in all of His mercy and love, people change, and their lifestyles are transformed. Wrongs are righted, and permanently so, only when Jesus and His power are truly revealed.

If the church is again to have the power that was unleashed by the Moravians and was evidenced at Cane Ridge and Azusa Street, then perhaps we need to relearn from the methods of prayer, dedication to the Word, and seeking the Lord that were used by the revivalists. The twenty-first century is groaning in anticipation, waiting for the manifestation of the children of God (see Romans 8:19)—those who walk in the power of Christ once again. I believe God is ready to anoint new revivalists. He only needs those who are willing to pick up the torch of these Generals and pay the same price for the power of God that they did. His ways and blessings have not changed—Jesus Christ is still *"the same yesterday, and to day, and for ever"* (Hebrews 13:8).

May God use you and me to change hearts in the ways they did, so that Jesus' will—His desire for healing, blessing, righting social wrongs, and touching humanity—can come again to our nations.

Further Readings

Batt, J. H. *Dwight L. Moody: The Life-work of a Modern Evangelist.* London: S. W. Partridge and Company, 1900.

Cox, F. Hayter. *He Was There! The Story of Brigadier Cox—Armour-bearer to William Booth.* London: Salvationist Publishing and Supplies, 1949.

Cross, Whitney R. *The Burned-over District: The Social and Intellectual History of Enthusiastic Religion in Western New York, 1800–1850.* Ithaca, NY: Cornell University Press, 1950.

Dallimore, Arnold A. *Susanna Wesley: The Mother of John and Charles Wesley.* Grand Rapids, MI: Baker Books, 1993.

Hankins, Barry. *The Second Great Awakening and the Transcendentalists.* Westport, CT: Greenwood Press, 2004.

Irvine, St. John. *God's Soldier: General William Booth.* 2 vols. London: William Heinemann, 1934.

Jennings, Daniel R. *The Supernatural Occurrences of John Wesley.* Sean Multimedia, 2005.

Kew, Clifford W., ed. *Catherine Booth—Her Continuing Relevance.* St. Albans, Great Britain: The Salvation Army International Headquarters, 1990.

Moody, William R. and A. P. Fitt. *The Life of D. L. Moody.* Kilmarnock, Scotland: John Ritchic, n.d., ca. 1910.

Northrop, Henry Davenport. *Life and Labors of Dwight L. Moody: The Great Evangelist*. Philadelphia: American Book and Bible House, 1899.

Regester, E. V., E. L. Watson, and H. K. Carroll, eds. *The Francis Asbury Monument in the National Capital*. Washington, DC: The Francis Asbury Memorial Association, Press of the Methodist Book Concern, 1925.

Watson, Bernard. *A Hundred Years War: The Salvation Army 1865–1965*. London: Hodder and Stoughton, 1964.

Photographic Credits for Portraits Featured in this Book

Front Cover: Billy Graham
Chuck Nacke / Alamy

Page 21: John Wesley
Reproduced with permission from the Methodist Collections of Drew University

Charles Wesley
Reproduced with permission from the Methodist Collections of Drew University

Page 91: George Whitefield
Reproduced with permission from the Methodist Collections of Drew University

Page 129: Jonathan Edwards
Public Domain

Page 173: Francis Asbury
Reproduced with permission from the Methodist Collections of Drew University

Page 209: The First Camp Meetings
Library of Congress, 3g03261

Page 245: Peter Cartwright
Reproduced with permission from the Methodist Collections of Drew University

Page 283: Charles Finney
Reproduced with permission from the Methodist Collections of Drew University

Page 335: Dwight L. Moody
Roberts Liardon Archives

Page 387: William and Catherine Booth
The Salvation Army Archives

Page 447: Billy Graham
Library of Congress, 03261

About the Author

Roberts Liardon

Roberts Liardon, author, public speaker, spiritual leader, church historian, and humanitarian, was born in Tulsa, Oklahoma, the first male child born at Oral Roberts University. For this distinction, he was named in honor of the university founder. Thus, from the start of his life, Roberts was destined to be one of the most well-known Christian authors and speakers of the turn of the millennium. To date, he has sold over six million books worldwide in over fifty languages and is internationally renowned.

An author of over four dozen Christian and self-help books, Roberts's career in ministry began when he gave his first public address at the age of thirteen. At seventeen, he published his first book, *I Saw Heaven*, which catapulted him into the public eye. By the time he was eighteen years old, he was one of the leading public speakers in the world. Later, he would write and produce a book and video series entitled *God's Generals*. This became one of the best-selling Christian series in history and established Roberts as a leading Protestant church historian.

Roberts's notoriety increased outside Christendom as well. Twice he was voted as Outstanding Young Man in America, and his career has taken him to over one hundred nations around the world, having been hosted by presidents, kings, leading political and religious leaders, and other world dignitaries. Roberts had an introduction with former President Ronald Reagan, Billy Graham, and with Former Prime Minister Lady Margaret Thatcher. Roberts received a letter from President George Bush honoring him for his commitment and contribution to improve the quality of life in his community.

In 1990, at the age of twenty-five, Roberts moved to Southern California and established his worldwide headquarters in Orange County. There, he founded Embassy Christian Center, which would become a base for his humanitarian work that would include assistance to the poor and needy, not only in Southern California, but throughout the world. He also built one of the largest Christian churches and Bible colleges in Orange County. He has established, financed, and sent forth more than 250 men and women to various nations. These humanitarian missionary teams have taken food, clothing, and medical supplies, along with the message of Jesus, to needy friends and neighbors worldwide.

As a church historian, Roberts also fervently pursues research of our Christian heritage. At age twelve, he received instruction from God to study past heroes of faith and gain insight into their successes and failures. The pursuit of Christian history became his passion, and, even as a young man, Roberts spent much of his free time with older Christians who knew the likes of William Branham, Kathryn Kuhlman, and Aimee Semple McPherson—great men and women of faith whose stories are told in the first *God's Generals* book and videos. Roberts possesses a wealth of knowledge regarding the great leaders of three Christian movements—Pentecostal, divine healing, and charismatic—and he has established ongoing research through the Reformers and Revivalists Historical Museum in California.

Overall, historian, humanitarian, pastor, teacher, and philanthropist Roberts Liardon has dedicated his entire life and finances to the work of God's kingdom and the welfare of his fellow man, keeping a watchful eye on those less fortunate and doing all he can to ease their pain and help their dreams come to pass.

Roberts Liardon Ministries

USA

Roberts Liardon
P.O. Box 2989
Sarasota, FL 34230
www.robertsliardon.com

United Kingdom/Europe

Roberts Liardon
P.O. Box 332
Knutsford, Cheshire
England WA169 WQ

If you desire additional information about the great God's Generals, such as voice recordings, film footage, and other related materials, please visit www.godsgenerals.org.